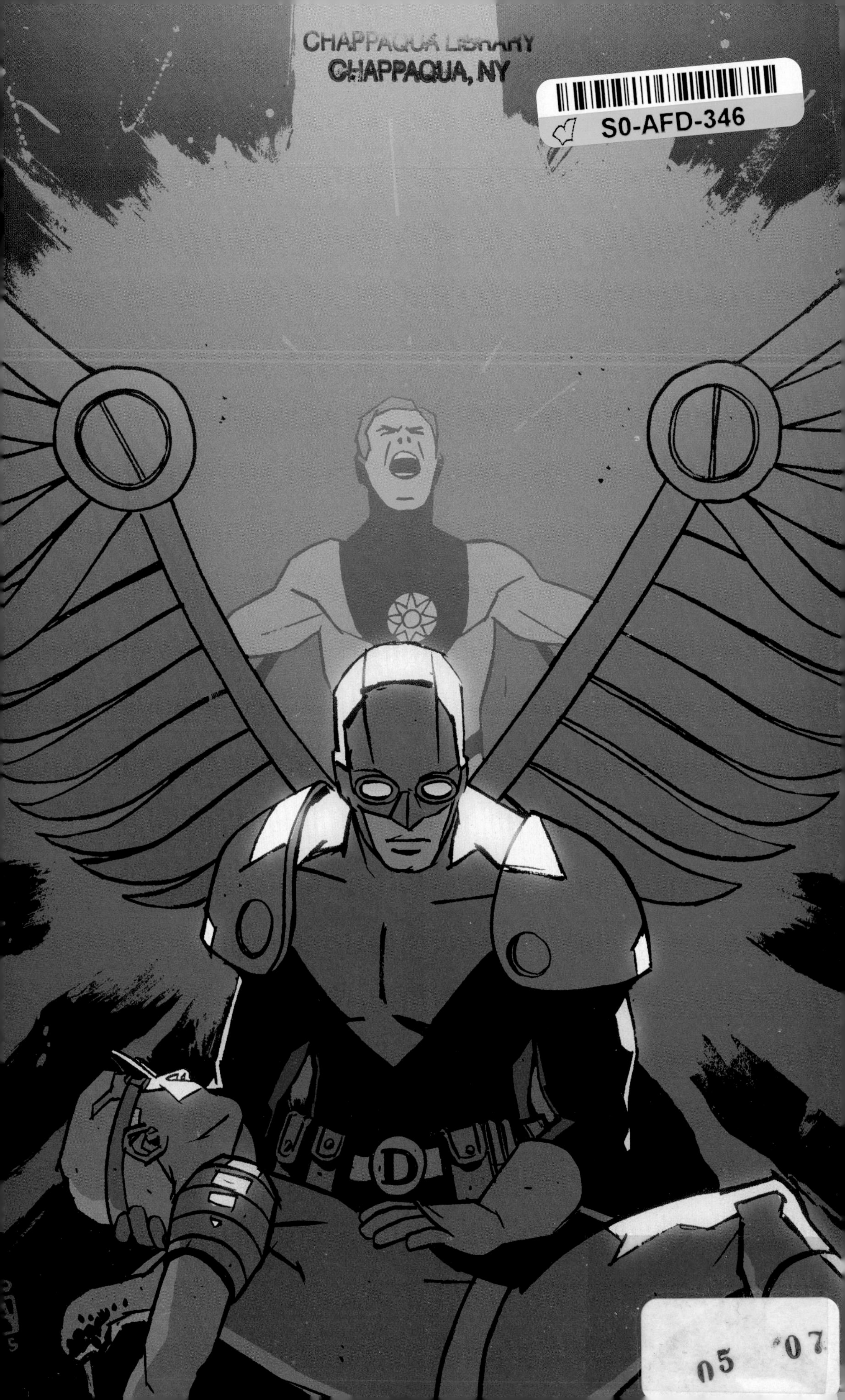

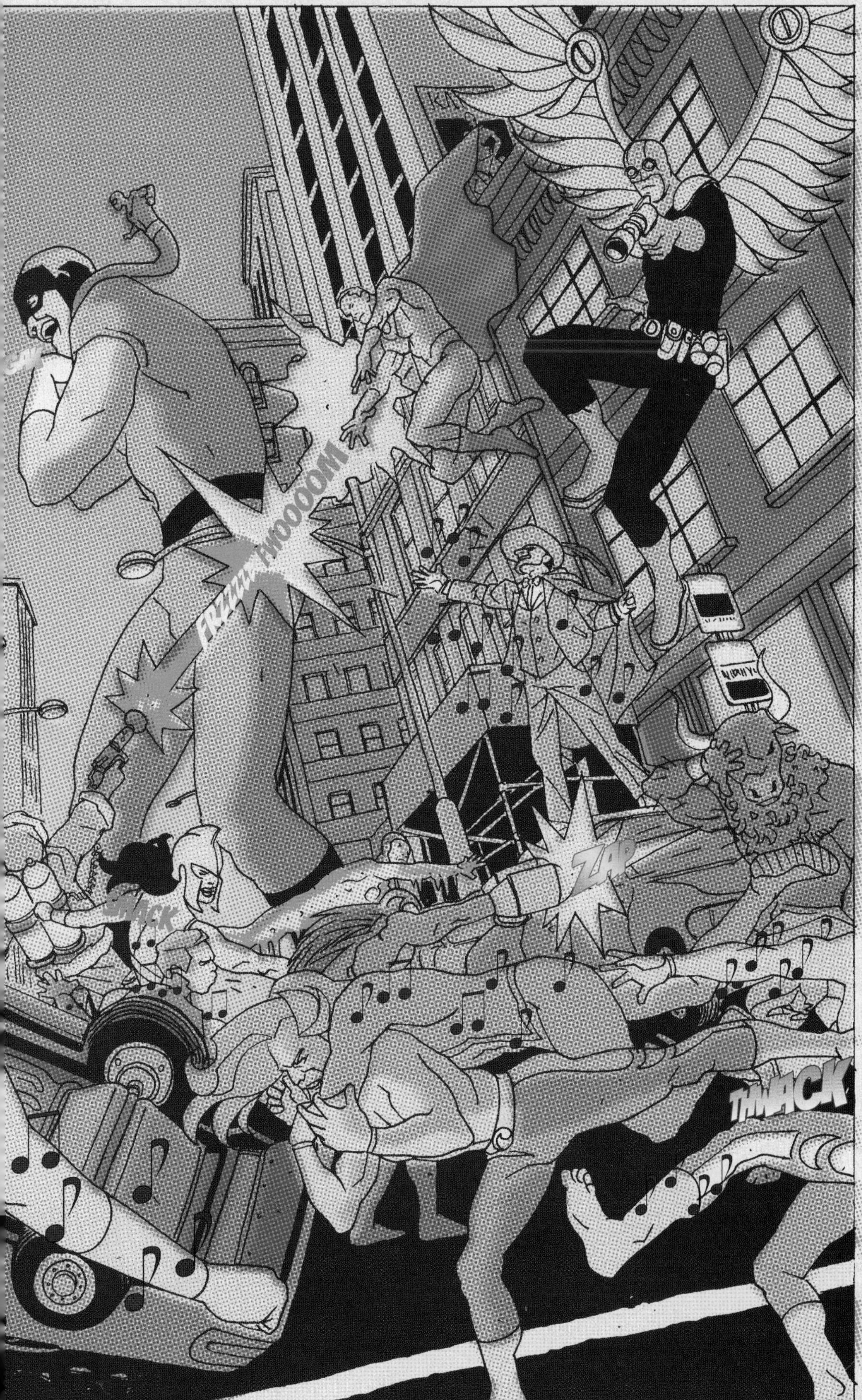
GAK
FRZZZZZ FWOOOOM
SMACK
ZAP
THWACK

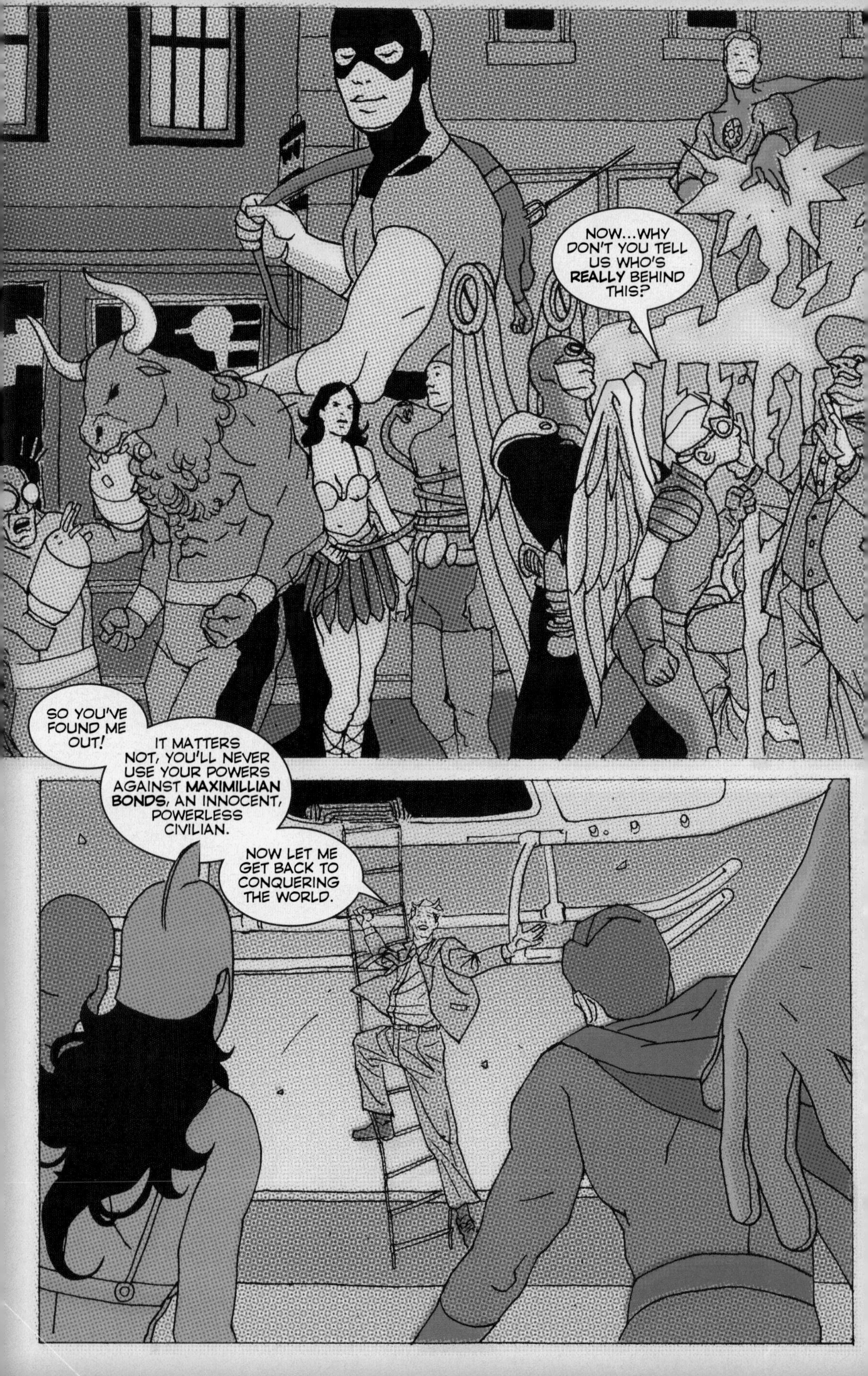
NOW...WHY DON'T YOU TELL US WHO'S **REALLY** BEHIND THIS?
SO YOU'VE FOUND ME OUT!
IT MATTERS NOT, YOU'LL NEVER USE YOUR POWERS AGAINST **MAXIMILLIAN BONDS**, AN INNOCENT, POWERLESS CIVILIAN.
NOW LET ME GET BACK TO CONQUERING THE WORLD.

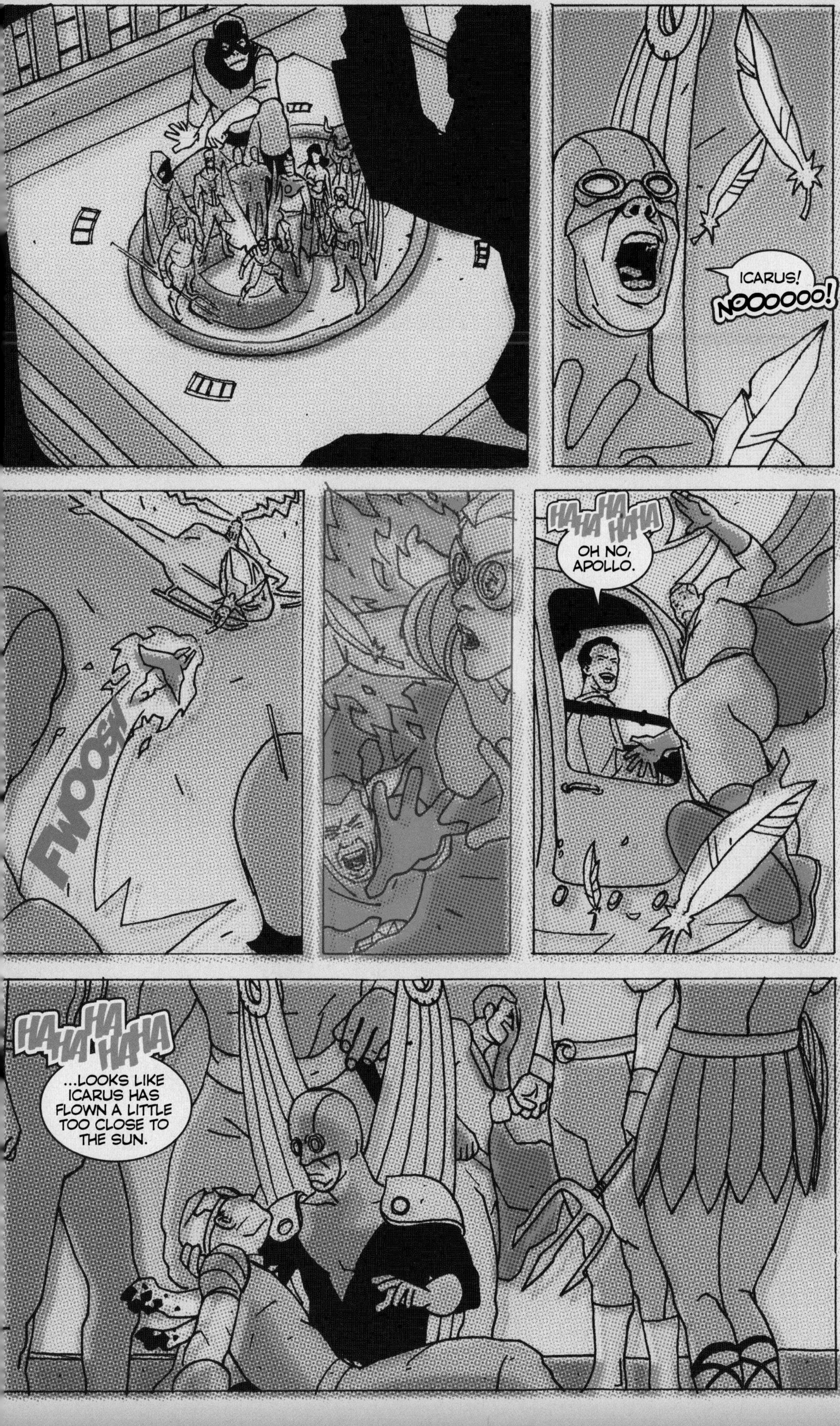
ICARUS!
NOOOOOO!
FWOOSH
HA HA HA HA HA HA
OH NO, APOLLO.
HA HA HA HA HA HA
...LOOKS LIKE ICARUS HAS FLOWN A LITTLE TOO CLOSE TO THE SUN.

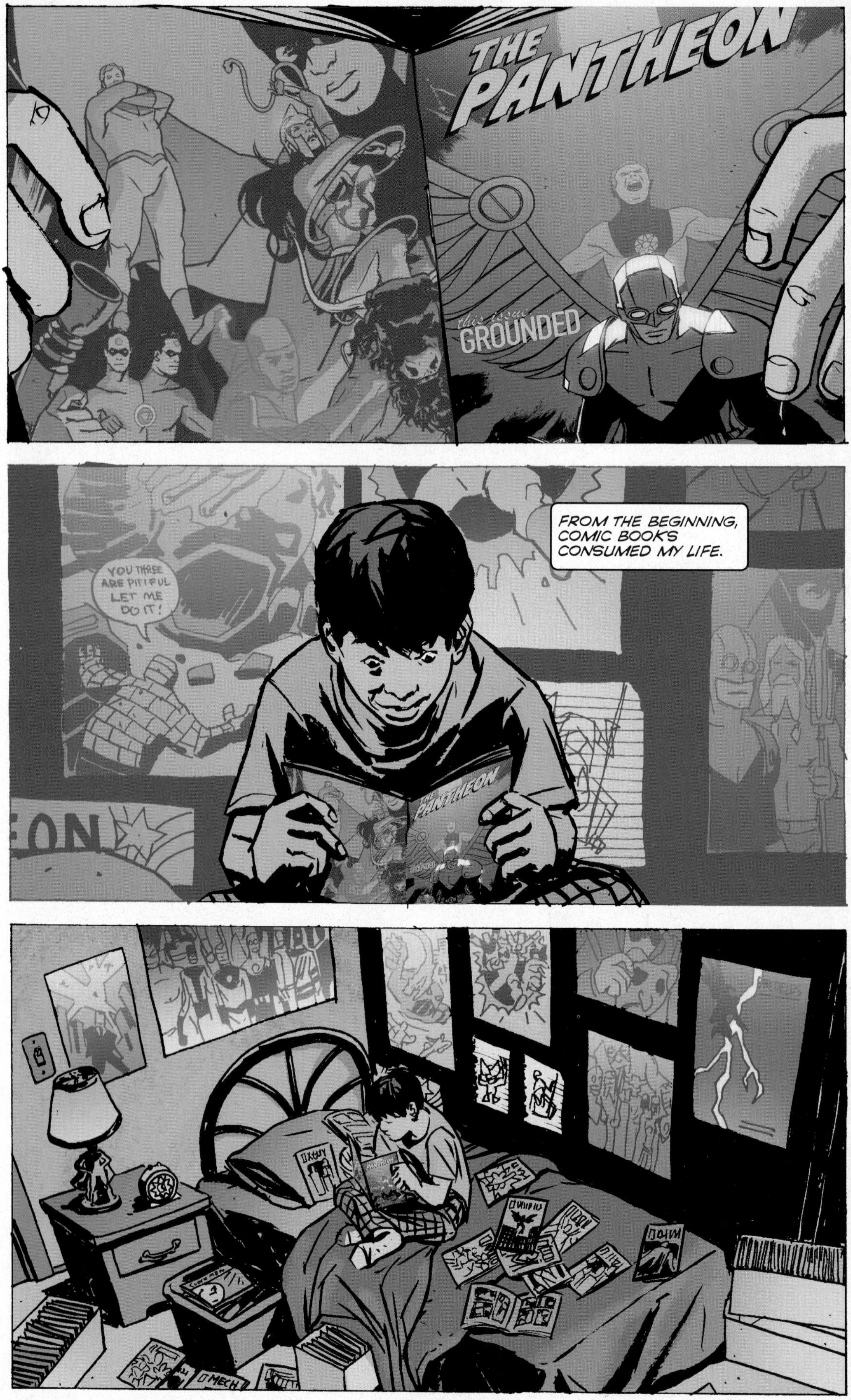
THE PANTHEON
this issue
GROUNDED
YOU THREE ARE PITIFUL LET ME DO IT!
FROM THE BEGINNING, COMIC BOOKS CONSUMED MY LIFE.
EON
THE PANTHEON
GROUNDED

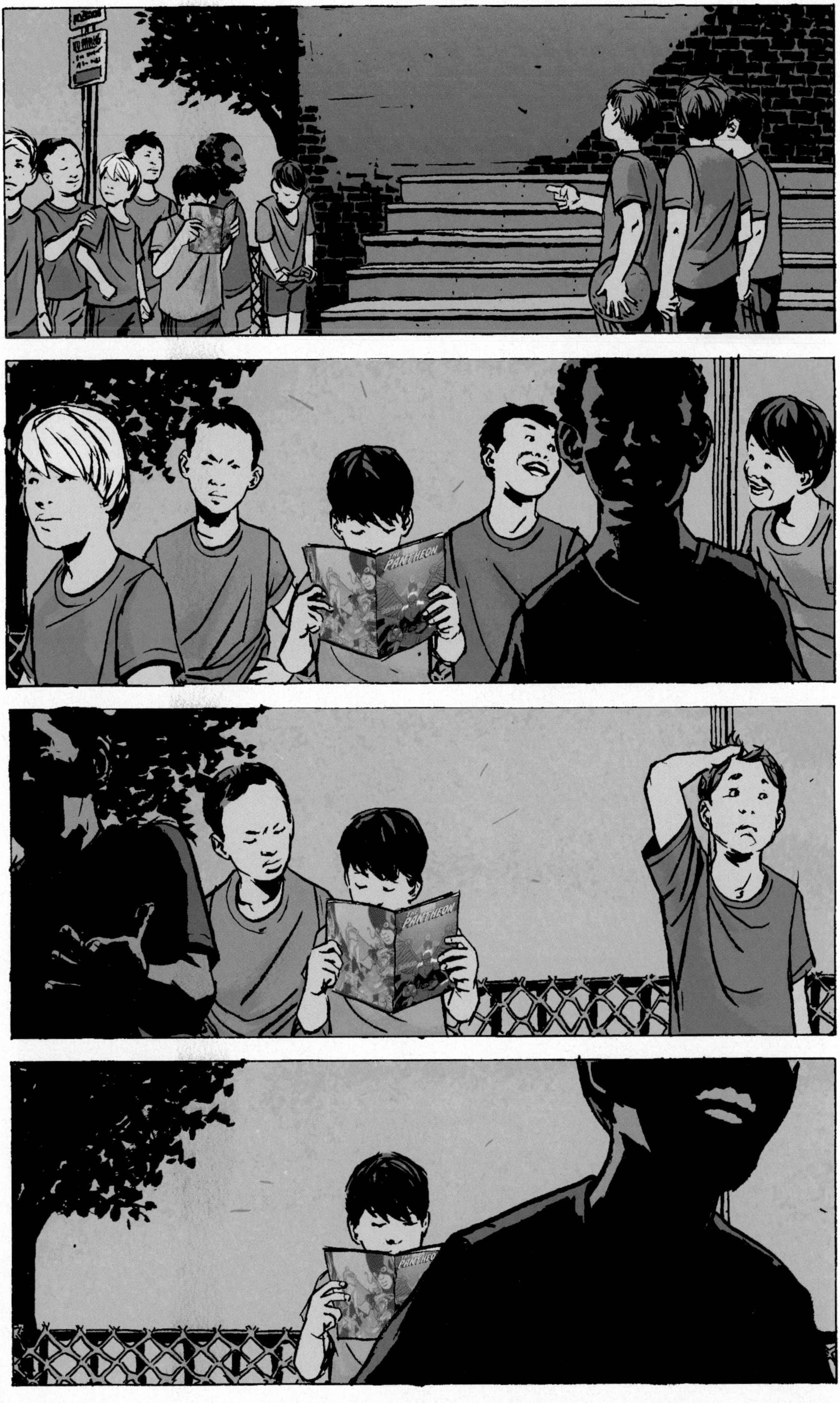
THE PANTHEON

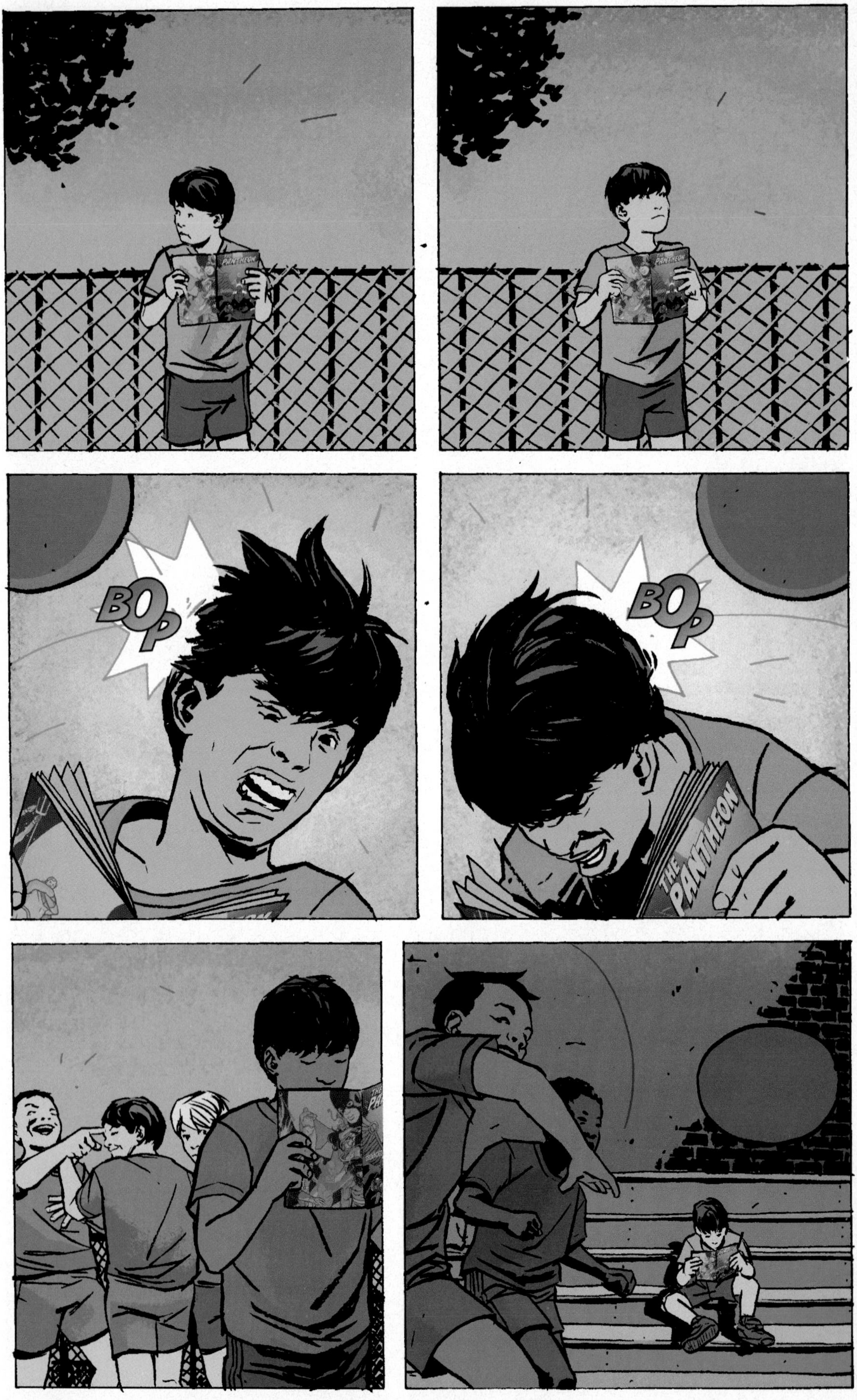
BOP
BOP
THE PANTHEON

NOT BECAUSE THEY REPRESENTED SOME KIND OF ESCAPE FROM REALITY...

POW

SMACK!

CRASH

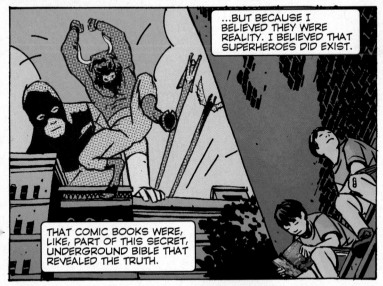

...BUT BECAUSE I BELIEVED THEY WERE REALITY. I BELIEVED THAT SUPERHEROES DID EXIST.

THAT COMIC BOOKS WERE, LIKE, PART OF THIS SECRET, UNDERGROUND BIBLE THAT REVEALED THE TRUTH.

THUD

BRWWWMBA

AND I BELIEVED IT WAS MY DUTY TO MAKE PEOPLE BELIEVE AS I DID, THAT HEROES WALKED AMONG US.

FWOOSH

PANTHEON

OF COURSE, I KNEW ALL THIS BECAUSE I WAS A SUPERHERO.

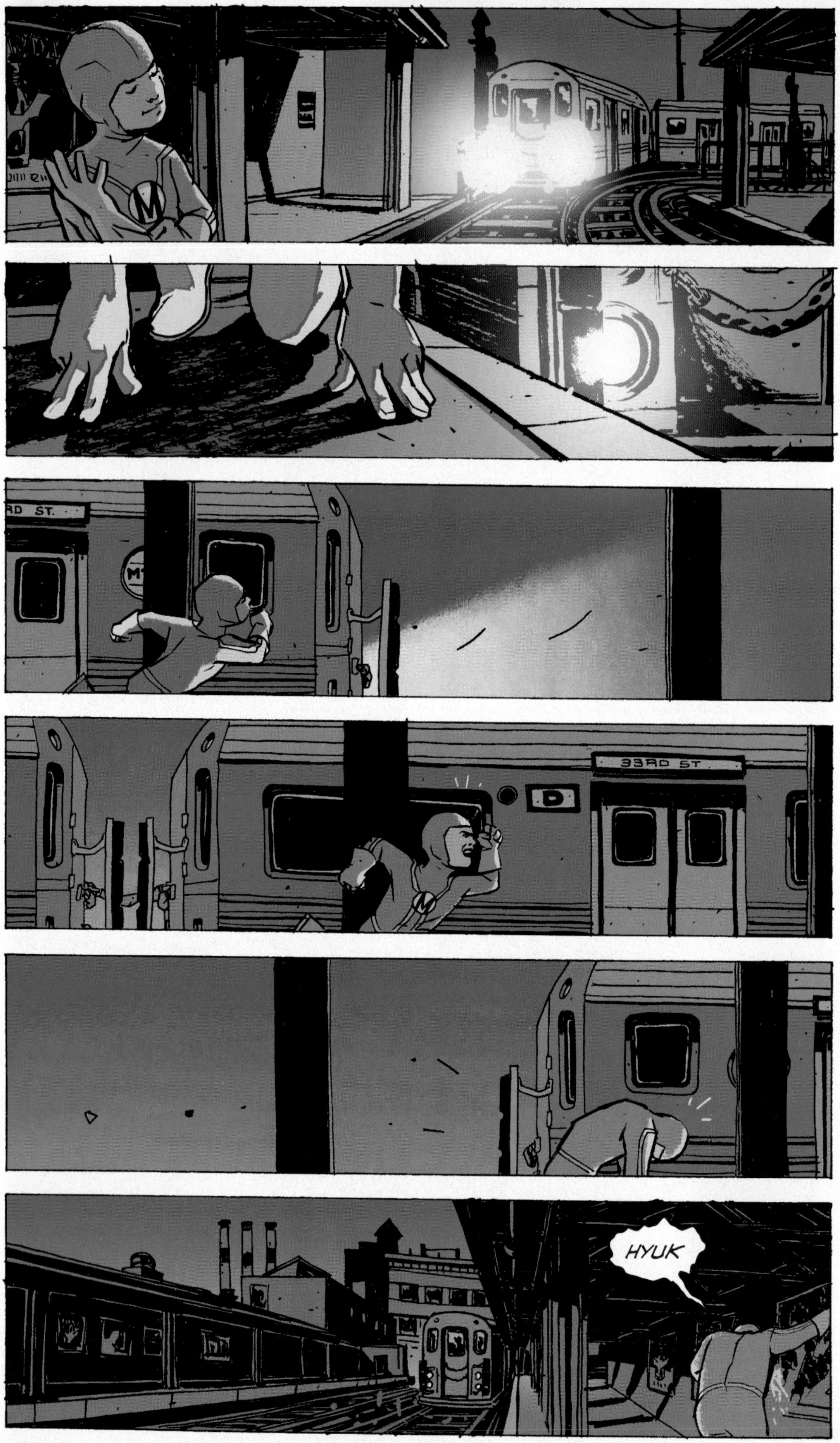
RD ST.
33RD ST
D
HYUK

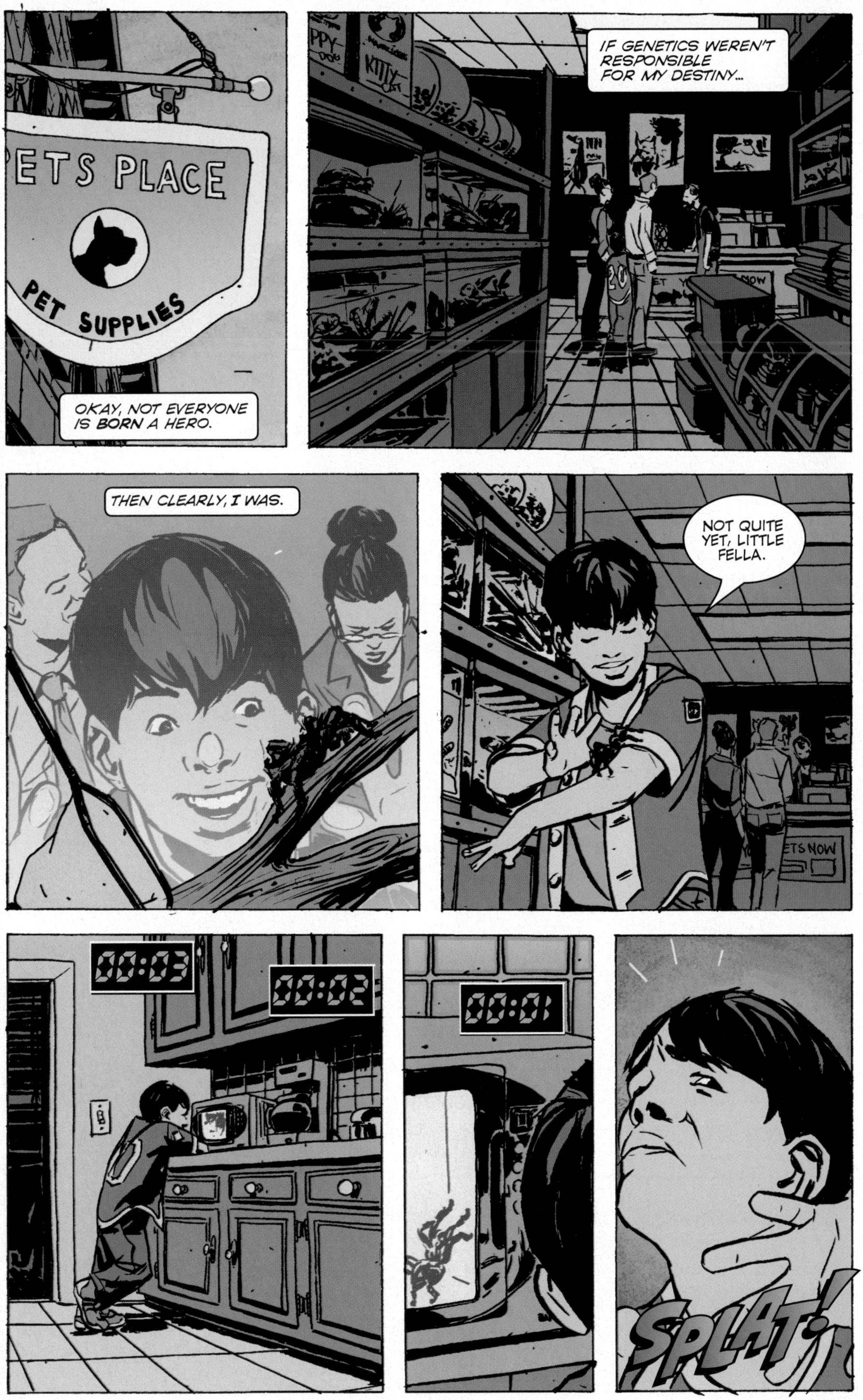

ETS PLACE
PET SUPPLIES
OKAY, NOT EVERYONE IS BORN A HERO.
IF GENETICS WEREN'T RESPONSIBLE FOR MY DESTINY...
THEN CLEARLY, I WAS.
NOT QUITE YET, LITTLE FELLA.
ETS NOW
00:03
00:02
00:01
SPLAT!

IT SOON BECAME APPARENT THAT MY LACK OF SCIENTIFIC KNOWLEDGE MIGHT BE SOMEWHAT OF A BARRIER TO GAINING THE ABILITIES I'D NEED.

TRAINING BECAME A PRIORITY...

Y THE SCHOOL FOR SPECIAL YOUNGSTERS

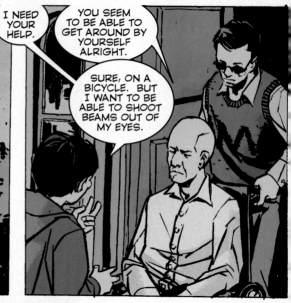

I NEED YOUR HELP.

YOU SEEM TO BE ABLE TO GET AROUND BY YOURSELF ALRIGHT.

SURE, ON A BICYCLE. BUT I WANT TO BE ABLE TO SHOOT BEAMS OUT OF MY EYES.

I THOUGHT THIS SCHOOL WAS FOR, YOU KNOW...

...SPECIAL PEOPLE.

YEAH, IT IS. LAST I HEARD THAT WAS THE POLITE TERM YOU PEOPLE CALL US HANDICAPS.

CAN'T YOU AT LEAST READ MINDS?

TAKE A GUESS AT WHAT I'M THINKING.

I AM NOT RETARDED.

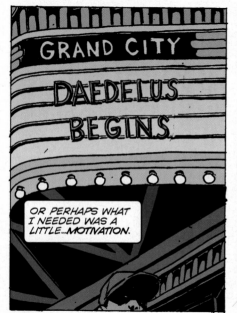

GRAND CITY

DAEDELUS

BEGINS

OR PERHAPS WHAT I NEEDED WAS A LITTLE...MOTIVATION.

GRAND CITY

DAEDELUS BEGINS

CAN'T WE TAKE THAT SHORTCUT OVER THERE?

SHRIEK!

BLAM BLAM BLAMMM

aaaahhh!

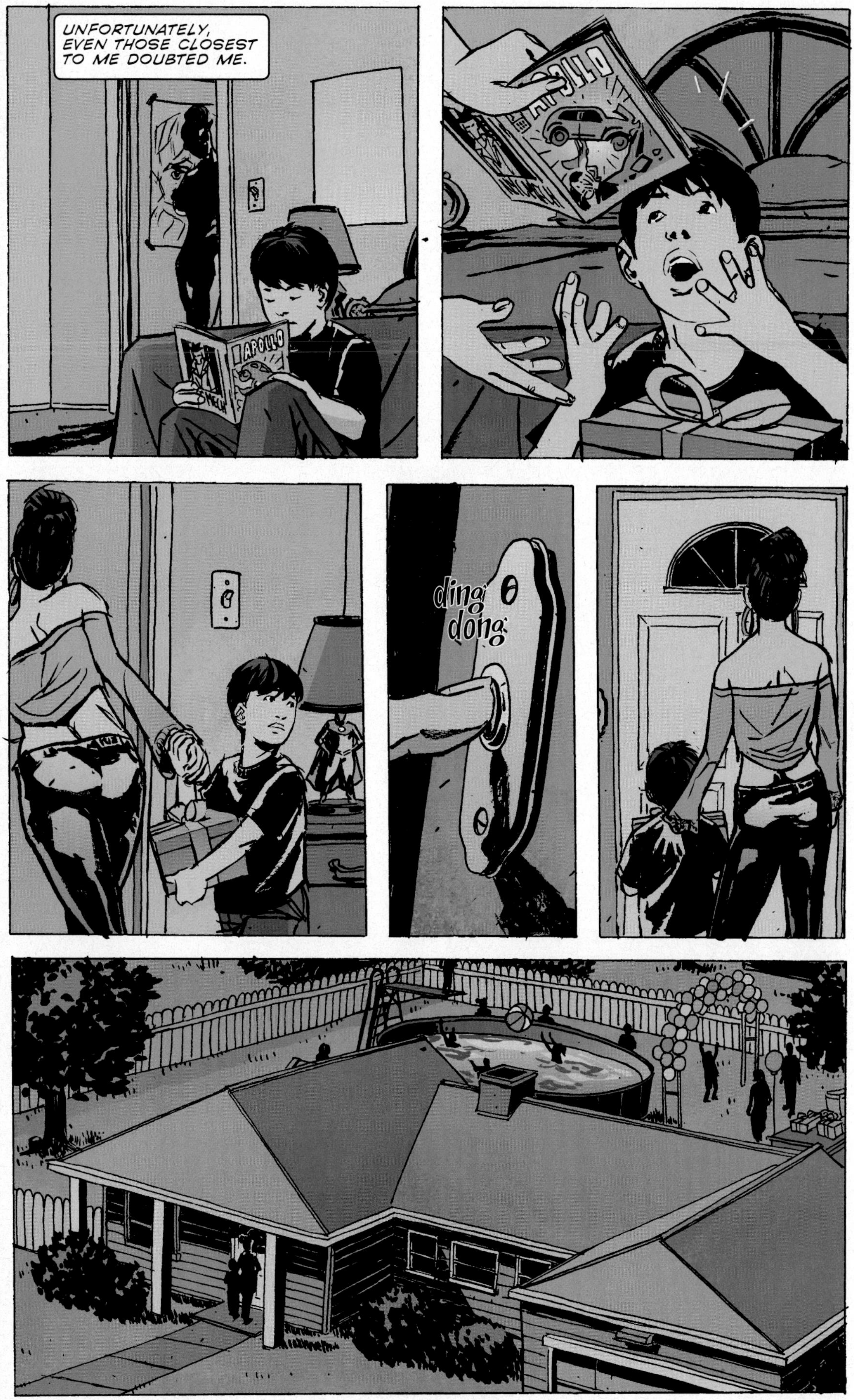
UNFORTUNATELY, EVEN THOSE CLOSEST TO ME DOUBTED ME.
APOLLO
APOLLO
ding
dong

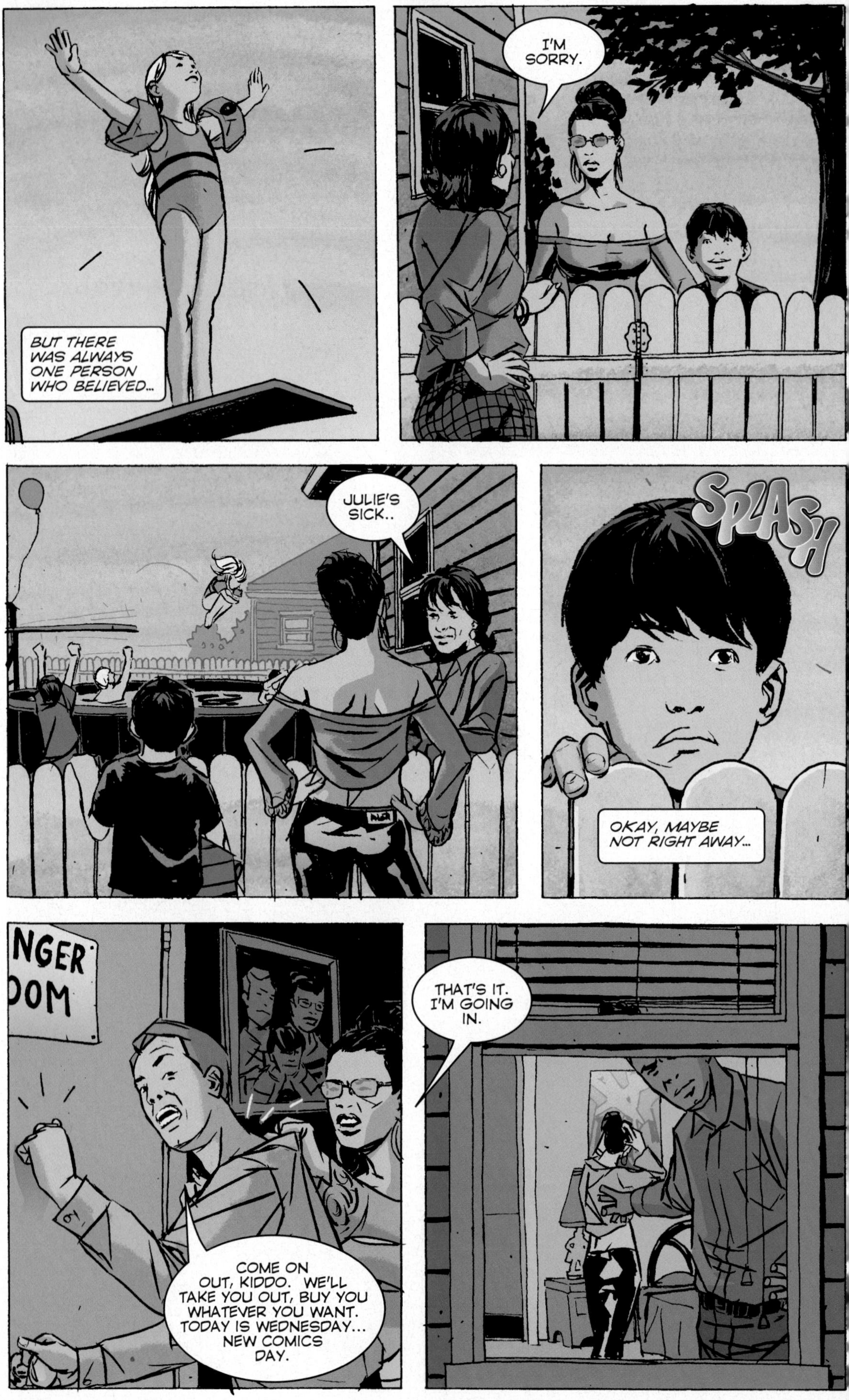
BUT THERE WAS ALWAYS ONE PERSON WHO BELIEVED...
I'M SORRY.
JULIE'S SICK..
SPLASH
OKAY, MAYBE NOT RIGHT AWAY...
NGER
OOM
COME ON OUT, KIDDO. WE'LL TAKE YOU OUT, BUY YOU WHATEVER YOU WANT. TODAY IS WEDNESDAY... NEW COMICS DAY.
THAT'S IT. I'M GOING IN.

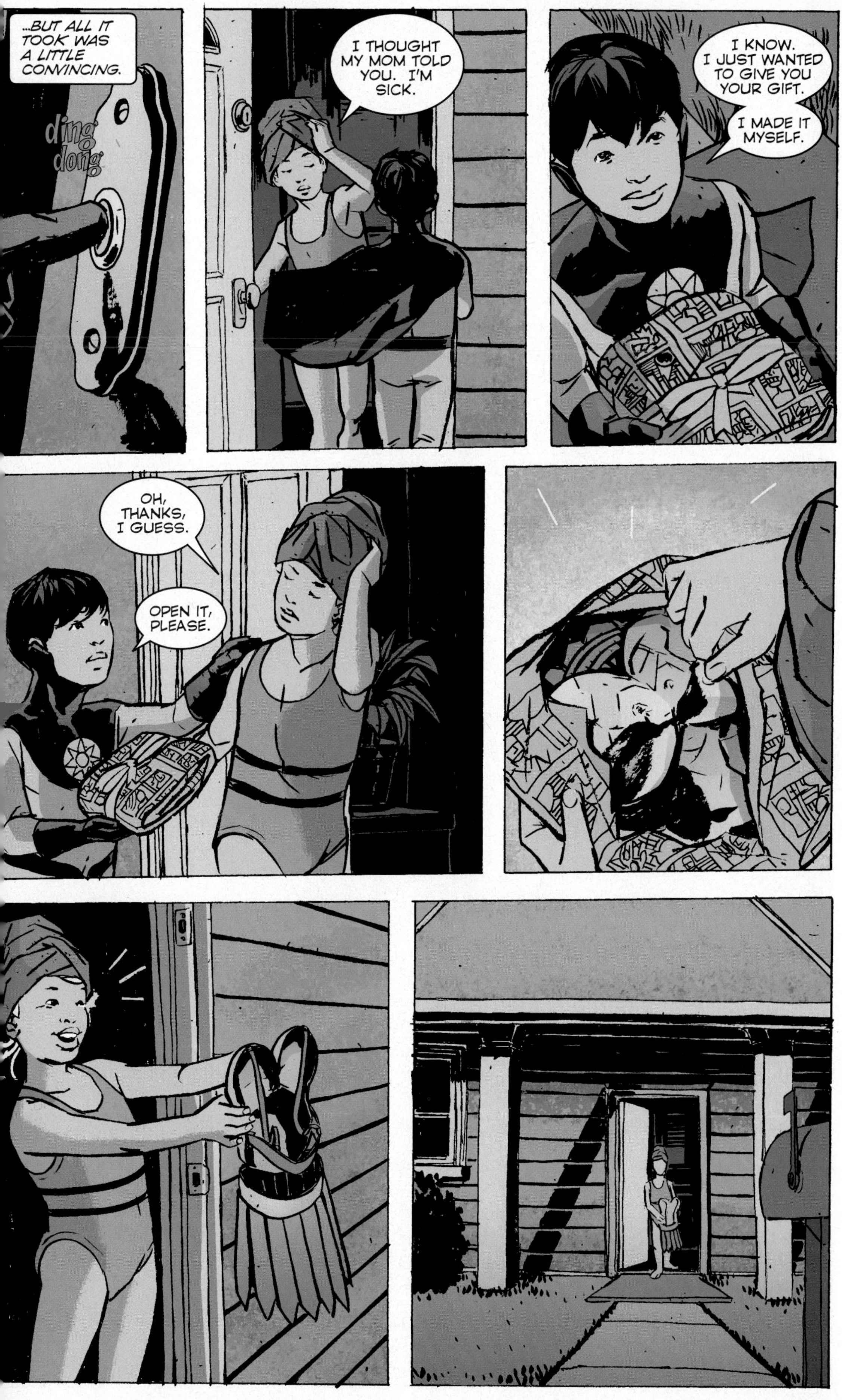
...BUT ALL IT TOOK WAS A LITTLE CONVINCING.
ding dong
I THOUGHT MY MOM TOLD YOU. I'M SICK.
I KNOW. I JUST WANTED TO GIVE YOU YOUR GIFT.
I MADE IT MYSELF.
OH, THANKS, I GUESS.
OPEN IT, PLEASE.

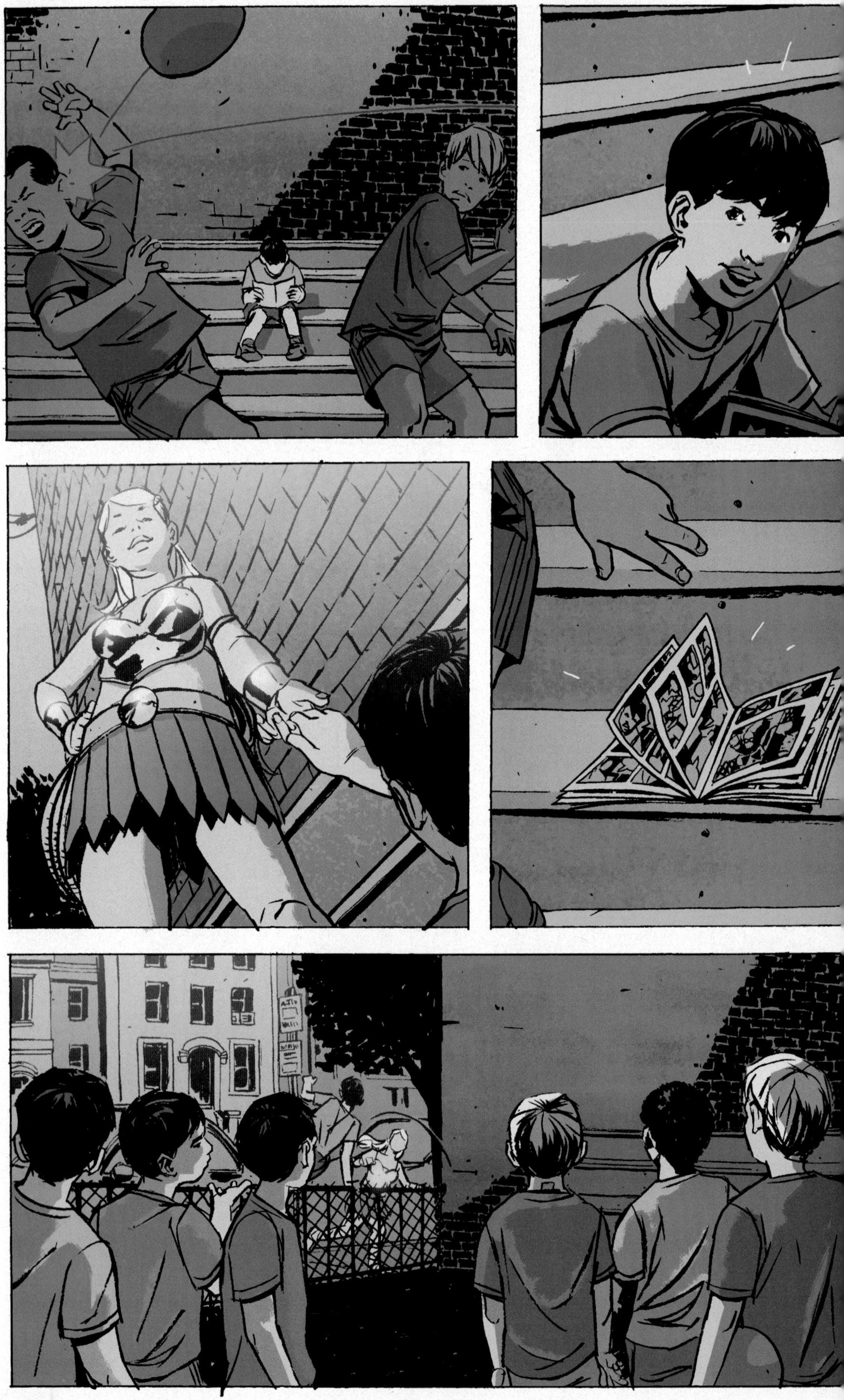

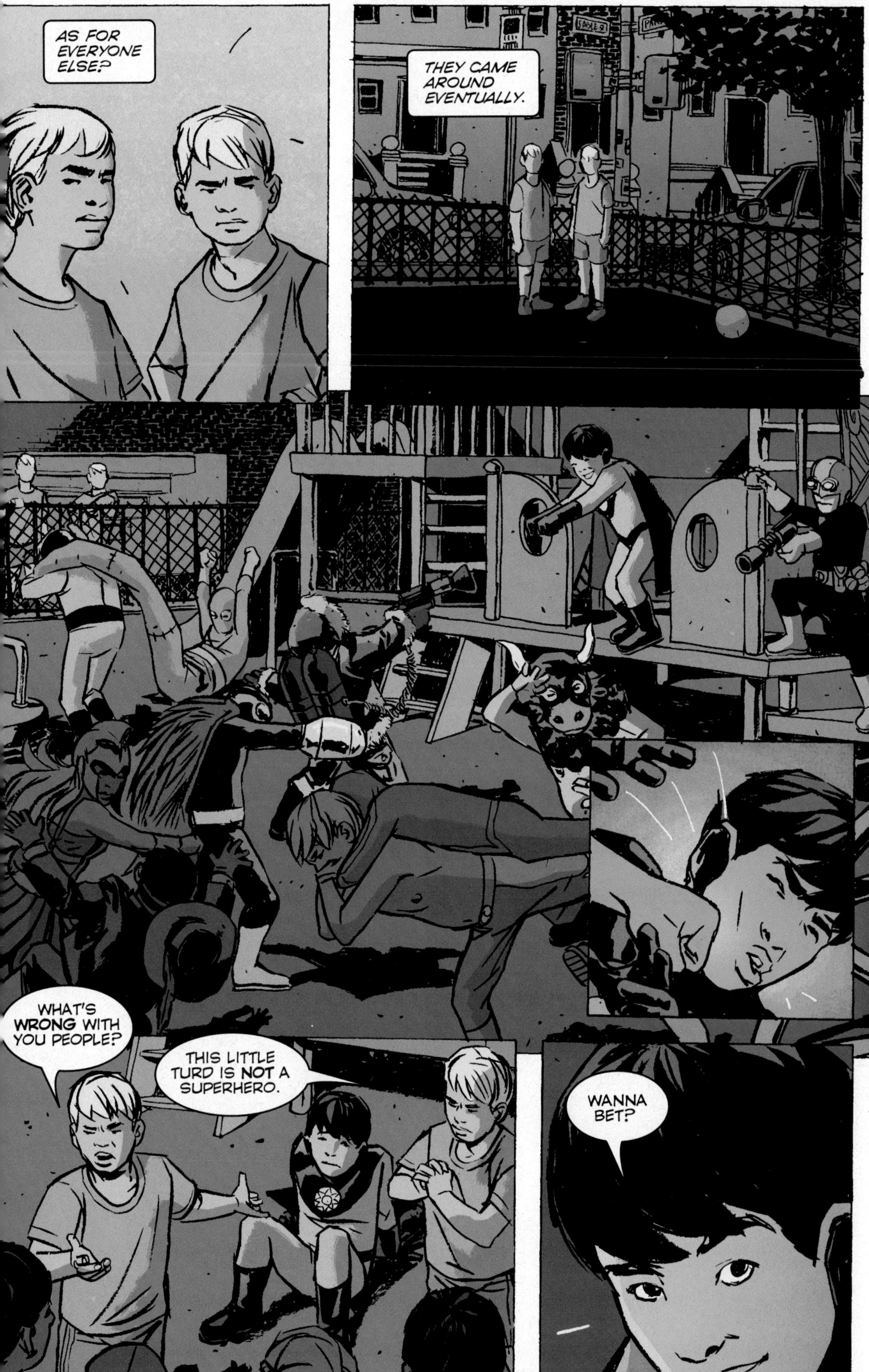
AS FOR EVERYONE ELSE?
THEY CAME AROUND EVENTUALLY.
WHAT'S WRONG WITH YOU PEOPLE?
THIS LITTLE TURD IS NOT A SUPERHERO.
WANNA BET?

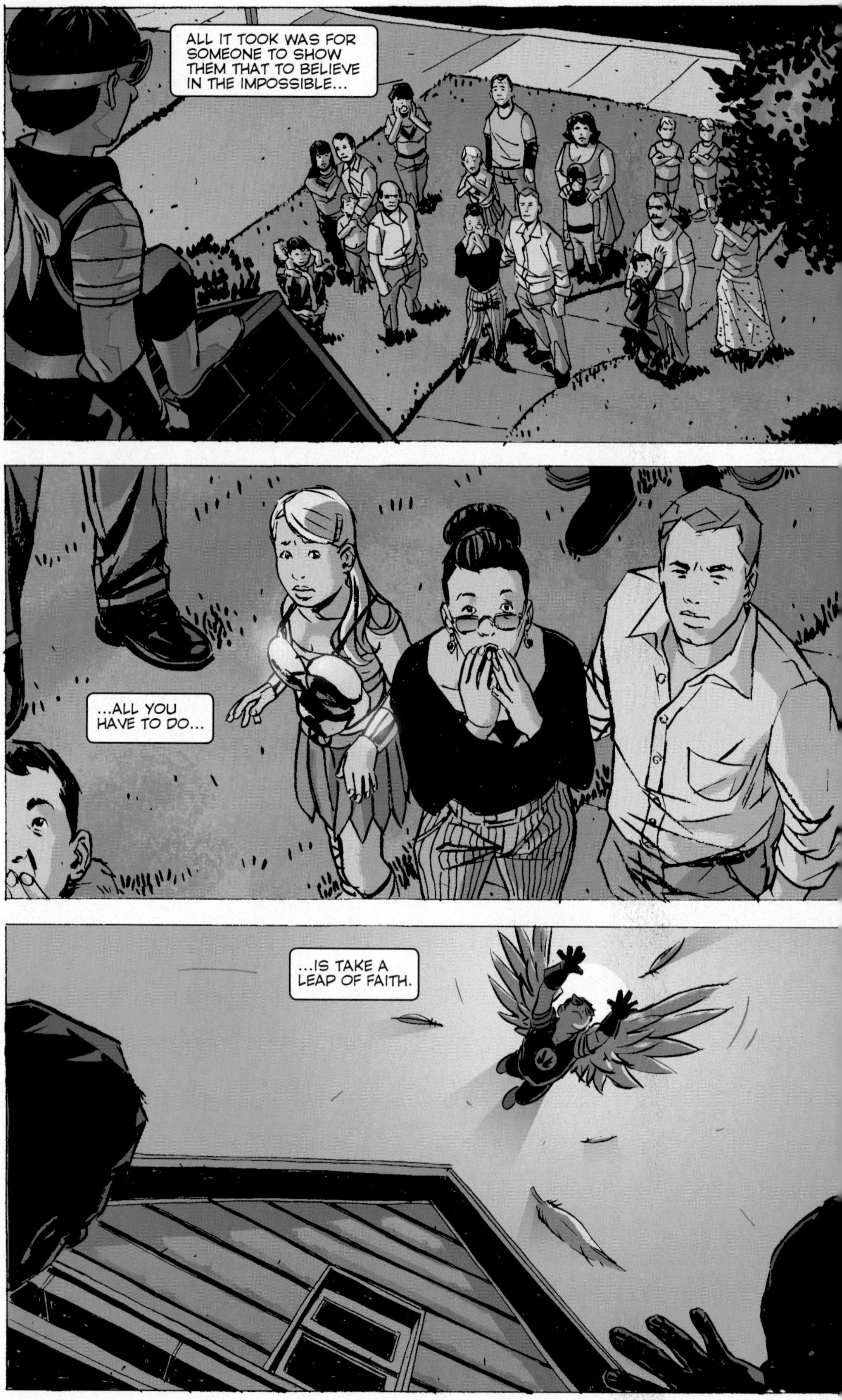
ALL IT TOOK WAS FOR SOMEONE TO SHOW THEM THAT TO BELIEVE IN THE IMPOSSIBLE...
...ALL YOU HAVE TO DO...
...IS TAKE A LEAP OF FAITH.

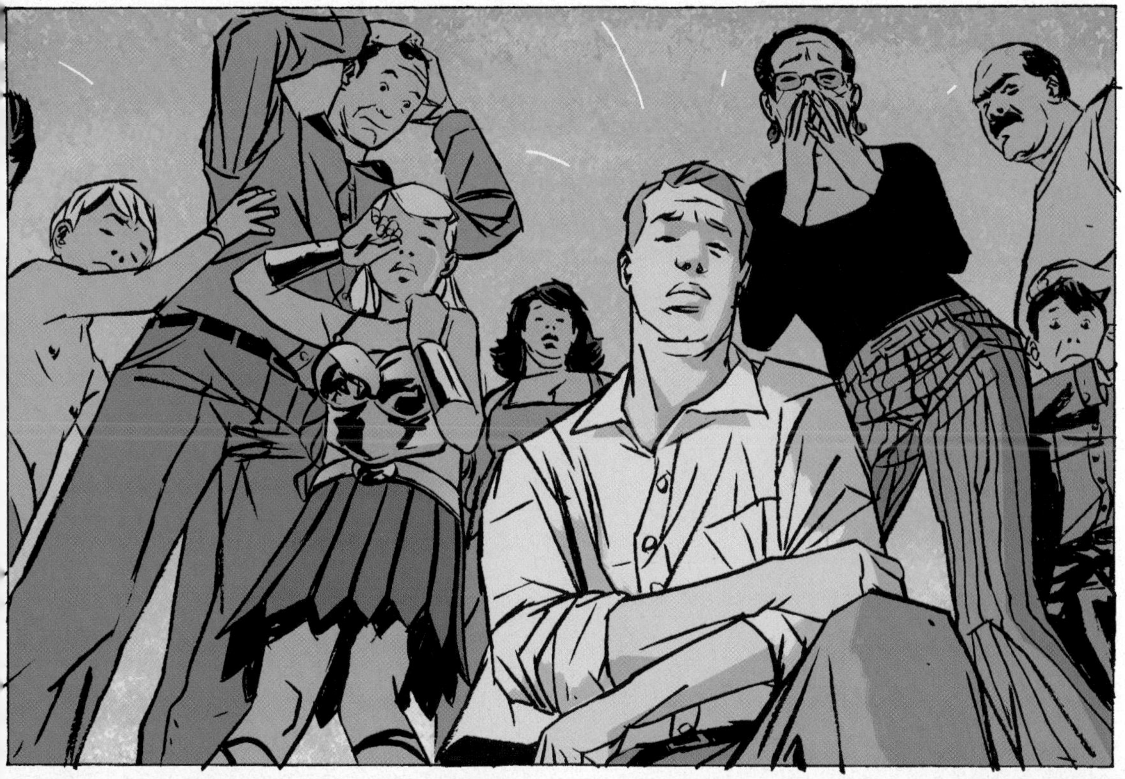

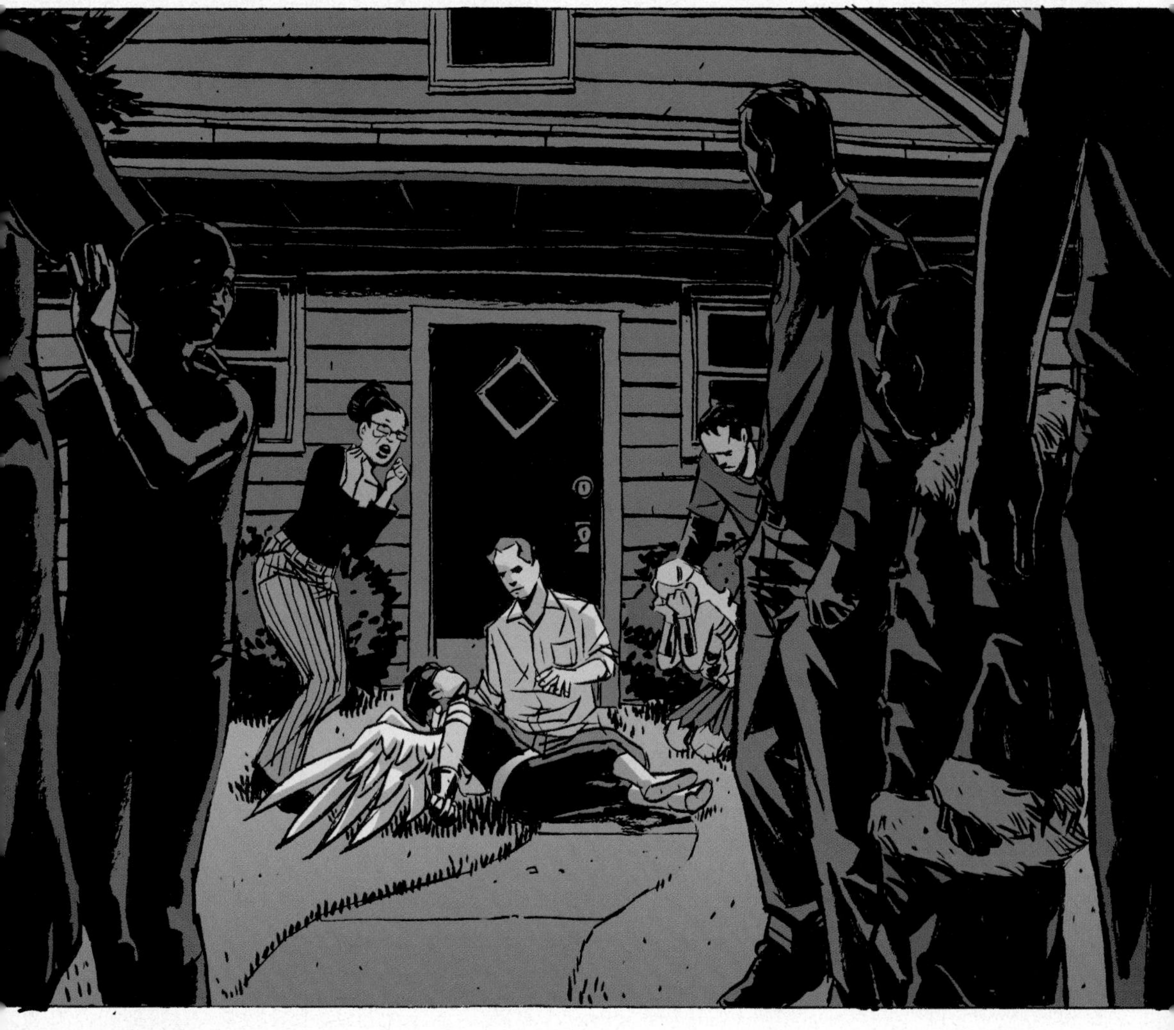

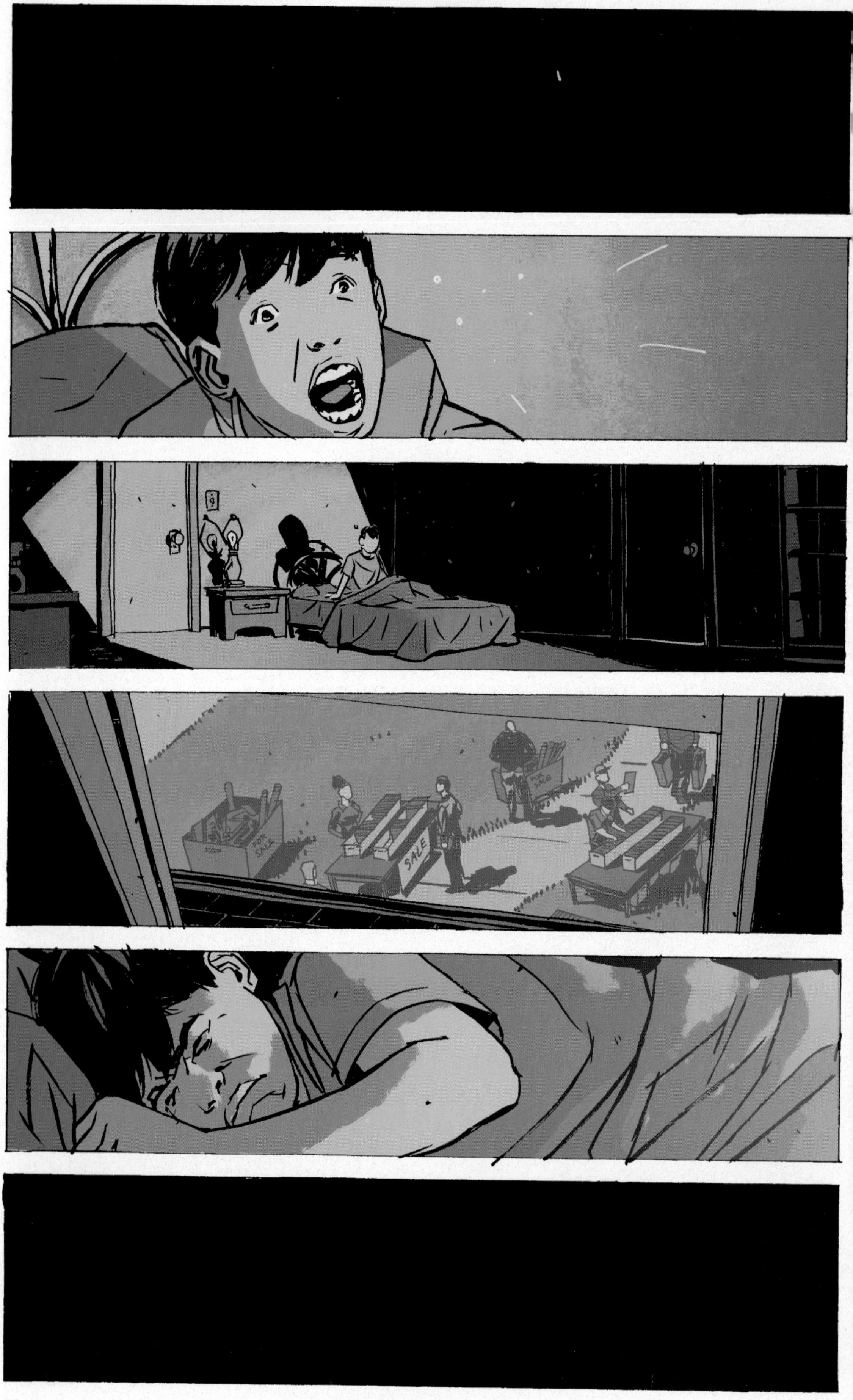
FOR SALE
SALE

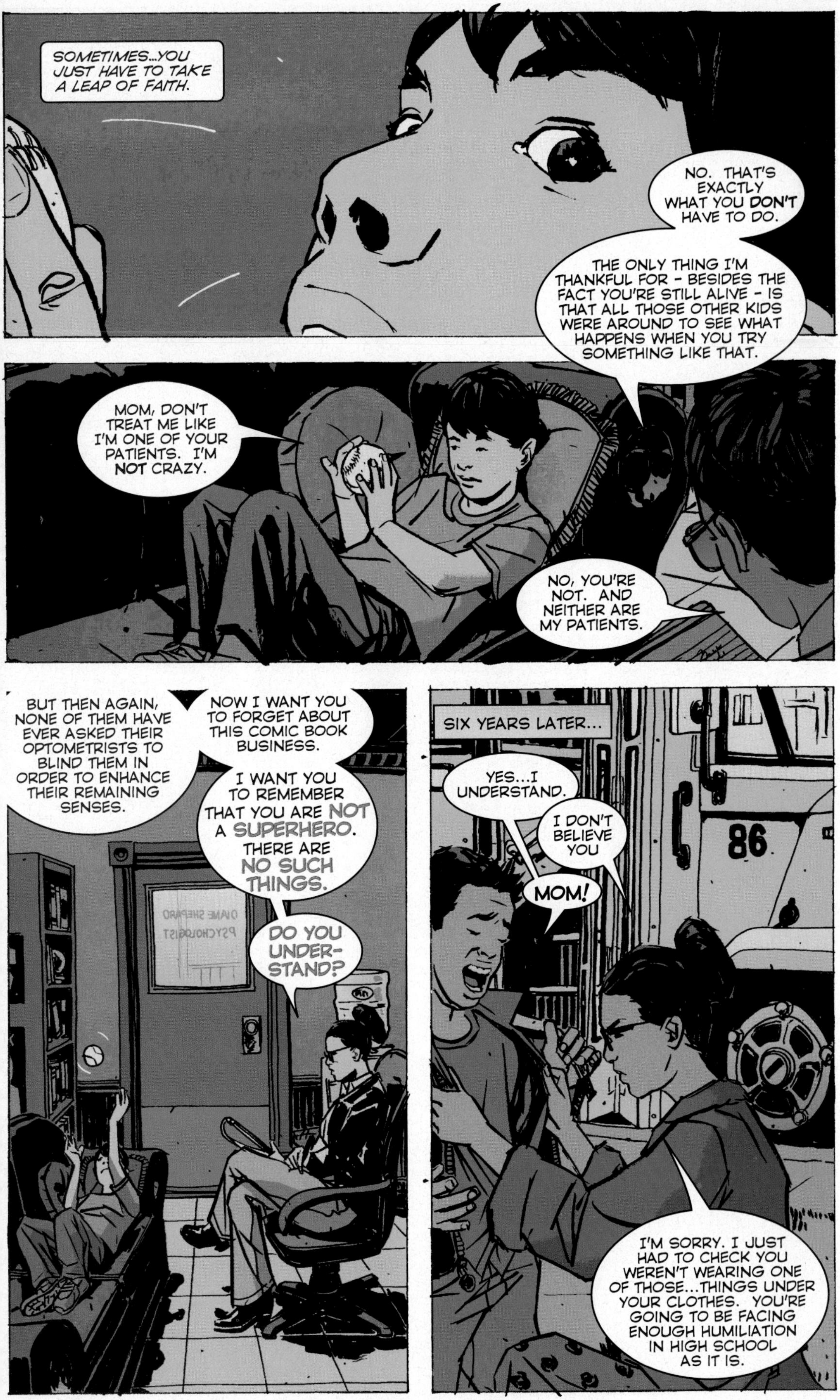
SOMETIMES...YOU JUST HAVE TO TAKE A LEAP OF FAITH.
NO. THAT'S EXACTLY WHAT YOU DON'T HAVE TO DO.
THE ONLY THING I'M THANKFUL FOR - BESIDES THE FACT YOU'RE STILL ALIVE - IS THAT ALL THOSE OTHER KIDS WERE AROUND TO SEE WHAT HAPPENS WHEN YOU TRY SOMETHING LIKE THAT.
MOM, DON'T TREAT ME LIKE I'M ONE OF YOUR PATIENTS. I'M NOT CRAZY.
NO, YOU'RE NOT. AND NEITHER ARE MY PATIENTS.
BUT THEN AGAIN, NONE OF THEM HAVE EVER ASKED THEIR OPTOMETRISTS TO BLIND THEM IN ORDER TO ENHANCE THEIR REMAINING SENSES.
NOW I WANT YOU TO FORGET ABOUT THIS COMIC BOOK BUSINESS.
I WANT YOU TO REMEMBER THAT YOU ARE NOT A SUPERHERO. THERE ARE NO SUCH THINGS.
DO YOU UNDER-STAND?
DIANE SHEPARD PSYCHOLOGIST
SIX YEARS LATER...
YES...I UNDERSTAND.
I DON'T BELIEVE YOU
MOM!
86
I'M SORRY. I JUST HAD TO CHECK YOU WEREN'T WEARING ONE OF THOSE...THINGS UNDER YOUR CLOTHES. YOU'RE GOING TO BE FACING ENOUGH HUMILIATION IN HIGH SCHOOL AS IT IS.

RRRIINNGG

WELL, IF IT ISN'T THE BOY WHO COULDN'T FLY.

WHAT YOU GOT IN THAT BAG?

OH COME ON, LIKE YOU DON'T KNOW WHAT'S IN HERE.

I'LL NEVER UNDERSTAND WHY STUPID PEOPLE FEEL THE NEED TO PLAY DUMB.

LET ME TELL YOU, IT CAN'T BE ANY MORE RIDICULOUS THAN WHAT YOU'RE WEARING.

WHAT DO THEY CALL THOSE THINGS BETWEEN YOUR CLEATS AND THE PINSTRIPES? KNICKERS, RIGHT?

I'M SAYING I HAVE JUST AS MUCH OF A CHANCE OF BECOMING A SUPERHERO AS YOU DO A PROFESSIONAL ATHLETE. AT LEAST MY UNIFORM **STANDS** FOR SOMETHING.

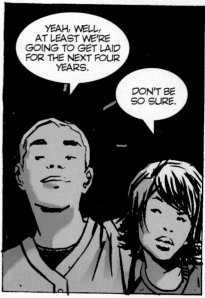

YEAH, WELL, AT LEAST WE'RE GOING TO GET LAID FOR THE NEXT FOUR YEARS.

DON'T BE SO SURE.

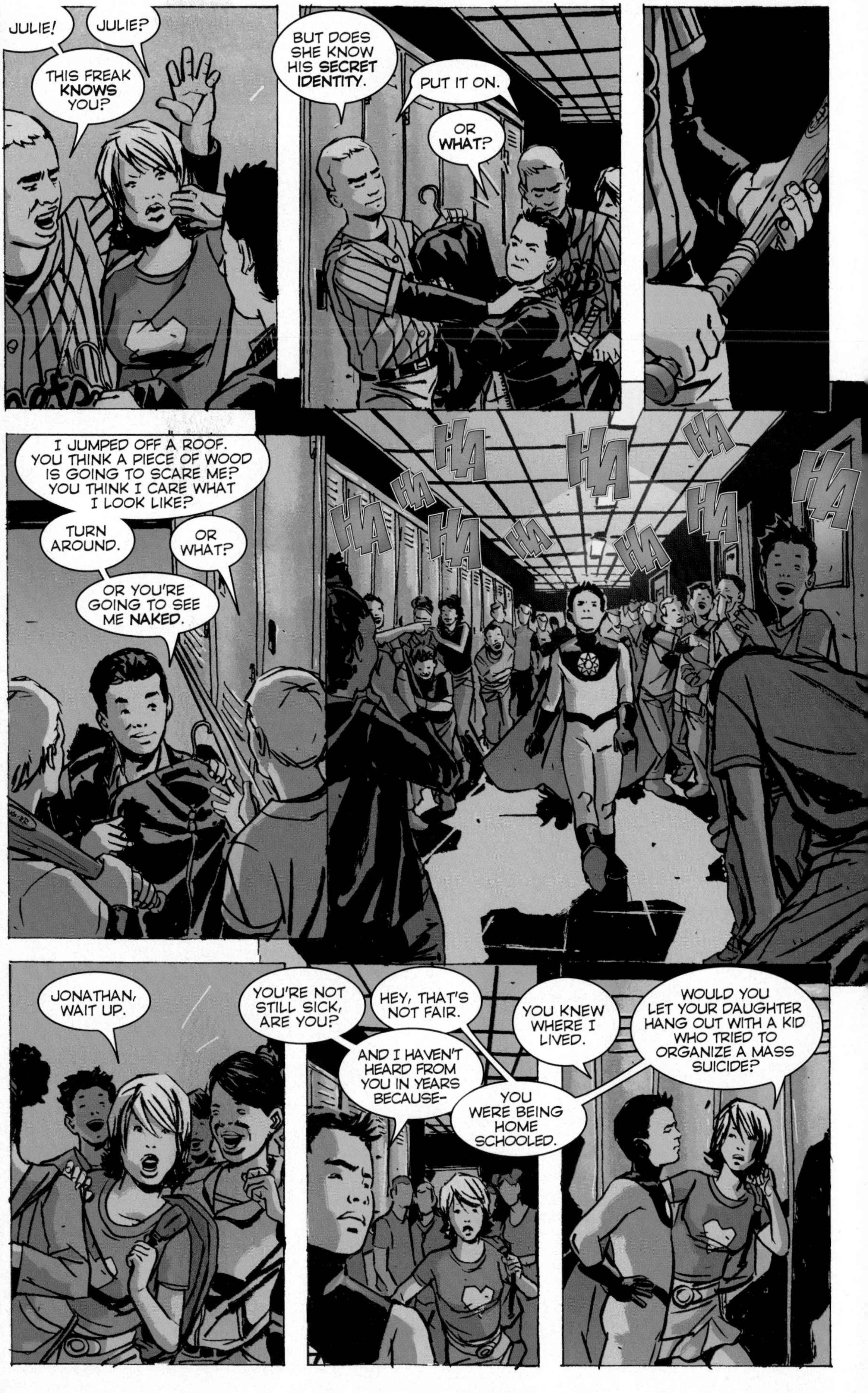

JULIE!
JULIE?
THIS FREAK **KNOWS** YOU?
BUT DOES SHE KNOW HIS **SECRET IDENTITY**.
PUT IT ON.
OR **WHAT?**
I JUMPED OFF A ROOF. YOU THINK A PIECE OF WOOD IS GOING TO SCARE ME? YOU THINK I CARE WHAT I LOOK LIKE?
TURN AROUND.
OR WHAT?
OR YOU'RE GOING TO SEE ME **NAKED**.
HA HA HA HA HA HA HA HA HA HA HA
JONATHAN, WAIT UP.
YOU'RE NOT STILL SICK, ARE YOU?
HEY, THAT'S NOT FAIR.
AND I HAVEN'T HEARD FROM YOU IN YEARS BECAUSE-
YOU WERE BEING HOME SCHOOLED.
YOU KNEW WHERE I LIVED.
WOULD YOU LET YOUR DAUGHTER HANG OUT WITH A KID WHO TRIED TO ORGANIZE A MASS SUICIDE?

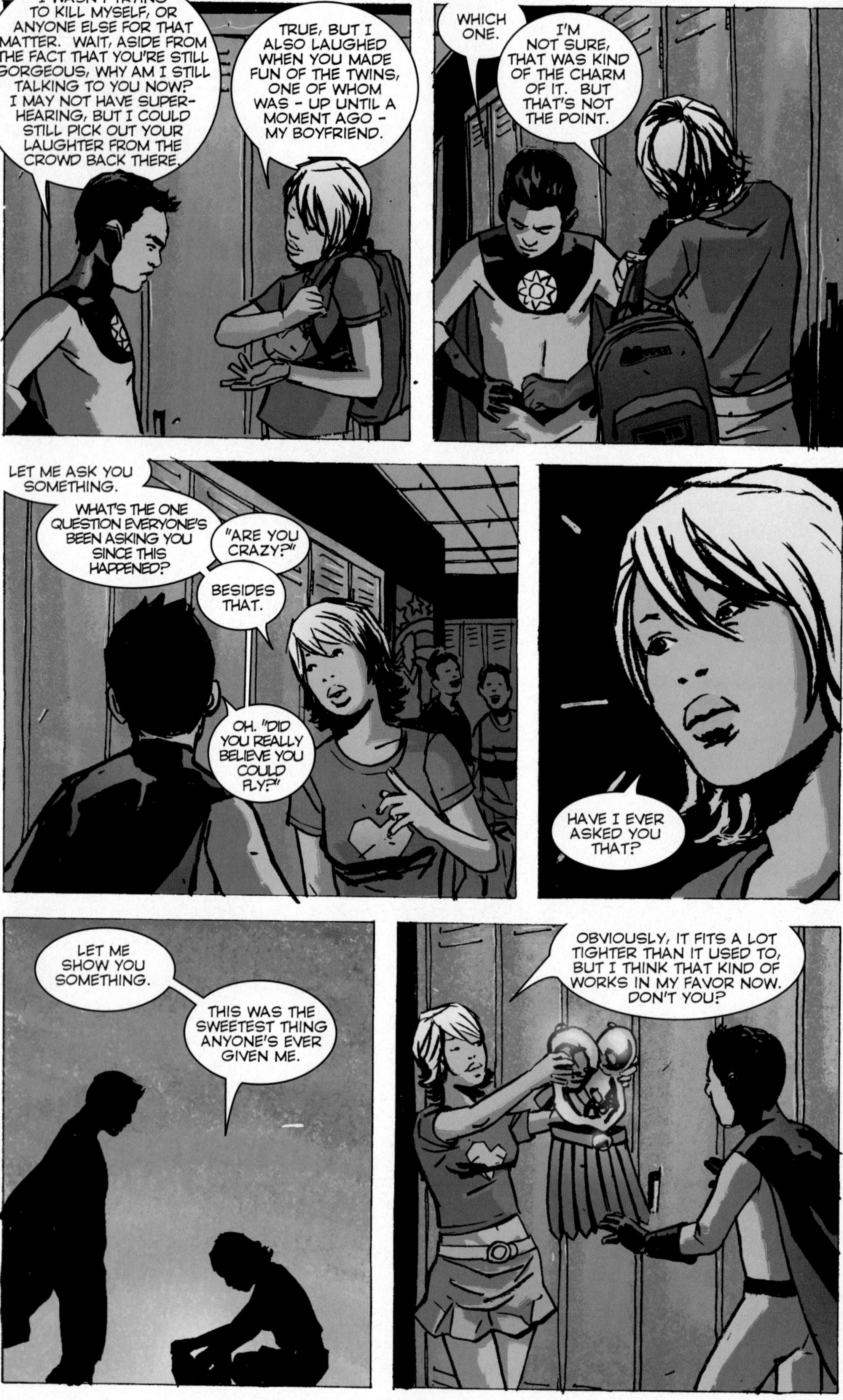
I WASN'T TRYING TO KILL MYSELF, OR ANYONE ELSE FOR THAT MATTER. WAIT, ASIDE FROM THE FACT THAT YOU'RE STILL GORGEOUS, WHY AM I STILL TALKING TO YOU NOW? I MAY NOT HAVE SUPER-HEARING, BUT I COULD STILL PICK OUT YOUR LAUGHTER FROM THE CROWD BACK THERE.
TRUE, BUT I ALSO LAUGHED WHEN YOU MADE FUN OF THE TWINS, ONE OF WHOM WAS - UP UNTIL A MOMENT AGO - MY BOYFRIEND.
WHICH ONE.
I'M NOT SURE, THAT WAS KIND OF THE CHARM OF IT. BUT THAT'S NOT THE POINT.
LET ME ASK YOU SOMETHING.
WHAT'S THE ONE QUESTION EVERYONE'S BEEN ASKING YOU SINCE THIS HAPPENED?
"ARE YOU CRAZY?"
BESIDES THAT.
OH. "DID YOU REALLY BELIEVE YOU COULD FLY?"
HAVE I EVER ASKED YOU THAT?
LET ME SHOW YOU SOMETHING.
THIS WAS THE SWEETEST THING ANYONE'S EVER GIVEN ME.
OBVIOUSLY, IT FITS A LOT TIGHTER THAN IT USED TO, BUT I THINK THAT KIND OF WORKS IN MY FAVOR NOW. DON'T YOU?

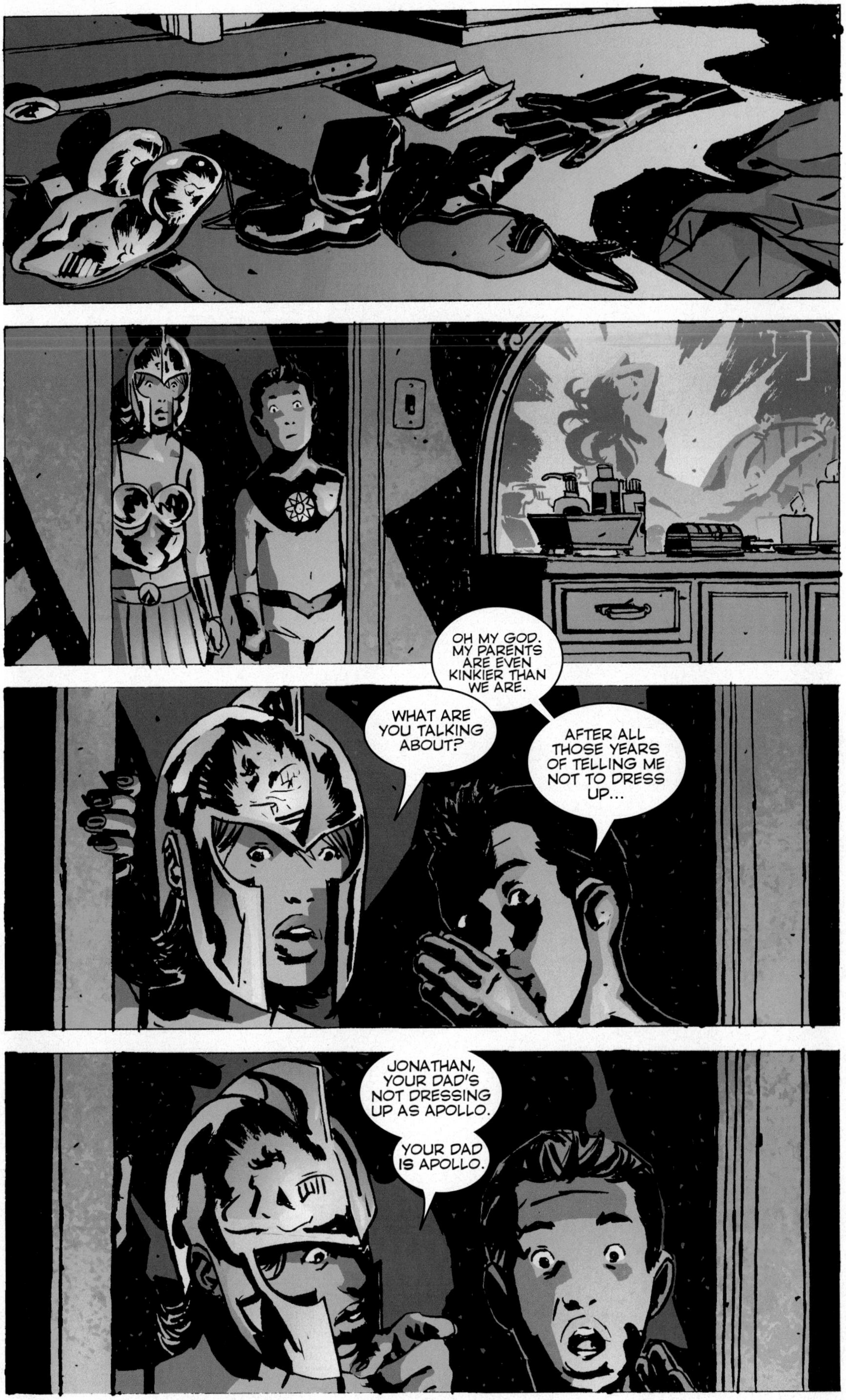
OH MY GOD. MY PARENTS ARE EVEN KINKIER THAN WE ARE.
WHAT ARE YOU TALKING ABOUT?
AFTER ALL THOSE YEARS OF TELLING ME NOT TO DRESS UP...
JONATHAN, YOUR DAD'S NOT DRESSING UP AS APOLLO.
YOUR DAD IS APOLLO.

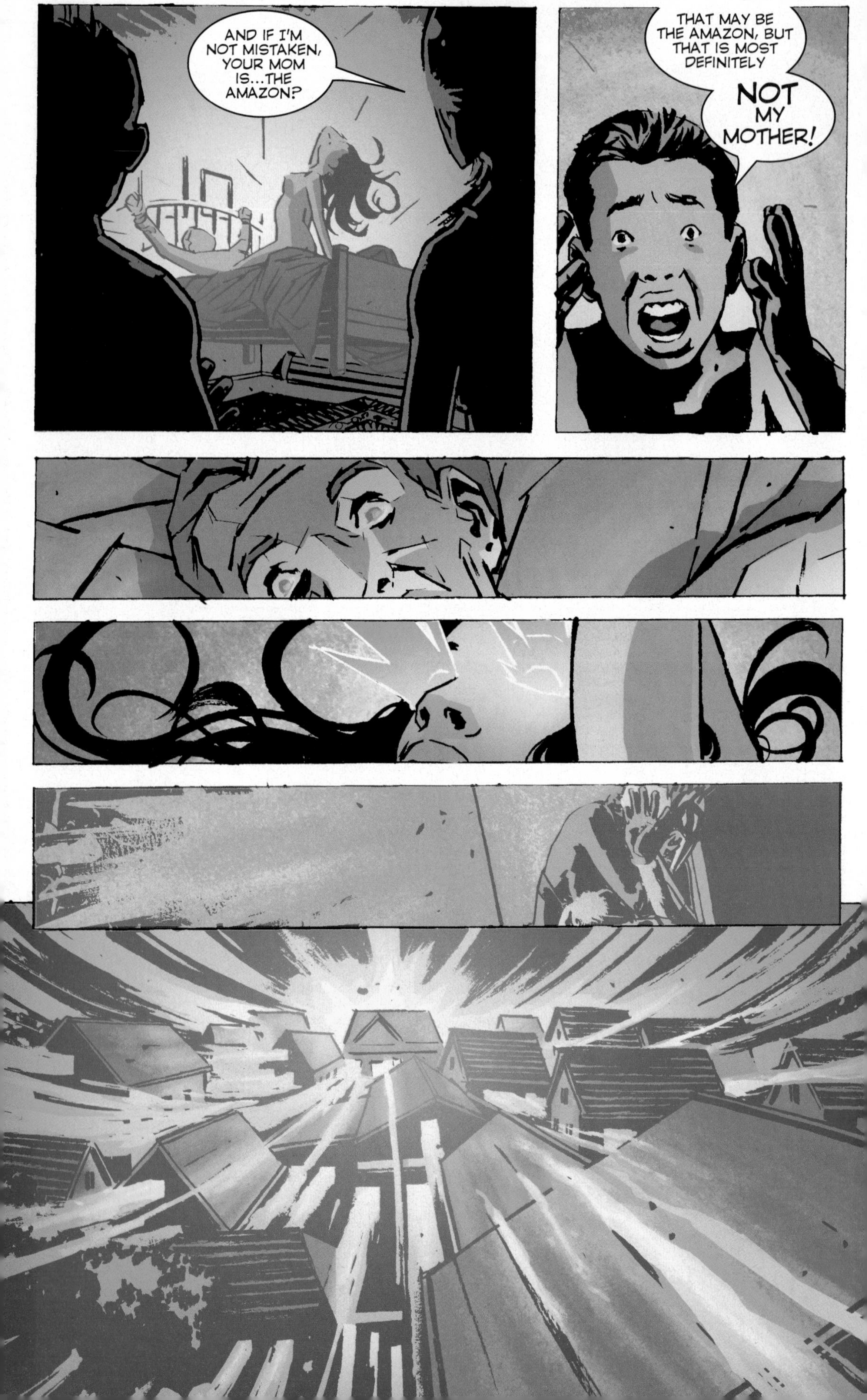
AND IF I'M NOT MISTAKEN, YOUR MOM IS...THE AMAZON?
THAT MAY BE THE AMAZON, BUT THAT IS MOST DEFINITELY NOT MY MOTHER!

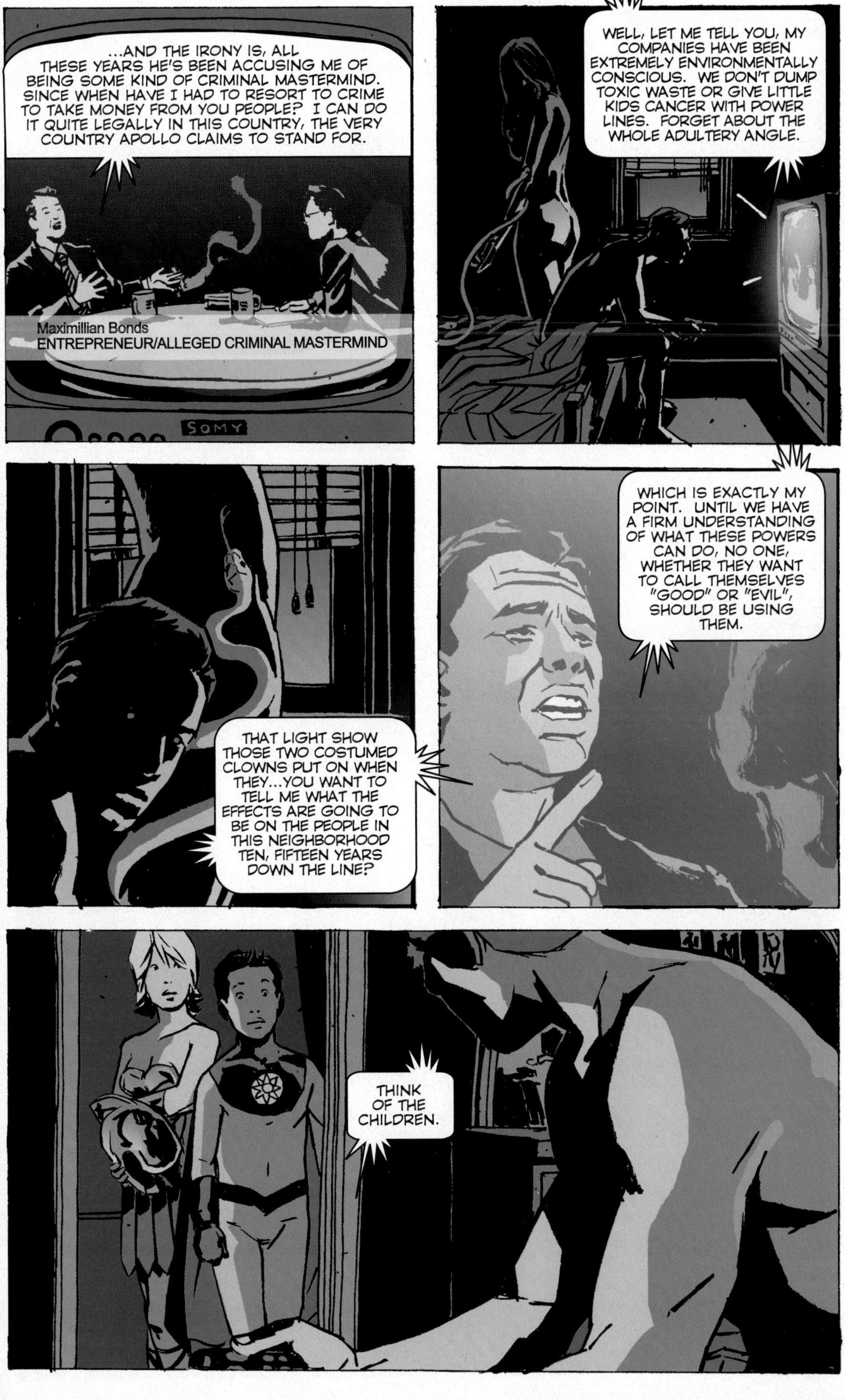
...AND THE IRONY IS, ALL THESE YEARS HE'S BEEN ACCUSING ME OF BEING SOME KIND OF CRIMINAL MASTERMIND. SINCE WHEN HAVE I HAD TO RESORT TO CRIME TO TAKE MONEY FROM YOU PEOPLE? I CAN DO IT QUITE LEGALLY IN THIS COUNTRY, THE VERY COUNTRY APOLLO CLAIMS TO STAND FOR.
Maximillian Bonds
ENTREPRENEUR/ALLEGED CRIMINAL MASTERMIND
SOMY
WELL, LET ME TELL YOU, MY COMPANIES HAVE BEEN EXTREMELY ENVIRONMENTALLY CONSCIOUS. WE DON'T DUMP TOXIC WASTE OR GIVE LITTLE KIDS CANCER WITH POWER LINES. FORGET ABOUT THE WHOLE ADULTERY ANGLE.
THAT LIGHT SHOW THOSE TWO COSTUMED CLOWNS PUT ON WHEN THEY...YOU WANT TO TELL ME WHAT THE EFFECTS ARE GOING TO BE ON THE PEOPLE IN THIS NEIGHBORHOOD TEN, FIFTEEN YEARS DOWN THE LINE?
WHICH IS EXACTLY MY POINT. UNTIL WE HAVE A FIRM UNDERSTANDING OF WHAT THESE POWERS CAN DO, NO ONE, WHETHER THEY WANT TO CALL THEMSELVES "GOOD" OR "EVIL", SHOULD BE USING THEM.
THINK OF THE CHILDREN.

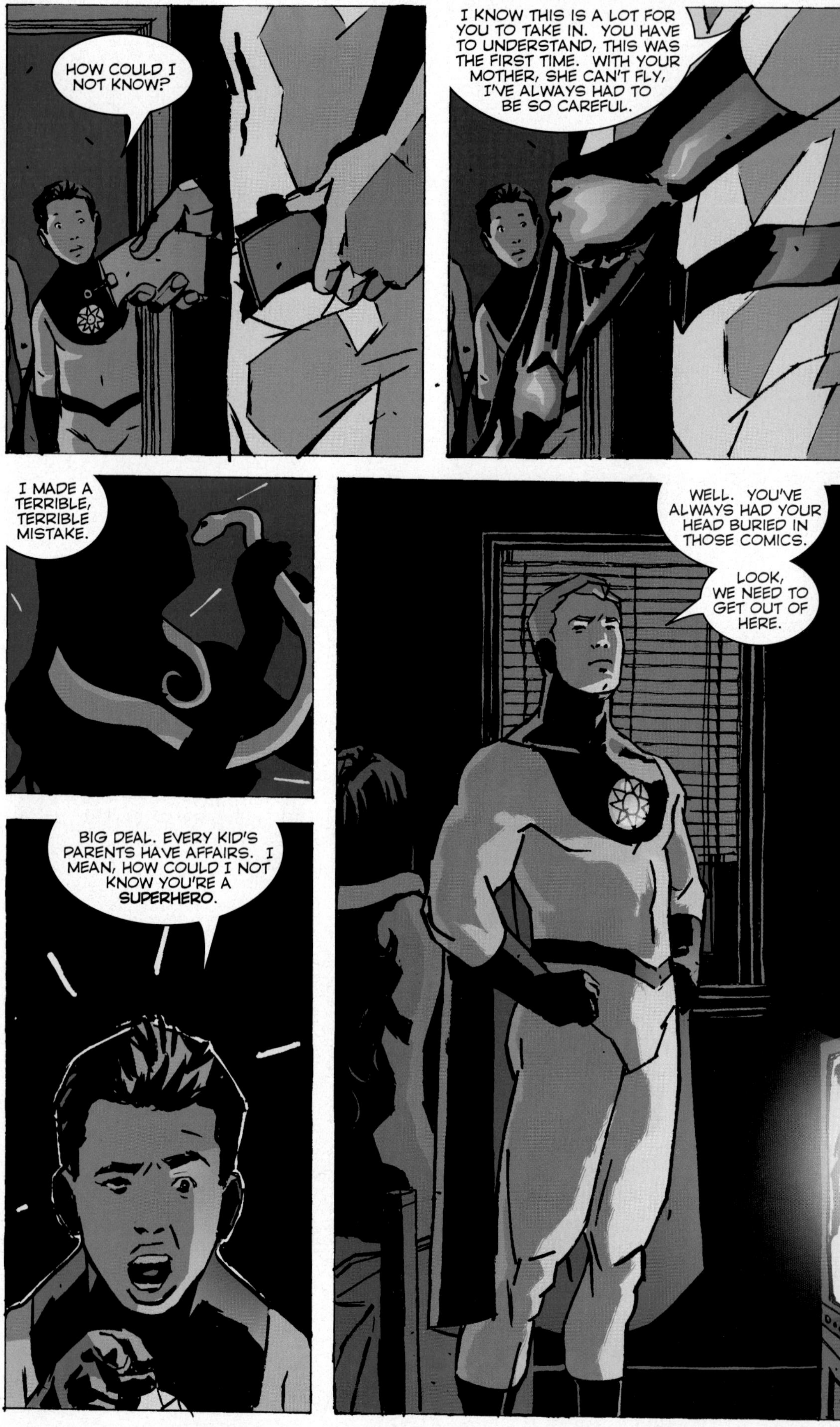
HOW COULD I NOT KNOW?
I KNOW THIS IS A LOT FOR YOU TO TAKE IN. YOU HAVE TO UNDERSTAND, THIS WAS THE FIRST TIME. WITH YOUR MOTHER, SHE CAN'T FLY, I'VE ALWAYS HAD TO BE SO CAREFUL.
I MADE A TERRIBLE, TERRIBLE MISTAKE.
BIG DEAL. EVERY KID'S PARENTS HAVE AFFAIRS. I MEAN, HOW COULD I NOT KNOW YOU'RE A SUPERHERO.
WELL. YOU'VE ALWAYS HAD YOUR HEAD BURIED IN THOSE COMICS.
LOOK, WE NEED TO GET OUT OF HERE.

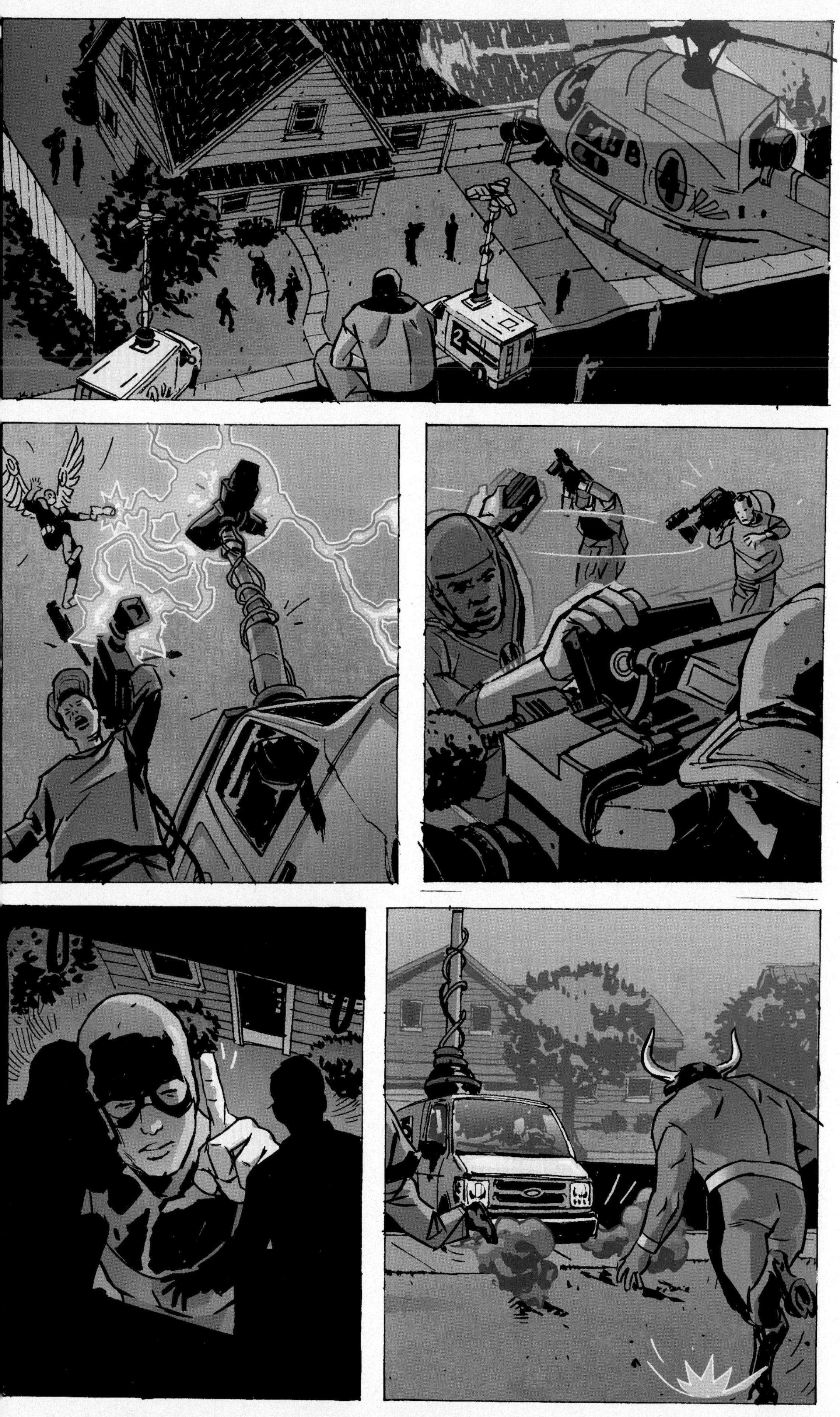

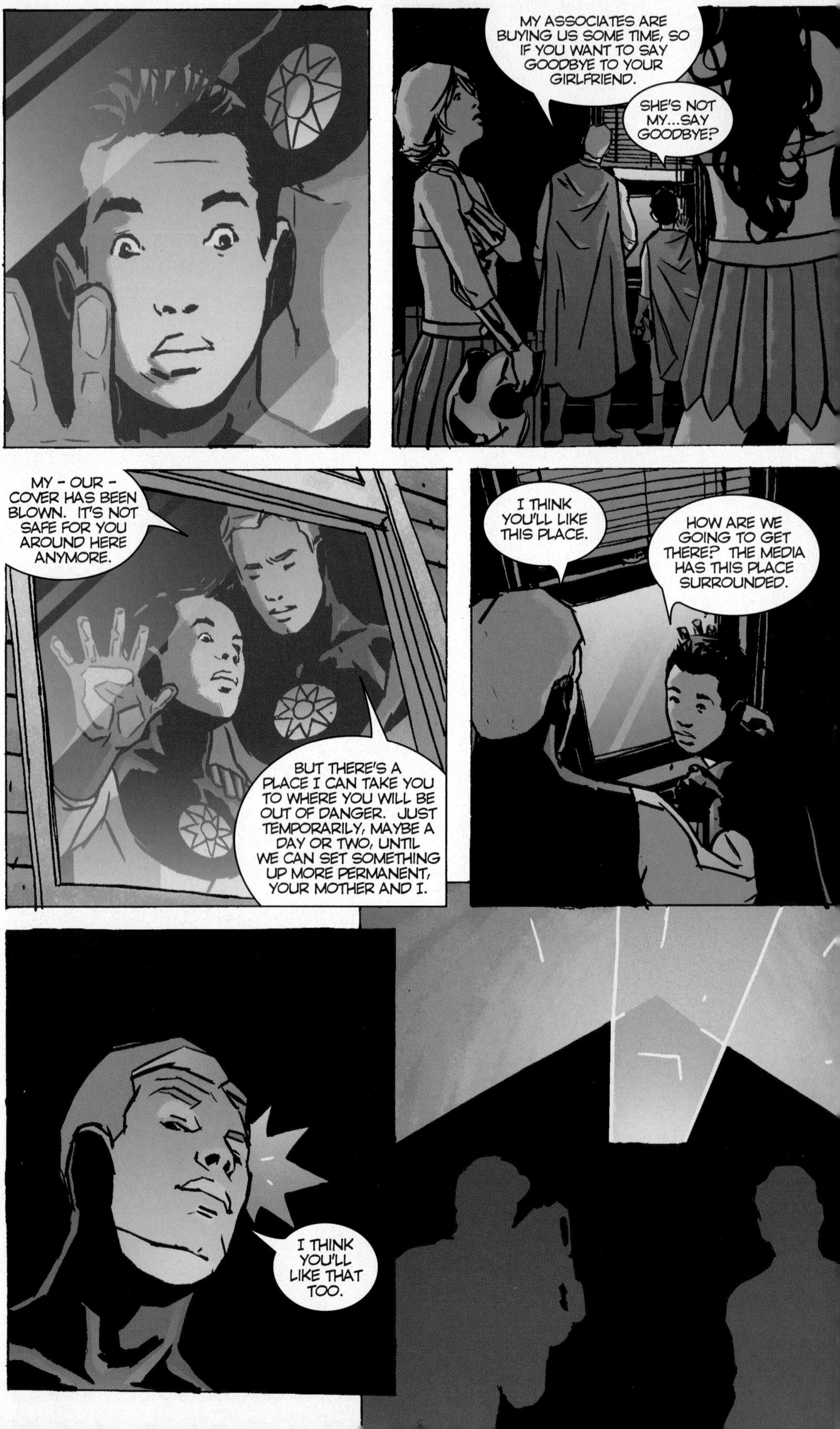
MY ASSOCIATES ARE BUYING US SOME TIME, SO IF YOU WANT TO SAY GOODBYE TO YOUR GIRLFRIEND.
SHE'S NOT MY...SAY GOODBYE?
MY - OUR - COVER HAS BEEN BLOWN. IT'S NOT SAFE FOR YOU AROUND HERE ANYMORE.
BUT THERE'S A PLACE I CAN TAKE YOU TO WHERE YOU WILL BE OUT OF DANGER. JUST TEMPORARILY, MAYBE A DAY OR TWO, UNTIL WE CAN SET SOMETHING UP MORE PERMANENT, YOUR MOTHER AND I.
I THINK YOU'LL LIKE THIS PLACE.
HOW ARE WE GOING TO GET THERE? THE MEDIA HAS THIS PLACE SURROUNDED.
I THINK YOU'LL LIKE THAT TOO.

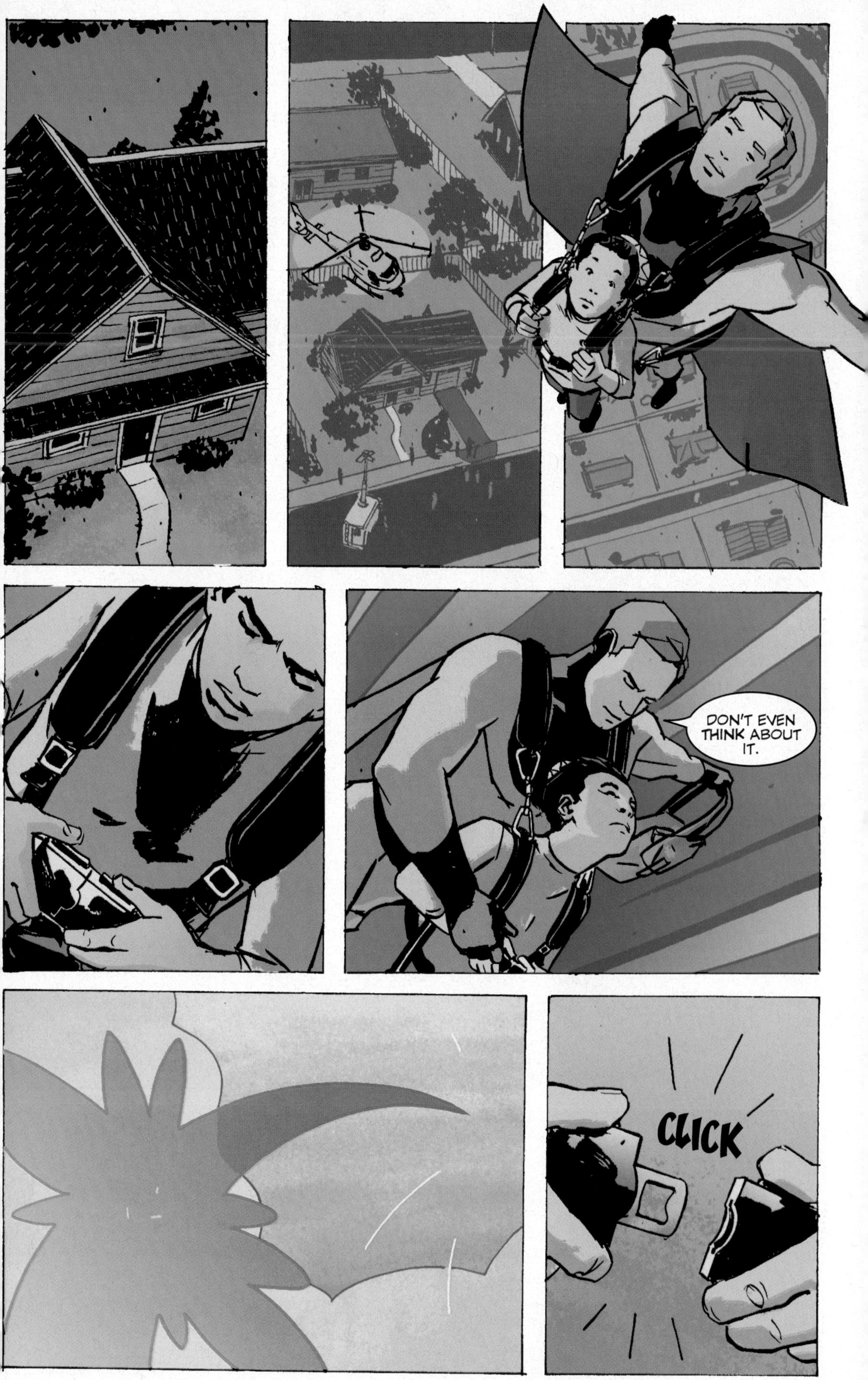

DON'T EVEN THINK ABOUT IT.
CLICK

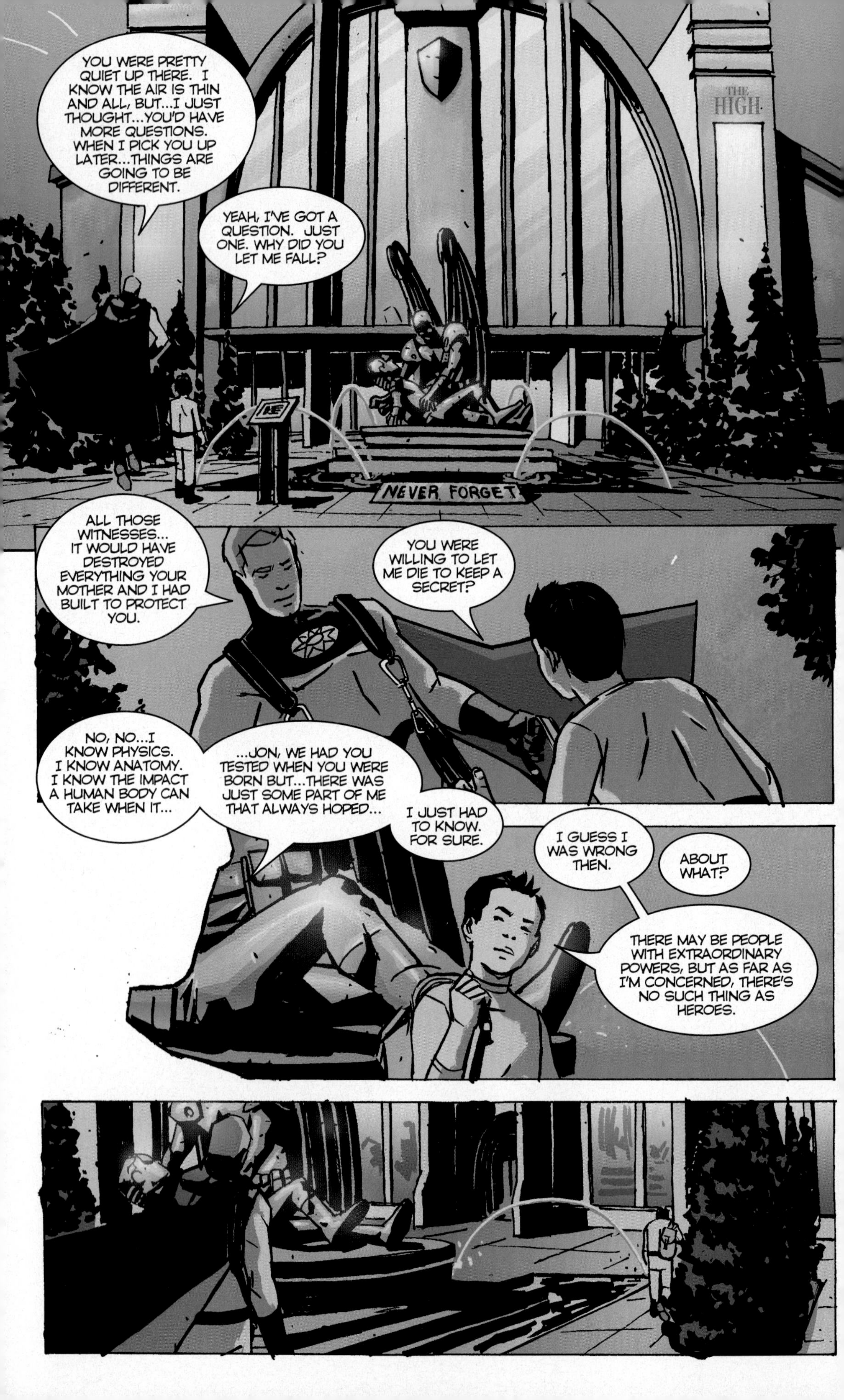
THE HIGH
YOU WERE PRETTY QUIET UP THERE. I KNOW THE AIR IS THIN AND ALL, BUT...I JUST THOUGHT...YOU'D HAVE MORE QUESTIONS. WHEN I PICK YOU UP LATER...THINGS ARE GOING TO BE DIFFERENT.
YEAH, I'VE GOT A QUESTION. JUST ONE. WHY DID YOU LET ME FALL?
NEVER FORGET
ALL THOSE WITNESSES... IT WOULD HAVE DESTROYED EVERYTHING YOUR MOTHER AND I HAD BUILT TO PROTECT YOU.
YOU WERE WILLING TO LET ME DIE TO KEEP A SECRET?
NO, NO...I KNOW PHYSICS. I KNOW ANATOMY. I KNOW THE IMPACT A HUMAN BODY CAN TAKE WHEN IT...
...JON, WE HAD YOU TESTED WHEN YOU WERE BORN BUT...THERE WAS JUST SOME PART OF ME THAT ALWAYS HOPED...
I JUST HAD TO KNOW. FOR SURE.
I GUESS I WAS WRONG THEN.
ABOUT WHAT?
THERE MAY BE PEOPLE WITH EXTRAORDINARY POWERS, BUT AS FAR AS I'M CONCERNED, THERE'S NO SUCH THING AS HEROES.

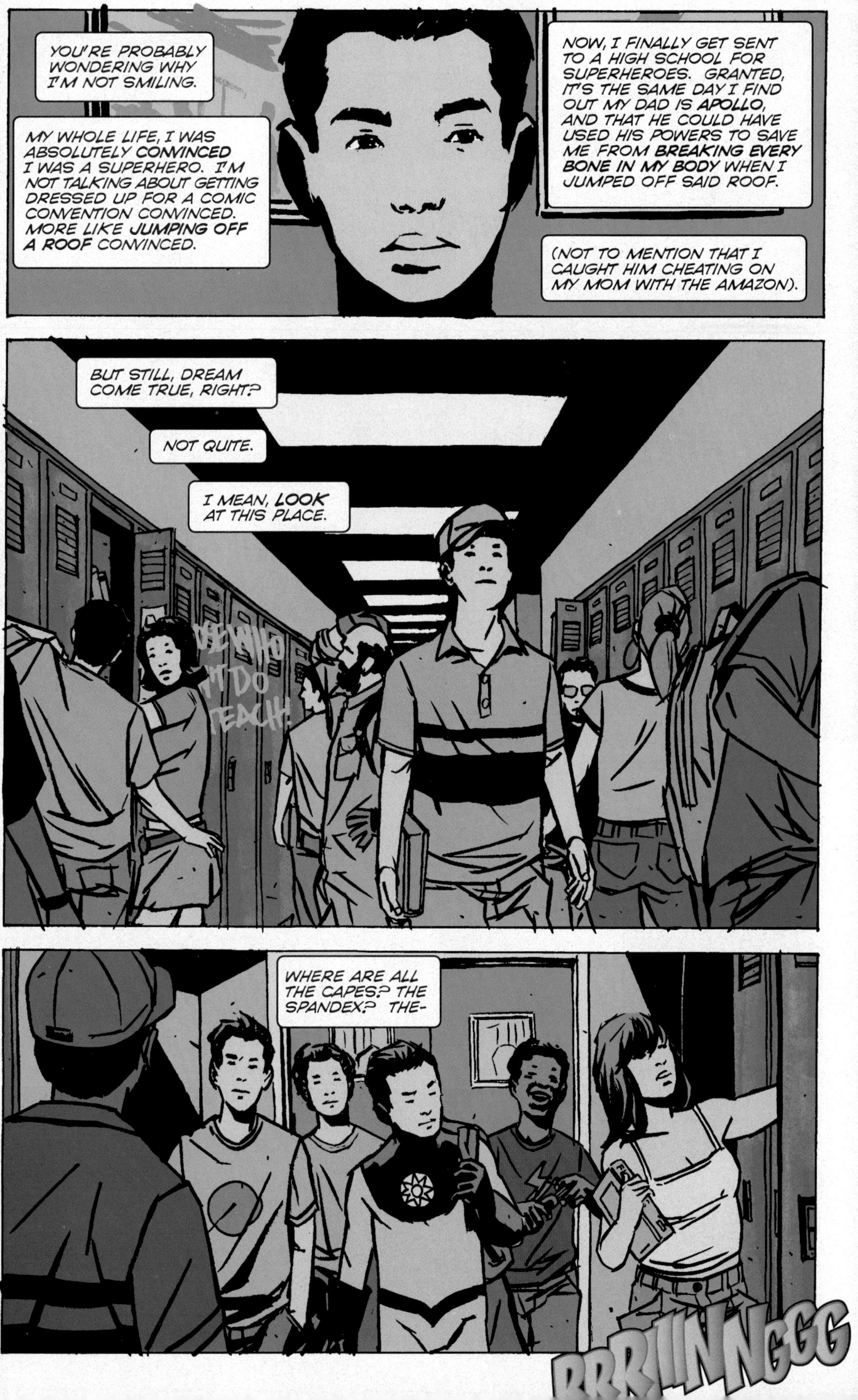
YOU'RE PROBABLY WONDERING WHY I'M NOT SMILING.
MY WHOLE LIFE, I WAS ABSOLUTELY **CONVINCED** I WAS A SUPERHERO. I'M NOT TALKING ABOUT GETTING DRESSED UP FOR A COMIC CONVENTION CONVINCED. MORE LIKE **JUMPING OFF A ROOF** CONVINCED.
NOW, I FINALLY GET SENT TO A HIGH SCHOOL FOR SUPERHEROES. GRANTED, IT'S THE SAME DAY I FIND OUT MY DAD IS **APOLLO**, AND THAT HE COULD HAVE USED HIS POWERS TO SAVE ME FROM **BREAKING EVERY BONE IN MY BODY** WHEN I JUMPED OFF SAID ROOF.
(NOT TO MENTION THAT I CAUGHT HIM CHEATING ON MY MOM WITH THE AMAZON).
BUT STILL, DREAM COME TRUE, RIGHT?
NOT QUITE.
I MEAN, **LOOK** AT THIS PLACE.
WHERE ARE ALL THE CAPES? THE SPANDEX? THE-
BRRIINNGGG

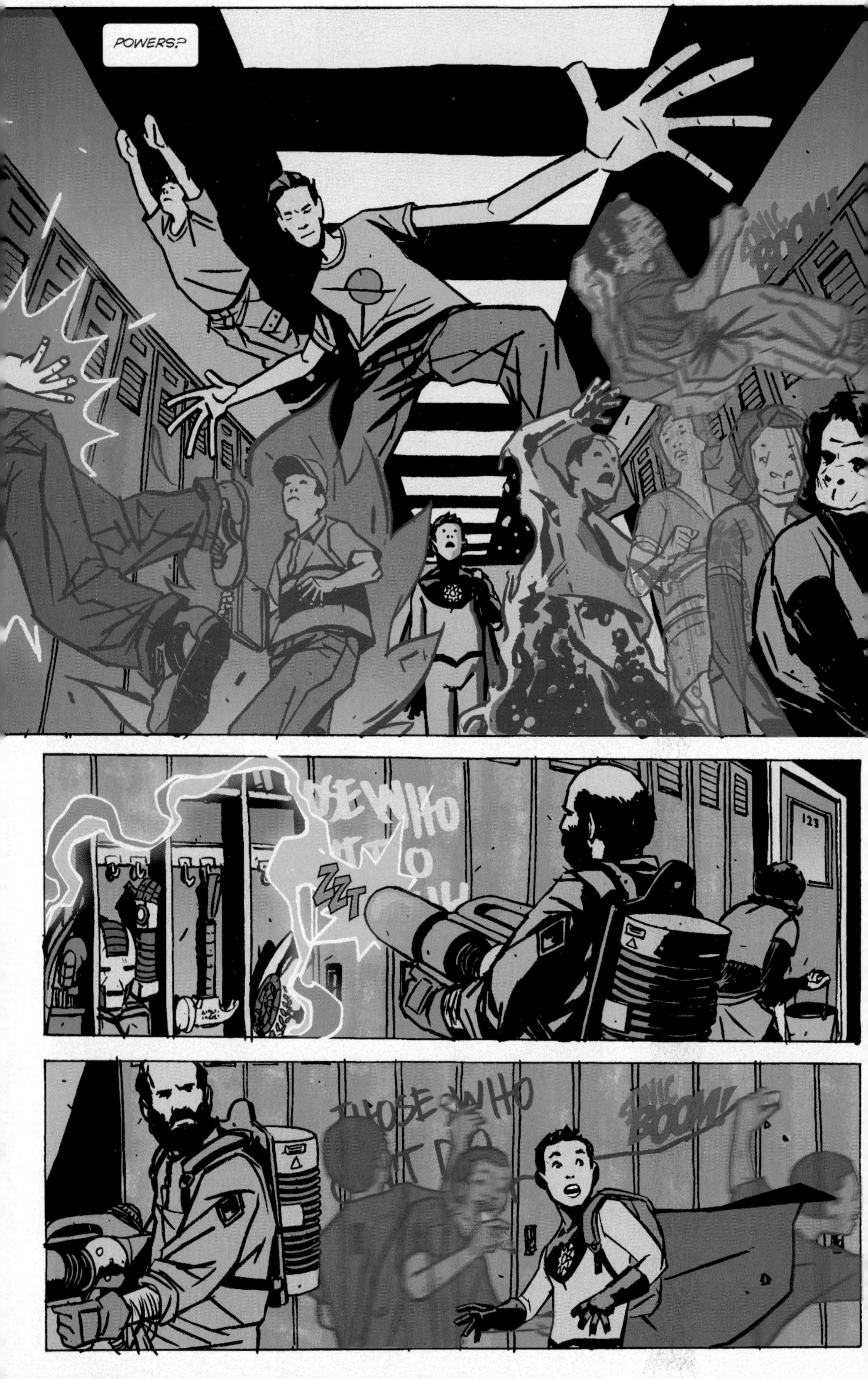
POWERS?
BOOM!
ZZT
BOOM!

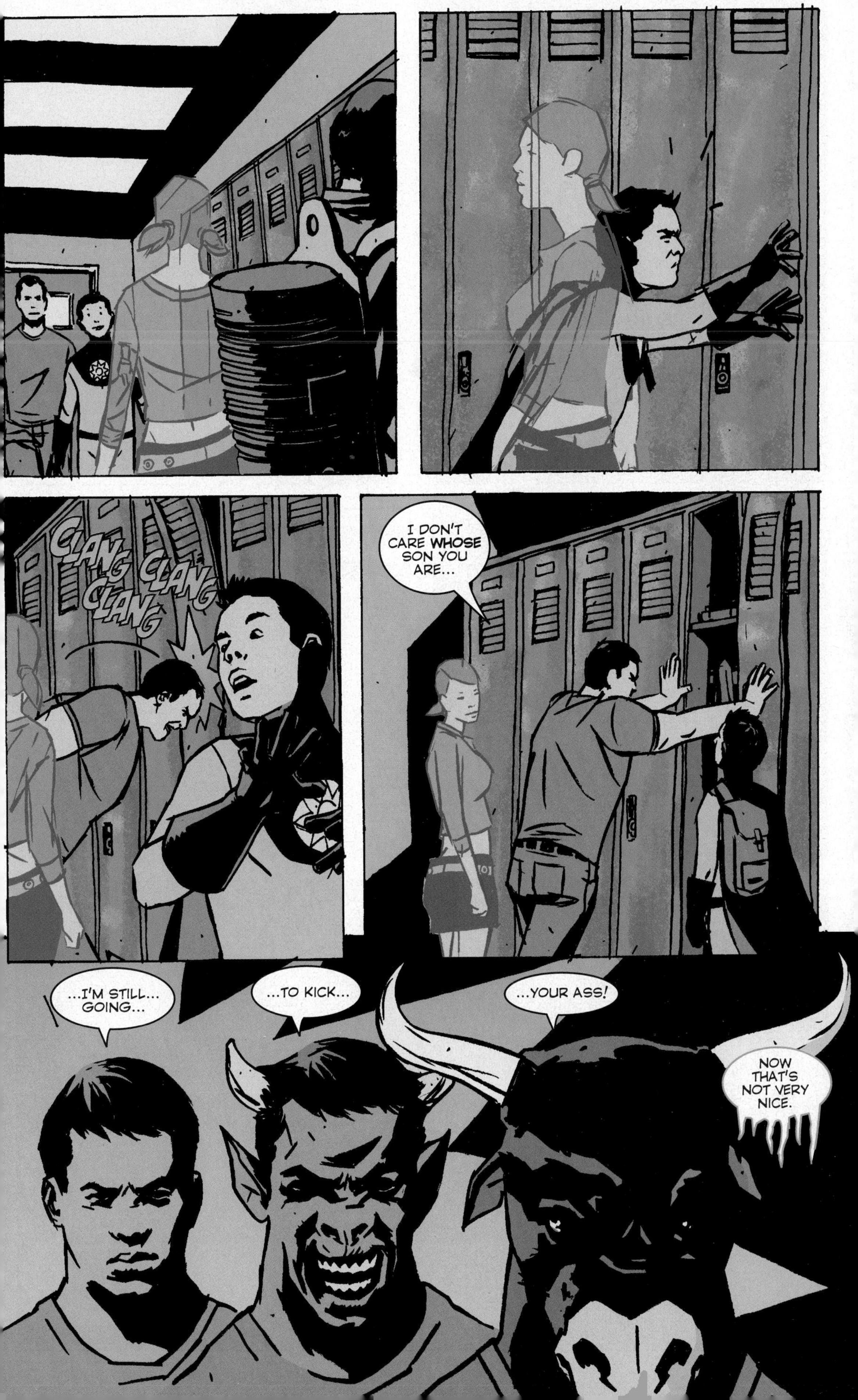
CLANG CLANG CLANG
I DON'T CARE WHOSE SON YOU ARE...
...I'M STILL... GOING...
...TO KICK...
...YOUR ASS!
NOW THAT'S NOT VERY NICE.

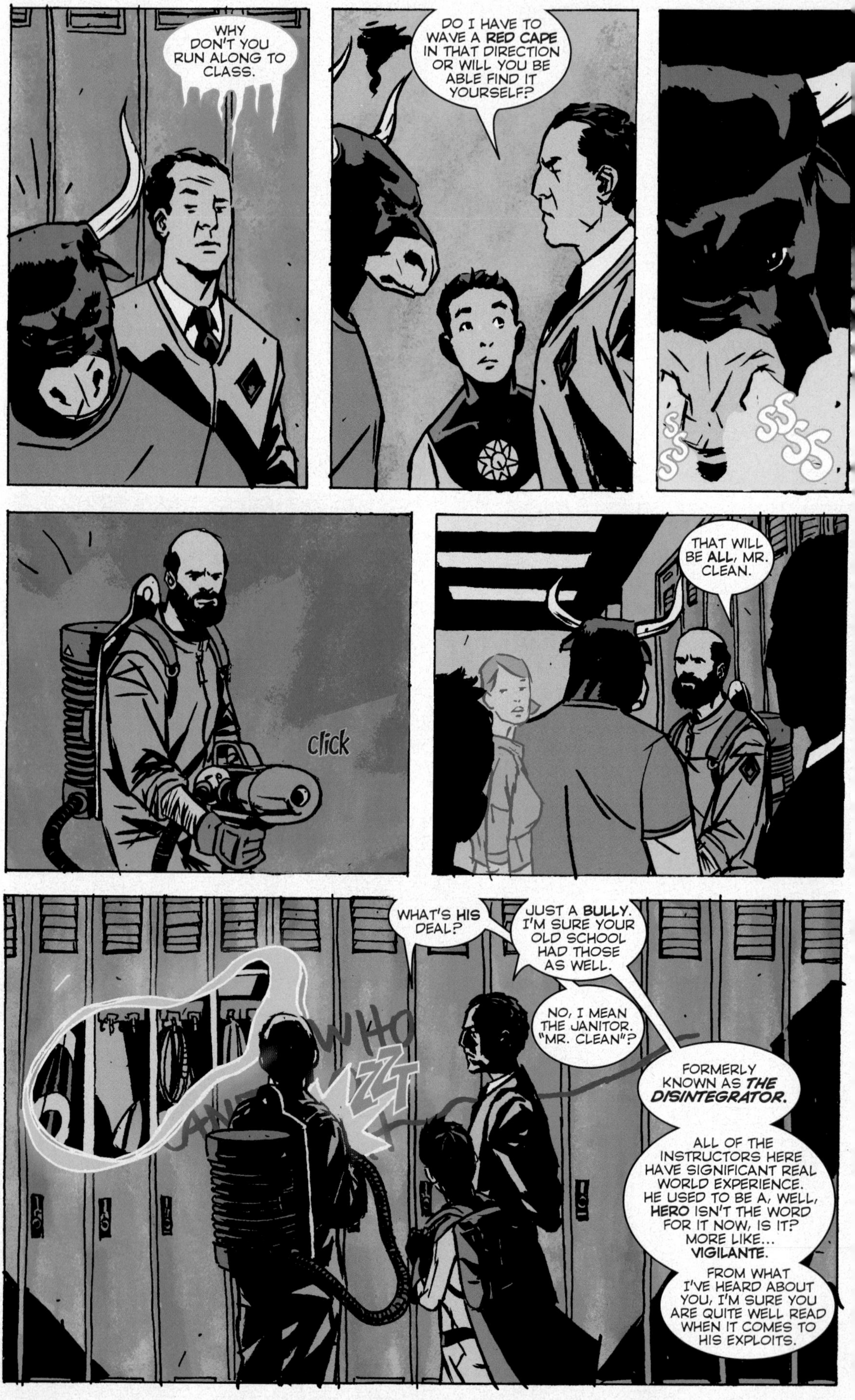

WHY DON'T YOU RUN ALONG TO CLASS.
DO I HAVE TO WAVE A **RED CAPE** IN THAT DIRECTION OR WILL YOU BE ABLE FIND IT YOURSELF?
SSSSS
CLICK
THAT WILL BE **ALL**, MR. CLEAN.
WHAT'S **HIS** DEAL?
JUST A **BULLY**. I'M SURE YOUR OLD SCHOOL HAD THOSE AS WELL.
NO, I MEAN THE JANITOR. "MR. CLEAN"?
FORMERLY KNOWN AS ***THE DISINTEGRATOR***.
ALL OF THE INSTRUCTORS HERE HAVE SIGNIFICANT REAL WORLD EXPERIENCE. HE USED TO BE A, WELL, **HERO** ISN'T THE WORD FOR IT NOW, IS IT? MORE LIKE... **VIGILANTE**.
FROM WHAT I'VE HEARD ABOUT YOU, I'M SURE YOU ARE QUITE WELL READ WHEN IT COMES TO HIS EXPLOITS.
WHO
ZZZT

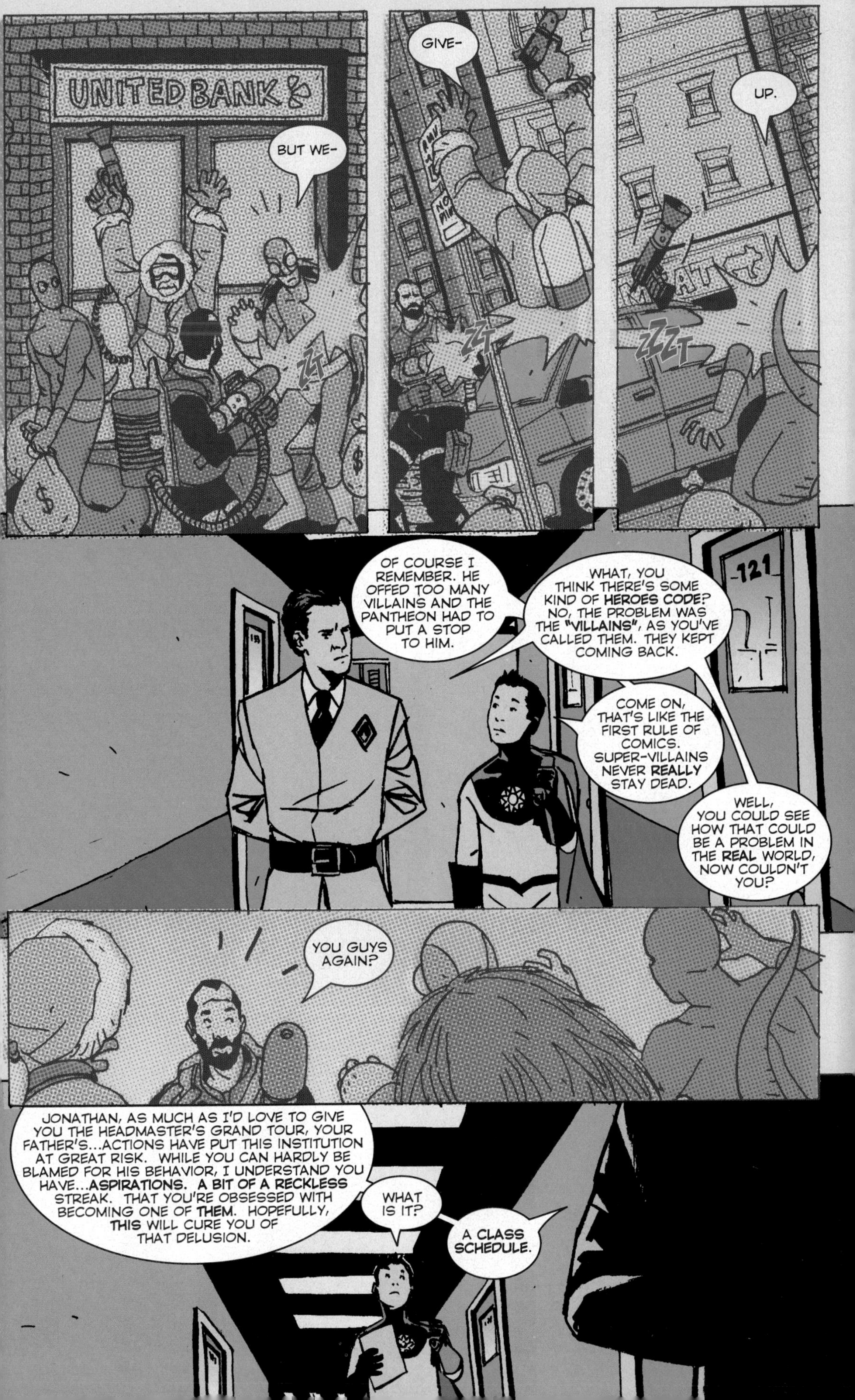
UNITED BANK
BUT WE-
ZZT
GIVE-
ZZT
UP.
ZZZT
OF COURSE I REMEMBER. HE OFFED TOO MANY VILLAINS AND THE PANTHEON HAD TO PUT A STOP TO HIM.
WHAT, YOU THINK THERE'S SOME KIND OF **HEROES CODE**? NO, THE PROBLEM WAS THE **"VILLAINS"**, AS YOU'VE CALLED THEM. THEY KEPT COMING BACK.
COME ON, THAT'S LIKE THE FIRST RULE OF COMICS. SUPER-VILLAINS NEVER **REALLY** STAY DEAD.
WELL, YOU COULD SEE HOW THAT COULD BE A PROBLEM IN THE **REAL** WORLD, NOW COULDN'T YOU?
121
YOU GUYS AGAIN?
JONATHAN, AS MUCH AS I'D LOVE TO GIVE YOU THE HEADMASTER'S GRAND TOUR, YOUR FATHER'S...ACTIONS HAVE PUT THIS INSTITUTION AT GREAT RISK. WHILE YOU CAN HARDLY BE BLAMED FOR HIS BEHAVIOR, I UNDERSTAND YOU HAVE...**ASPIRATIONS. A BIT OF A RECKLESS** STREAK. THAT YOU'RE OBSESSED WITH BECOMING ONE OF **THEM**. HOPEFULLY, **THIS** WILL CURE YOU OF THAT DELUSION.
WHAT IS IT?
A **CLASS SCHEDULE**.

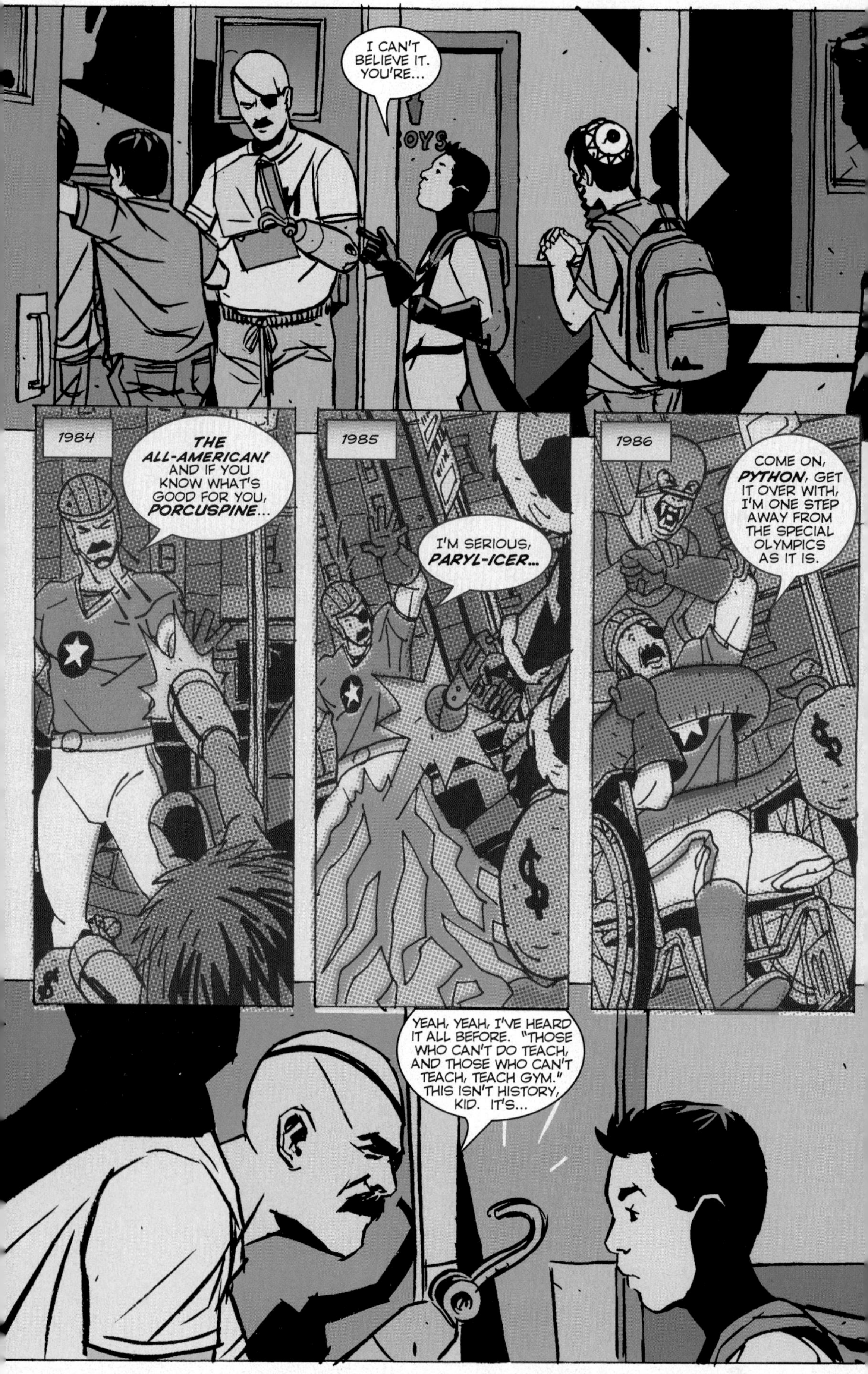

I CAN'T BELIEVE IT. YOU'RE...
OYS
1984
THE ALL-AMERICAN! AND IF YOU KNOW WHAT'S GOOD FOR YOU, PORCUSPINE...
1985
I'M SERIOUS, PARYL-ICER...
1986
COME ON, PYTHON, GET IT OVER WITH, I'M ONE STEP AWAY FROM THE SPECIAL OLYMPICS AS IT IS.
YEAH, YEAH, I'VE HEARD IT ALL BEFORE. "THOSE WHO CAN'T DO TEACH, AND THOSE WHO CAN'T TEACH, TEACH GYM." THIS ISN'T HISTORY, KID. IT'S...

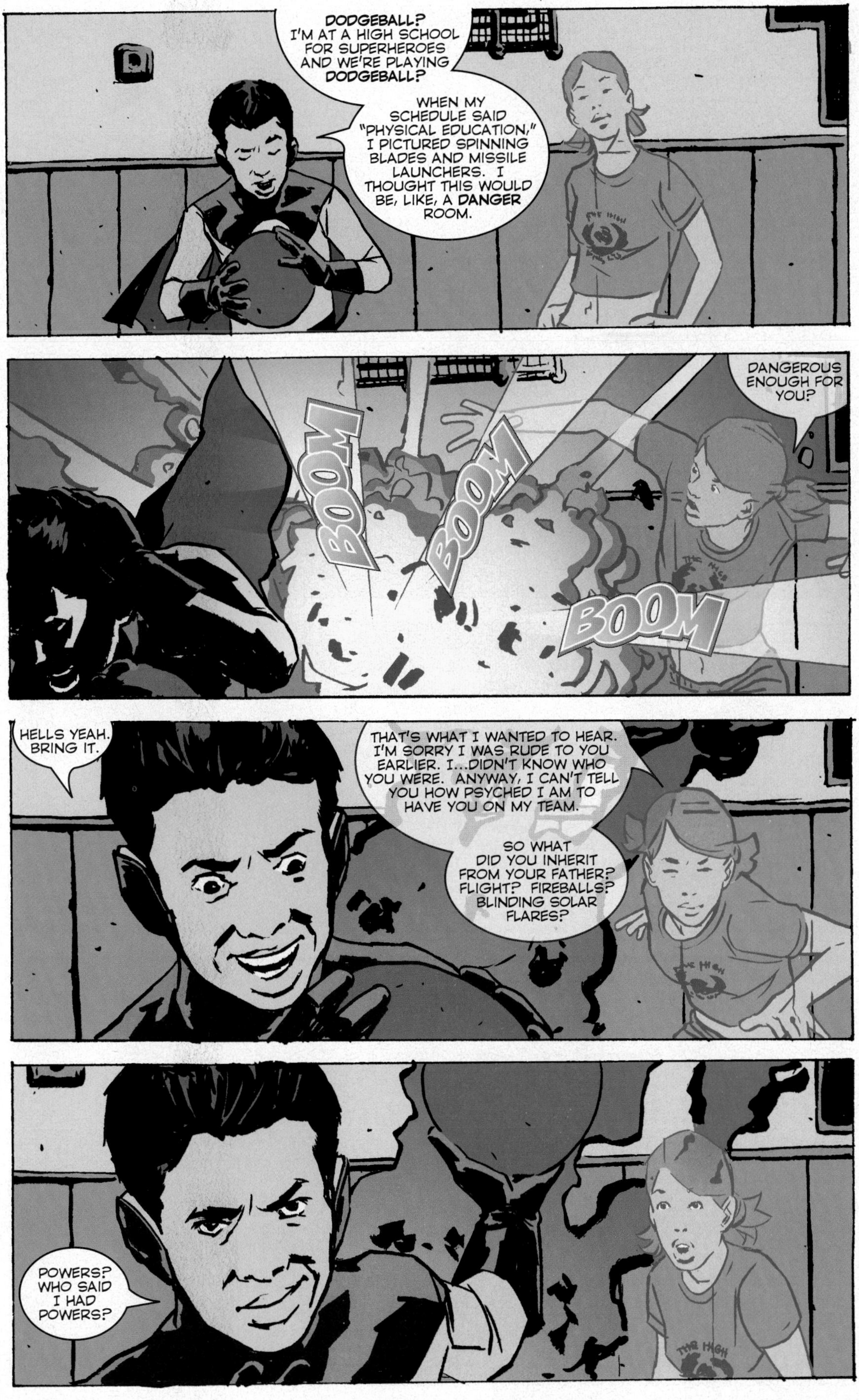
DODGEBALL? I'M AT A HIGH SCHOOL FOR SUPERHEROES AND WE'RE PLAYING DODGEBALL?
WHEN MY SCHEDULE SAID "PHYSICAL EDUCATION," I PICTURED SPINNING BLADES AND MISSILE LAUNCHERS. I THOUGHT THIS WOULD BE, LIKE, A DANGER ROOM.
BOOM
BOOM
BOOM
DANGEROUS ENOUGH FOR YOU?
HELLS YEAH. BRING IT.
THAT'S WHAT I WANTED TO HEAR. I'M SORRY I WAS RUDE TO YOU EARLIER. I...DIDN'T KNOW WHO YOU WERE. ANYWAY, I CAN'T TELL YOU HOW PSYCHED I AM TO HAVE YOU ON MY TEAM.
SO WHAT DID YOU INHERIT FROM YOUR FATHER? FLIGHT? FIREBALLS? BLINDING SOLAR FLARES?
POWERS? WHO SAID I HAD POWERS?

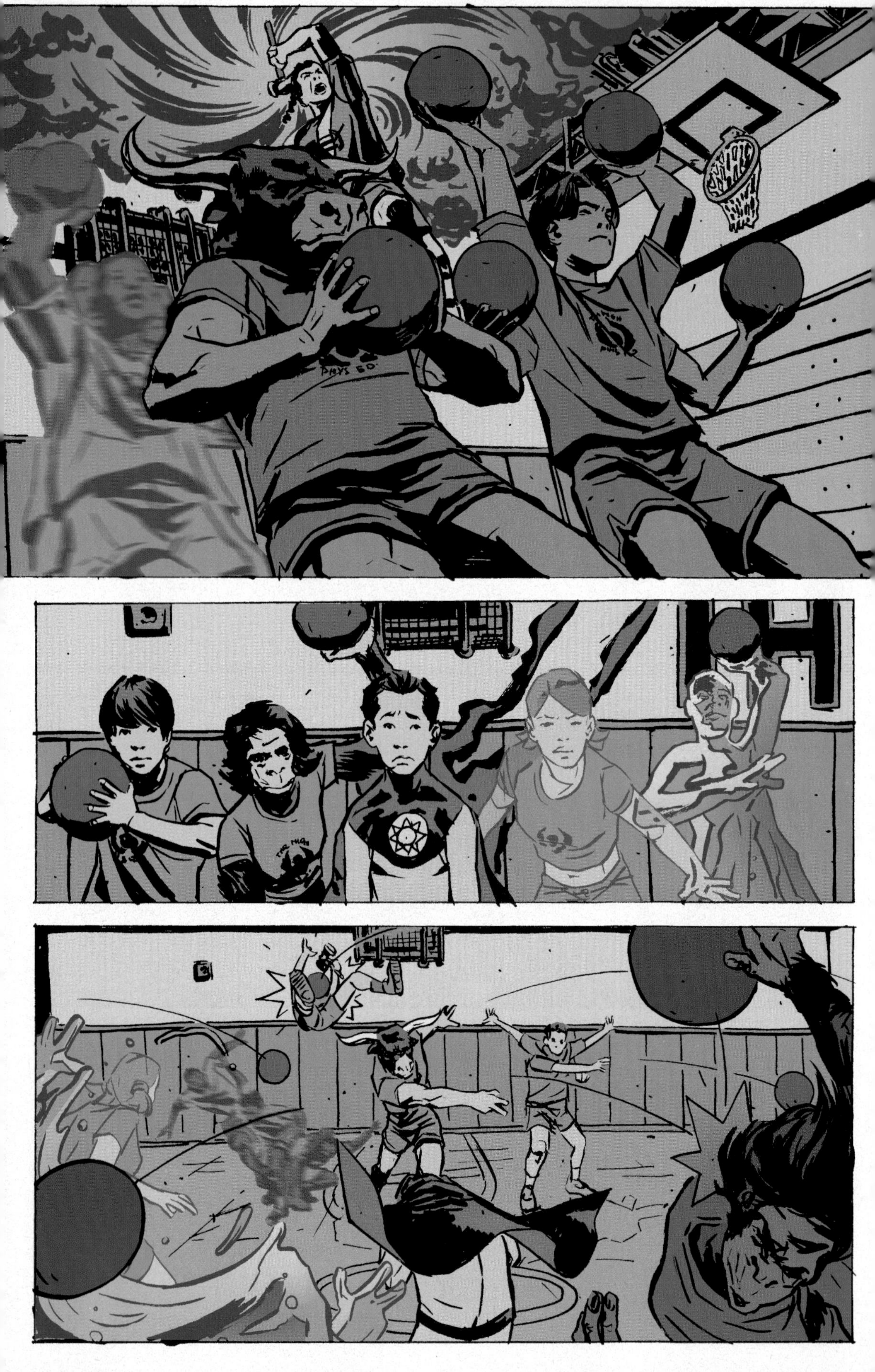
PHYS ED

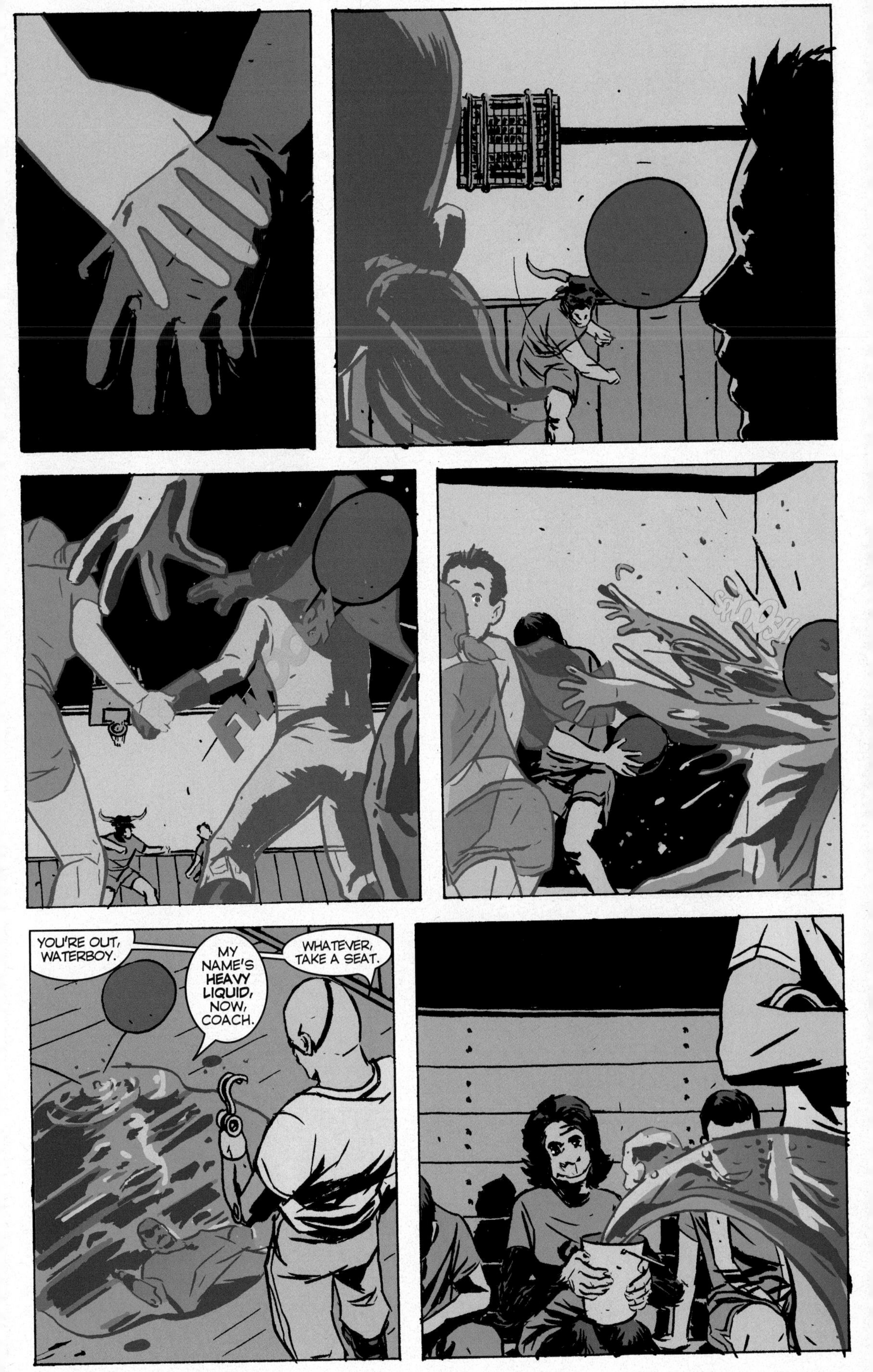
YOU'RE OUT, WATERBOY.
MY NAME'S **HEAVY LIQUID,** NOW, COACH.
WHATEVER, TAKE A SEAT.

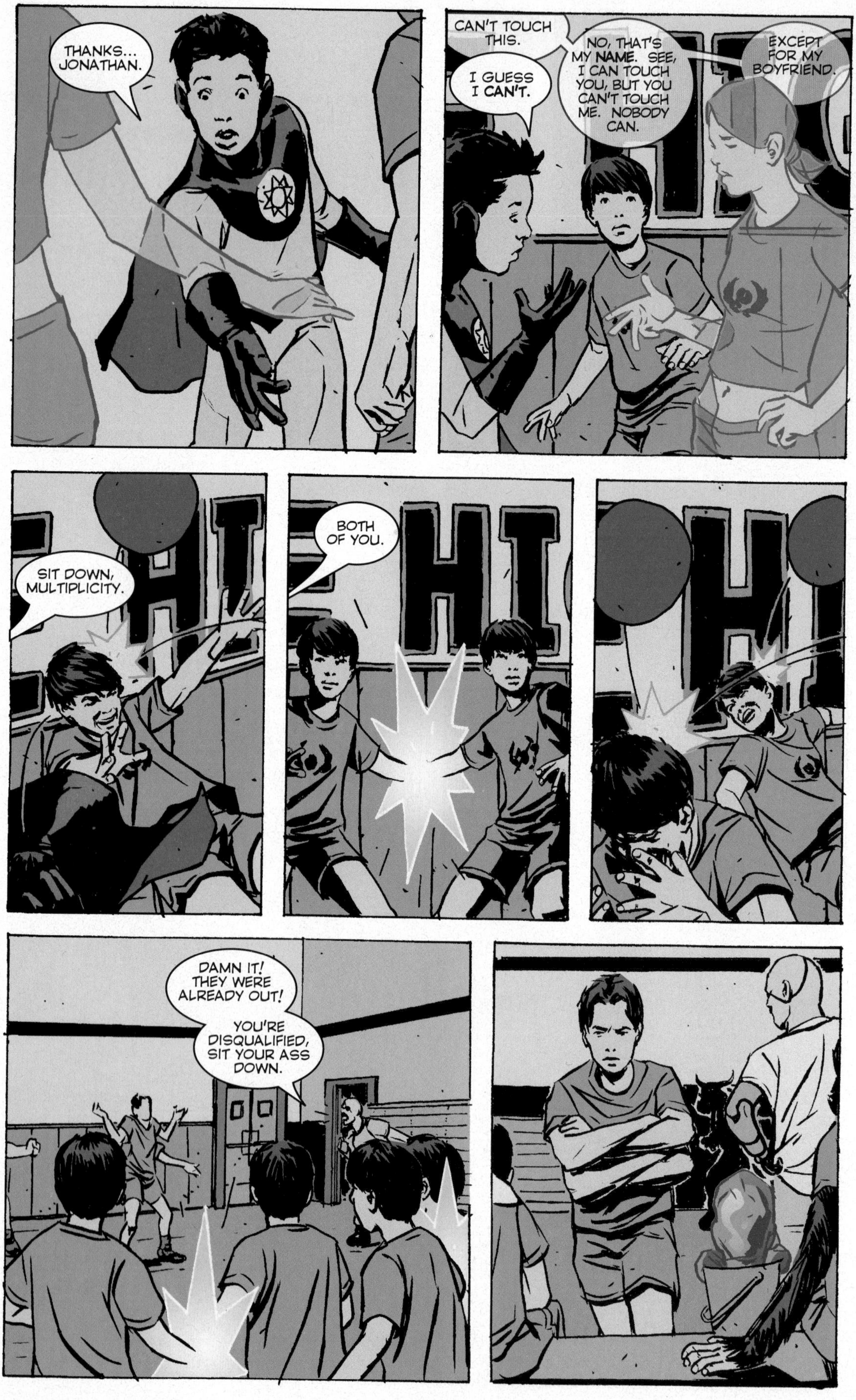
THANKS... JONATHAN.
CAN'T TOUCH THIS.
I GUESS I **CAN'T.**
NO, THAT'S MY **NAME**. SEE, I CAN TOUCH YOU, BUT YOU CAN'T TOUCH ME. NOBODY CAN.
EXCEPT FOR MY BOYFRIEND.
SIT DOWN, MULTIPLICITY.
BOTH OF YOU.
DAMN IT! THEY WERE ALREADY OUT!
YOU'RE DISQUALIFIED, SIT YOUR ASS DOWN.

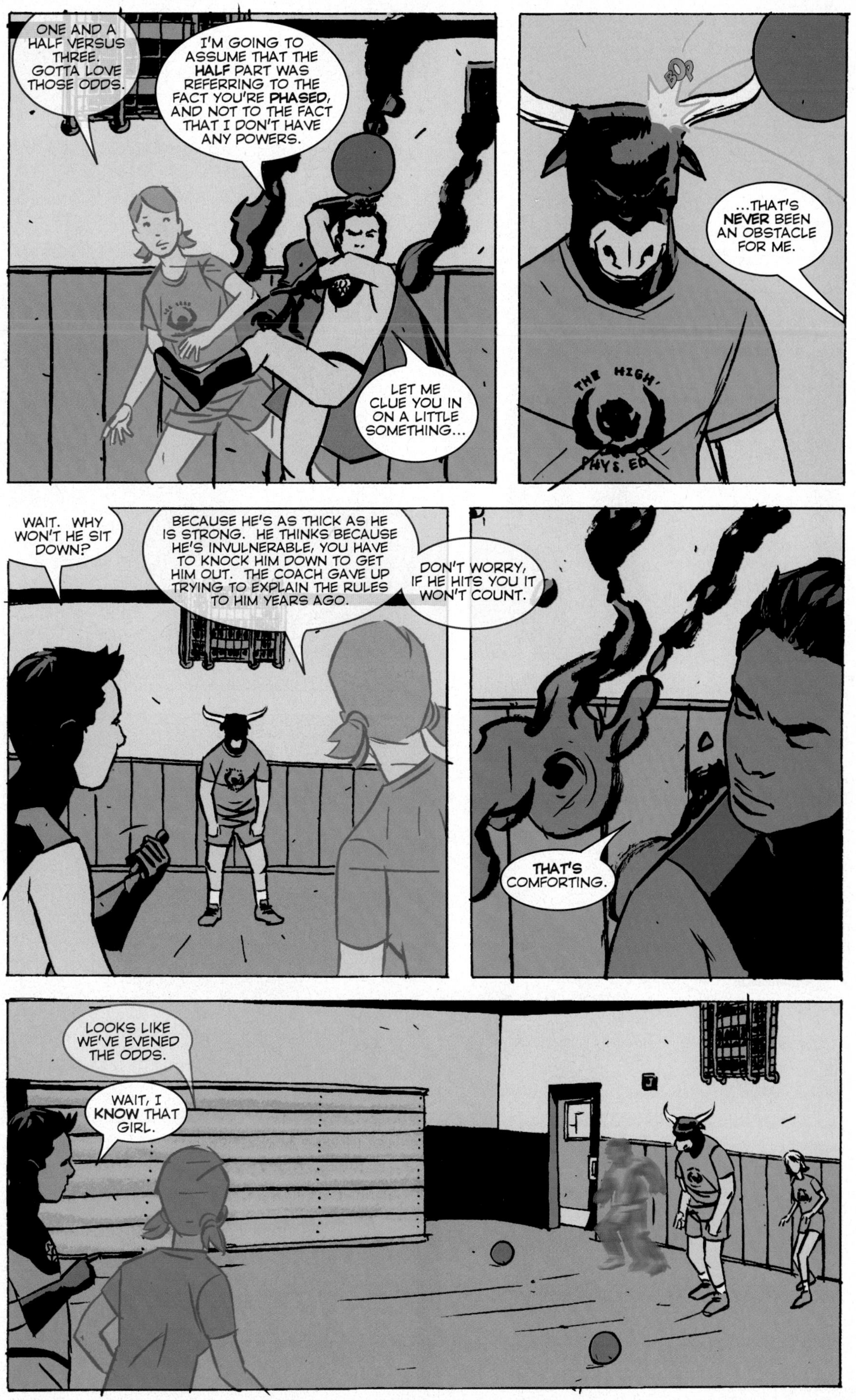
ONE AND A HALF VERSUS THREE. GOTTA LOVE THOSE ODDS.
I'M GOING TO ASSUME THAT THE HALF PART WAS REFERRING TO THE FACT YOU'RE PHASED, AND NOT TO THE FACT THAT I DON'T HAVE ANY POWERS.
LET ME CLUE YOU IN ON A LITTLE SOMETHING...
BOP
...THAT'S NEVER BEEN AN OBSTACLE FOR ME.
THE HIGH PHYS. ED
WAIT. WHY WON'T HE SIT DOWN?
BECAUSE HE'S AS THICK AS HE IS STRONG. HE THINKS BECAUSE HE'S INVULNERABLE, YOU HAVE TO KNOCK HIM DOWN TO GET HIM OUT. THE COACH GAVE UP TRYING TO EXPLAIN THE RULES TO HIM YEARS AGO.
DON'T WORRY, IF HE HITS YOU IT WON'T COUNT.
THAT'S COMFORTING.
LOOKS LIKE WE'VE EVENED THE ODDS.
WAIT, I KNOW THAT GIRL.

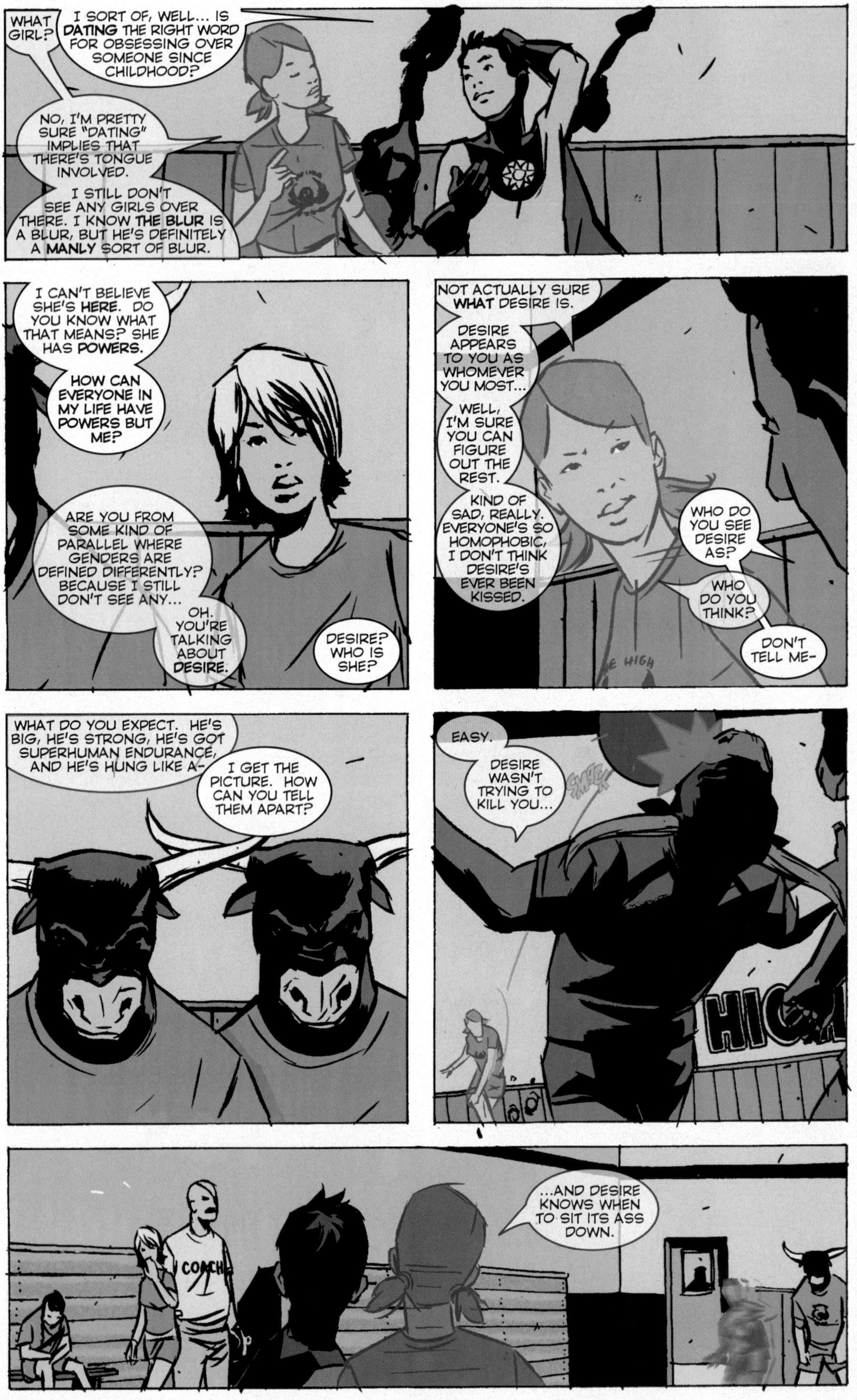
WHAT GIRL?
I SORT OF, WELL... IS DATING THE RIGHT WORD FOR OBSESSING OVER SOMEONE SINCE CHILDHOOD?
NO, I'M PRETTY SURE "DATING" IMPLIES THAT THERE'S TONGUE INVOLVED.
I STILL DON'T SEE ANY GIRLS OVER THERE. I KNOW THE BLUR IS A BLUR, BUT HE'S DEFINITELY A MANLY SORT OF BLUR.
I CAN'T BELIEVE SHE'S HERE. DO YOU KNOW WHAT THAT MEANS? SHE HAS POWERS.
HOW CAN EVERYONE IN MY LIFE HAVE POWERS BUT ME?
ARE YOU FROM SOME KIND OF PARALLEL WHERE GENDERS ARE DEFINED DIFFERENTLY? BECAUSE I STILL DON'T SEE ANY...
OH. YOU'RE TALKING ABOUT DESIRE.
DESIRE? WHO IS SHE?
NOT ACTUALLY SURE WHAT DESIRE IS.
DESIRE APPEARS TO YOU AS WHOMEVER YOU MOST...
WELL, I'M SURE YOU CAN FIGURE OUT THE REST.
KIND OF SAD, REALLY. EVERYONE'S SO HOMOPHOBIC, I DON'T THINK DESIRE'S EVER BEEN KISSED.
WHO DO YOU SEE DESIRE AS?
WHO DO YOU THINK?
DON'T TELL ME-
WHAT DO YOU EXPECT. HE'S BIG, HE'S STRONG, HE'S GOT SUPERHUMAN ENDURANCE, AND HE'S HUNG LIKE A-
I GET THE PICTURE. HOW CAN YOU TELL THEM APART?
EASY.
DESIRE WASN'T TRYING TO KILL YOU...
SMACK
HIGH
...AND DESIRE KNOWS WHEN TO SIT ITS ASS DOWN.
COACH

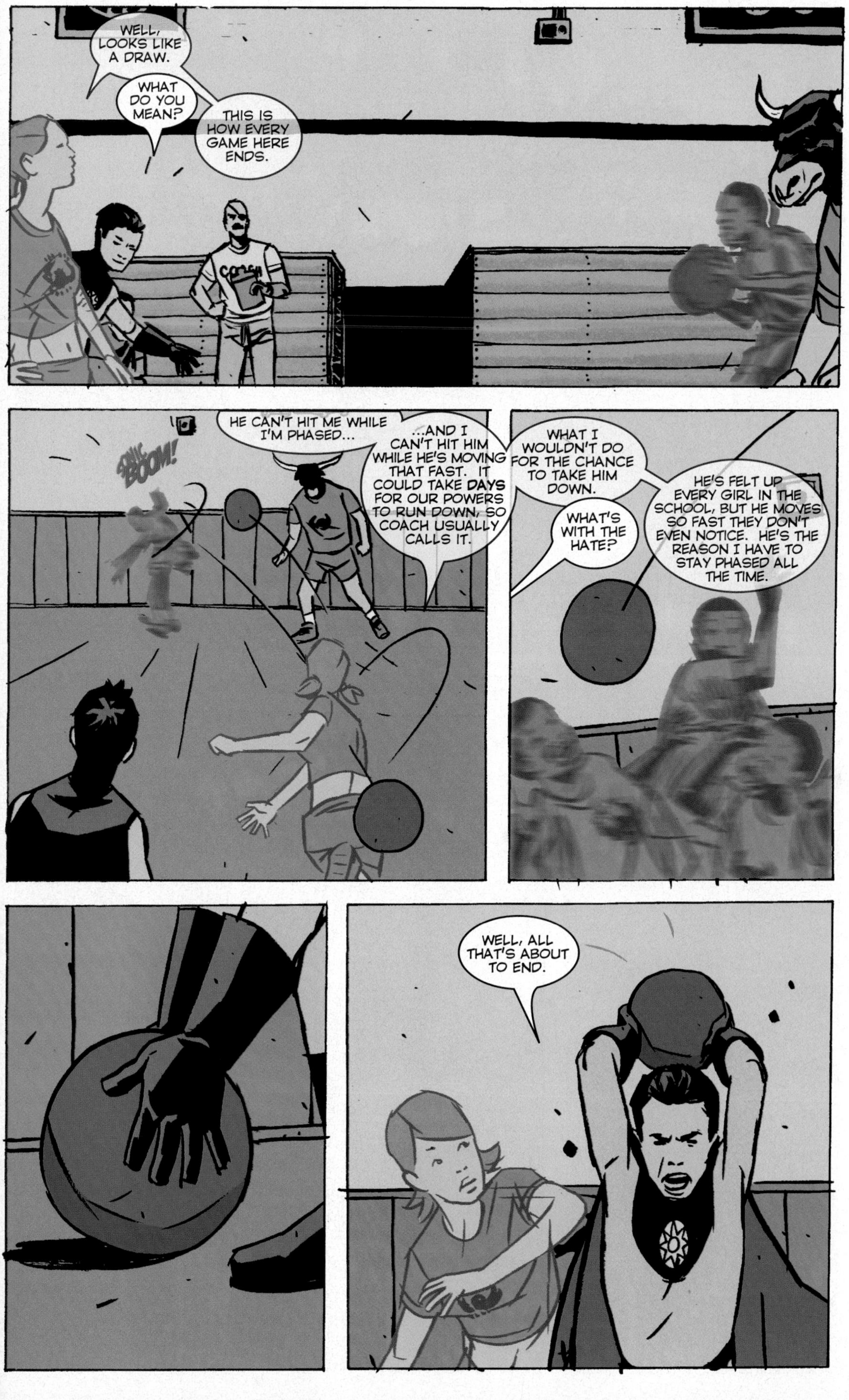
WELL, LOOKS LIKE A DRAW.
WHAT DO YOU MEAN?
THIS IS HOW EVERY GAME HERE ENDS.
SONIC BOOM!
HE CAN'T HIT ME WHILE I'M PHASED...
...AND I CAN'T HIT HIM WHILE HE'S MOVING THAT FAST. IT COULD TAKE DAYS FOR OUR POWERS TO RUN DOWN, SO COACH USUALLY CALLS IT.
WHAT I WOULDN'T DO FOR THE CHANCE TO TAKE HIM DOWN.
WHAT'S WITH THE HATE?
HE'S FELT UP EVERY GIRL IN THE SCHOOL, BUT HE MOVES SO FAST THEY DON'T EVEN NOTICE. HE'S THE REASON I HAVE TO STAY PHASED ALL THE TIME.
WELL, ALL THAT'S ABOUT TO END.

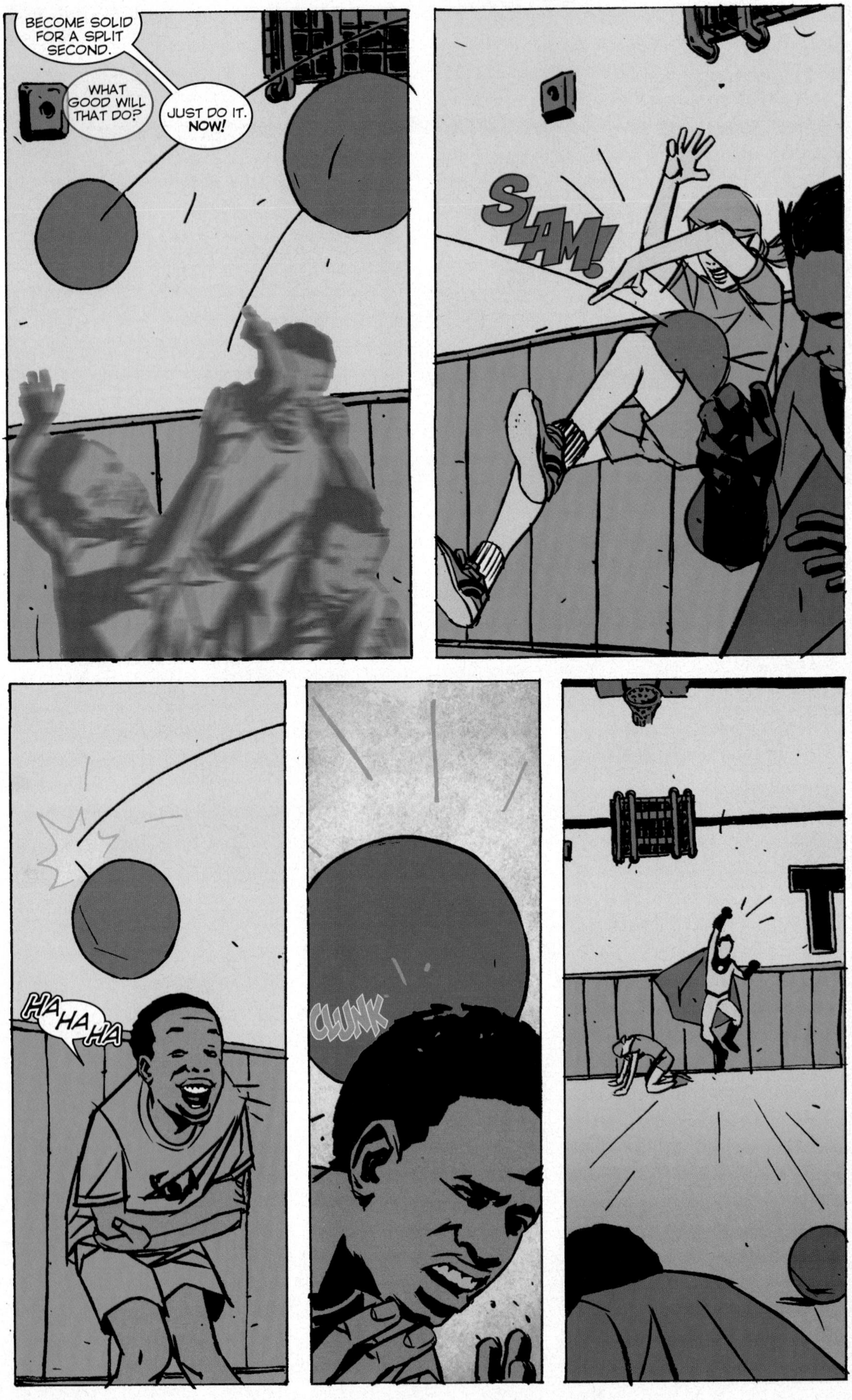

BECOME SOLID FOR A SPLIT SECOND.
WHAT GOOD WILL THAT DO?
JUST DO IT. NOW!
SLAM!
HA HA HA
CLUNK

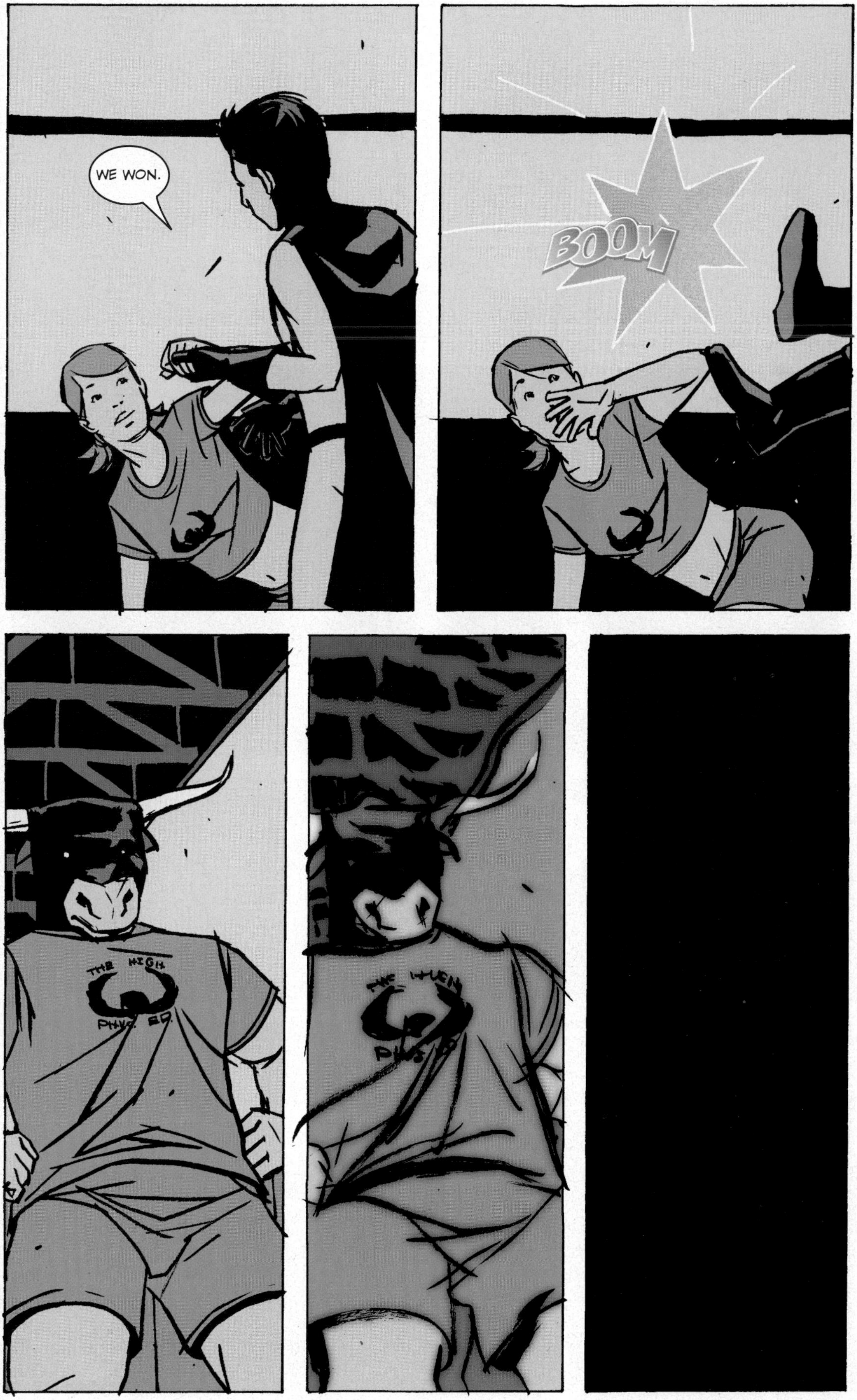
WE WON.
BOOM
THE HIGH
PHYS. ED.

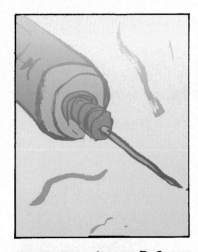

COME TO FINISH ME OFF?

RELAX. I'M JUST BORROWING HIS BODY. HE'S SUPPOSED TO BE IN DETENTION FOR WHAT HE DID TO YOU.

AT THIS POINT, I'M MORE THAN WILLING TO ACCEPT THE FACT THAT THE SCHOOL NURSE HERE CAN POSSESS STUDENT BODIES. BUT ARE YOU SURE YOU SHOULD BE TREATING ME? YOU LOOK PRETTY SICK THERE YOURSELF.

HOW SICK EXACTLY? LIKE COMMON COLD SICK, OR EBOLA SICK?

I'D GO WITH THE FLU.

A-CHOO

THANK YOU.

BUT I DIDN'T SAY BLESS YOU YET. ISN'T THAT SUPPOSED TO BE BAD LUCK?

NO. I MEAN, THANKS. I'VE BEEN TRYING TO BECOME LESS SYMPTOMATIC. IT'S EASIER ON THE HOSTS. I'M A VIRUS.

IS THAT YOUR NAME, OR–

WELL, YES, ACTUALLY THAT IS MY NAME, I'M THE VIRUS, BUT I'M ALSO A VIRUS. LITERALLY. DON'T WORRY, I'M ONLY CONTAGIOUS WHEN I WANT TO BE.

THAT'S REASSURING.

YOU MEAN I'M REALLY AN INFECTIOUS DISEASE?

YOU KNOW, YOU AND I, WE HAVE SOMETHING IN COMMON.

NO, YOU LIKE COMIC BOOKS, RIGHT? YOU'RE, LIKE, A HUGE FAN?

WELL, I WAS...YOU TOO?

NOT EXACTLY. REMEMBER...

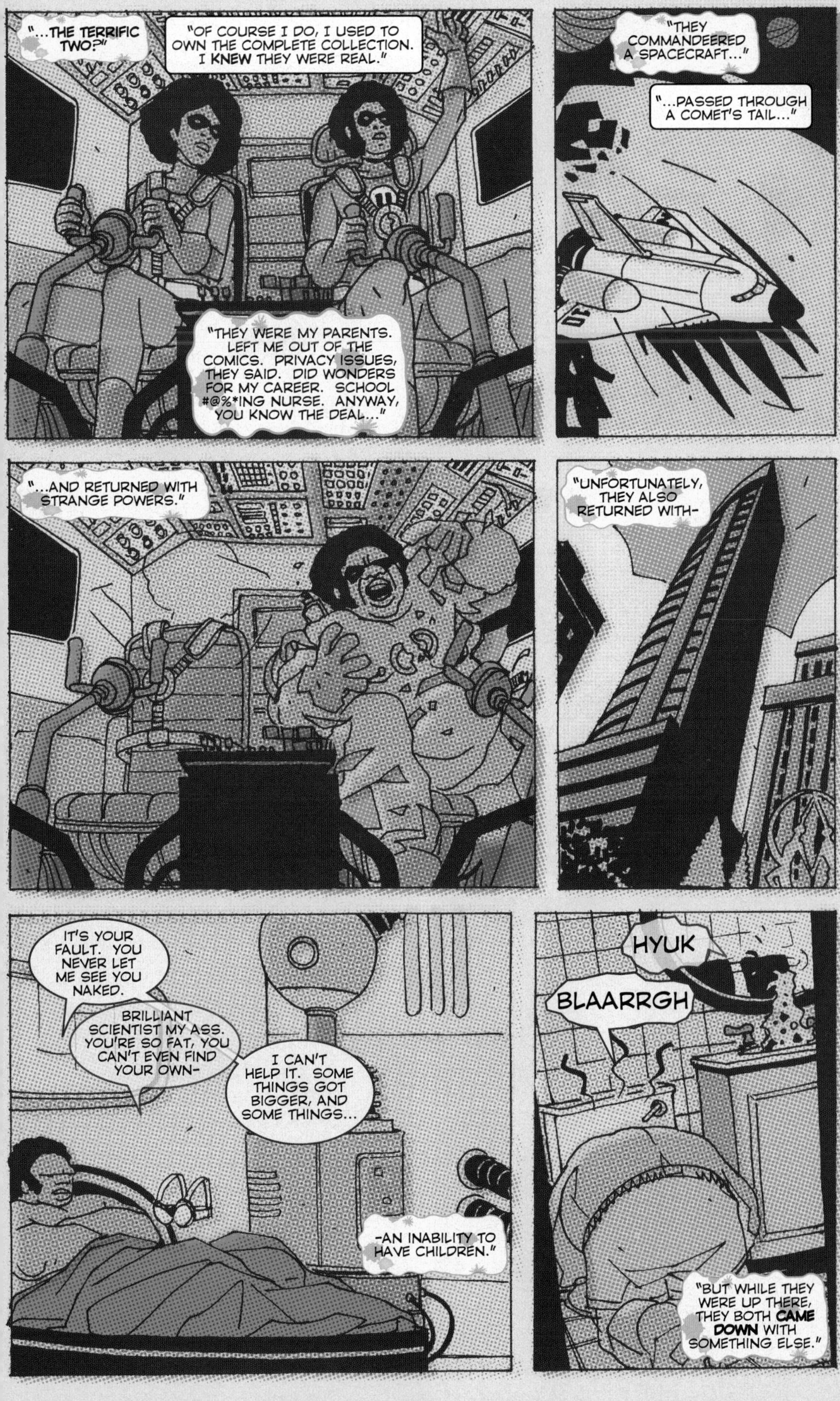
"...THE TERRIFIC TWO?"
"OF COURSE I DO, I USED TO OWN THE COMPLETE COLLECTION. I KNEW THEY WERE REAL."
"THEY WERE MY PARENTS. LEFT ME OUT OF THE COMICS. PRIVACY ISSUES, THEY SAID. DID WONDERS FOR MY CAREER. SCHOOL #@%*ING NURSE. ANYWAY, YOU KNOW THE DEAL..."
"THEY COMMANDEERED A SPACECRAFT..."
"...PASSED THROUGH A COMET'S TAIL..."
"...AND RETURNED WITH STRANGE POWERS."
"UNFORTUNATELY, THEY ALSO RETURNED WITH-
IT'S YOUR FAULT. YOU NEVER LET ME SEE YOU NAKED.
BRILLIANT SCIENTIST MY ASS. YOU'RE SO FAT, YOU CAN'T EVEN FIND YOUR OWN-
I CAN'T HELP IT. SOME THINGS GOT BIGGER, AND SOME THINGS...
-AN INABILITY TO HAVE CHILDREN."
HYUK
BLAARRGH
"BUT WHILE THEY WERE UP THERE, THEY BOTH CAME DOWN WITH SOMETHING ELSE."

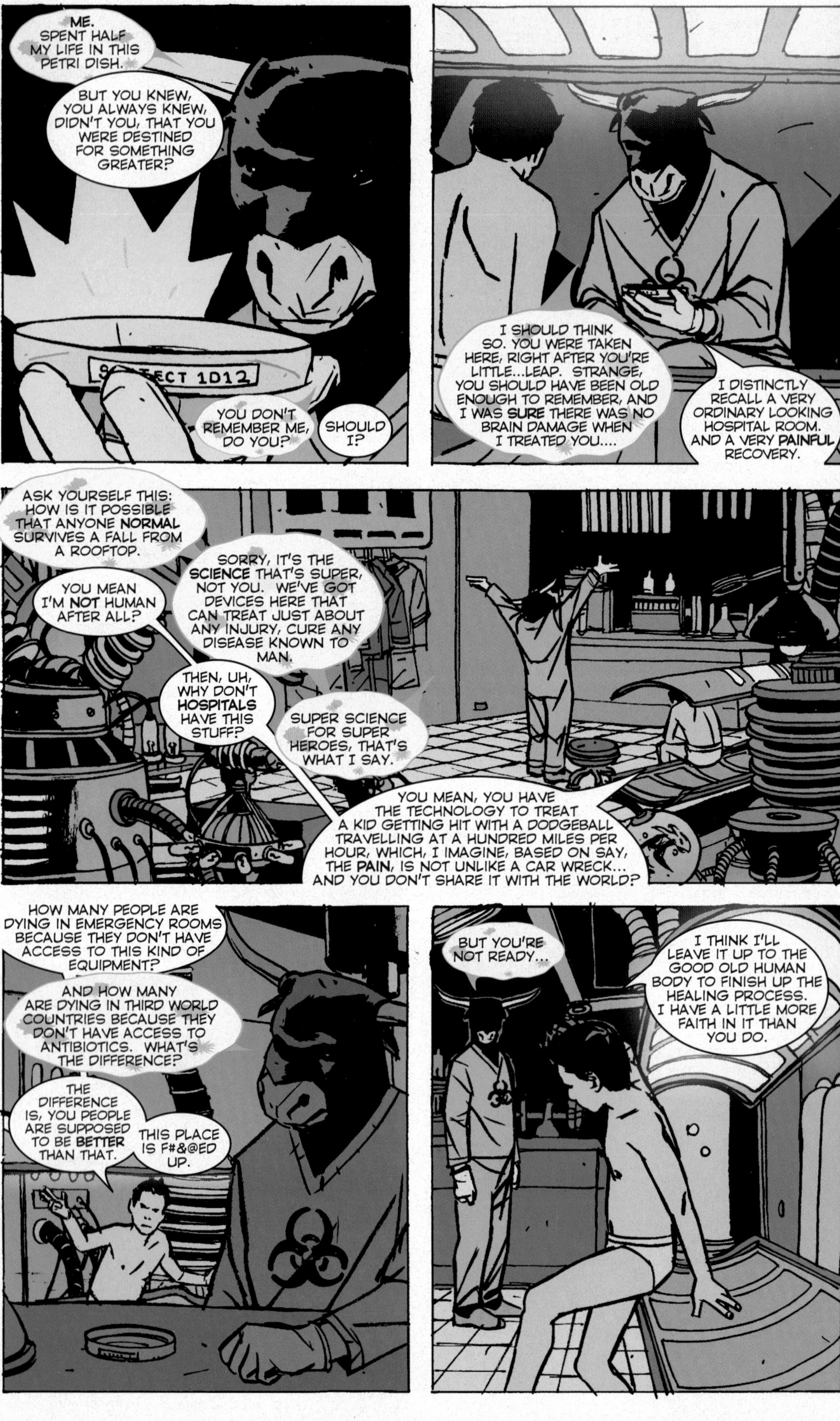
ME. SPENT HALF MY LIFE IN THIS PETRI DISH.
BUT YOU KNEW, YOU ALWAYS KNEW, DIDN'T YOU, THAT YOU WERE DESTINED FOR SOMETHING GREATER?
YOU DON'T REMEMBER ME, DO YOU?
SHOULD I?
I SHOULD THINK SO. YOU WERE TAKEN HERE, RIGHT AFTER YOU'RE LITTLE...LEAP. STRANGE, YOU SHOULD HAVE BEEN OLD ENOUGH TO REMEMBER, AND I WAS SURE THERE WAS NO BRAIN DAMAGE WHEN I TREATED YOU....
I DISTINCTLY RECALL A VERY ORDINARY LOOKING HOSPITAL ROOM. AND A VERY PAINFUL RECOVERY.
ASK YOURSELF THIS: HOW IS IT POSSIBLE THAT ANYONE NORMAL SURVIVES A FALL FROM A ROOFTOP.
YOU MEAN I'M NOT HUMAN AFTER ALL?
SORRY, IT'S THE SCIENCE THAT'S SUPER, NOT YOU. WE'VE GOT DEVICES HERE THAT CAN TREAT JUST ABOUT ANY INJURY, CURE ANY DISEASE KNOWN TO MAN.
THEN, UH, WHY DON'T HOSPITALS HAVE THIS STUFF?
SUPER SCIENCE FOR SUPER HEROES, THAT'S WHAT I SAY.
YOU MEAN, YOU HAVE THE TECHNOLOGY TO TREAT A KID GETTING HIT WITH A DODGEBALL TRAVELLING AT A HUNDRED MILES PER HOUR, WHICH, I IMAGINE, BASED ON SAY, THE PAIN, IS NOT UNLIKE A CAR WRECK... AND YOU DON'T SHARE IT WITH THE WORLD?
HOW MANY PEOPLE ARE DYING IN EMERGENCY ROOMS BECAUSE THEY DON'T HAVE ACCESS TO THIS KIND OF EQUIPMENT?
AND HOW MANY ARE DYING IN THIRD WORLD COUNTRIES BECAUSE THEY DON'T HAVE ACCESS TO ANTIBIOTICS. WHAT'S THE DIFFERENCE?
THE DIFFERENCE IS, YOU PEOPLE ARE SUPPOSED TO BE BETTER THAN THAT.
THIS PLACE IS F#&@ED UP.
BUT YOU'RE NOT READY...
I THINK I'LL LEAVE IT UP TO THE GOOD OLD HUMAN BODY TO FINISH UP THE HEALING PROCESS. I HAVE A LITTLE MORE FAITH IN IT THAN YOU DO.

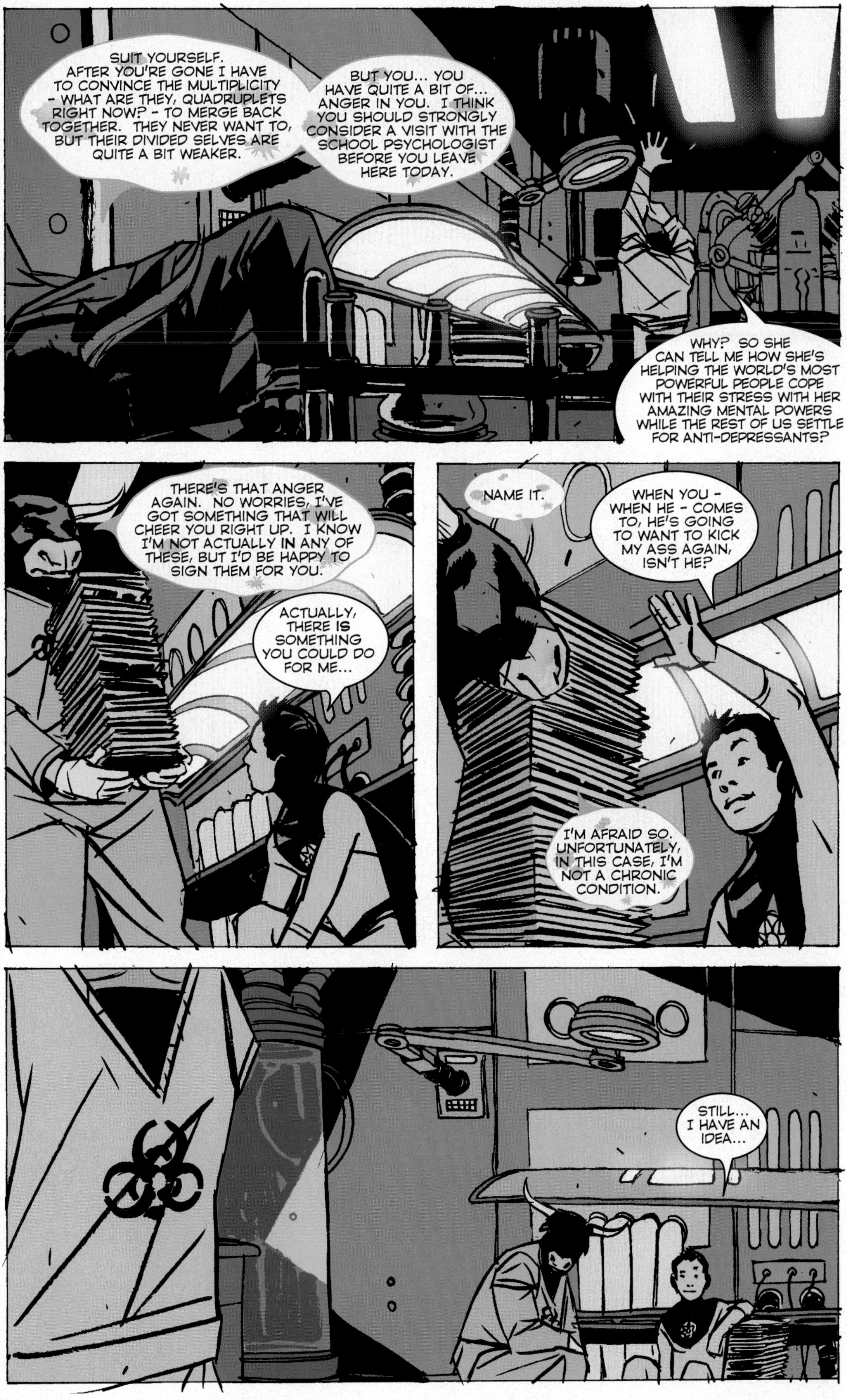

SUIT YOURSELF. AFTER YOU'RE GONE I HAVE TO CONVINCE THE MULTIPLICITY - WHAT ARE THEY, QUADRUPLETS RIGHT NOW? - TO MERGE BACK TOGETHER. THEY NEVER WANT TO, BUT THEIR DIVIDED SELVES ARE QUITE A BIT WEAKER.
BUT YOU... YOU HAVE QUITE A BIT OF... ANGER IN YOU. I THINK YOU SHOULD STRONGLY CONSIDER A VISIT WITH THE SCHOOL PSYCHOLOGIST BEFORE YOU LEAVE HERE TODAY.
WHY? SO SHE CAN TELL ME HOW SHE'S HELPING THE WORLD'S MOST POWERFUL PEOPLE COPE WITH THEIR STRESS WITH HER AMAZING MENTAL POWERS WHILE THE REST OF US SETTLE FOR ANTI-DEPRESSANTS?
THERE'S THAT ANGER AGAIN. NO WORRIES, I'VE GOT SOMETHING THAT WILL CHEER YOU RIGHT UP. I KNOW I'M NOT ACTUALLY **IN** ANY OF THESE, BUT I'D BE HAPPY TO SIGN THEM FOR YOU.
ACTUALLY, THERE **IS** SOMETHING YOU COULD DO FOR ME...
NAME IT.
WHEN YOU - WHEN HE - COMES TO, HE'S GOING TO WANT TO KICK MY ASS AGAIN, ISN'T HE?
I'M AFRAID SO. UNFORTUNATELY, IN THIS CASE, I'M NOT A CHRONIC CONDITION.
STILL... I HAVE AN IDEA...

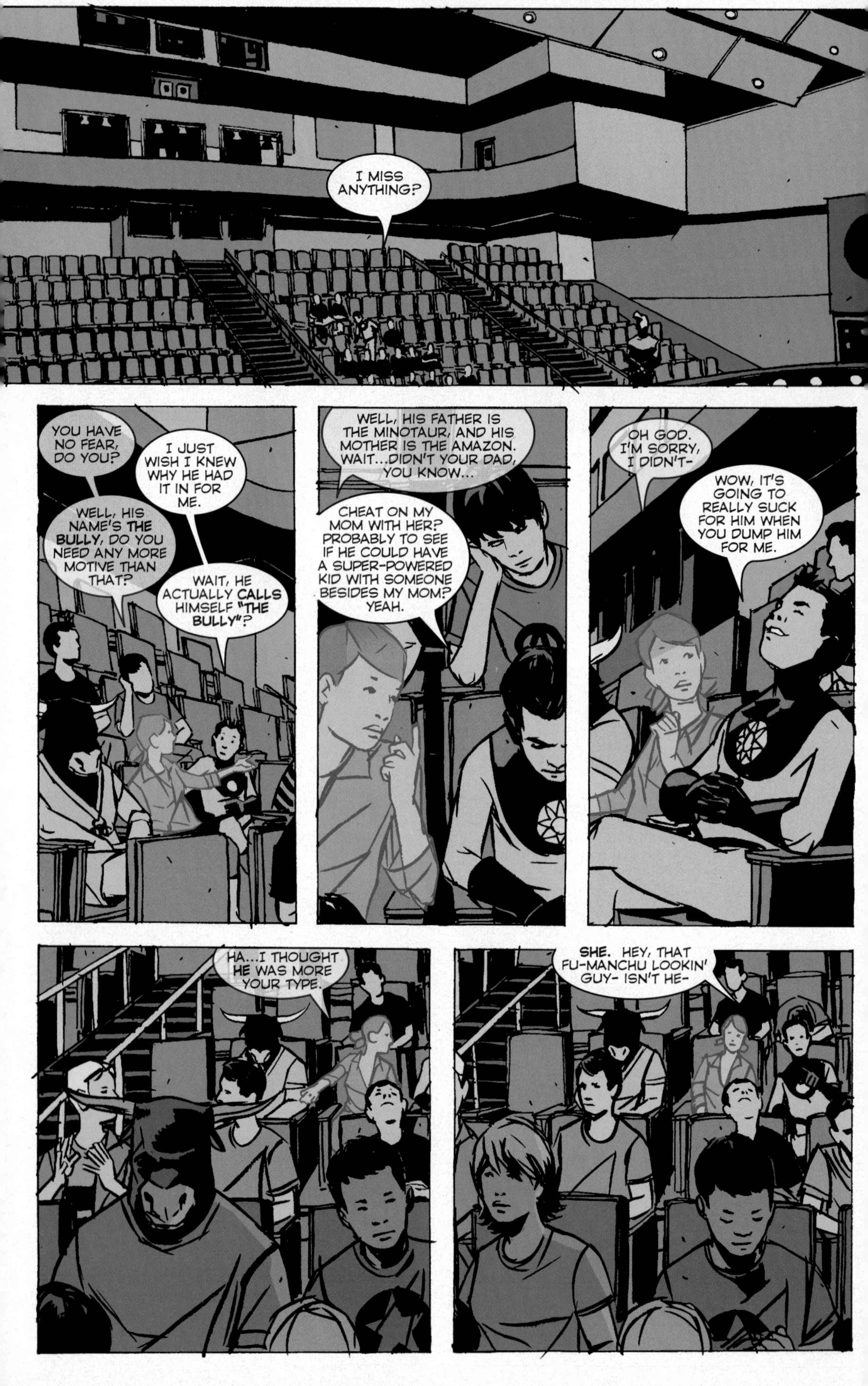
I MISS ANYTHING?
YOU HAVE NO FEAR, DO YOU?
I JUST WISH I KNEW WHY HE HAD IT IN FOR ME.
WELL, HIS NAME'S **THE BULLY**, DO YOU NEED ANY MORE MOTIVE THAN THAT?
WAIT, HE ACTUALLY **CALLS** HIMSELF **"THE BULLY"**?
WELL, HIS FATHER IS THE MINOTAUR, AND HIS MOTHER IS THE AMAZON. WAIT...DIDN'T YOUR DAD, YOU KNOW...
CHEAT ON MY MOM WITH HER? PROBABLY TO SEE IF HE COULD HAVE A SUPER-POWERED KID WITH SOMEONE BESIDES MY MOM? YEAH.
OH GOD. I'M SORRY, I DIDN'T-
WOW, IT'S GOING TO REALLY SUCK FOR HIM WHEN YOU DUMP HIM FOR ME.
HA...I THOUGHT **HE** WAS MORE YOUR TYPE.
SHE. HEY, THAT FU-MANCHU LOOKIN' GUY- ISN'T HE-

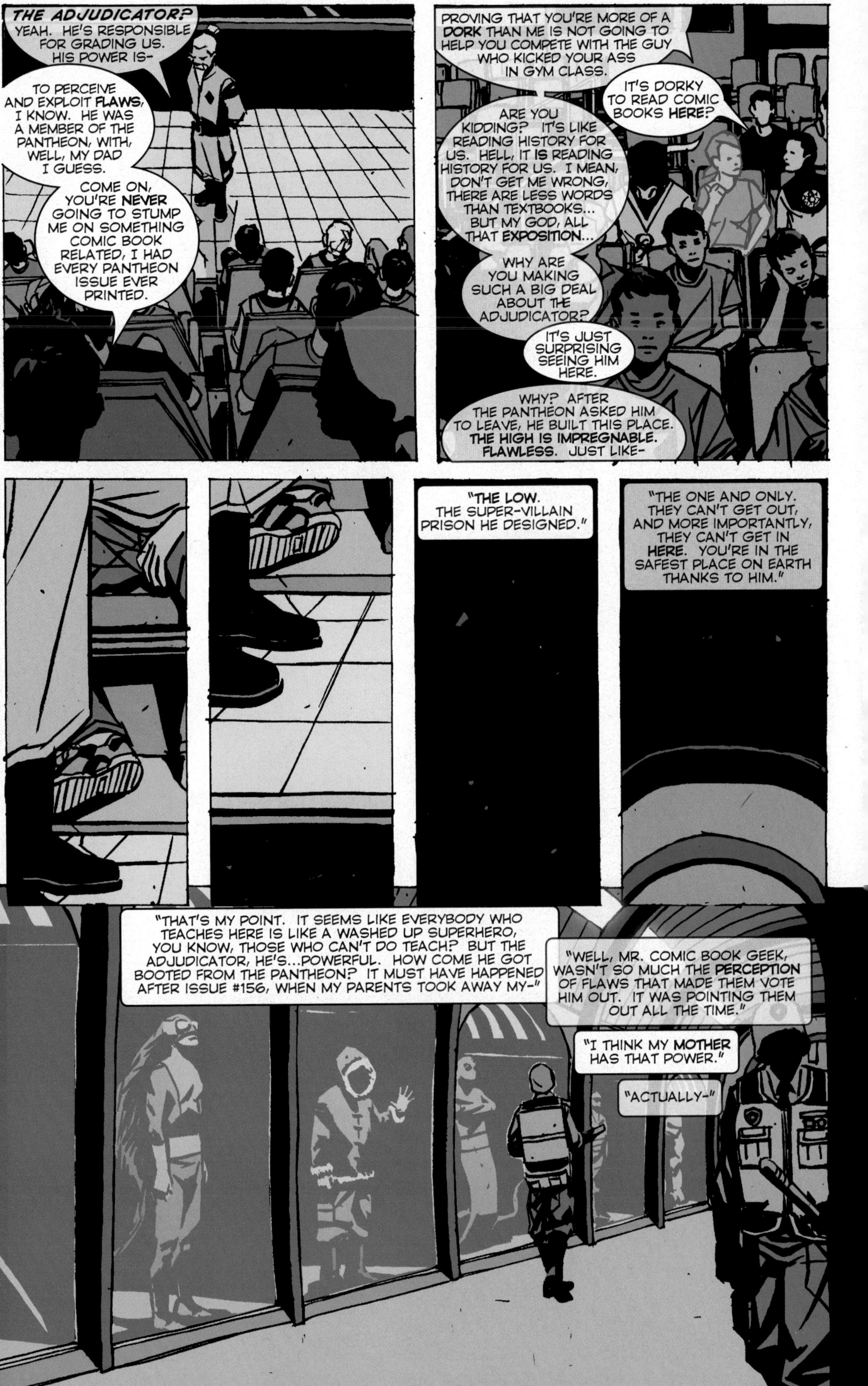
THE ADJUDICATOR? YEAH. HE'S RESPONSIBLE FOR GRADING US. HIS POWER IS-
TO PERCEIVE AND EXPLOIT FLAWS, I KNOW. HE WAS A MEMBER OF THE PANTHEON, WITH, WELL, MY DAD I GUESS.
COME ON, YOU'RE NEVER GOING TO STUMP ME ON SOMETHING COMIC BOOK RELATED, I HAD EVERY PANTHEON ISSUE EVER PRINTED.
PROVING THAT YOU'RE MORE OF A DORK THAN ME IS NOT GOING TO HELP YOU COMPETE WITH THE GUY WHO KICKED YOUR ASS IN GYM CLASS.
IT'S DORKY TO READ COMIC BOOKS HERE?
ARE YOU KIDDING? IT'S LIKE READING HISTORY FOR US. HELL, IT IS READING HISTORY FOR US. I MEAN, DON'T GET ME WRONG, THERE ARE LESS WORDS THAN TEXTBOOKS... BUT MY GOD, ALL THAT EXPOSITION...
WHY ARE YOU MAKING SUCH A BIG DEAL ABOUT THE ADJUDICATOR?
IT'S JUST SURPRISING SEEING HIM HERE.
WHY? AFTER THE PANTHEON ASKED HIM TO LEAVE, HE BUILT THIS PLACE. THE HIGH IS IMPREGNABLE. FLAWLESS. JUST LIKE-
"THE LOW. THE SUPER-VILLAIN PRISON HE DESIGNED."
"THE ONE AND ONLY. THEY CAN'T GET OUT, AND MORE IMPORTANTLY, THEY CAN'T GET IN HERE. YOU'RE IN THE SAFEST PLACE ON EARTH THANKS TO HIM."
"THAT'S MY POINT. IT SEEMS LIKE EVERYBODY WHO TEACHES HERE IS LIKE A WASHED UP SUPERHERO, YOU KNOW, THOSE WHO CAN'T DO TEACH? BUT THE ADJUDICATOR, HE'S...POWERFUL. HOW COME HE GOT BOOTED FROM THE PANTHEON? IT MUST HAVE HAPPENED AFTER ISSUE #156, WHEN MY PARENTS TOOK AWAY MY-"
"WELL, MR. COMIC BOOK GEEK, WASN'T SO MUCH THE PERCEPTION OF FLAWS THAT MADE THEM VOTE HIM OUT. IT WAS POINTING THEM OUT ALL THE TIME."
"I THINK MY MOTHER HAS THAT POWER."
"ACTUALLY-"

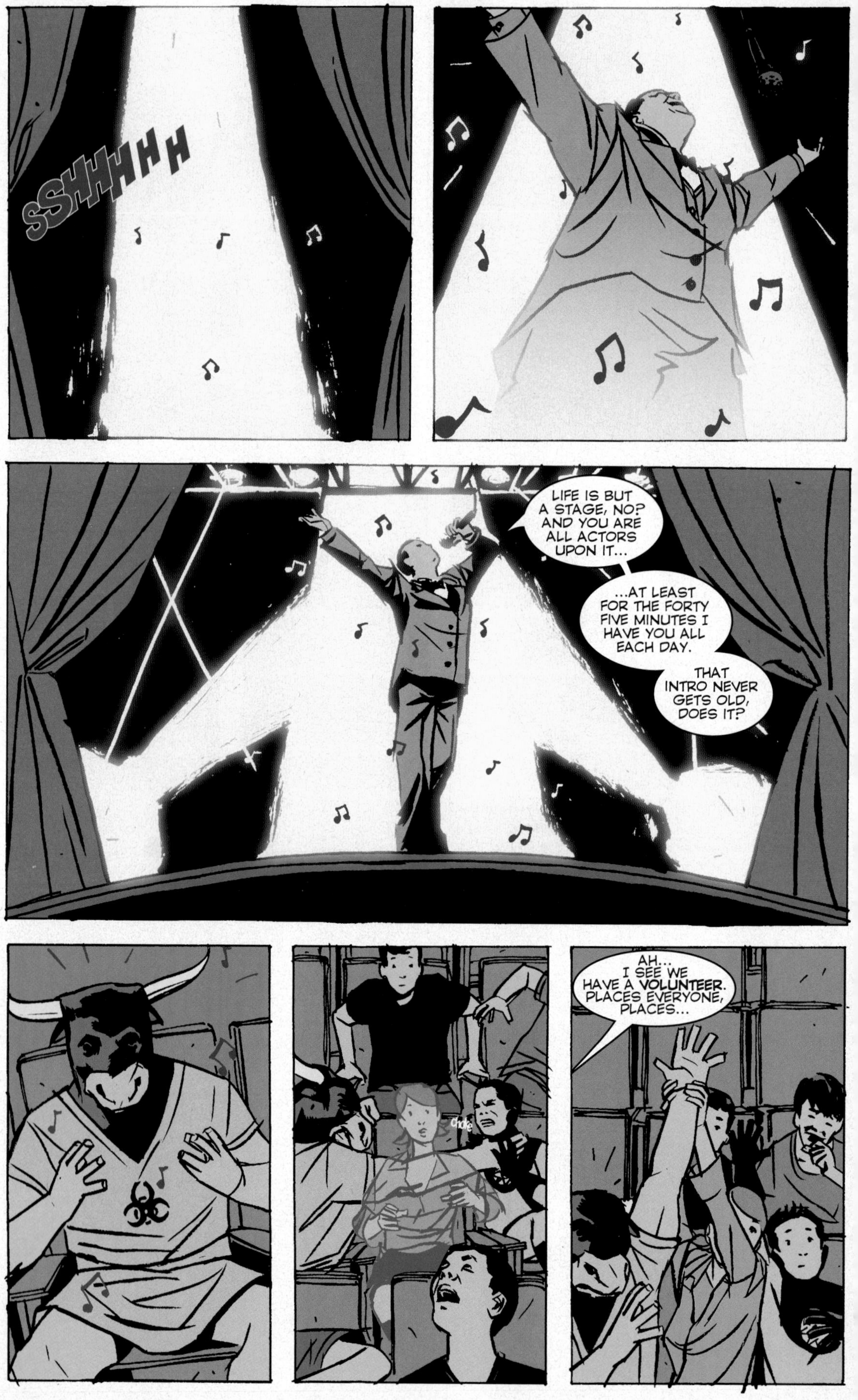
SSHHHHHH
LIFE IS BUT A STAGE, NO? AND YOU ARE ALL ACTORS UPON IT...
...AT LEAST FOR THE FORTY FIVE MINUTES I HAVE YOU ALL EACH DAY.
THAT INTRO NEVER GETS OLD, DOES IT?
AH... I SEE WE HAVE A **VOLUNTEER.** PLACES EVERYONE, PLACES...

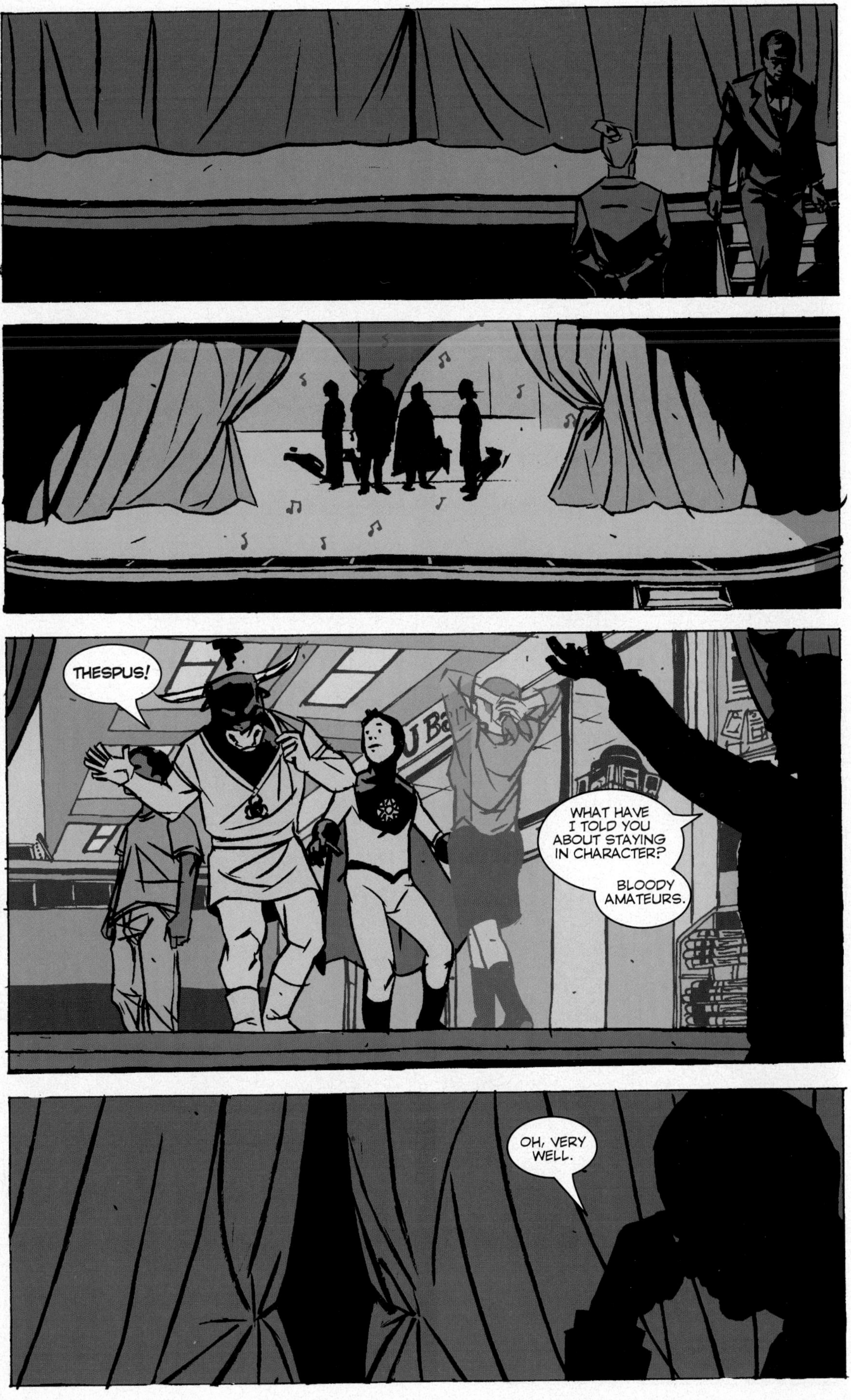
THESPUS!
WHAT HAVE I TOLD YOU ABOUT STAYING IN CHARACTER?
BLOODY AMATEURS.
OH, VERY WELL.

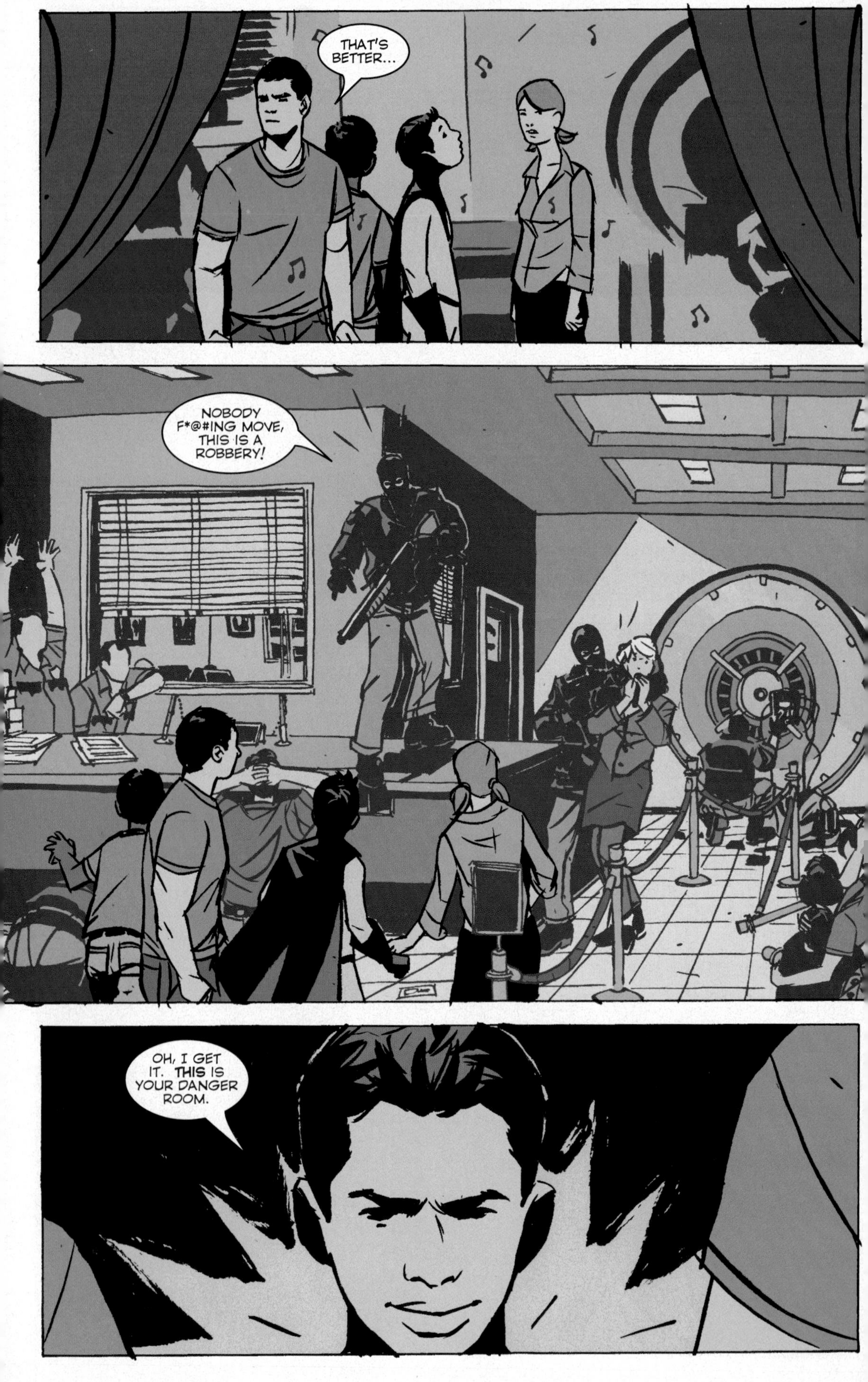
THAT'S BETTER...
NOBODY F*@#ING MOVE, THIS IS A ROBBERY!
OH, I GET IT. THIS IS YOUR DANGER ROOM.

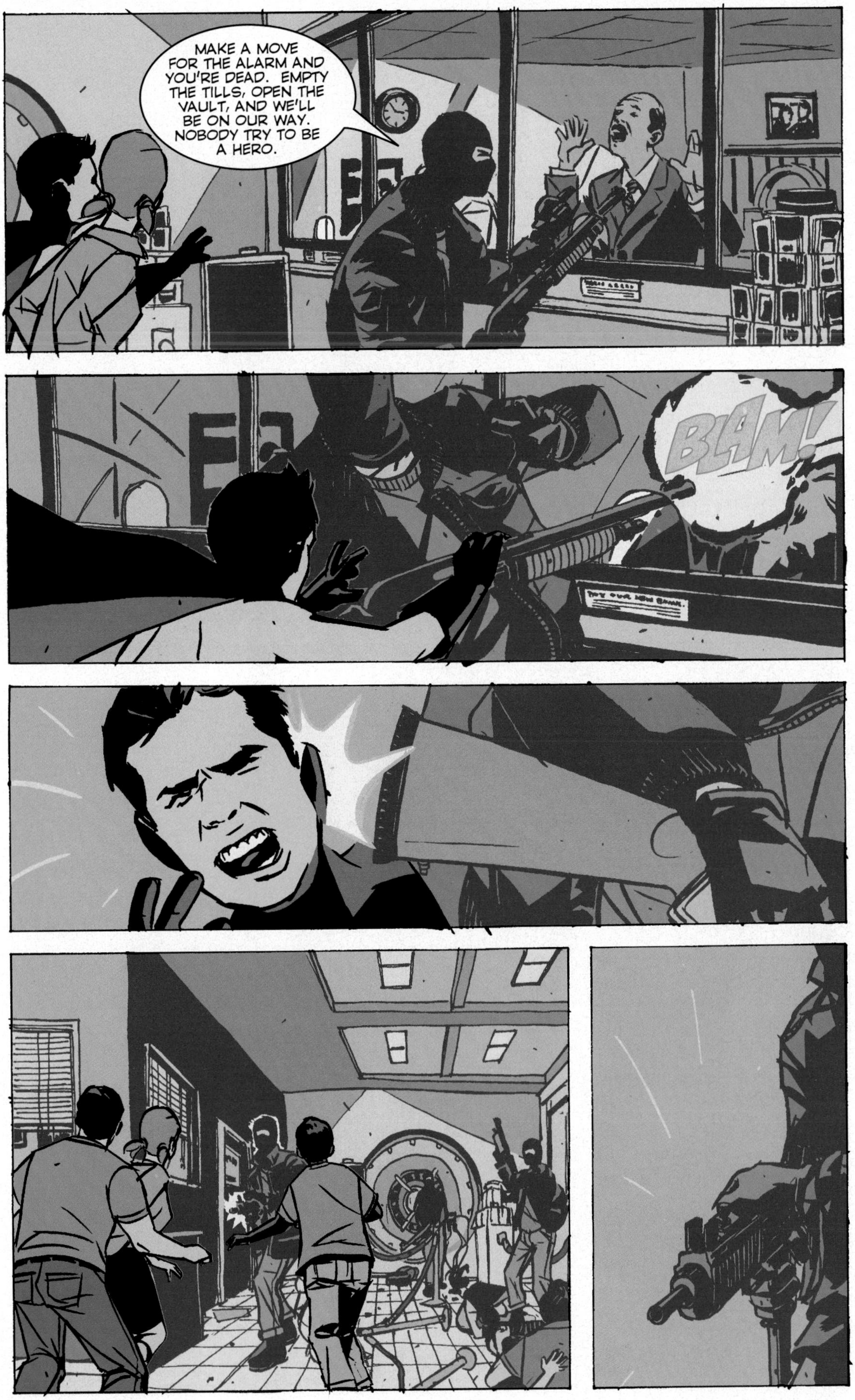
MAKE A MOVE FOR THE ALARM AND YOU'RE DEAD. EMPTY THE TILLS, OPEN THE VAULT, AND WE'LL BE ON OUR WAY. NOBODY TRY TO BE A HERO.
BLAM!

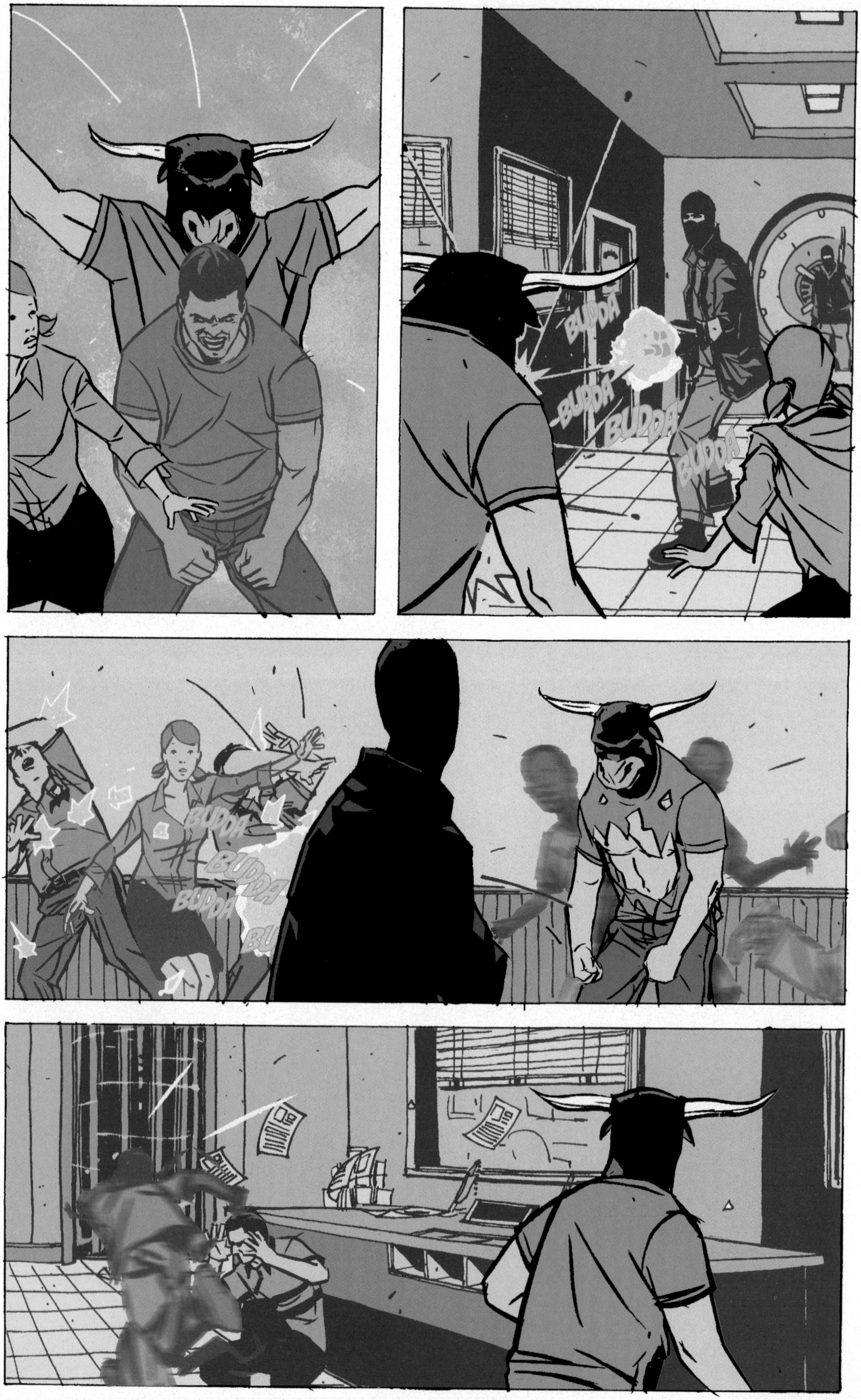
BUDDA
BUDDA
BUDDA
BUDDA
BUDDA
BUDDA
BUDDA

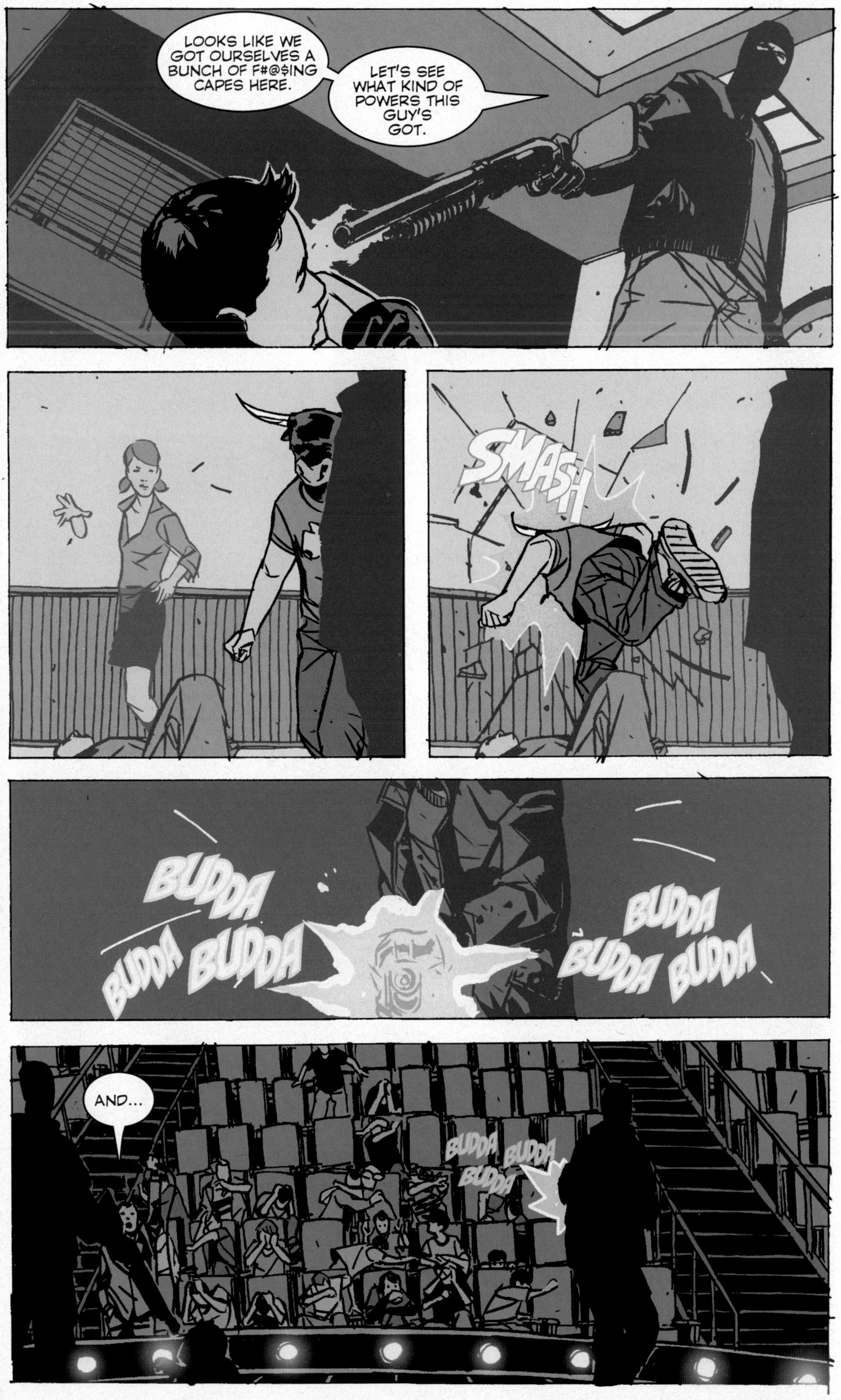
LOOKS LIKE WE GOT OURSELVES A BUNCH OF F#@$ING CAPES HERE.
LET'S SEE WHAT KIND OF POWERS THIS GUY'S GOT.
SMASH
BUDDA BUDDA BUDDA
BUDDA BUDDA BUDDA
AND...
BUDDA BUDDA BUDDA

...SCeNe.

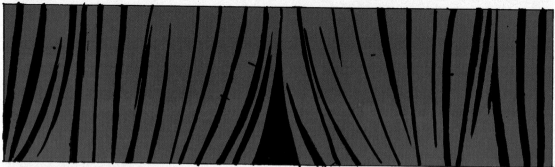

NOW, CAN ANYONE TELL ME WHAT WENT WRONG WITH THAT SCENE?

I CAN.

IF THIS WERE NOT A SIMULATION, YOU, POWERLESS ONE, WOULD BE DEAD.

THE REST OF YOU, THERE WERE SECURITY CAMERAS EVERYWHERE. AT BEST, YOUR IDENTITIES WOULD HAVE BEEN SEVERELY COMPROMISED.

OK, OK, I WAS RECKLESS, BUT I THOUGHT I HAD SERIOUS BACK-UP. SHOULDN'T THEY HAVE AT LEAST **TRIED** TO STOP THE ROBBERY? ISN'T THAT WHAT YOU'RE TRAINING THEM FOR?

OF COURSE NOT. DON'T BE ABSURD.

THEN WHAT THE HELL IS THE POINT OF THIS PLACE?

NOW THAT... THAT IS A VERY GOOD QUESTION.

THESPUS? HOUSE LIGHTS, PLEASE.

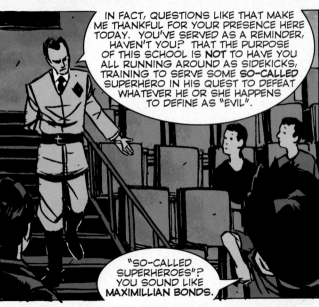

IN FACT, QUESTIONS LIKE THAT MAKE ME THANKFUL FOR YOUR PRESENCE HERE TODAY. YOU'VE SERVED AS A REMINDER, HAVEN'T YOU? THAT THE PURPOSE OF THIS SCHOOL IS **NOT** TO HAVE YOU ALL RUNNING AROUND AS SIDEKICKS, TRAINING TO SERVE SOME **SO-CALLED** SUPERHERO IN HIS QUEST TO DEFEAT WHATEVER HE OR SHE HAPPENS TO DEFINE AS "EVIL".

"SO-CALLED SUPERHEROES"? YOU SOUND LIKE **MAXIMILLIAN BONDS.**

HOW DARE YOU MENTION THAT NAME IN MY - OUR PURPOSE IS TO INSTILL SOMETHING YOU SEEM TO LACK - A **SURVIVAL INSTINCT.**

IF YOU WANT TO PARADE AROUND IN THOSE TIGHTS, GO AHEAD. AS FAR AS I CAN TELL, THEY SEEM TO PROVIDE LITTLE PROTECTION FROM SAY, **FALLING FROM GREAT HEIGHTS.**

IS THIS TRUE? YOU GUYS HAVE POWERS, BUT YOU DON'T WANT TO BE HEROES?

WHAT'S THE UPSIDE? LAST I HEARD, CRIMEFIGHTING WAS A HIGH RISK, NON-PAYING JOB. AND IF OUR PARENTS, IF YOUR **FATHER** IS ANY EXAMPLE-

THEN WHAT IS IT YOU **DO** WANT?

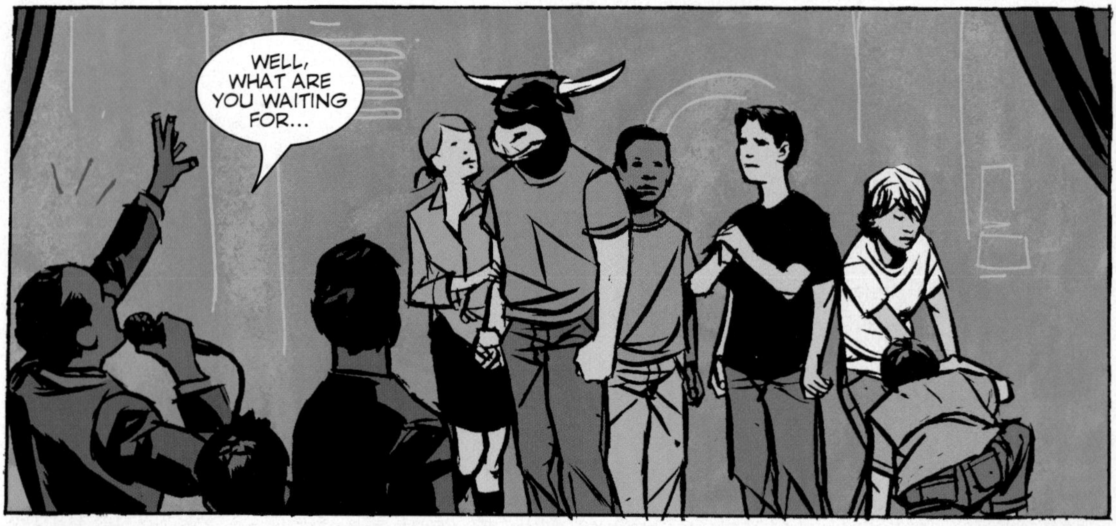
WELL, WHAT ARE YOU WAITING FOR...

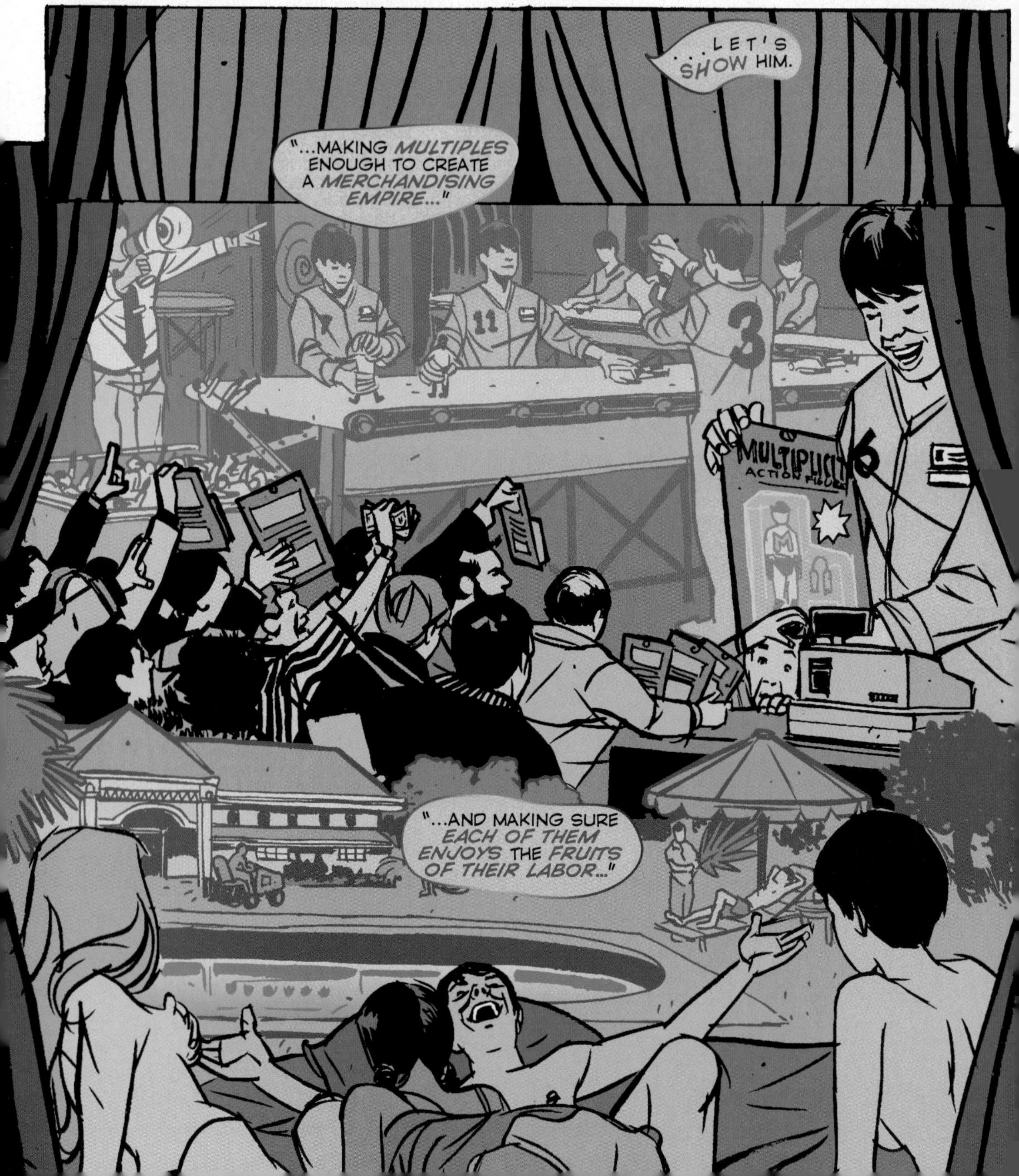
...LET'S SHOW HIM.
"...MAKING MULTIPLES ENOUGH TO CREATE A MERCHANDISING EMPIRE..."
MULTIPLICITY
ACTION FIGURES
"...AND MAKING SURE EACH OF THEM ENJOYS THE FRUITS OF THEIR LABOR..."

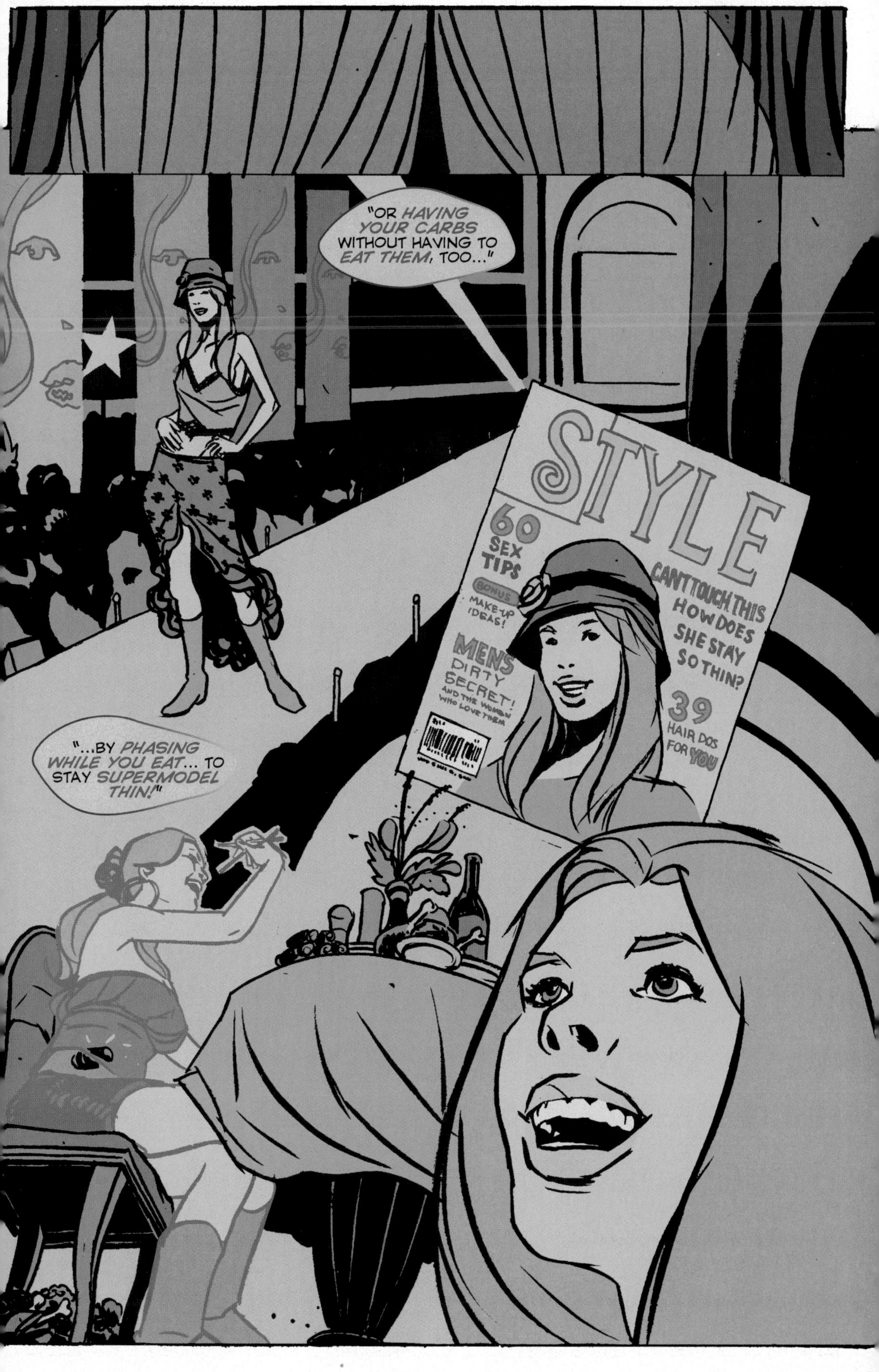
"OR HAVING YOUR CARBS WITHOUT HAVING TO EAT THEM, TOO..."
STYLE
60 SEX TIPS
BONUS MAKE-UP IDEAS!
MENS DIRTY SECRET! AND THE WOMEN WHO LOVE THEM
CAN'T TOUCH THIS HOW DOES SHE STAY SO THIN?
39 HAIR DOS FOR YOU
"...BY PHASING WHILE YOU EAT... TO STAY SUPERMODEL THIN!"

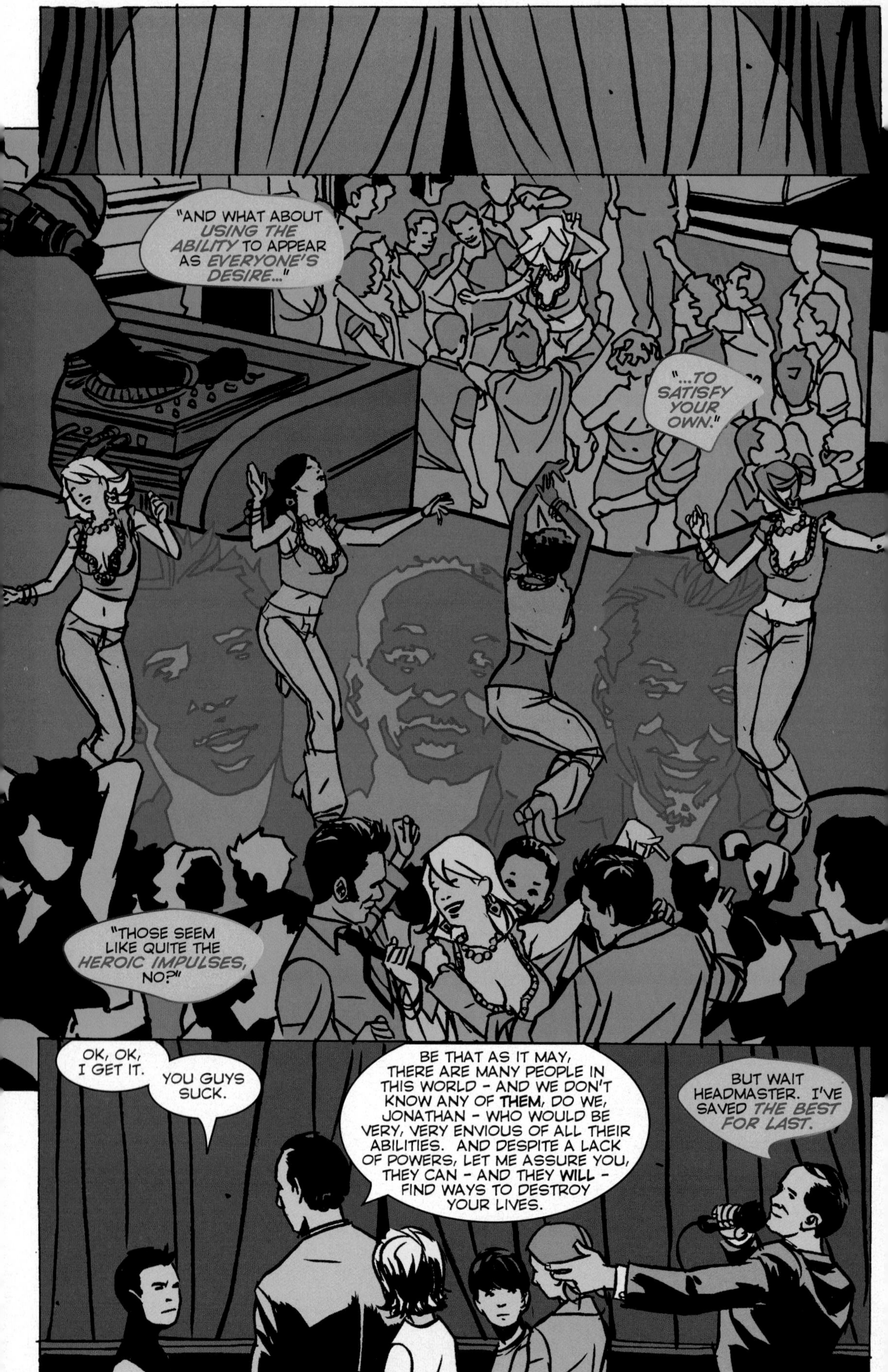
"AND WHAT ABOUT USING THE ABILITY TO APPEAR AS EVERYONE'S DESIRE..."
"...TO SATISFY YOUR OWN."
"THOSE SEEM LIKE QUITE THE HEROIC IMPULSES, NO?"
OK, OK, I GET IT.
YOU GUYS SUCK.
BE THAT AS IT MAY, THERE ARE MANY PEOPLE IN THIS WORLD - AND WE DON'T KNOW ANY OF THEM, DO WE, JONATHAN - WHO WOULD BE VERY, VERY ENVIOUS OF ALL THEIR ABILITIES. AND DESPITE A LACK OF POWERS, LET ME ASSURE YOU, THEY CAN - AND THEY WILL - FIND WAYS TO DESTROY YOUR LIVES.
BUT WAIT HEADMASTER. I'VE SAVED THE BEST FOR LAST.

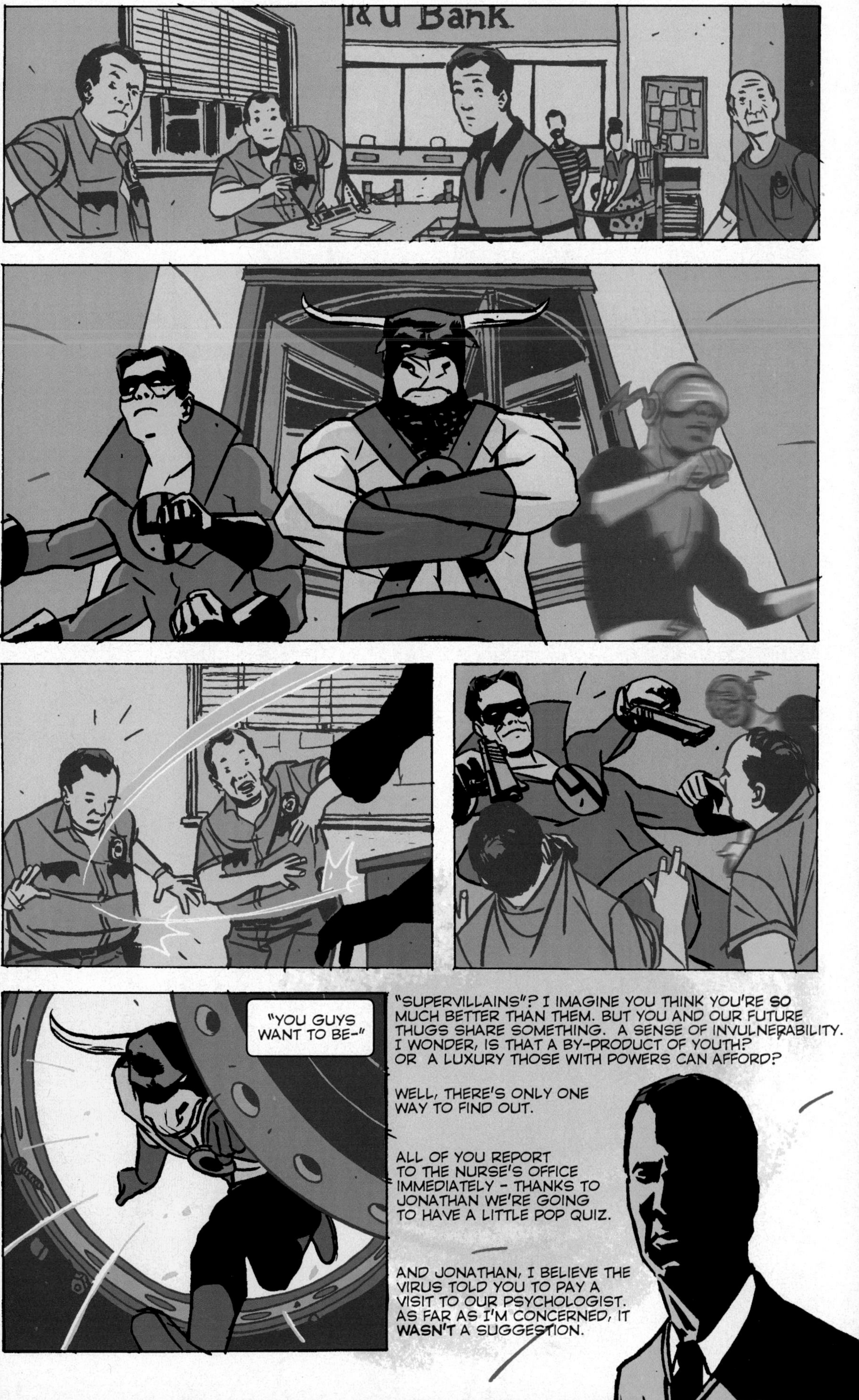
I&U Bank
"YOU GUYS WANT TO BE-"
"SUPERVILLAINS"? I IMAGINE YOU THINK YOU'RE SO MUCH BETTER THAN THEM. BUT YOU AND OUR FUTURE THUGS SHARE SOMETHING. A SENSE OF INVULNERABILITY. I WONDER, IS THAT A BY-PRODUCT OF YOUTH? OR A LUXURY THOSE WITH POWERS CAN AFFORD?
WELL, THERE'S ONLY ONE WAY TO FIND OUT.
ALL OF YOU REPORT TO THE NURSE'S OFFICE IMMEDIATELY - THANKS TO JONATHAN WE'RE GOING TO HAVE A LITTLE POP QUIZ.
AND JONATHAN, I BELIEVE THE VIRUS TOLD YOU TO PAY A VISIT TO OUR PSYCHOLOGIST. AS FAR AS I'M CONCERNED, IT **WASN'T** A SUGGESTION.

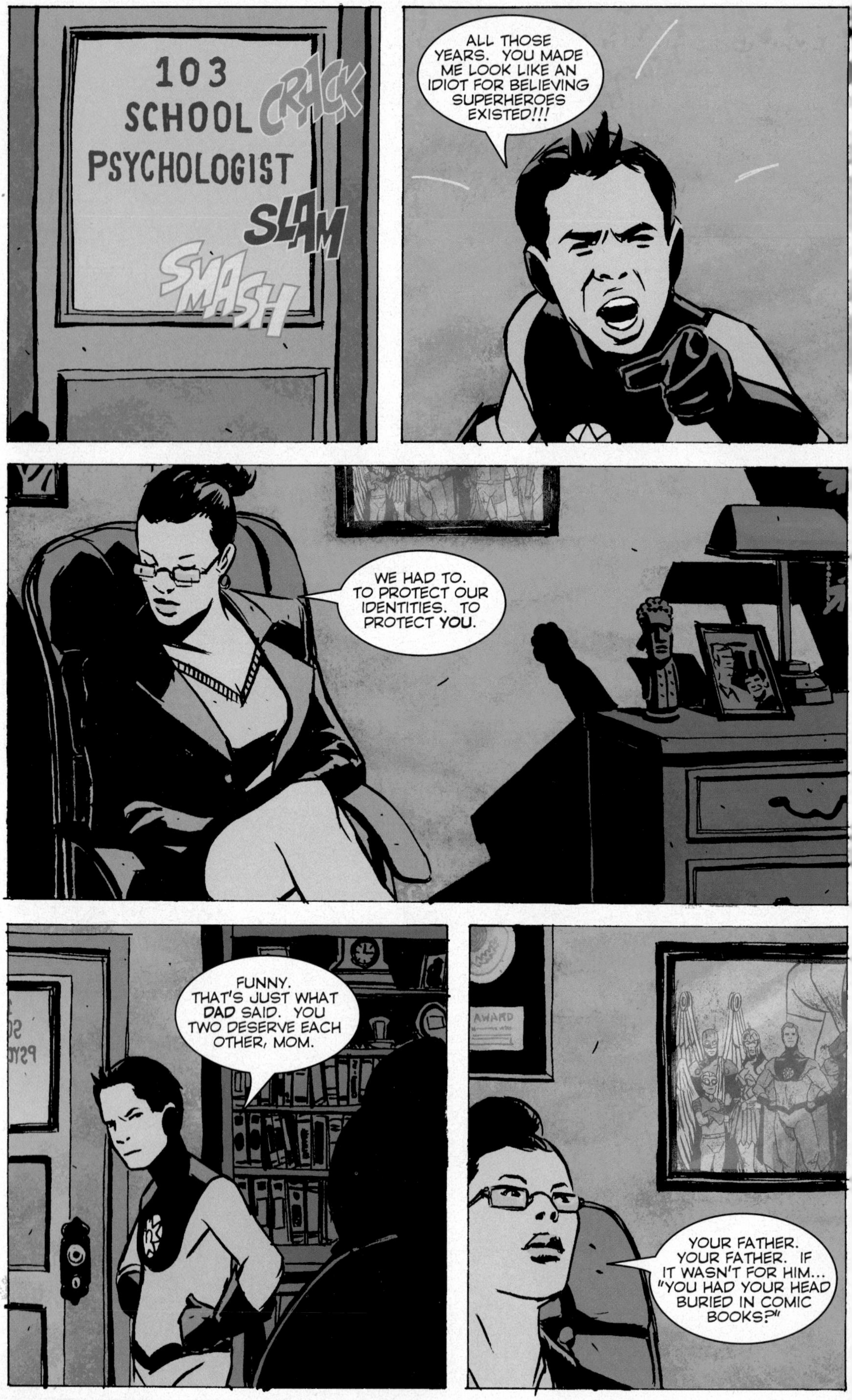
103
SCHOOL
PSYCHOLOGIST
CRACK
SLAM
SMASH
ALL THOSE YEARS. YOU MADE ME LOOK LIKE AN IDIOT FOR BELIEVING SUPERHEROES EXISTED!!!
WE HAD TO. TO PROTECT OUR IDENTITIES. TO PROTECT YOU.
FUNNY. THAT'S JUST WHAT DAD SAID. YOU TWO DESERVE EACH OTHER, MOM.
AWARD
YOUR FATHER. YOUR FATHER. IF IT WASN'T FOR HIM... "YOU HAD YOUR HEAD BURIED IN COMIC BOOKS?"

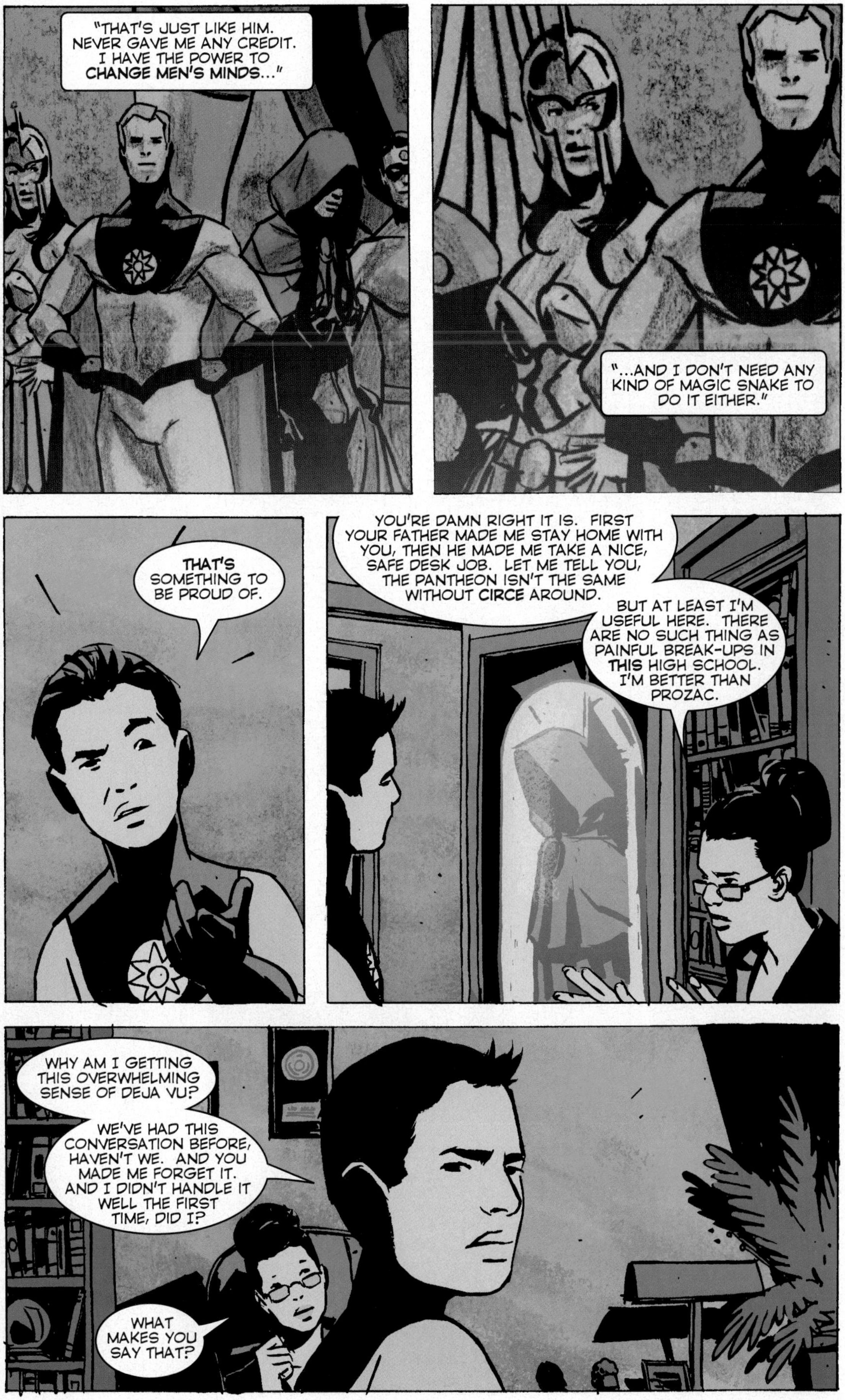
"THAT'S JUST LIKE HIM. NEVER GAVE ME ANY CREDIT. I HAVE THE POWER TO **CHANGE MEN'S MINDS...**"
"...AND I DON'T NEED ANY KIND OF MAGIC SNAKE TO DO IT EITHER."
THAT'S SOMETHING TO BE PROUD OF.
YOU'RE DAMN RIGHT IT IS. FIRST YOUR FATHER MADE ME STAY HOME WITH YOU, THEN HE MADE ME TAKE A NICE, SAFE DESK JOB. LET ME TELL YOU, THE PANTHEON ISN'T THE SAME WITHOUT **CIRCE** AROUND.
BUT AT LEAST I'M USEFUL HERE. THERE ARE NO SUCH THING AS PAINFUL BREAK-UPS IN **THIS** HIGH SCHOOL. I'M BETTER THAN PROZAC.
WHY AM I GETTING THIS OVERWHELMING SENSE OF DEJA VU?
WE'VE HAD THIS CONVERSATION BEFORE, HAVEN'T WE. AND YOU MADE ME FORGET IT. AND I DIDN'T HANDLE IT WELL THE FIRST TIME, DID I?
WHAT MAKES YOU SAY THAT?

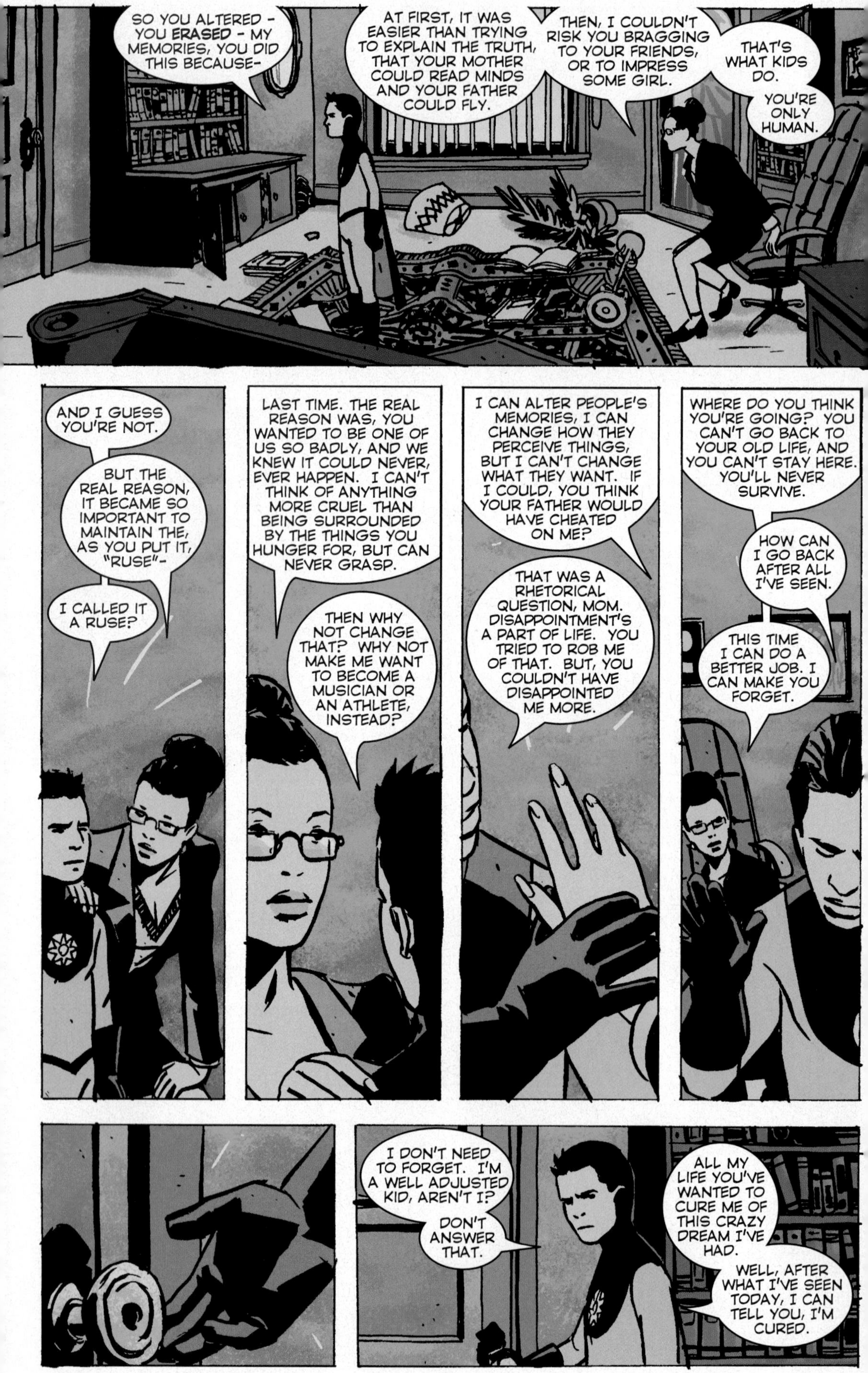
SO YOU ALTERED - YOU **ERASED** - MY MEMORIES, YOU DID THIS BECAUSE-
AT FIRST, IT WAS EASIER THAN TRYING TO EXPLAIN THE TRUTH, THAT YOUR MOTHER COULD READ MINDS AND YOUR FATHER COULD FLY.
THEN, I COULDN'T RISK YOU BRAGGING TO YOUR FRIENDS, OR TO IMPRESS SOME GIRL.
THAT'S WHAT KIDS DO.
YOU'RE ONLY HUMAN.
AND I GUESS YOU'RE NOT.
BUT THE REAL REASON, IT BECAME SO IMPORTANT TO MAINTAIN THE, AS YOU PUT IT, "RUSE"-
I CALLED IT A RUSE?
LAST TIME. THE REAL REASON WAS, YOU WANTED TO BE ONE OF US SO BADLY, AND WE KNEW IT COULD NEVER, EVER HAPPEN. I CAN'T THINK OF ANYTHING MORE CRUEL THAN BEING SURROUNDED BY THE THINGS YOU HUNGER FOR, BUT CAN NEVER GRASP.
THEN WHY NOT CHANGE THAT? WHY NOT MAKE ME WANT TO BECOME A MUSICIAN OR AN ATHLETE, INSTEAD?
I CAN ALTER PEOPLE'S MEMORIES, I CAN CHANGE HOW THEY PERCEIVE THINGS, BUT I CAN'T CHANGE WHAT THEY WANT. IF I COULD, YOU THINK YOUR FATHER WOULD HAVE CHEATED ON ME?
THAT WAS A RHETORICAL QUESTION, MOM. DISAPPOINTMENT'S A PART OF LIFE. YOU TRIED TO ROB ME OF THAT. BUT, YOU COULDN'T HAVE DISAPPOINTED ME MORE.
WHERE DO YOU THINK YOU'RE GOING? YOU CAN'T GO BACK TO YOUR OLD LIFE, AND YOU CAN'T STAY HERE. YOU'LL NEVER SURVIVE.
HOW CAN I GO BACK AFTER ALL I'VE SEEN.
THIS TIME I CAN DO A BETTER JOB. I CAN MAKE YOU FORGET.
I DON'T NEED TO FORGET. I'M A WELL ADJUSTED KID, AREN'T I?
DON'T ANSWER THAT.
ALL MY LIFE YOU'VE WANTED TO CURE ME OF THIS CRAZY DREAM I'VE HAD.
WELL, AFTER WHAT I'VE SEEN TODAY, I CAN TELL YOU, I'M CURED.

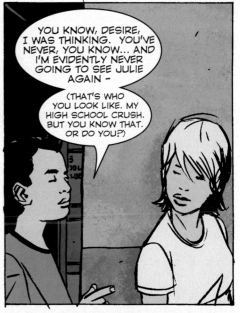

YOU KNOW, DESIRE, I WAS THINKING. YOU'VE NEVER, YOU KNOW... AND I'M EVIDENTLY NEVER GOING TO SEE JULIE AGAIN —

(THAT'S WHO YOU LOOK LIKE. MY HIGH SCHOOL CRUSH. BUT YOU KNOW THAT. OR DO YOU?)

ANYWAY, IF I ASKED TO KISS YOU, IT WOULDN'T BE FAIR TO EITHER OF US, WOULD IT?

NURSES OFFICE

ONE MORE ACT OF HEROISM BEFORE YOU LEAVE US ALL BEHIND?

SOMEONE HAS TO SET AN EXAMPLE FOR YOU GUYS.

WELL, CONGRATULATIONS. NOW YOU'VE MADE THE REST OF US LIKE YOU.

YOU'VE CHANGED YOUR MINDS? YOU WANT TO BE HEROES?

THE NURSE IS GIVING US SHOTS. THEY'RE TAKING OUR POWERS AWAY.

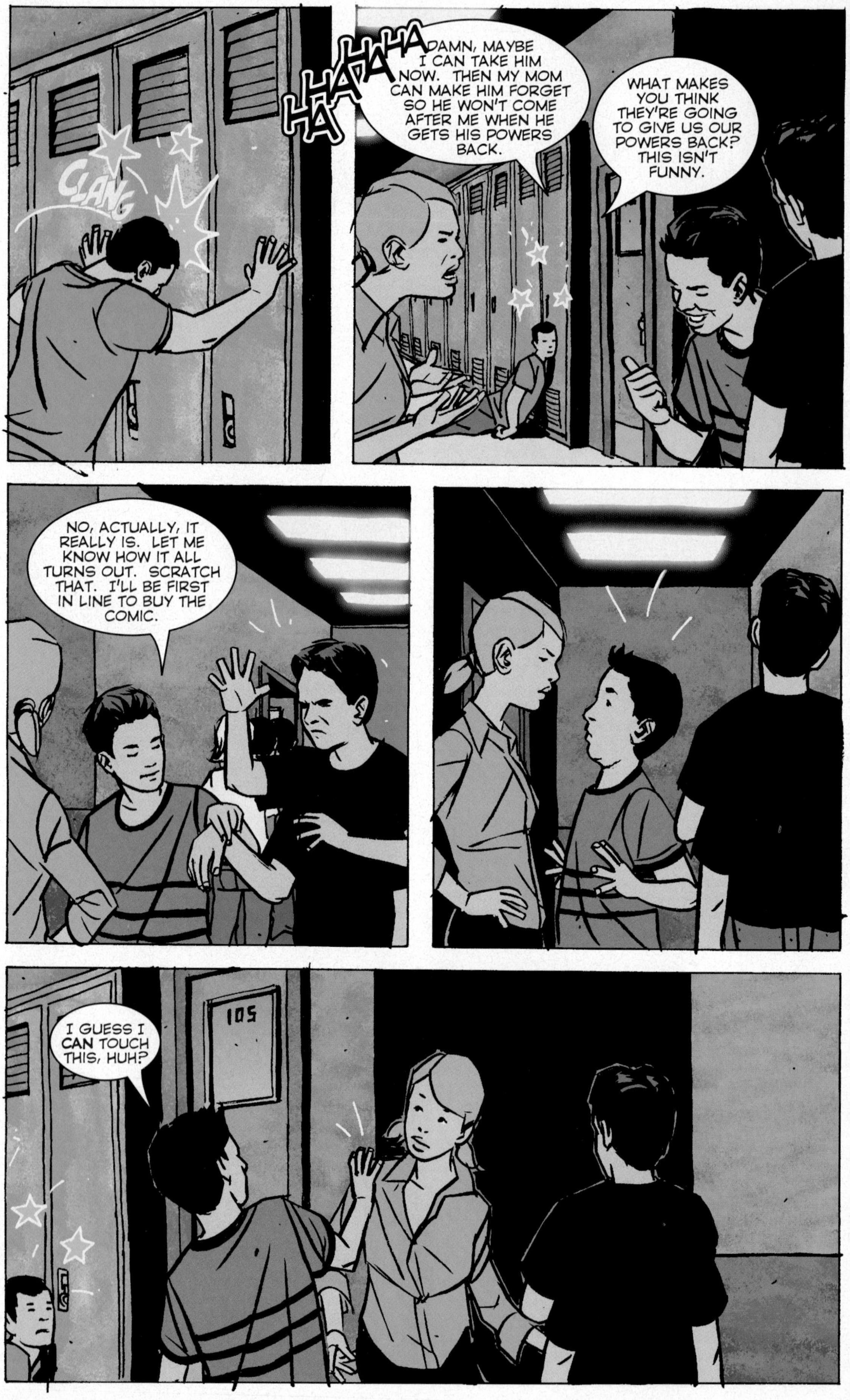
CLANG
HA HA HA HA HA
DAMN, MAYBE I CAN TAKE HIM NOW. THEN MY MOM CAN MAKE HIM FORGET SO HE WON'T COME AFTER ME WHEN HE GETS HIS POWERS BACK.
WHAT MAKES YOU THINK THEY'RE GOING TO GIVE US OUR POWERS BACK? THIS ISN'T FUNNY.
NO, ACTUALLY, IT REALLY IS. LET ME KNOW HOW IT ALL TURNS OUT. SCRATCH THAT. I'LL BE FIRST IN LINE TO BUY THE COMIC.
105
I GUESS I **CAN** TOUCH THIS, HUH?

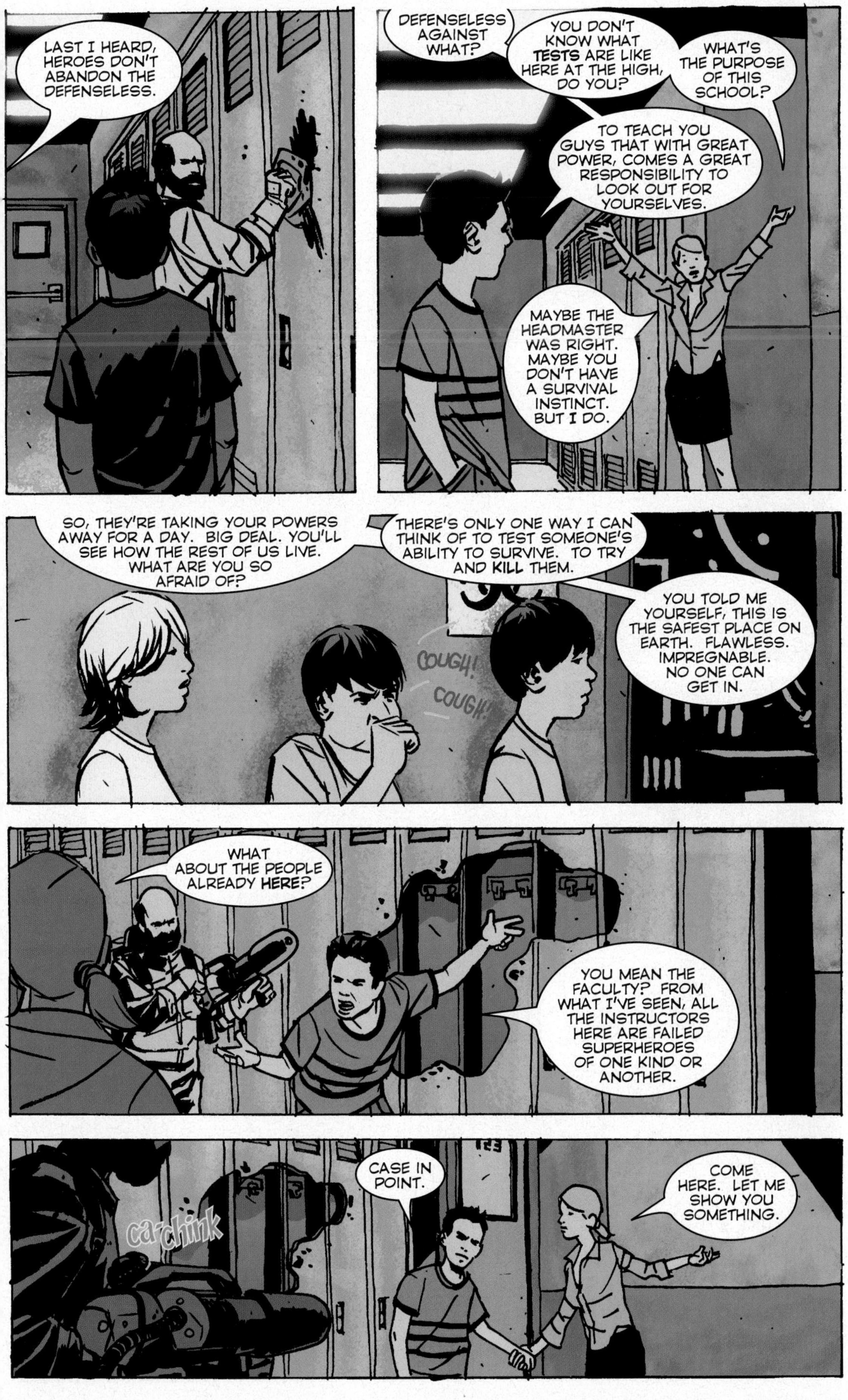
LAST I HEARD, HEROES DON'T ABANDON THE DEFENSELESS.
DEFENSELESS AGAINST WHAT?
YOU DON'T KNOW WHAT TESTS ARE LIKE HERE AT THE HIGH, DO YOU?
WHAT'S THE PURPOSE OF THIS SCHOOL?
TO TEACH YOU GUYS THAT WITH GREAT POWER, COMES A GREAT RESPONSIBILITY TO LOOK OUT FOR YOURSELVES.
MAYBE THE HEADMASTER WAS RIGHT. MAYBE YOU DON'T HAVE A SURVIVAL INSTINCT. BUT I DO.
SO, THEY'RE TAKING YOUR POWERS AWAY FOR A DAY. BIG DEAL. YOU'LL SEE HOW THE REST OF US LIVE. WHAT ARE YOU SO AFRAID OF?
THERE'S ONLY ONE WAY I CAN THINK OF TO TEST SOMEONE'S ABILITY TO SURVIVE. TO TRY AND KILL THEM.
COUGH!
COUGH!
YOU TOLD ME YOURSELF, THIS IS THE SAFEST PLACE ON EARTH. FLAWLESS. IMPREGNABLE. NO ONE CAN GET IN.
WHAT ABOUT THE PEOPLE ALREADY HERE?
YOU MEAN THE FACULTY? FROM WHAT I'VE SEEN, ALL THE INSTRUCTORS HERE ARE FAILED SUPERHEROES OF ONE KIND OR ANOTHER.
ca-chink
CASE IN POINT.
COME HERE. LET ME SHOW YOU SOMETHING.

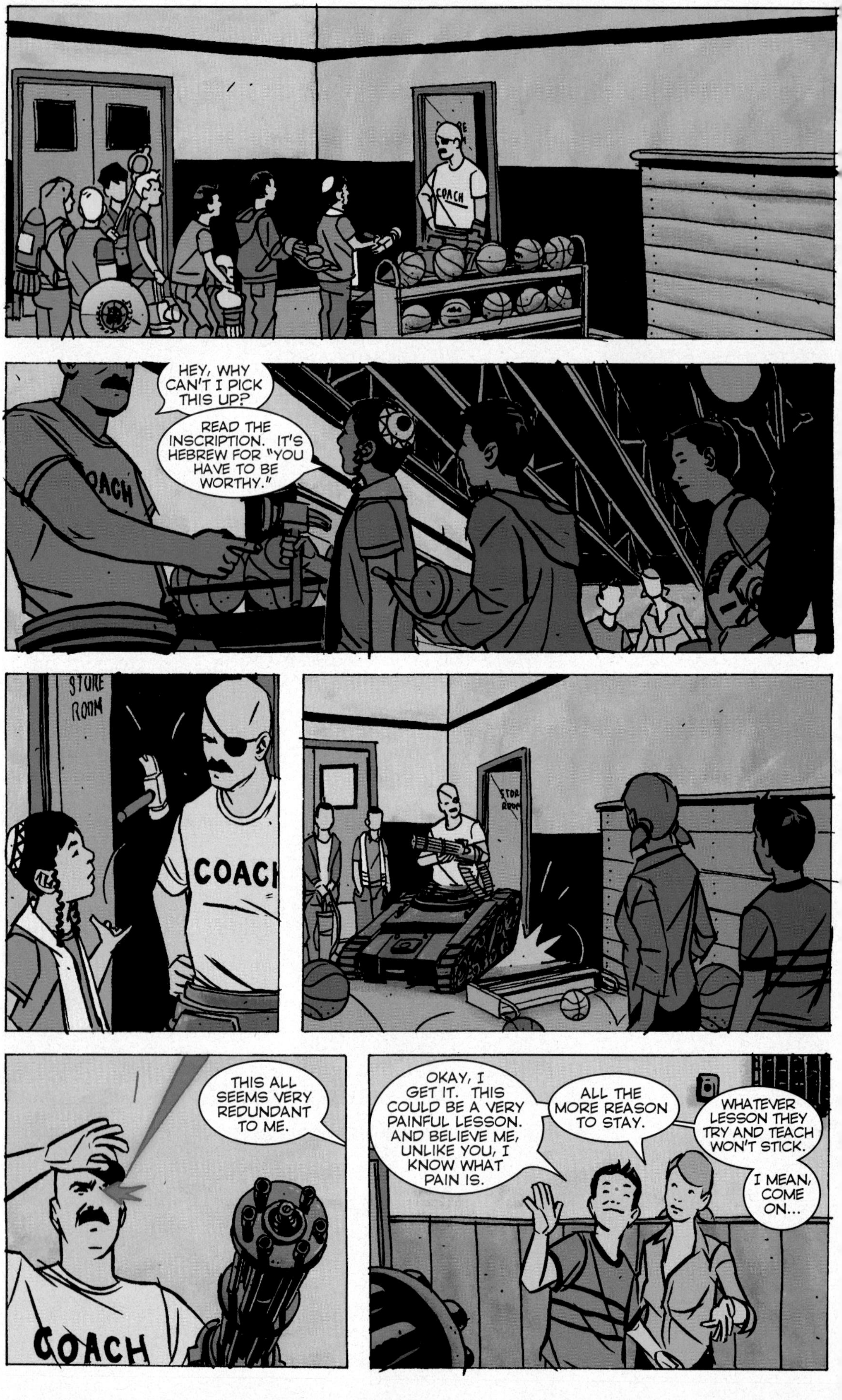
COACH
HEY, WHY CAN'T I PICK THIS UP?
READ THE INSCRIPTION. IT'S HEBREW FOR "YOU HAVE TO BE WORTHY."
STORE ROOM
COACH
THIS ALL SEEMS VERY REDUNDANT TO ME.
COACH
OKAY, I GET IT. THIS COULD BE A VERY PAINFUL LESSON. AND BELIEVE ME, UNLIKE YOU, I KNOW WHAT PAIN IS.
ALL THE MORE REASON TO STAY.
WHATEVER LESSON THEY TRY AND TEACH WON'T STICK.
I MEAN, COME ON...

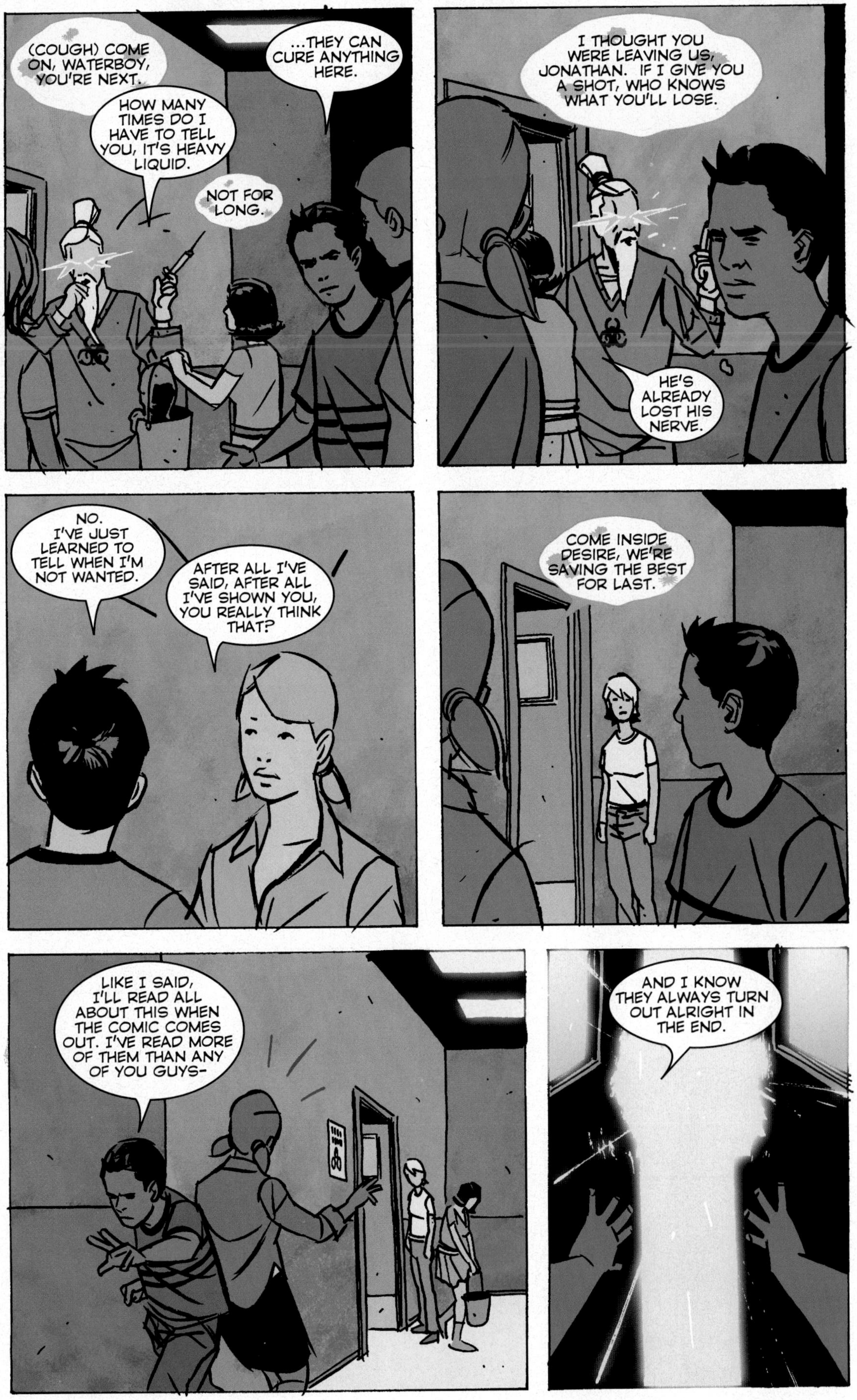
(COUGH) COME ON, WATERBOY, YOU'RE NEXT.
HOW MANY TIMES DO I HAVE TO TELL YOU, IT'S HEAVY LIQUID.
...THEY CAN CURE ANYTHING HERE.
NOT FOR LONG.
I THOUGHT YOU WERE LEAVING US, JONATHAN. IF I GIVE YOU A SHOT, WHO KNOWS WHAT YOU'LL LOSE.
HE'S ALREADY LOST HIS NERVE.
NO. I'VE JUST LEARNED TO TELL WHEN I'M NOT WANTED.
AFTER ALL I'VE SAID, AFTER ALL I'VE SHOWN YOU, YOU REALLY THINK THAT?
COME INSIDE DESIRE, WE'RE SAVING THE BEST FOR LAST.
LIKE I SAID, I'LL READ ALL ABOUT THIS WHEN THE COMIC COMES OUT. I'VE READ MORE OF THEM THAN ANY OF YOU GUYS-
AND I KNOW THEY ALWAYS TURN OUT ALRIGHT IN THE END.

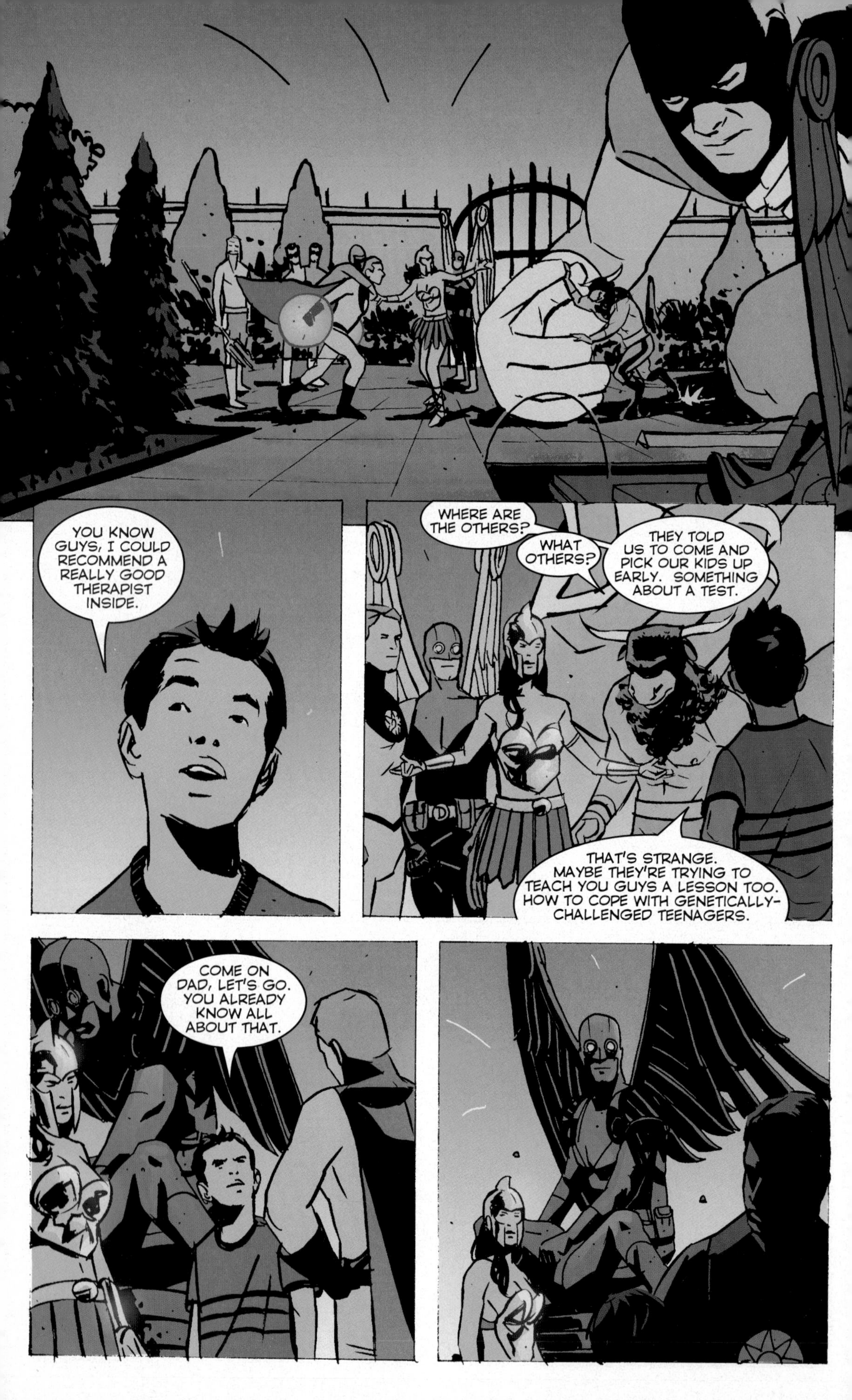

YOU KNOW GUYS, I COULD RECOMMEND A REALLY GOOD THERAPIST INSIDE.
WHERE ARE THE OTHERS?
WHAT OTHERS?
THEY TOLD US TO COME AND PICK OUR KIDS UP EARLY. SOMETHING ABOUT A TEST.
THAT'S STRANGE. MAYBE THEY'RE TRYING TO TEACH YOU GUYS A LESSON TOO. HOW TO COPE WITH GENETICALLY-CHALLENGED TEENAGERS.
COME ON DAD, LET'S GO. YOU ALREADY KNOW ALL ABOUT THAT.

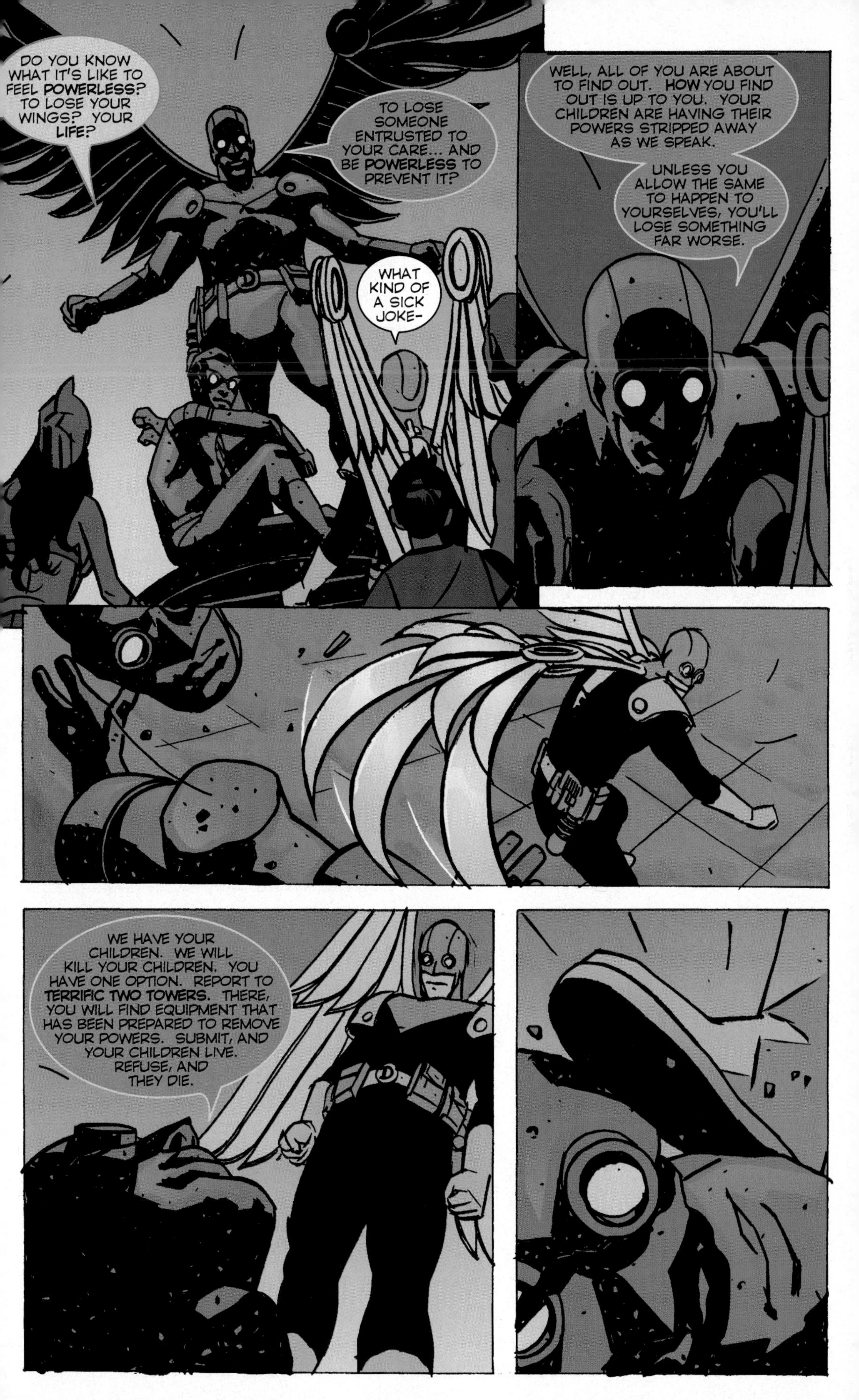

DO YOU KNOW WHAT IT'S LIKE TO FEEL **POWERLESS**? TO LOSE YOUR WINGS? YOUR **LIFE**?
TO LOSE SOMEONE ENTRUSTED TO YOUR CARE... AND BE **POWERLESS** TO PREVENT IT?
WHAT KIND OF A SICK JOKE-
WELL, ALL OF YOU ARE ABOUT TO FIND OUT. **HOW** YOU FIND OUT IS UP TO YOU. YOUR CHILDREN ARE HAVING THEIR POWERS STRIPPED AWAY AS WE SPEAK.
UNLESS YOU ALLOW THE SAME TO HAPPEN TO YOURSELVES, YOU'LL LOSE SOMETHING FAR WORSE.
WE HAVE YOUR CHILDREN. WE WILL KILL YOUR CHILDREN. YOU HAVE ONE OPTION. REPORT TO **TERRIFIC TWO TOWERS**. THERE, YOU WILL FIND EQUIPMENT THAT HAS BEEN PREPARED TO REMOVE YOUR POWERS. SUBMIT, AND YOUR CHILDREN LIVE. REFUSE, AND THEY DIE.

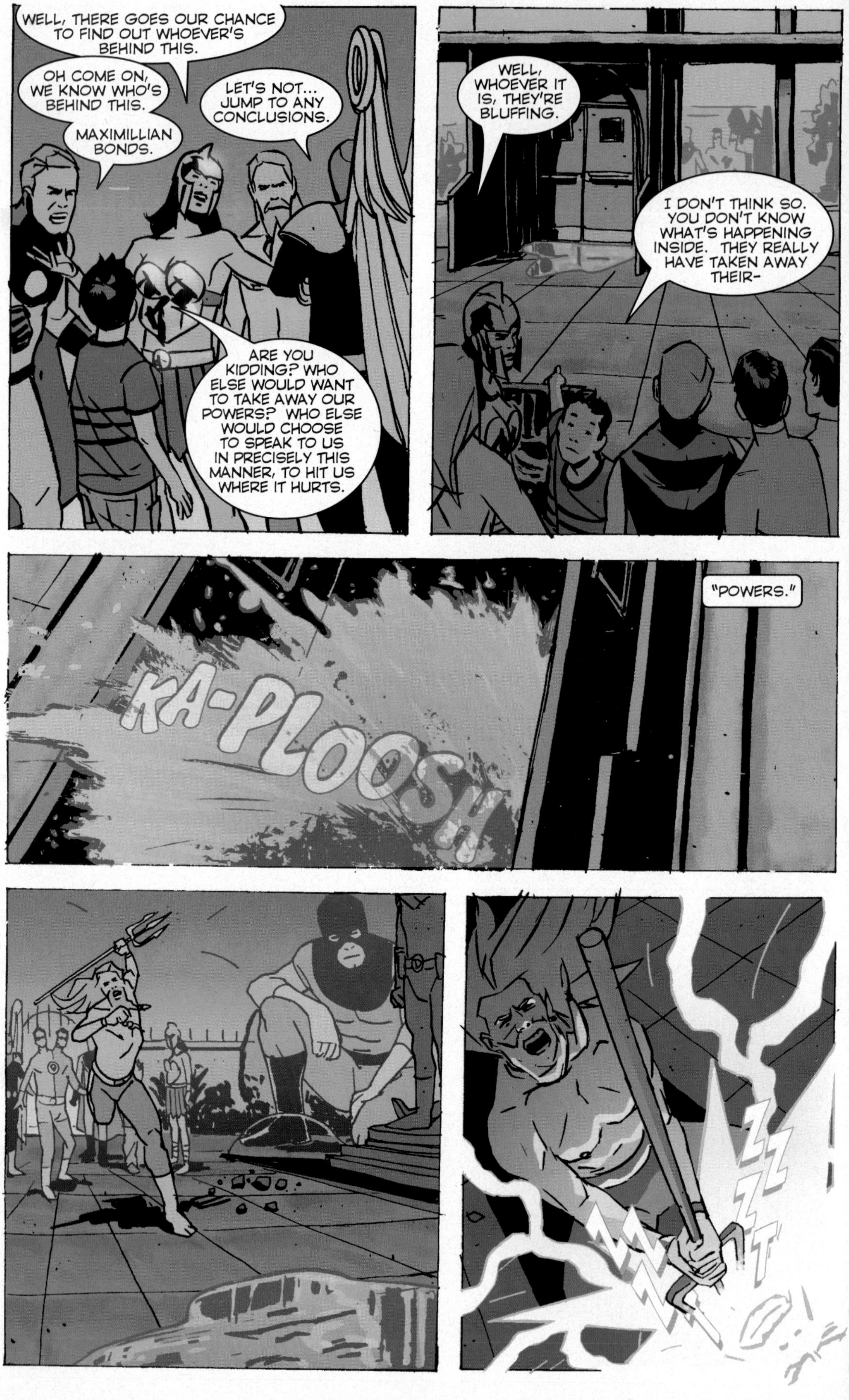

WELL, THERE GOES OUR CHANCE TO FIND OUT WHOEVER'S BEHIND THIS.
OH COME ON, WE KNOW WHO'S BEHIND THIS.
MAXIMILLIAN BONDS.
LET'S NOT... JUMP TO ANY CONCLUSIONS.
ARE YOU KIDDING? WHO ELSE WOULD WANT TO TAKE AWAY OUR POWERS? WHO ELSE WOULD CHOOSE TO SPEAK TO US IN PRECISELY THIS MANNER, TO HIT US WHERE IT HURTS.
WELL, WHOEVER IT IS, THEY'RE BLUFFING.
I DON'T THINK SO. YOU DON'T KNOW WHAT'S HAPPENING INSIDE. THEY REALLY HAVE TAKEN AWAY THEIR-
"POWERS."
KA-PLOOSH
ZZZT

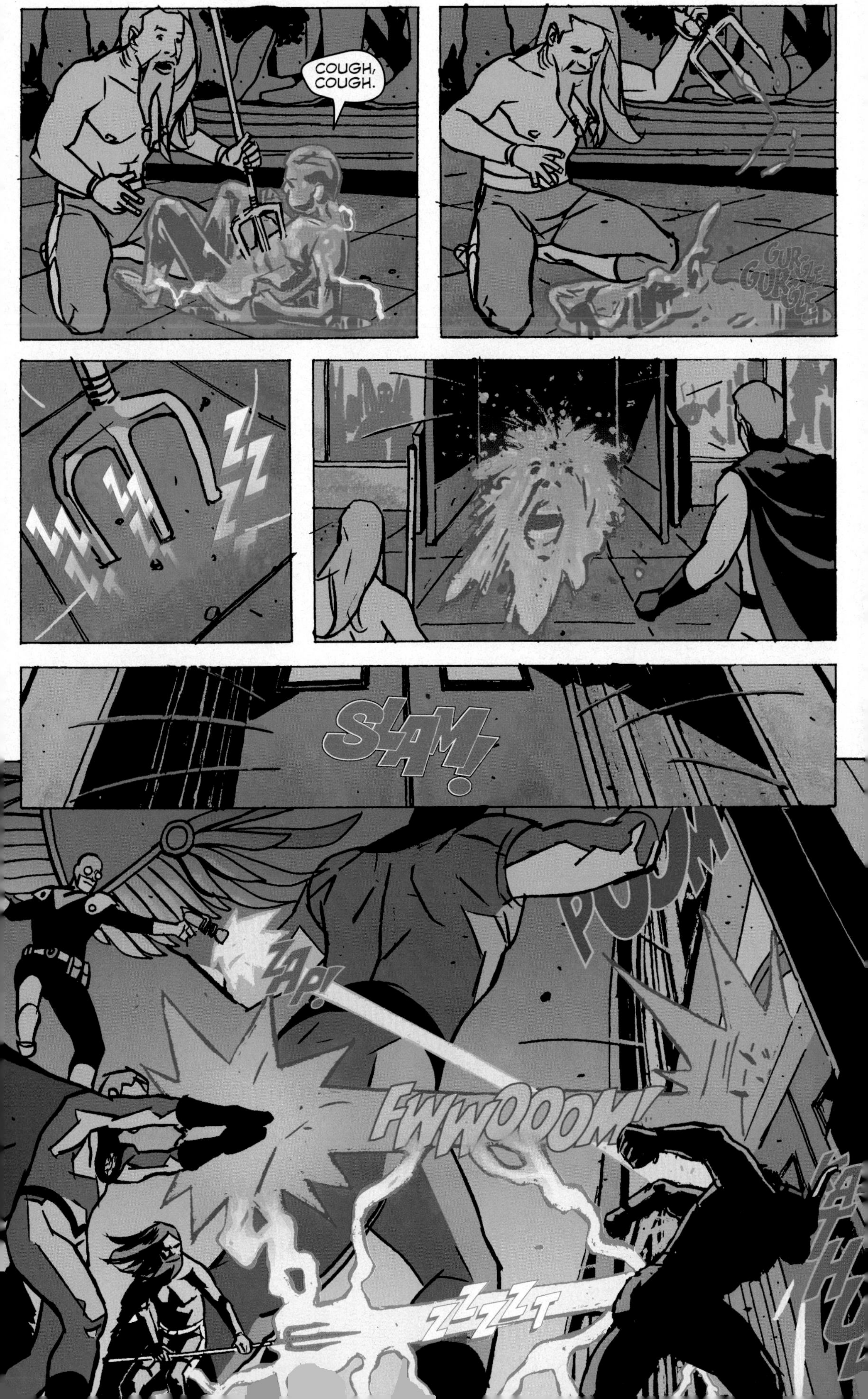
COUGH, COUGH.
GURGLE GURGLE
SLAM!
ZAP!
POOM
FWWOOOM!
ZZZZZT

HOW MANY TIMES DO WE HAVE TO TELL YOU? NO ONE WITH POWERS ENTERS. IF YOU WANT TO SEE YOUR CHILDREN ALIVE–

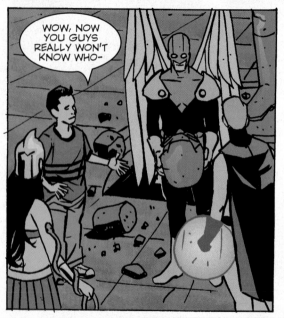

WOW, NOW YOU GUYS REALLY WON'T KNOW WHO–

I GUESS WE CAN RULE OUT THE USUAL SUSPECTS.

WHAT DO YOU MEAN?

I JUST CAME BACK FROM THE LOW.

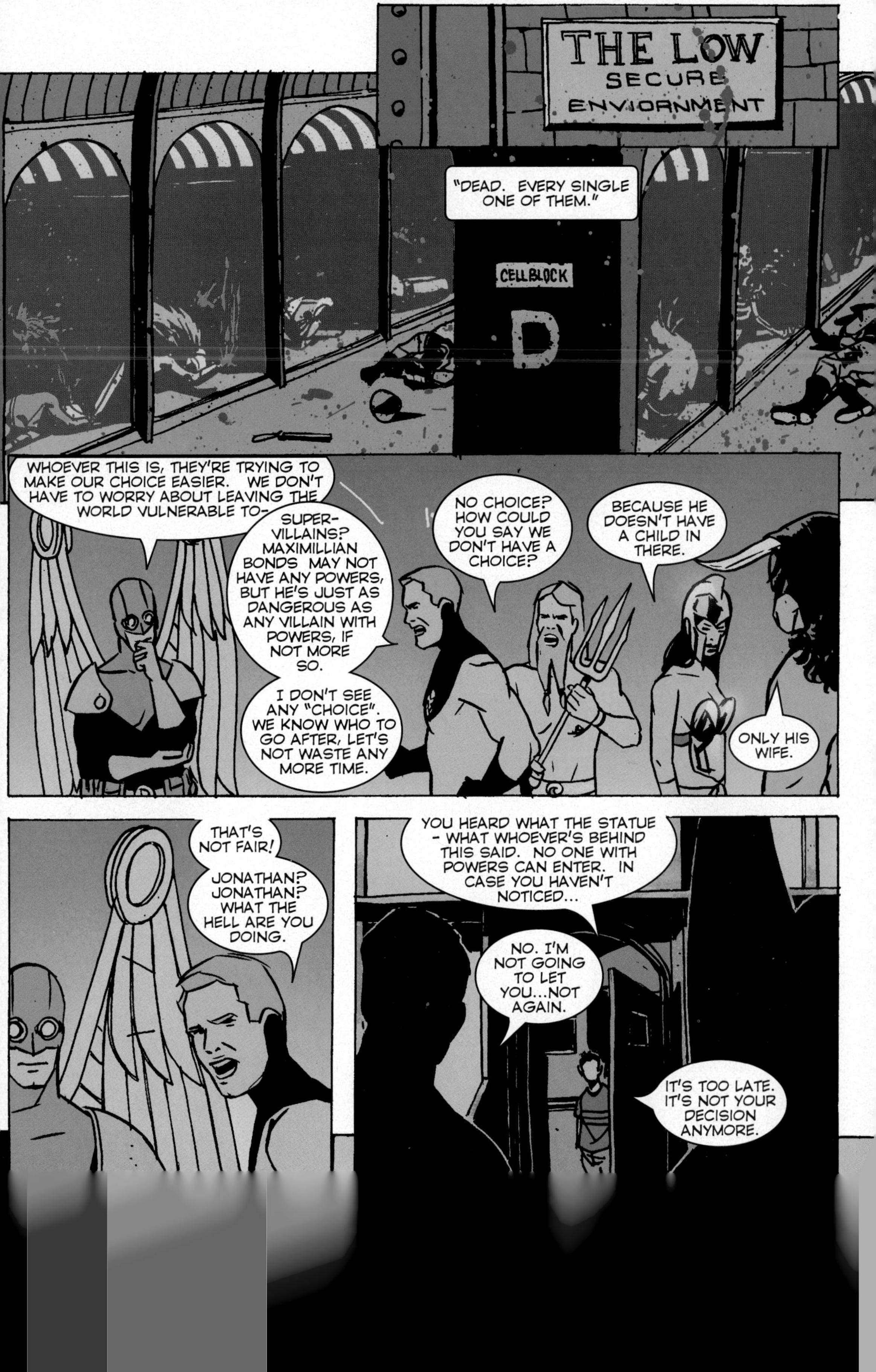
THE LOW
SECURE
ENVIORNMENT
"DEAD. EVERY SINGLE ONE OF THEM."
CELLBLOCK
D
WHOEVER THIS IS, THEY'RE TRYING TO MAKE OUR CHOICE EASIER. WE DON'T HAVE TO WORRY ABOUT LEAVING THE WORLD VULNERABLE TO-
SUPER-VILLAINS? MAXIMILLIAN BONDS MAY NOT HAVE ANY POWERS, BUT HE'S JUST AS DANGEROUS AS ANY VILLAIN WITH POWERS, IF NOT MORE SO.
I DON'T SEE ANY "CHOICE". WE KNOW WHO TO GO AFTER, LET'S NOT WASTE ANY MORE TIME.
NO CHOICE? HOW COULD YOU SAY WE DON'T HAVE A CHOICE?
BECAUSE HE DOESN'T HAVE A CHILD IN THERE.
ONLY HIS WIFE.
THAT'S NOT FAIR!
JONATHAN? JONATHAN? WHAT THE HELL ARE YOU DOING.
YOU HEARD WHAT THE STATUE - WHAT WHOEVER'S BEHIND THIS SAID. NO ONE WITH POWERS CAN ENTER. IN CASE YOU HAVEN'T NOTICED...
NO. I'M NOT GOING TO LET YOU...NOT AGAIN.
IT'S TOO LATE. IT'S NOT YOUR DECISION ANYMORE.

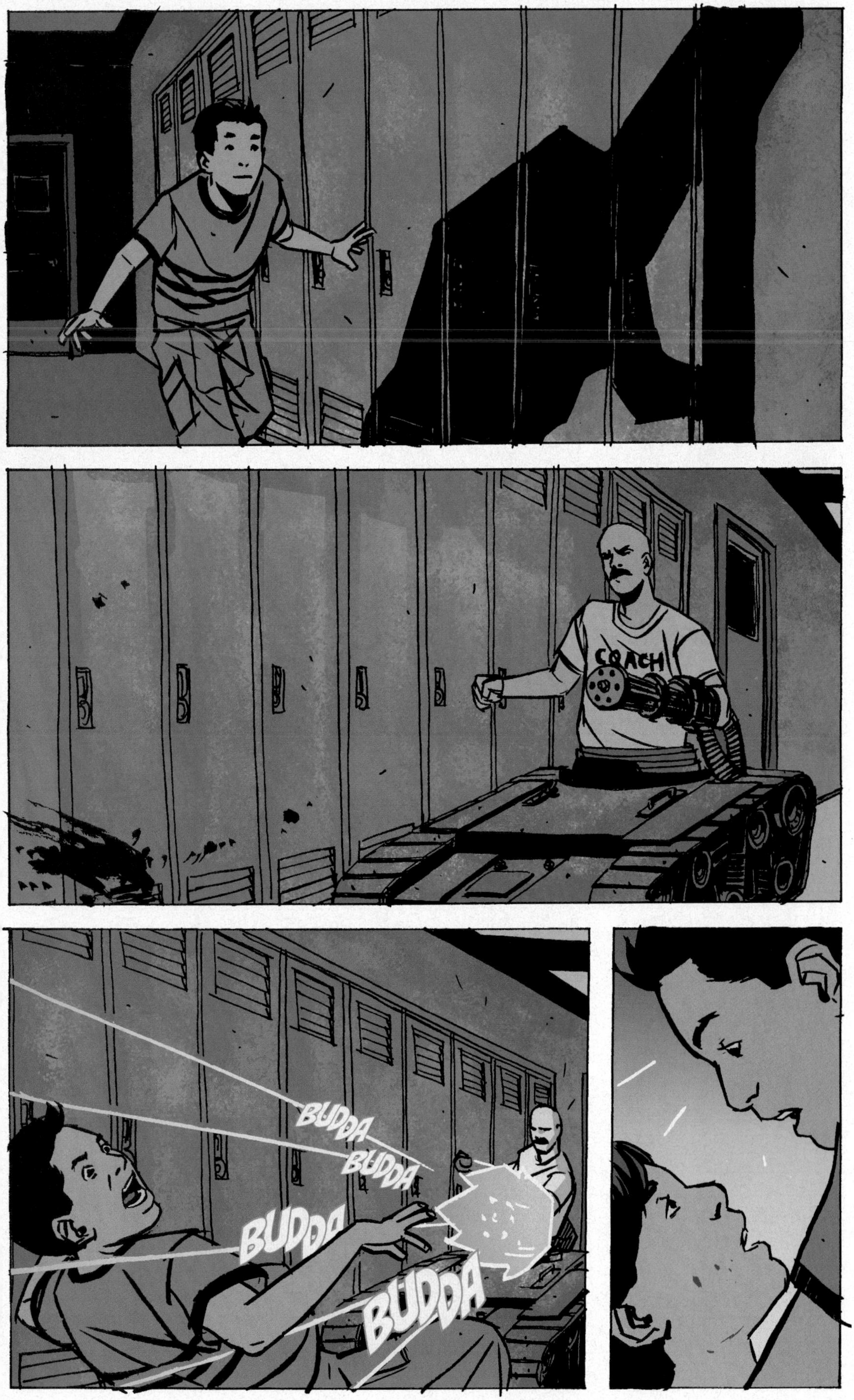
COACH
BUDDA
BUDDA
BUDDA
BUDDA

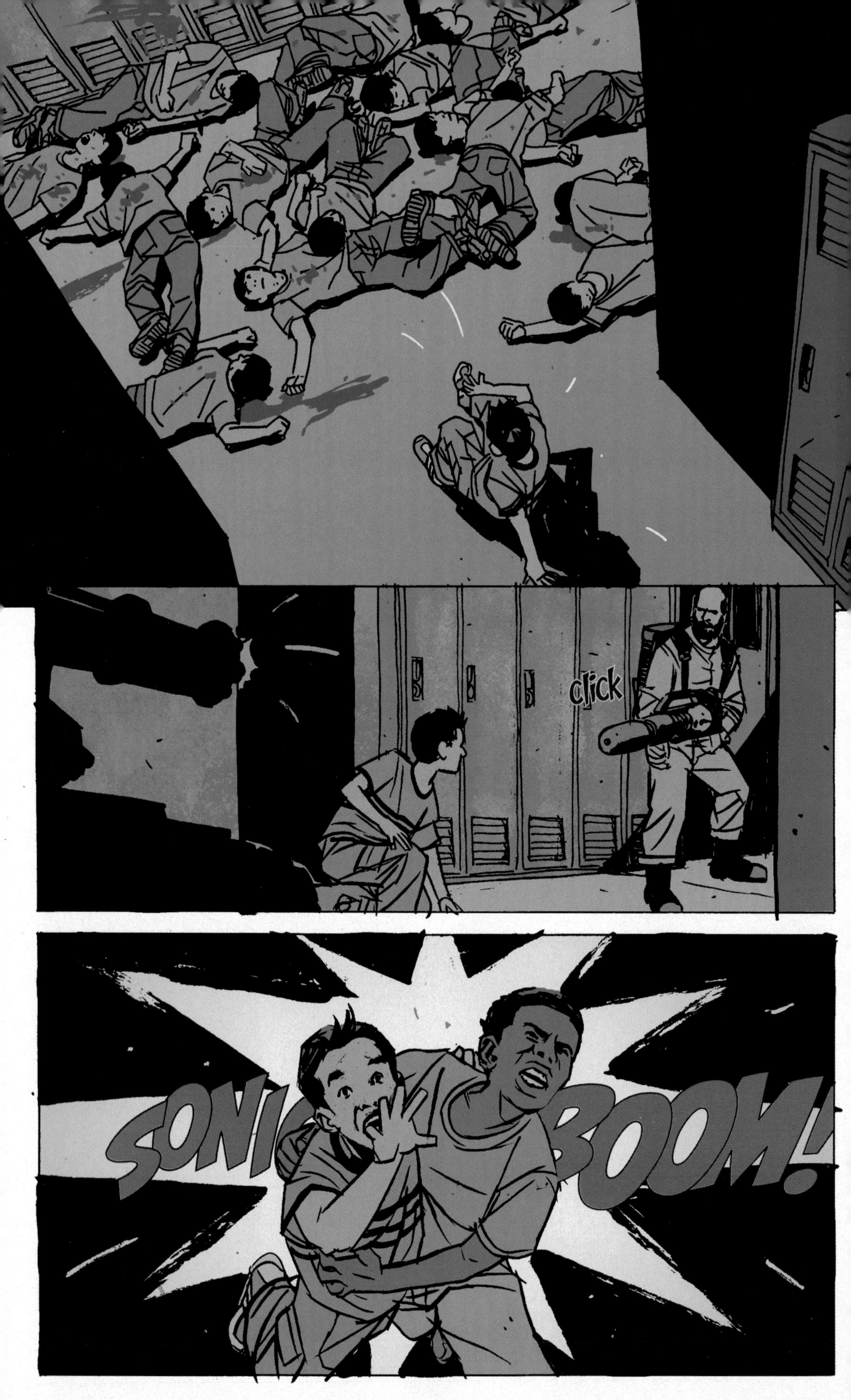
CLICK
SONIC BOOM!

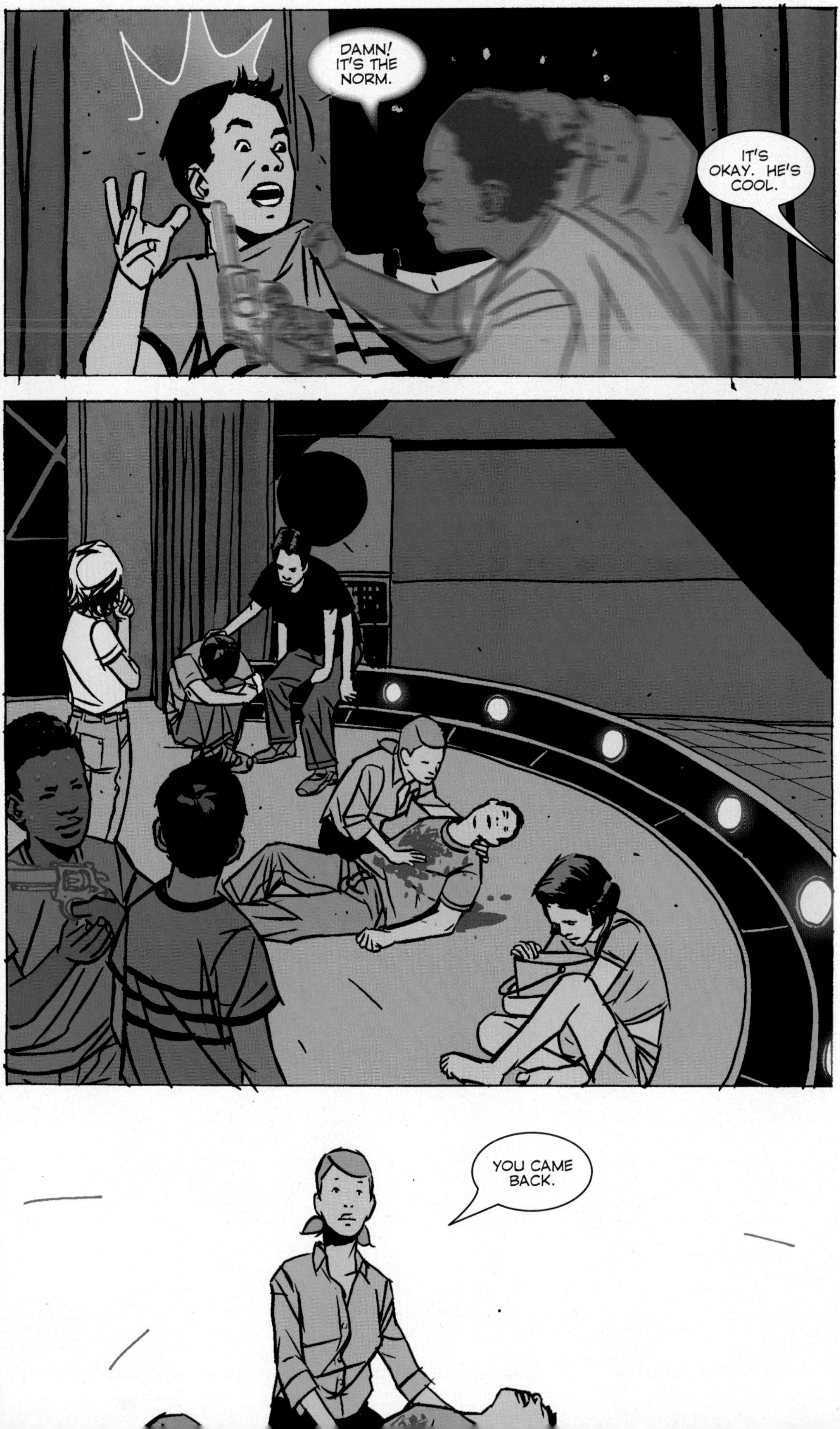
DAMN! IT'S THE NORM.
IT'S OKAY. HE'S COOL.
YOU CAME BACK.

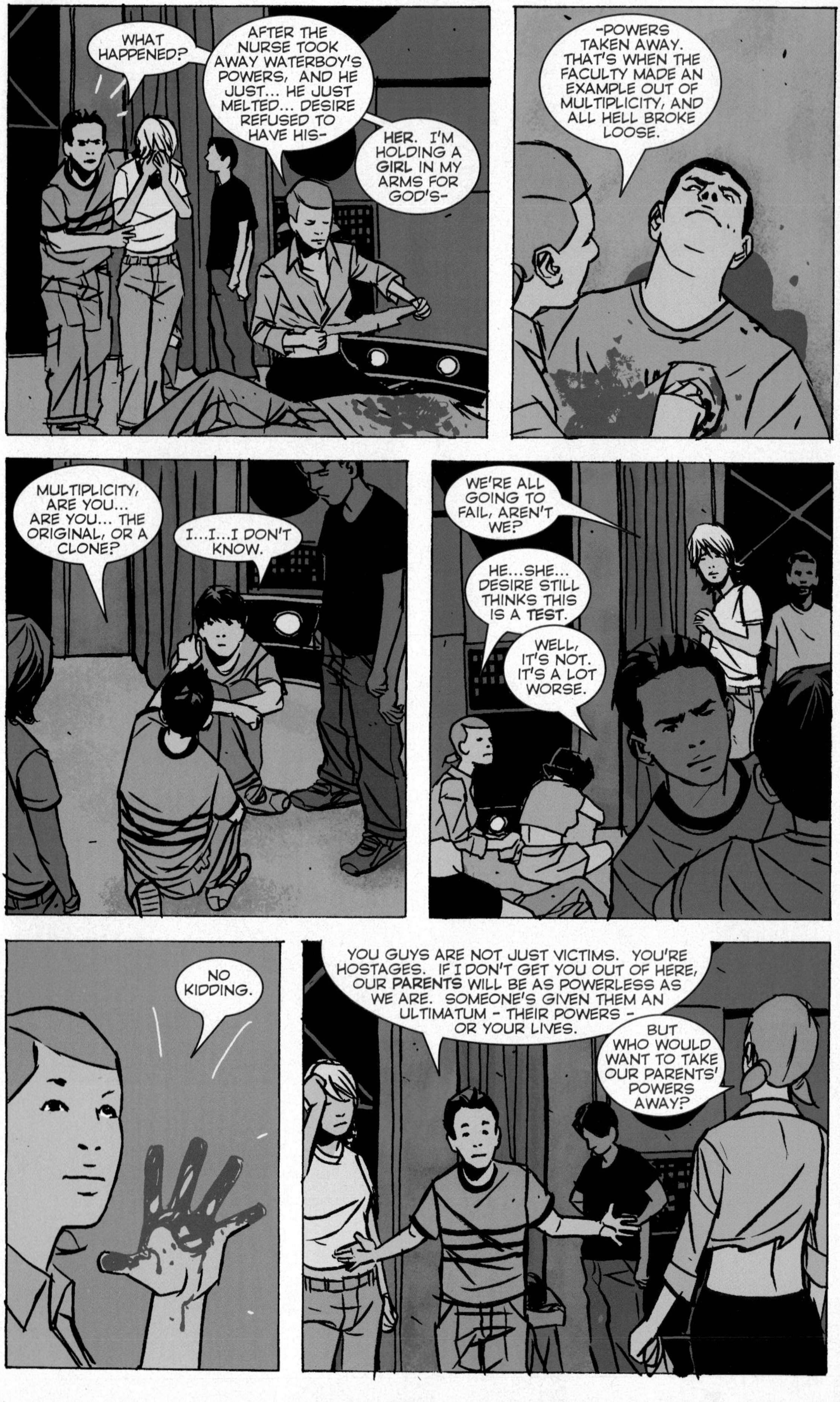

WHAT HAPPENED?
AFTER THE NURSE TOOK AWAY WATERBOY'S POWERS, AND HE JUST... HE JUST MELTED... DESIRE REFUSED TO HAVE HIS-
HER. I'M HOLDING A GIRL IN MY ARMS FOR GOD'S-
-POWERS TAKEN AWAY. THAT'S WHEN THE FACULTY MADE AN EXAMPLE OUT OF MULTIPLICITY, AND ALL HELL BROKE LOOSE.
MULTIPLICITY, ARE YOU... ARE YOU... THE ORIGINAL, OR A CLONE?
I...I...I DON'T KNOW.
WE'RE ALL GOING TO FAIL, AREN'T WE?
HE...SHE... DESIRE STILL THINKS THIS IS A TEST.
WELL, IT'S NOT. IT'S A LOT WORSE.
NO KIDDING.
YOU GUYS ARE NOT JUST VICTIMS. YOU'RE HOSTAGES. IF I DON'T GET YOU OUT OF HERE, OUR PARENTS WILL BE AS POWERLESS AS WE ARE. SOMEONE'S GIVEN THEM AN ULTIMATUM - THEIR POWERS - OR YOUR LIVES.
BUT WHO WOULD WANT TO TAKE OUR PARENTS' POWERS AWAY?

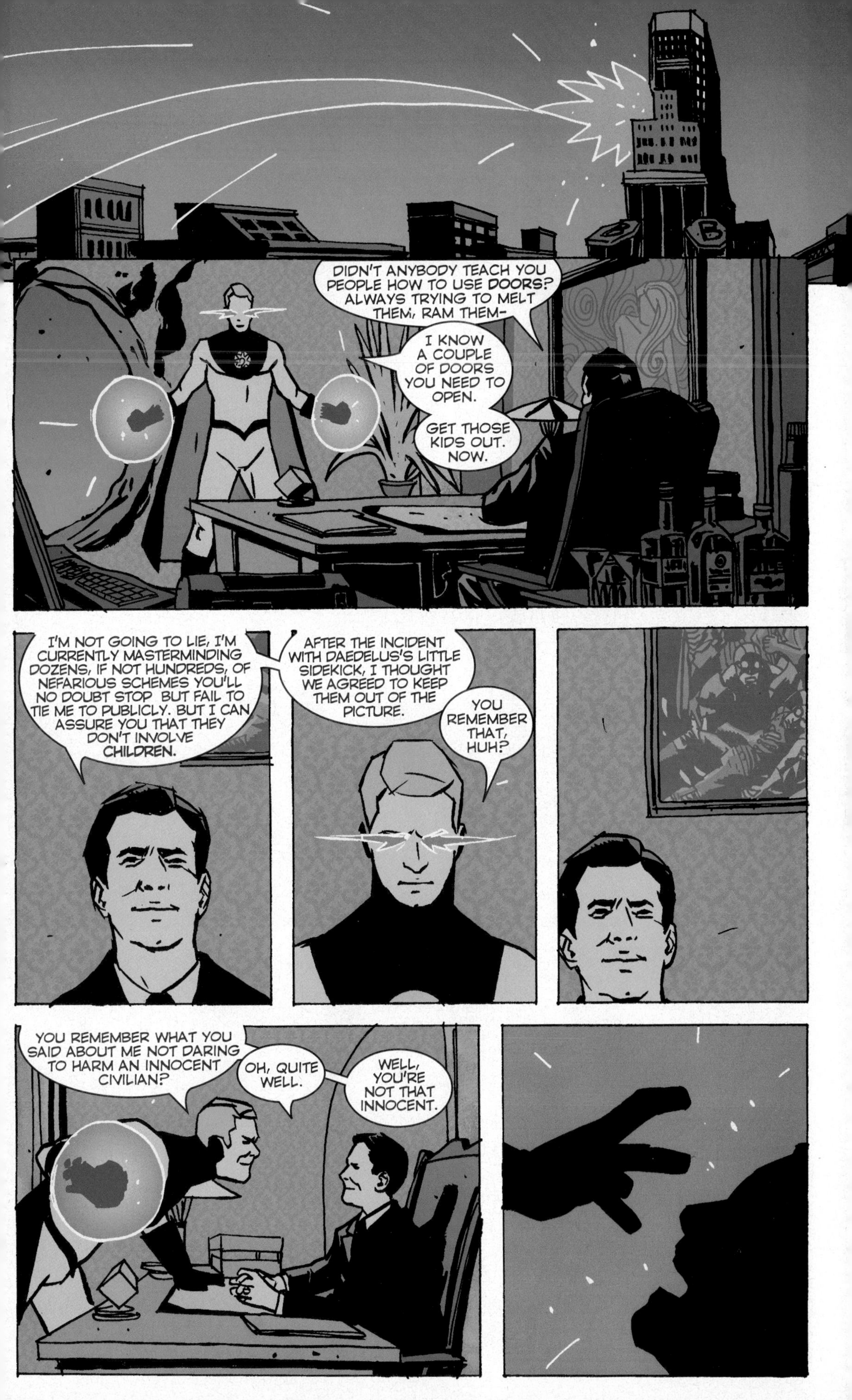
DIDN'T ANYBODY TEACH YOU PEOPLE HOW TO USE DOORS? ALWAYS TRYING TO MELT THEM, RAM THEM-
I KNOW A COUPLE OF DOORS YOU NEED TO OPEN.
GET THOSE KIDS OUT. NOW.
I'M NOT GOING TO LIE, I'M CURRENTLY MASTERMINDING DOZENS, IF NOT HUNDREDS, OF NEFARIOUS SCHEMES YOU'LL NO DOUBT STOP BUT FAIL TO TIE ME TO PUBLICLY. BUT I CAN ASSURE YOU THAT THEY DON'T INVOLVE CHILDREN.
AFTER THE INCIDENT WITH DAEDELUS'S LITTLE SIDEKICK, I THOUGHT WE AGREED TO KEEP THEM OUT OF THE PICTURE.
YOU REMEMBER THAT, HUH?
YOU REMEMBER WHAT YOU SAID ABOUT ME NOT DARING TO HARM AN INNOCENT CIVILIAN?
OH, QUITE WELL.
WELL, YOU'RE NOT THAT INNOCENT.

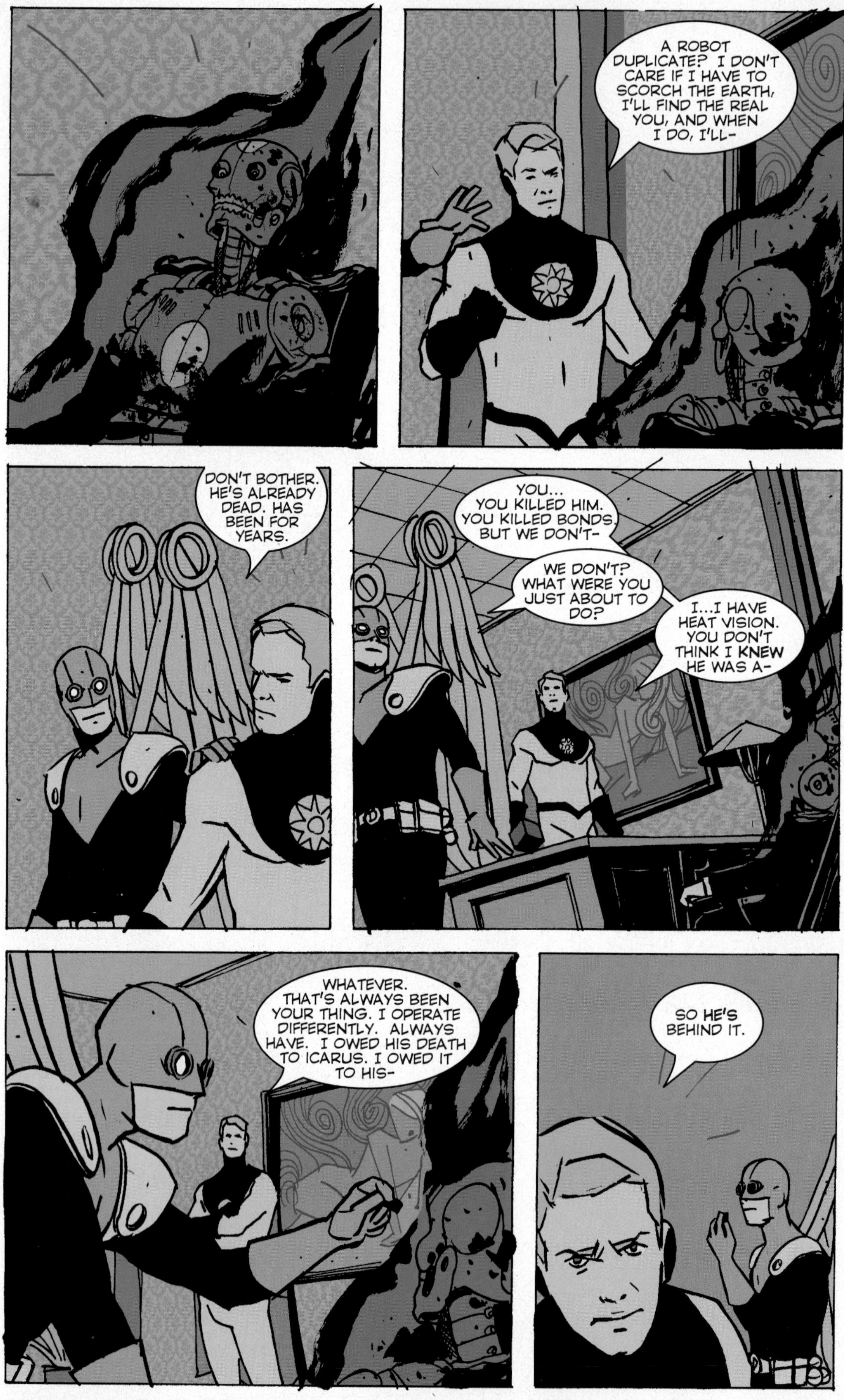
A ROBOT DUPLICATE? I DON'T CARE IF I HAVE TO SCORCH THE EARTH, I'LL FIND THE REAL YOU, AND WHEN I DO, I'LL-
DON'T BOTHER. HE'S ALREADY DEAD. HAS BEEN FOR YEARS.
YOU... YOU KILLED HIM. YOU KILLED BONDS. BUT WE DON'T-
WE DON'T? WHAT WERE YOU JUST ABOUT TO DO?
I...I HAVE HEAT VISION. YOU DON'T THINK I KNEW HE WAS A-
WHATEVER. THAT'S ALWAYS BEEN YOUR THING. I OPERATE DIFFERENTLY. ALWAYS HAVE. I OWED HIS DEATH TO ICARUS. I OWED IT TO HIS-
SO HE'S BEHIND IT.

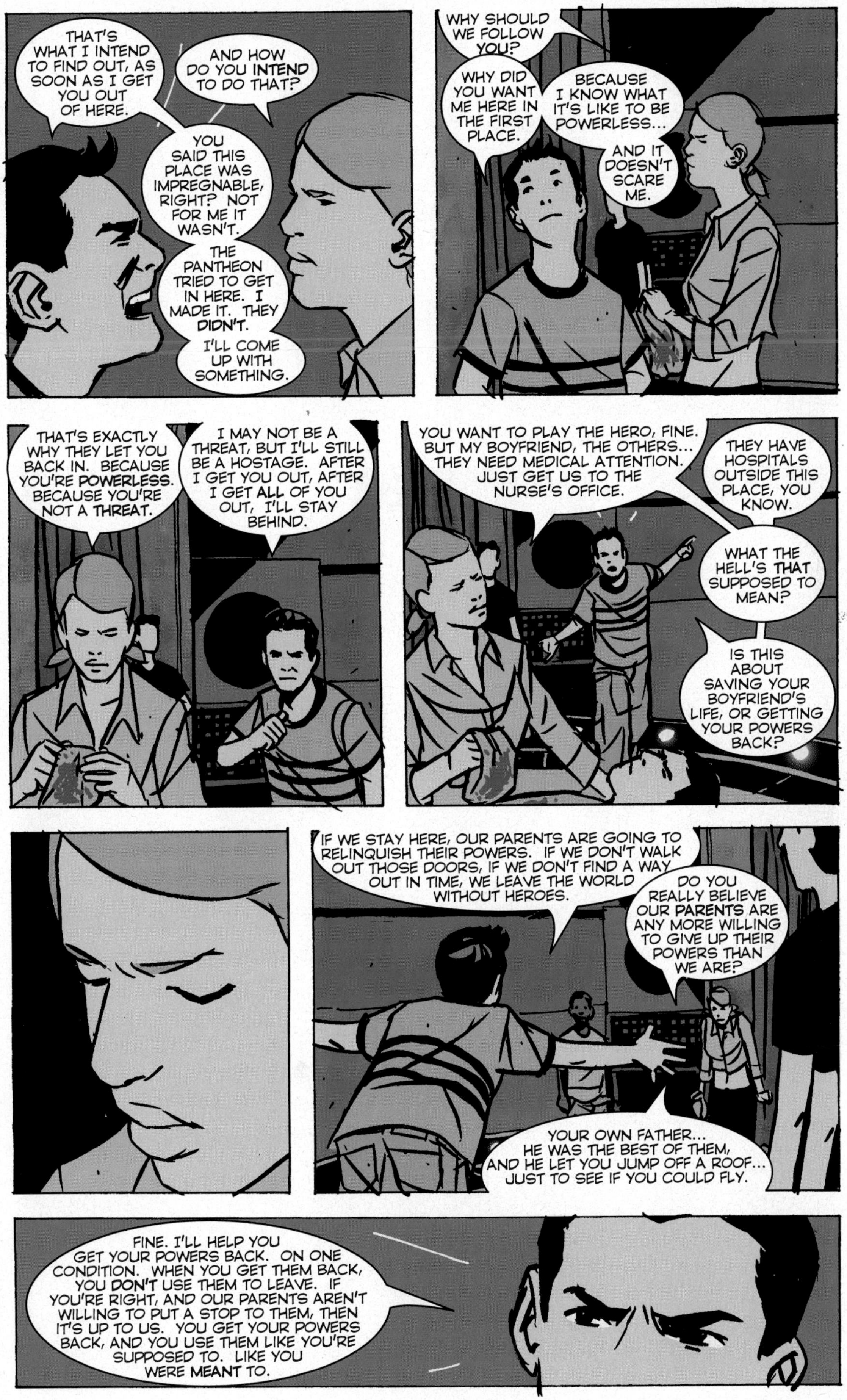
THAT'S WHAT I INTEND TO FIND OUT, AS SOON AS I GET YOU OUT OF HERE.
AND HOW DO YOU INTEND TO DO THAT?
YOU SAID THIS PLACE WAS IMPREGNABLE, RIGHT? NOT FOR ME IT WASN'T.
THE PANTHEON TRIED TO GET IN HERE. I MADE IT. THEY DIDN'T.
I'LL COME UP WITH SOMETHING.
WHY SHOULD WE FOLLOW YOU?
WHY DID YOU WANT ME HERE IN THE FIRST PLACE.
BECAUSE I KNOW WHAT IT'S LIKE TO BE POWERLESS...
AND IT DOESN'T SCARE ME.
THAT'S EXACTLY WHY THEY LET YOU BACK IN. BECAUSE YOU'RE POWERLESS. BECAUSE YOU'RE NOT A THREAT.
I MAY NOT BE A THREAT, BUT I'LL STILL BE A HOSTAGE. AFTER I GET YOU OUT, AFTER I GET ALL OF YOU OUT, I'LL STAY BEHIND.
YOU WANT TO PLAY THE HERO, FINE. BUT MY BOYFRIEND, THE OTHERS... THEY NEED MEDICAL ATTENTION. JUST GET US TO THE NURSE'S OFFICE.
THEY HAVE HOSPITALS OUTSIDE THIS PLACE, YOU KNOW.
WHAT THE HELL'S THAT SUPPOSED TO MEAN?
IS THIS ABOUT SAVING YOUR BOYFRIEND'S LIFE, OR GETTING YOUR POWERS BACK?
IF WE STAY HERE, OUR PARENTS ARE GOING TO RELINQUISH THEIR POWERS. IF WE DON'T WALK OUT THOSE DOORS, IF WE DON'T FIND A WAY OUT IN TIME, WE LEAVE THE WORLD WITHOUT HEROES.
DO YOU REALLY BELIEVE OUR PARENTS ARE ANY MORE WILLING TO GIVE UP THEIR POWERS THAN WE ARE?
YOUR OWN FATHER... HE WAS THE BEST OF THEM, AND HE LET YOU JUMP OFF A ROOF... JUST TO SEE IF YOU COULD FLY.
FINE. I'LL HELP YOU GET YOUR POWERS BACK. ON ONE CONDITION. WHEN YOU GET THEM BACK, YOU DON'T USE THEM TO LEAVE. IF YOU'RE RIGHT, AND OUR PARENTS AREN'T WILLING TO PUT A STOP TO THEM, THEN IT'S UP TO US. YOU GET YOUR POWERS BACK, AND YOU USE THEM LIKE YOU'RE SUPPOSED TO. LIKE YOU WERE MEANT TO.

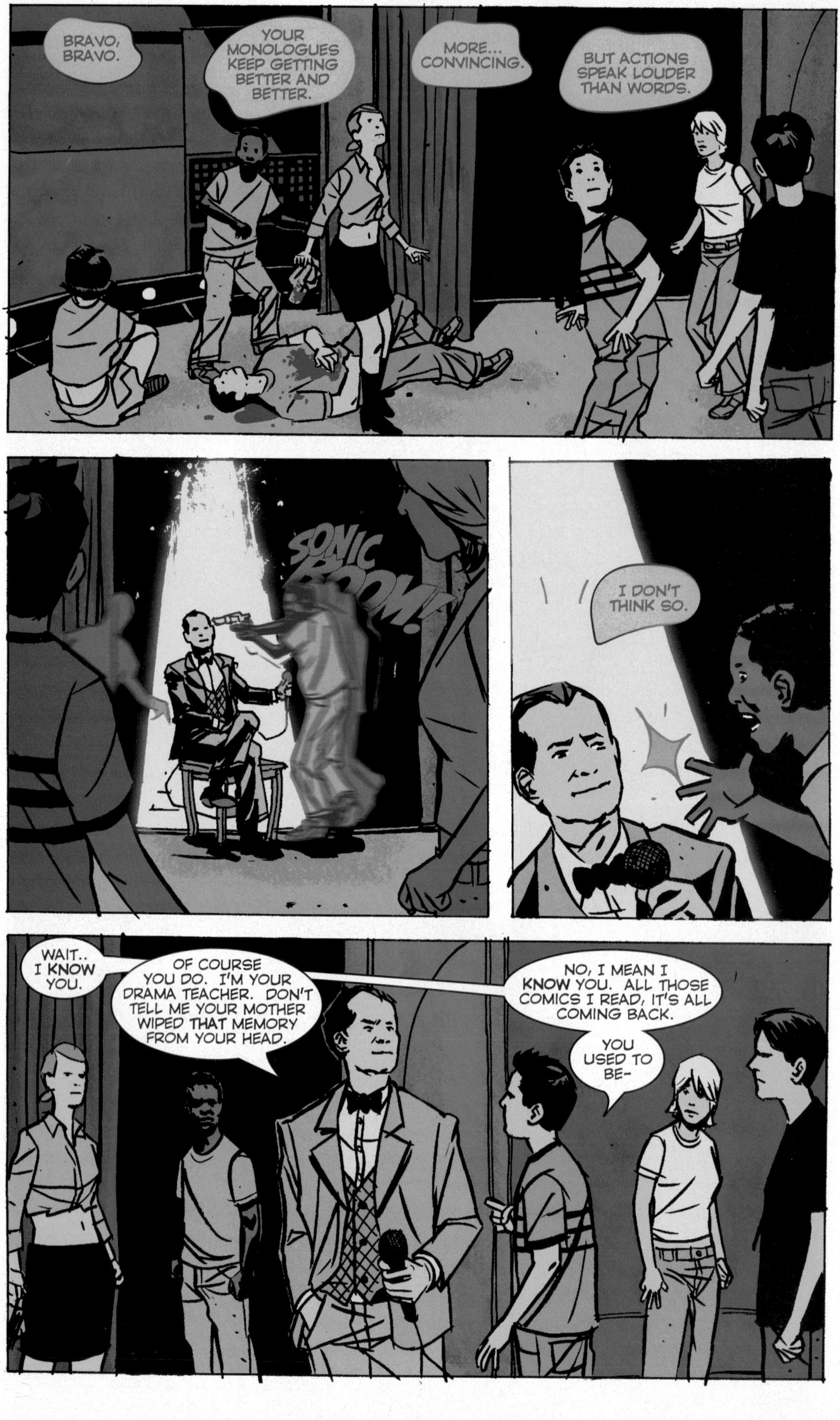
BRAVO, BRAVO.
YOUR MONOLOGUES KEEP GETTING BETTER AND BETTER.
MORE... CONVINCING.
BUT ACTIONS SPEAK LOUDER THAN WORDS.
SONIC BOOM!
I DON'T THINK SO.
WAIT.. I KNOW YOU.
OF COURSE YOU DO. I'M YOUR DRAMA TEACHER. DON'T TELL ME YOUR MOTHER WIPED THAT MEMORY FROM YOUR HEAD.
NO, I MEAN I KNOW YOU. ALL THOSE COMICS I READ, IT'S ALL COMING BACK.
YOU USED TO BE-

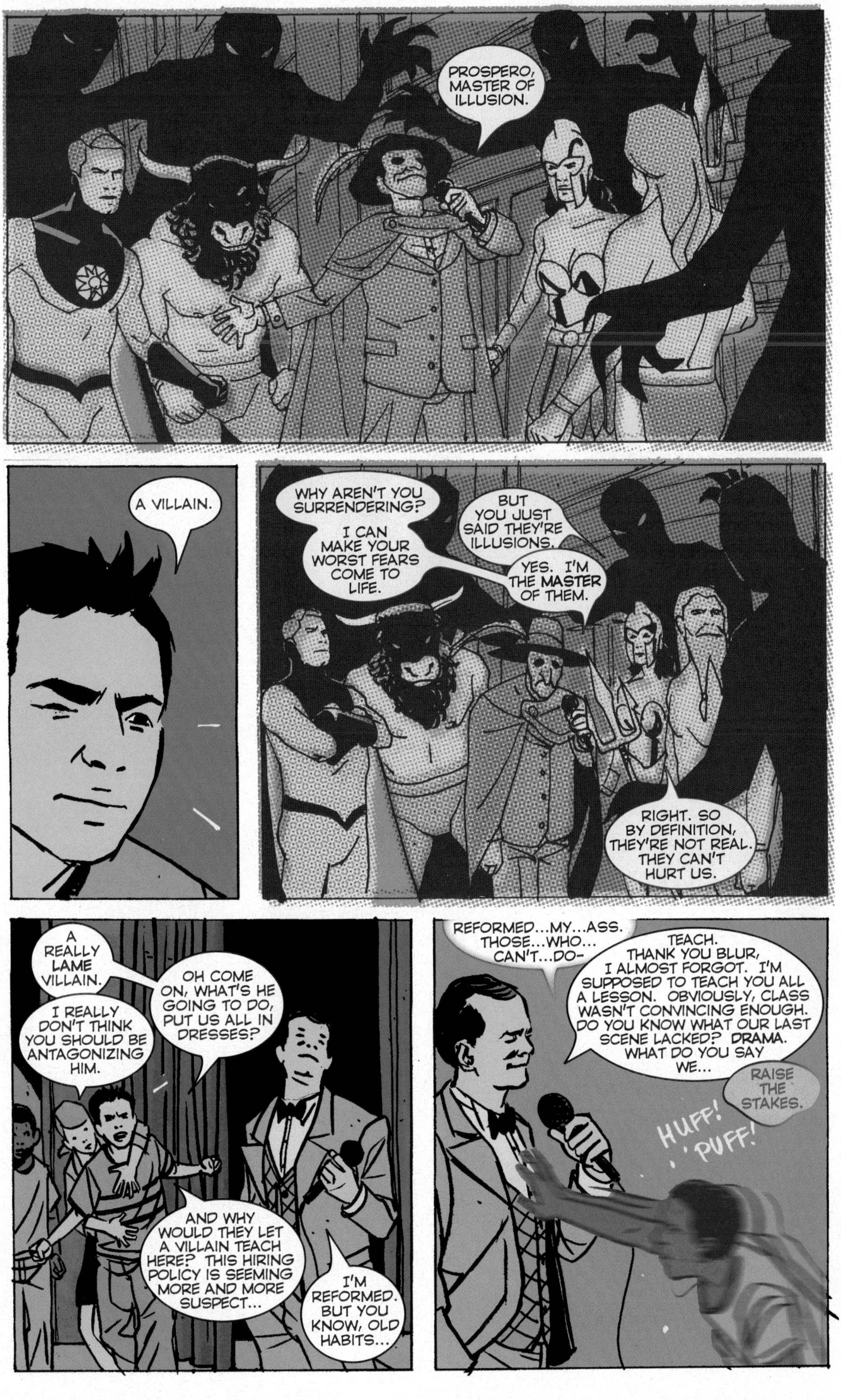
PROSPERO, MASTER OF ILLUSION.
A VILLAIN.
WHY AREN'T YOU SURRENDERING?
I CAN MAKE YOUR WORST FEARS COME TO LIFE.
BUT YOU JUST SAID THEY'RE ILLUSIONS.
YES. I'M THE MASTER OF THEM.
RIGHT. SO BY DEFINITION, THEY'RE NOT REAL. THEY CAN'T HURT US.
A REALLY LAME VILLAIN.
I REALLY DON'T THINK YOU SHOULD BE ANTAGONIZING HIM.
OH COME ON, WHAT'S HE GOING TO DO, PUT US ALL IN DRESSES?
AND WHY WOULD THEY LET A VILLAIN TEACH HERE? THIS HIRING POLICY IS SEEMING MORE AND MORE SUSPECT...
I'M REFORMED. BUT YOU KNOW, OLD HABITS...
REFORMED...MY...ASS. THOSE...WHO... CAN'T...DO-
TEACH. THANK YOU BLUR, I ALMOST FORGOT. I'M SUPPOSED TO TEACH YOU ALL A LESSON. OBVIOUSLY, CLASS WASN'T CONVINCING ENOUGH. DO YOU KNOW WHAT OUR LAST SCENE LACKED? DRAMA. WHAT DO YOU SAY WE...
RAISE THE STAKES.
HUFF! PUFF!

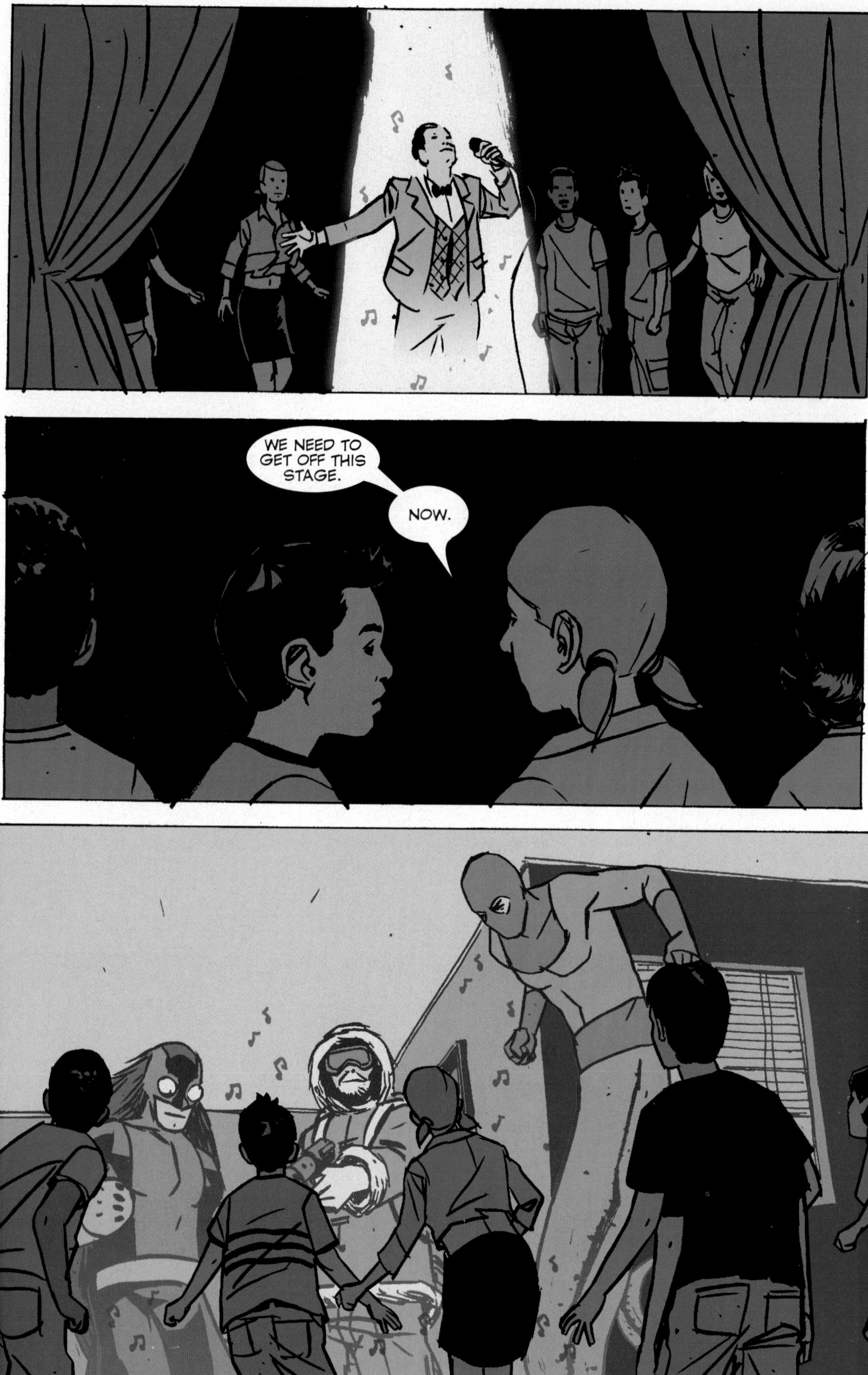
WE NEED TO GET OFF THIS STAGE.
NOW.

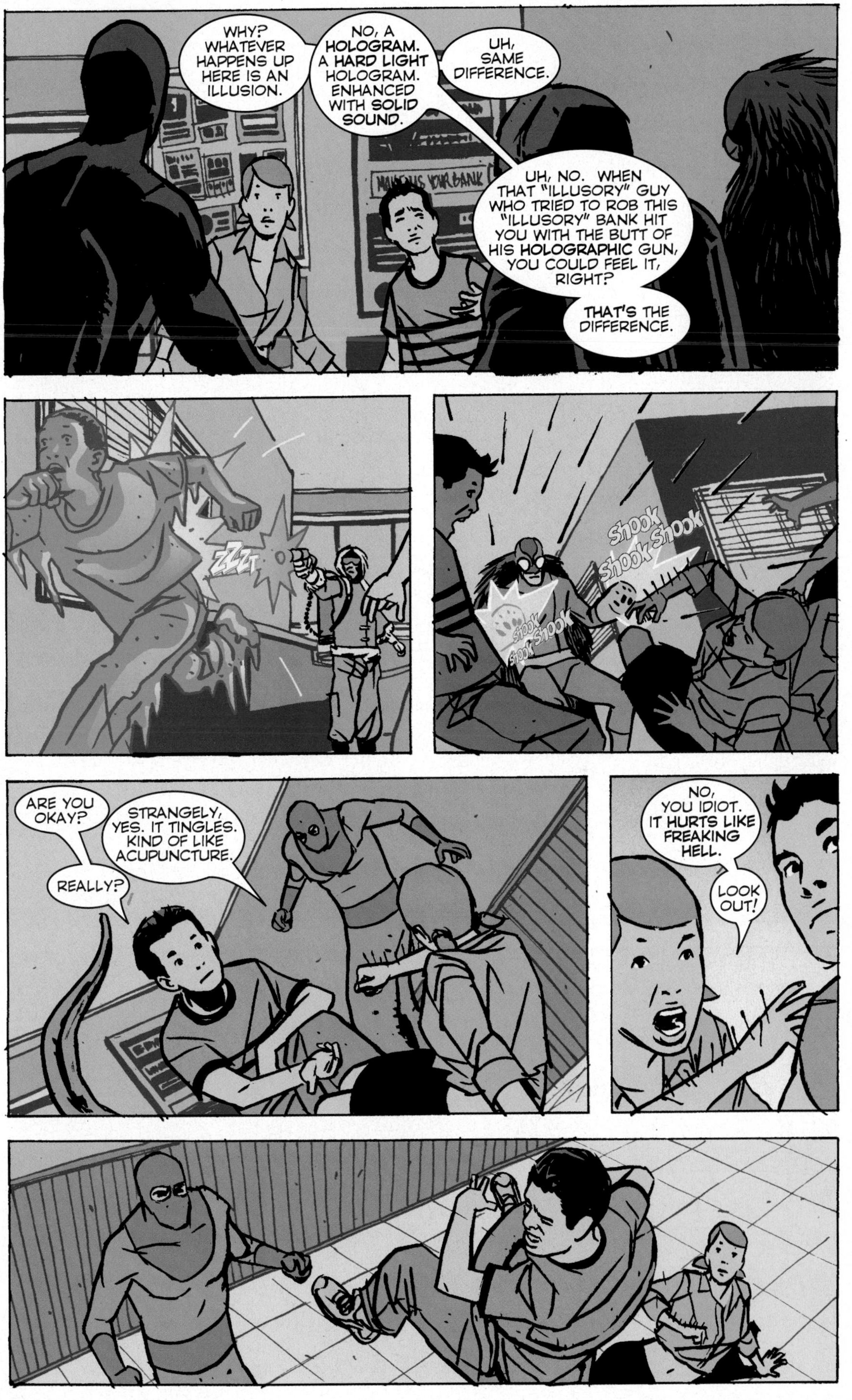
WHY? WHATEVER HAPPENS UP HERE IS AN ILLUSION.
NO, A HOLOGRAM. A HARD LIGHT HOLOGRAM. ENHANCED WITH SOLID SOUND.
UH, SAME DIFFERENCE.
UH, NO. WHEN THAT "ILLUSORY" GUY WHO TRIED TO ROB THIS "ILLUSORY" BANK HIT YOU WITH THE BUTT OF HIS HOLOGRAPHIC GUN, YOU COULD FEEL IT, RIGHT?
THAT'S THE DIFFERENCE.
ZZZT
SHOOK SHOOK SHOOK
SHOOK SHOOK SHOOK
ARE YOU OKAY?
STRANGELY, YES. IT TINGLES. KIND OF LIKE ACUPUNCTURE.
REALLY?
NO, YOU IDIOT. IT HURTS LIKE FREAKING HELL.
LOOK OUT!

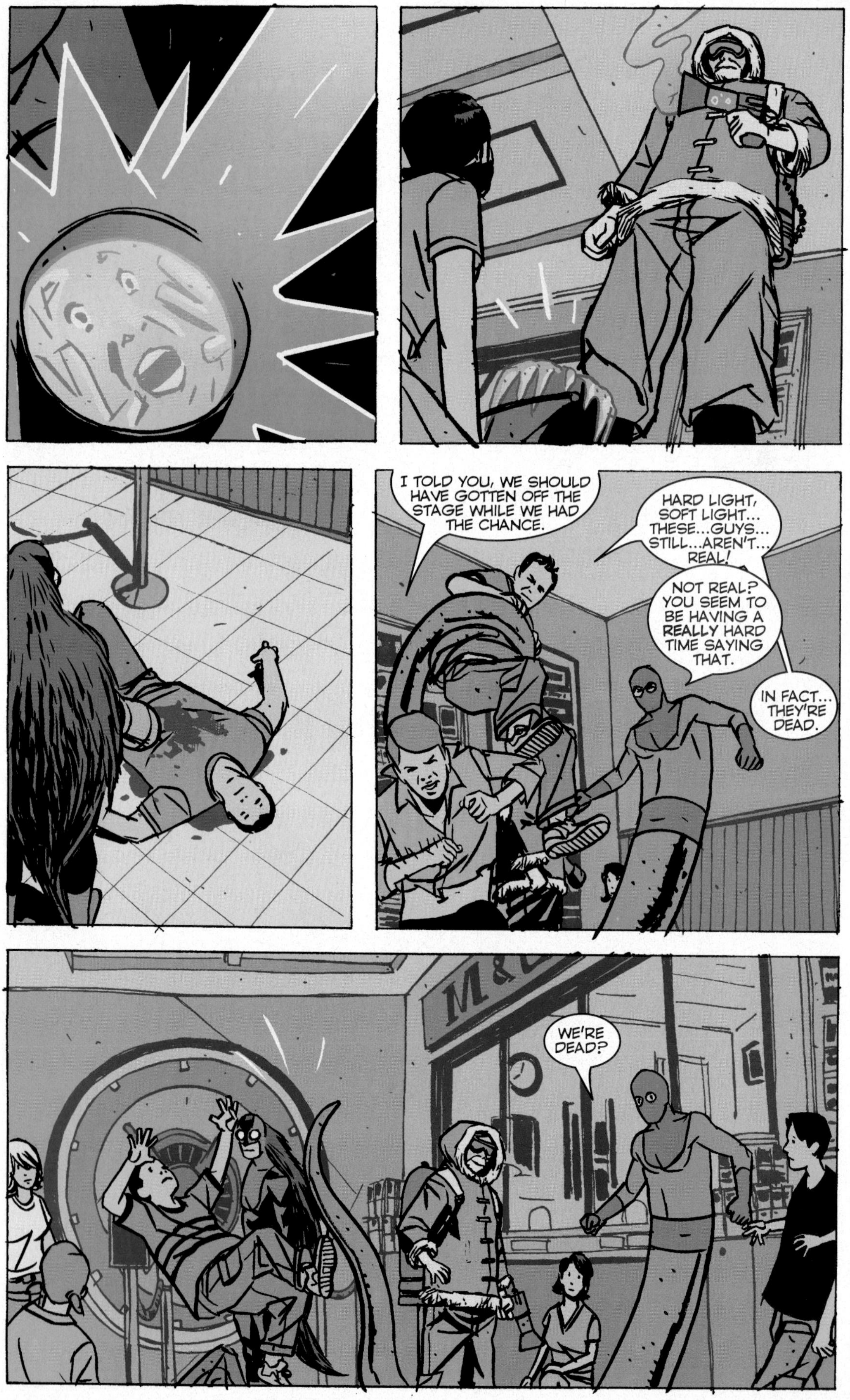
I TOLD YOU, WE SHOULD HAVE GOTTEN OFF THE STAGE WHILE WE HAD THE CHANCE.
HARD LIGHT, SOFT LIGHT... THESE...GUYS... STILL...AREN'T... REAL!
NOT REAL? YOU SEEM TO BE HAVING A REALLY HARD TIME SAYING THAT.
IN FACT... THEY'RE DEAD.
WE'RE DEAD?

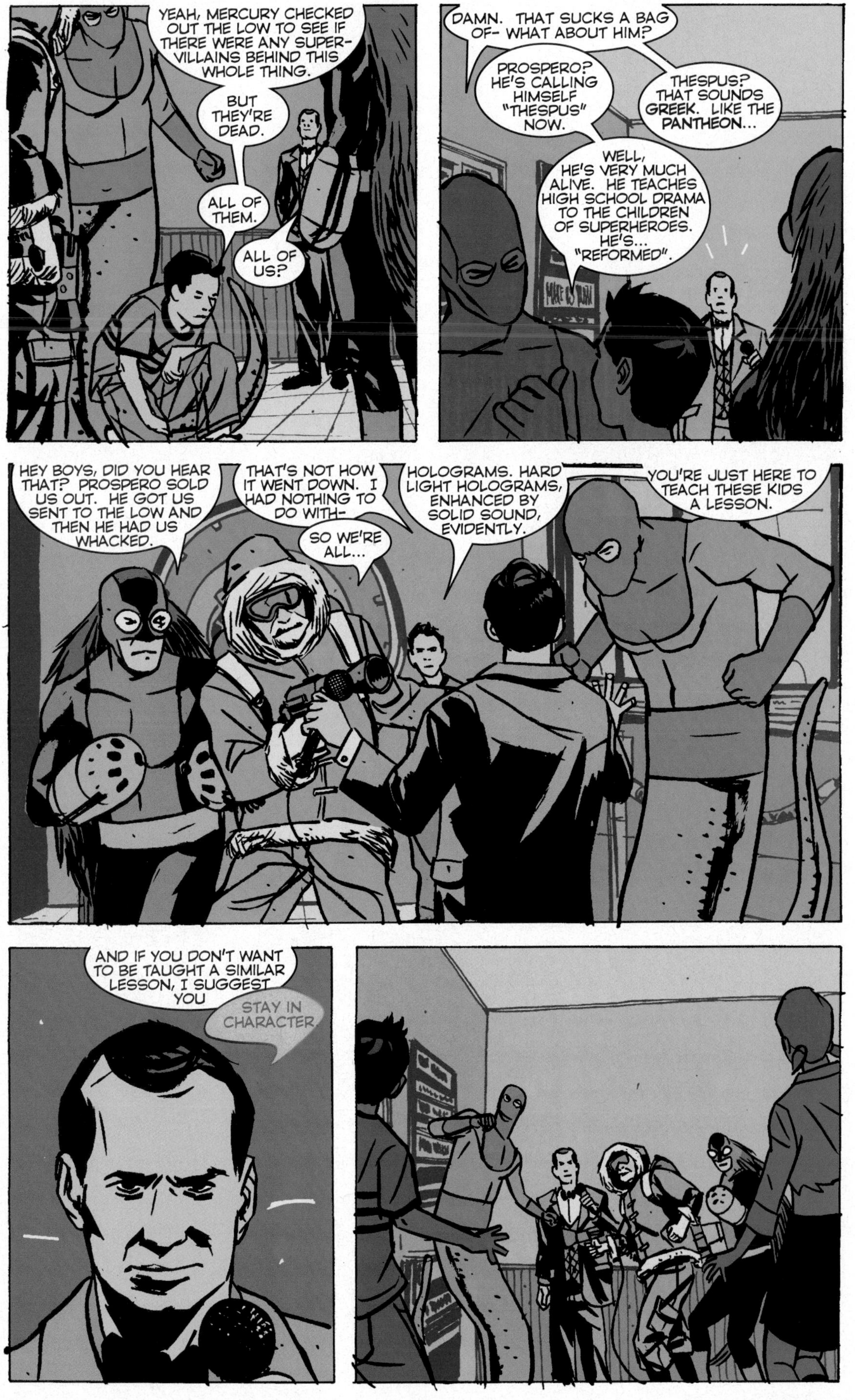
YEAH, MERCURY CHECKED OUT THE LOW TO SEE IF THERE WERE ANY SUPER-VILLAINS BEHIND THIS WHOLE THING.
BUT THEY'RE DEAD.
ALL OF THEM.
ALL OF US?
DAMN. THAT SUCKS A BAG OF- WHAT ABOUT HIM?
PROSPERO? HE'S CALLING HIMSELF "THESPUS" NOW.
THESPUS? THAT SOUNDS GREEK. LIKE THE PANTHEON...
WELL, HE'S VERY MUCH ALIVE. HE TEACHES HIGH SCHOOL DRAMA TO THE CHILDREN OF SUPERHEROES. HE'S... "REFORMED".
HEY BOYS, DID YOU HEAR THAT? PROSPERO SOLD US OUT. HE GOT US SENT TO THE LOW AND THEN HE HAD US WHACKED.
THAT'S NOT HOW IT WENT DOWN. I HAD NOTHING TO DO WITH-
SO WE'RE ALL...
HOLOGRAMS. HARD LIGHT HOLOGRAMS, ENHANCED BY SOLID SOUND, EVIDENTLY.
YOU'RE JUST HERE TO TEACH THESE KIDS A LESSON.
AND IF YOU DON'T WANT TO BE TAUGHT A SIMILAR LESSON, I SUGGEST YOU
STAY IN CHARACTER.

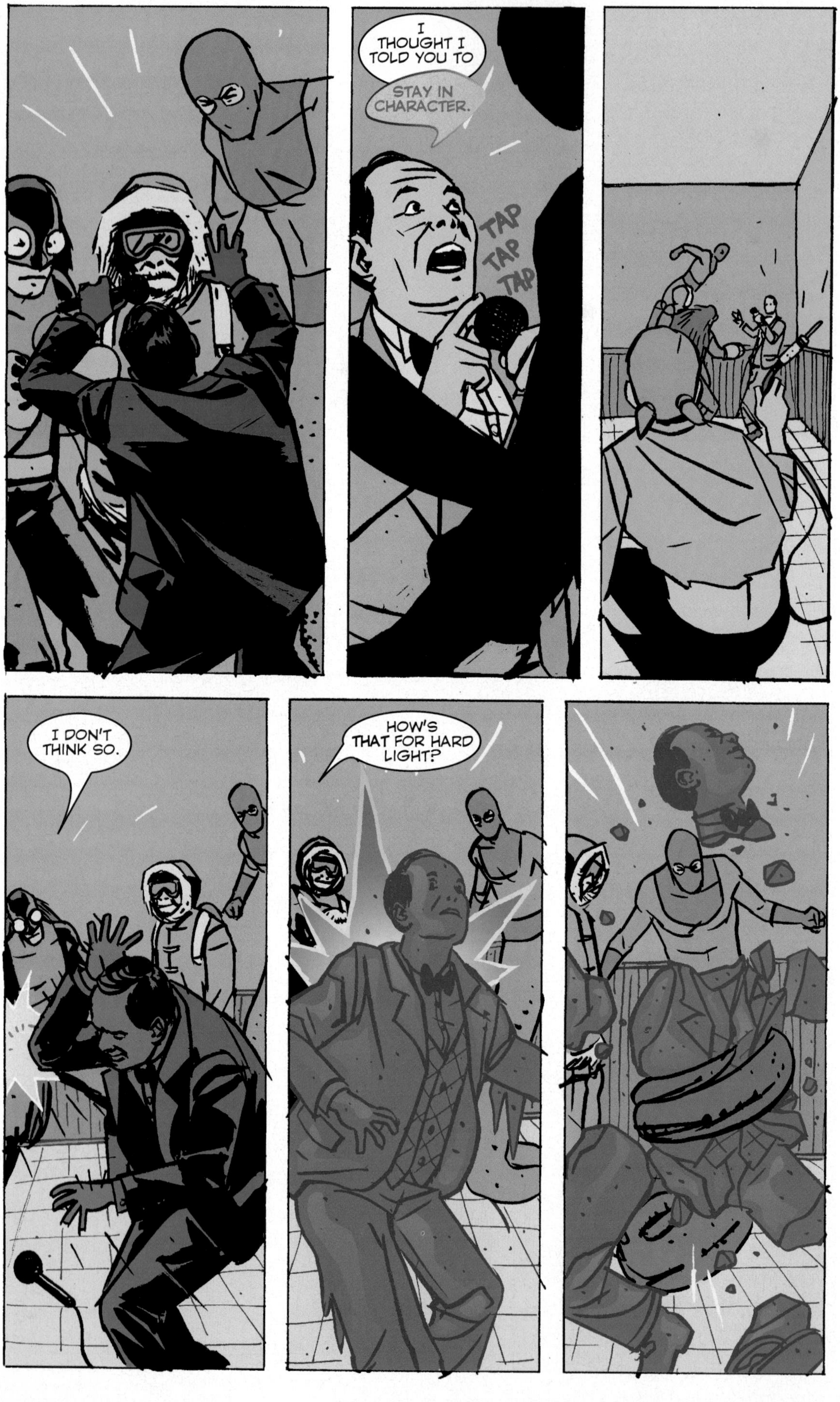
I THOUGHT I TOLD YOU TO
STAY IN CHARACTER.
TAP TAP TAP
I DON'T THINK SO.
HOW'S THAT FOR HARD LIGHT?

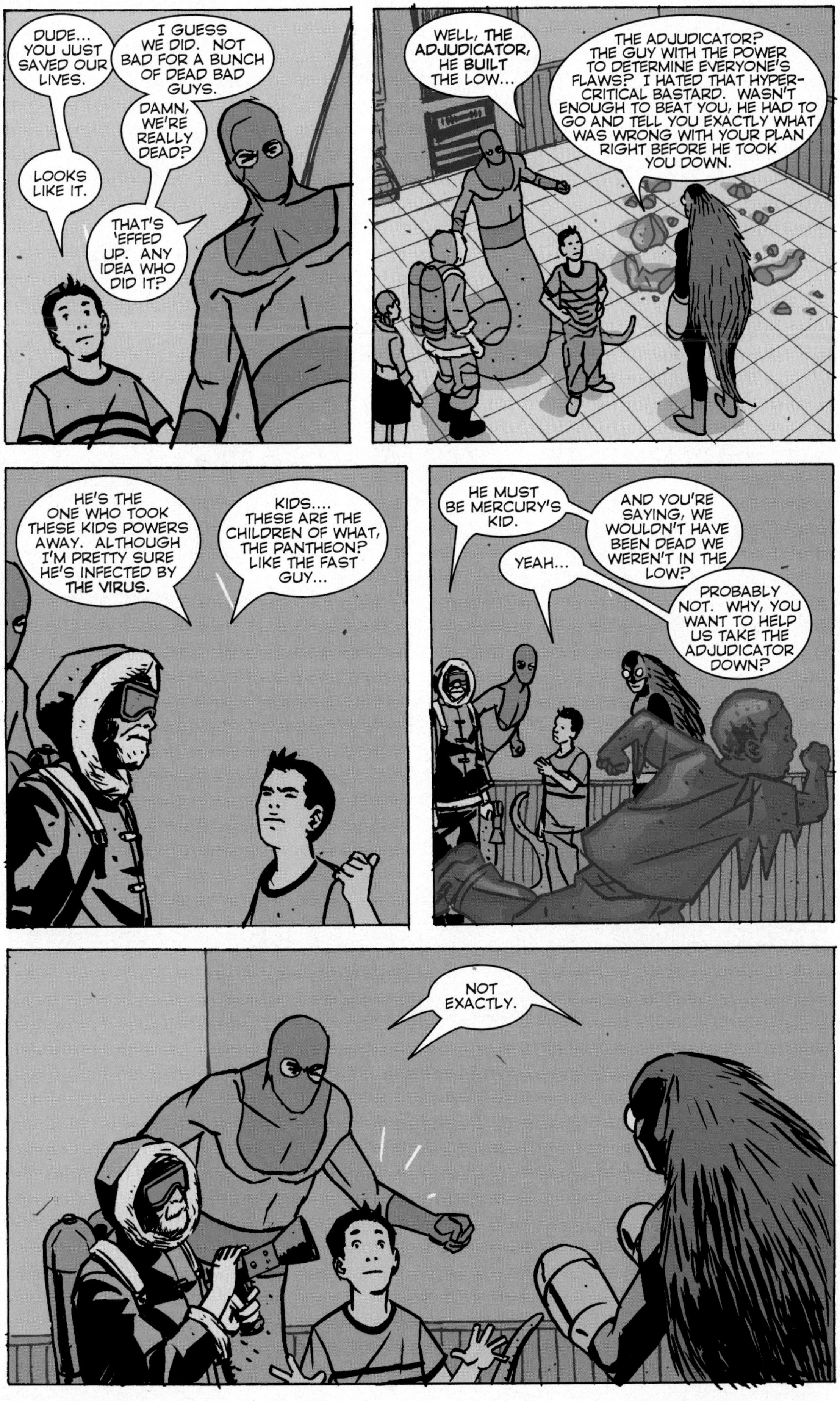
DUDE... YOU JUST SAVED OUR LIVES.
I GUESS WE DID. NOT BAD FOR A BUNCH OF DEAD BAD GUYS.
DAMN, WE'RE REALLY DEAD?
LOOKS LIKE IT.
THAT'S 'EFFED UP. ANY IDEA WHO DID IT?
WELL, THE ADJUDICATOR, HE BUILT THE LOW...
THE ADJUDICATOR? THE GUY WITH THE POWER TO DETERMINE EVERYONE'S FLAWS? I HATED THAT HYPER-CRITICAL BASTARD. WASN'T ENOUGH TO BEAT YOU, HE HAD TO GO AND TELL YOU EXACTLY WHAT WAS WRONG WITH YOUR PLAN RIGHT BEFORE HE TOOK YOU DOWN.
HE'S THE ONE WHO TOOK THESE KIDS POWERS AWAY. ALTHOUGH I'M PRETTY SURE HE'S INFECTED BY THE VIRUS.
KIDS.... THESE ARE THE CHILDREN OF WHAT, THE PANTHEON? LIKE THE FAST GUY...
HE MUST BE MERCURY'S KID.
AND YOU'RE SAYING, WE WOULDN'T HAVE BEEN DEAD WE WEREN'T IN THE LOW?
YEAH...
PROBABLY NOT. WHY, YOU WANT TO HELP US TAKE THE ADJUDICATOR DOWN?
NOT EXACTLY.

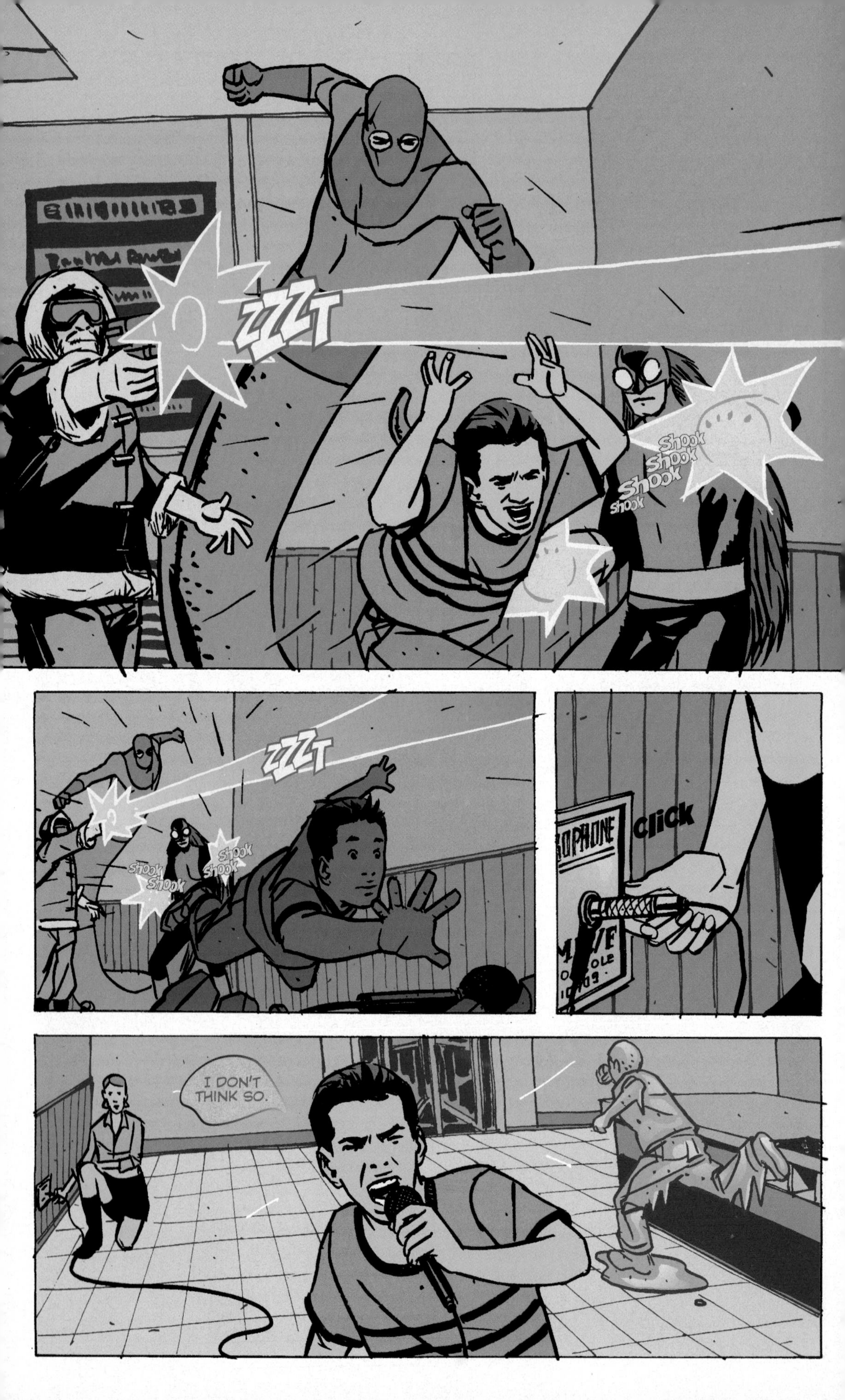
ZZZT
Shook
Shook
Shook
Shook
ZZZT
Shook
Shook
Shook
Shook
Click
I DON'T THINK SO.

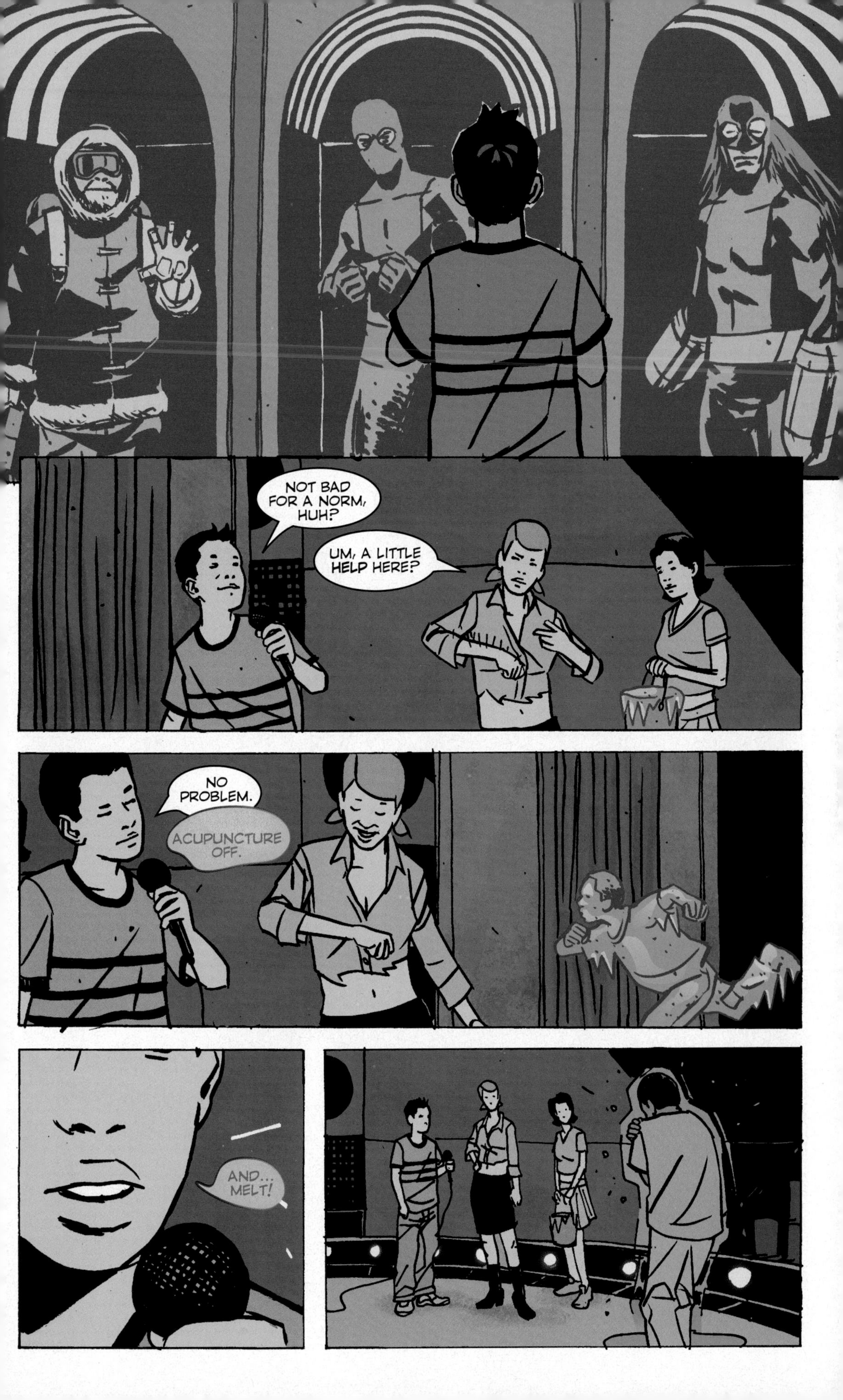
NOT BAD FOR A NORM, HUH?
UM, A LITTLE HELP HERE?
NO PROBLEM.
ACUPUNCTURE OFF.
AND... MELT!

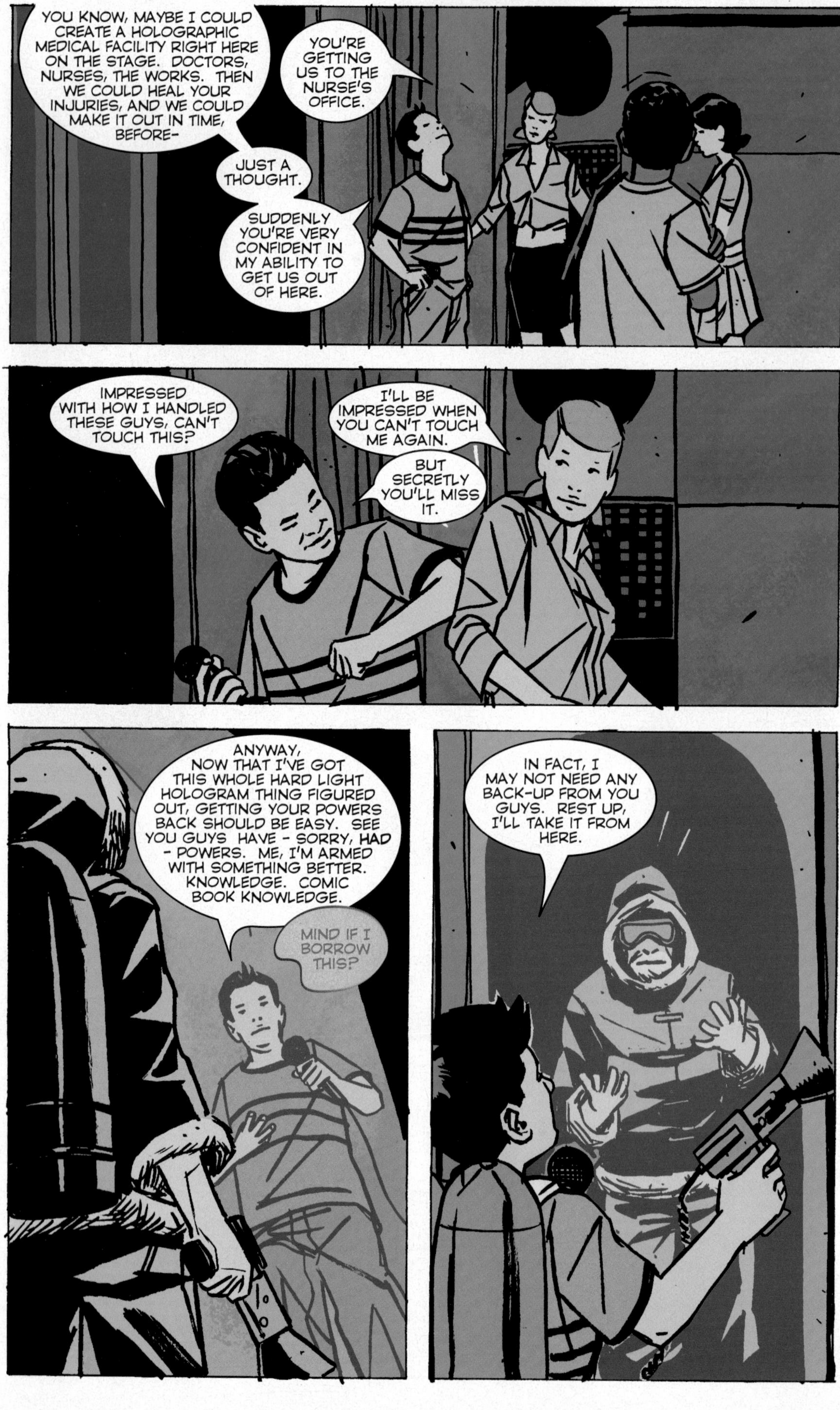
YOU KNOW, MAYBE I COULD CREATE A HOLOGRAPHIC MEDICAL FACILITY RIGHT HERE ON THE STAGE. DOCTORS, NURSES, THE WORKS. THEN WE COULD HEAL YOUR INJURIES, AND WE COULD MAKE IT OUT IN TIME, BEFORE-
YOU'RE GETTING US TO THE NURSE'S OFFICE.
JUST A THOUGHT.
SUDDENLY YOU'RE VERY CONFIDENT IN MY ABILITY TO GET US OUT OF HERE.
IMPRESSED WITH HOW I HANDLED THESE GUYS, CAN'T TOUCH THIS?
I'LL BE IMPRESSED WHEN YOU CAN'T TOUCH ME AGAIN.
BUT SECRETLY YOU'LL MISS IT.
ANYWAY, NOW THAT I'VE GOT THIS WHOLE HARD LIGHT HOLOGRAM THING FIGURED OUT, GETTING YOUR POWERS BACK SHOULD BE EASY. SEE YOU GUYS HAVE - SORRY, **HAD** - POWERS. ME, I'M ARMED WITH SOMETHING BETTER. KNOWLEDGE. COMIC BOOK KNOWLEDGE.
MIND IF I BORROW THIS?
IN FACT, I MAY NOT NEED ANY BACK-UP FROM YOU GUYS. REST UP, I'LL TAKE IT FROM HERE.

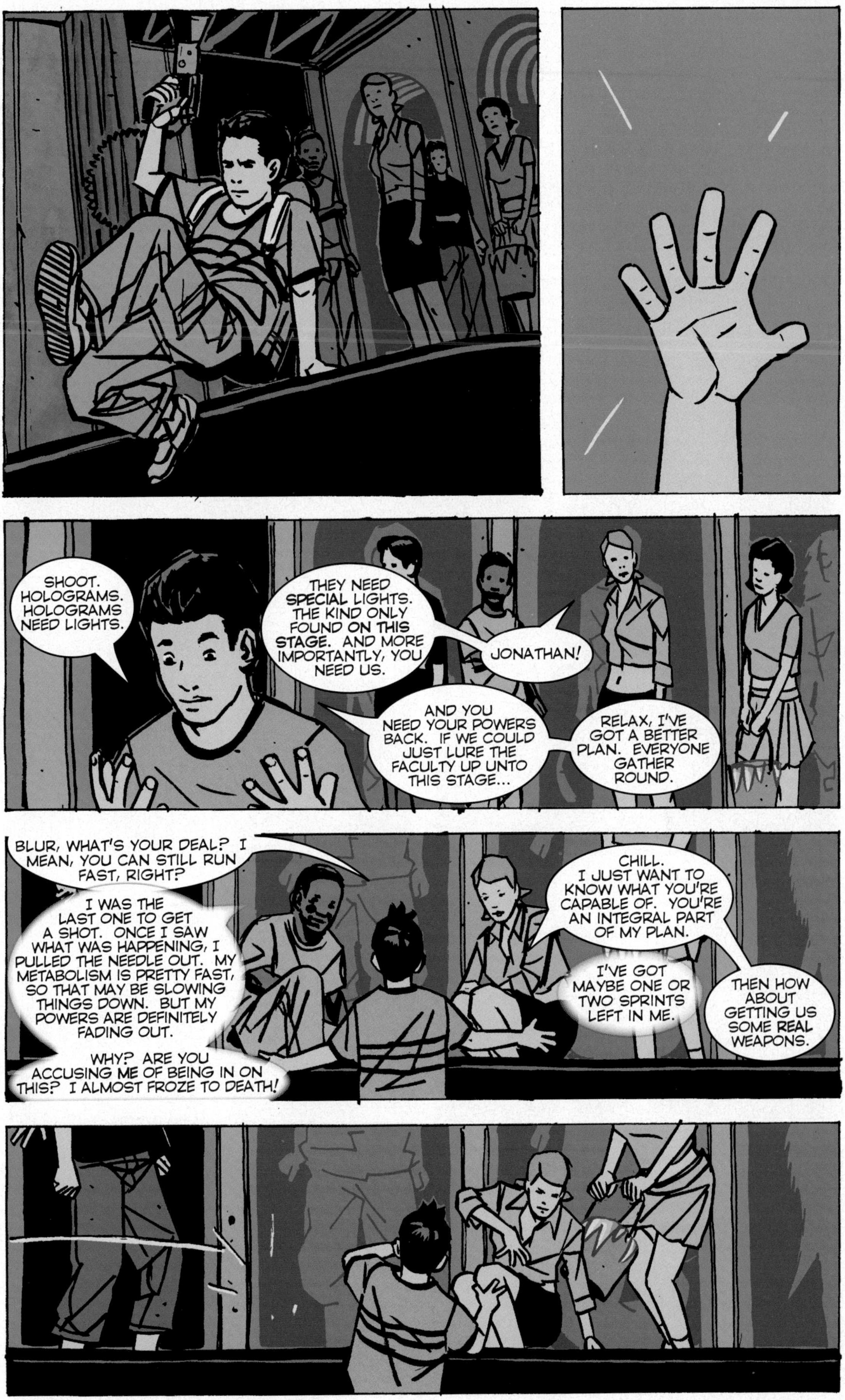
SHOOT. HOLOGRAMS. HOLOGRAMS NEED LIGHTS.
THEY NEED SPECIAL LIGHTS. THE KIND ONLY FOUND ON THIS STAGE. AND MORE IMPORTANTLY, YOU NEED US.
JONATHAN!
AND YOU NEED YOUR POWERS BACK. IF WE COULD JUST LURE THE FACULTY UP UNTO THIS STAGE...
RELAX, I'VE GOT A BETTER PLAN. EVERYONE GATHER ROUND.
BLUR, WHAT'S YOUR DEAL? I MEAN, YOU CAN STILL RUN FAST, RIGHT?
I WAS THE LAST ONE TO GET A SHOT. ONCE I SAW WHAT WAS HAPPENING, I PULLED THE NEEDLE OUT. MY METABOLISM IS PRETTY FAST, SO THAT MAY BE SLOWING THINGS DOWN. BUT MY POWERS ARE DEFINITELY FADING OUT.
WHY? ARE YOU ACCUSING ME OF BEING IN ON THIS? I ALMOST FROZE TO DEATH!
CHILL. I JUST WANT TO KNOW WHAT YOU'RE CAPABLE OF. YOU'RE AN INTEGRAL PART OF MY PLAN.
I'VE GOT MAYBE ONE OR TWO SPRINTS LEFT IN ME.
THEN HOW ABOUT GETTING US SOME REAL WEAPONS.

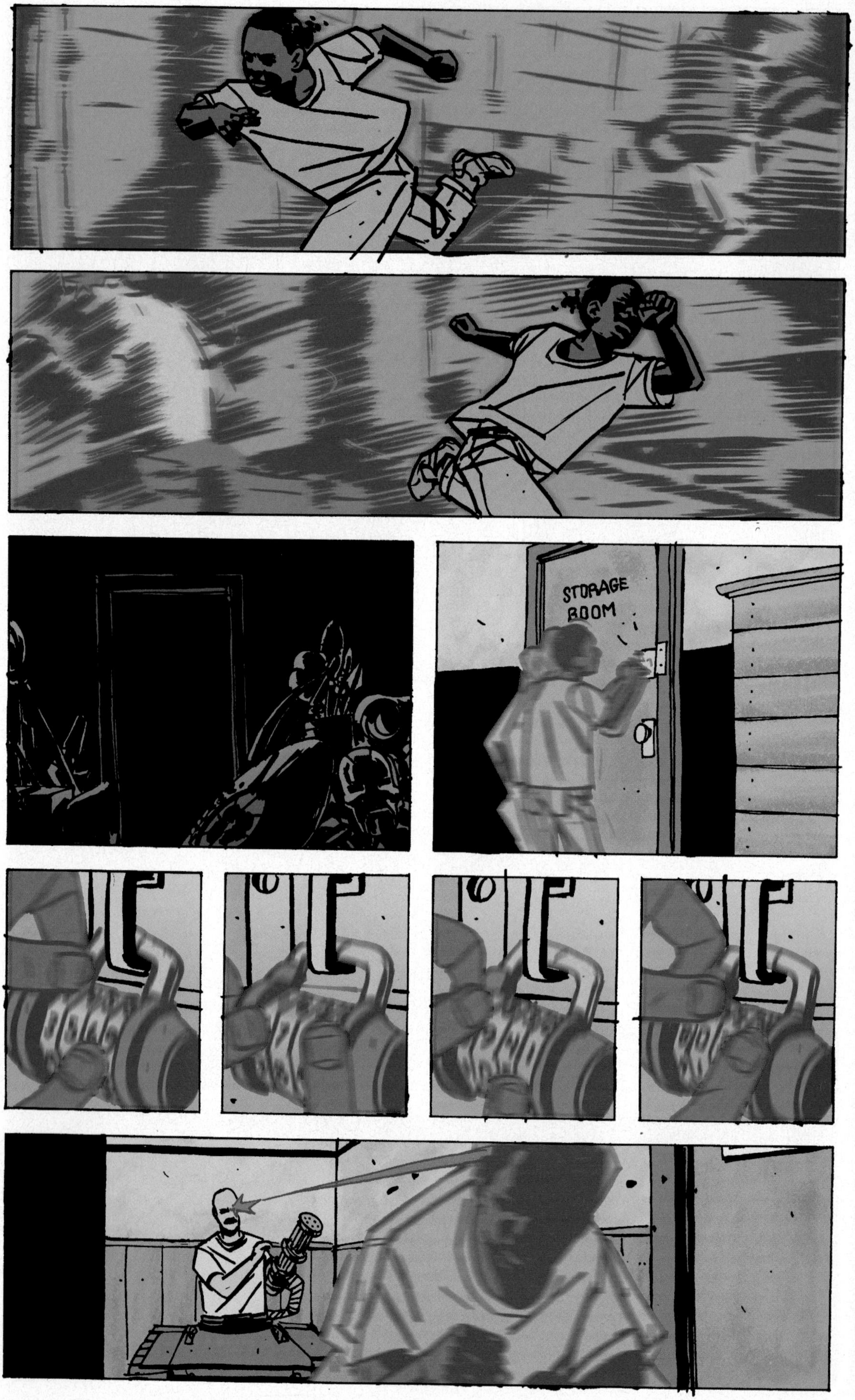
STORAGE
ROOM

WHATEVER YOU JUST DID... THAT WASN'T THE PLAN I HAD IN MIND. YOU GOT ONE MORE SPRINT IN YOU?

OKAY, LISTEN THIS TIME BEFORE YOU SPEED OFF. LET ME ASK YOU A QUESTION,

HOW MANY SUPERHEROES DOES IT TAKE TO SCREW IN A LIGHTBULB?

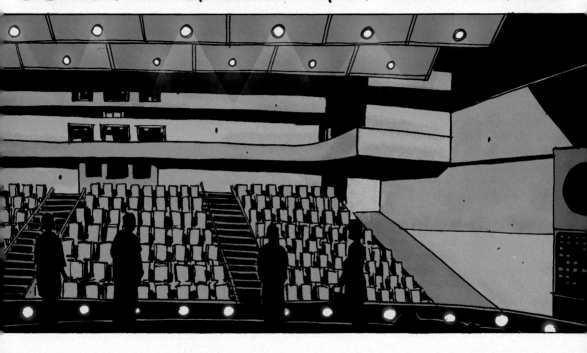

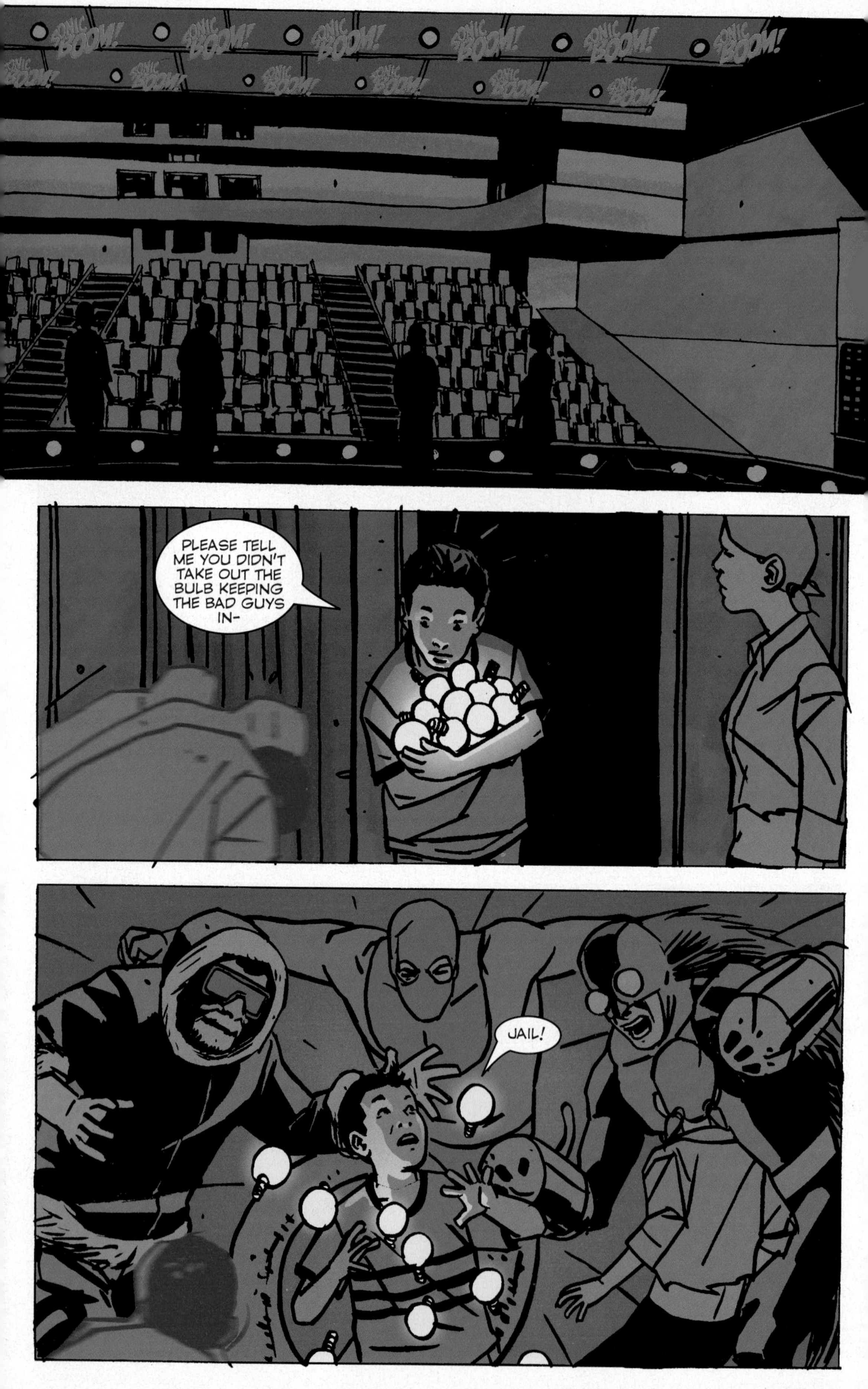
SONIC BOOM!
PLEASE TELL ME YOU DIDN'T TAKE OUT THE BULB KEEPING THE BAD GUYS IN-
JAIL!

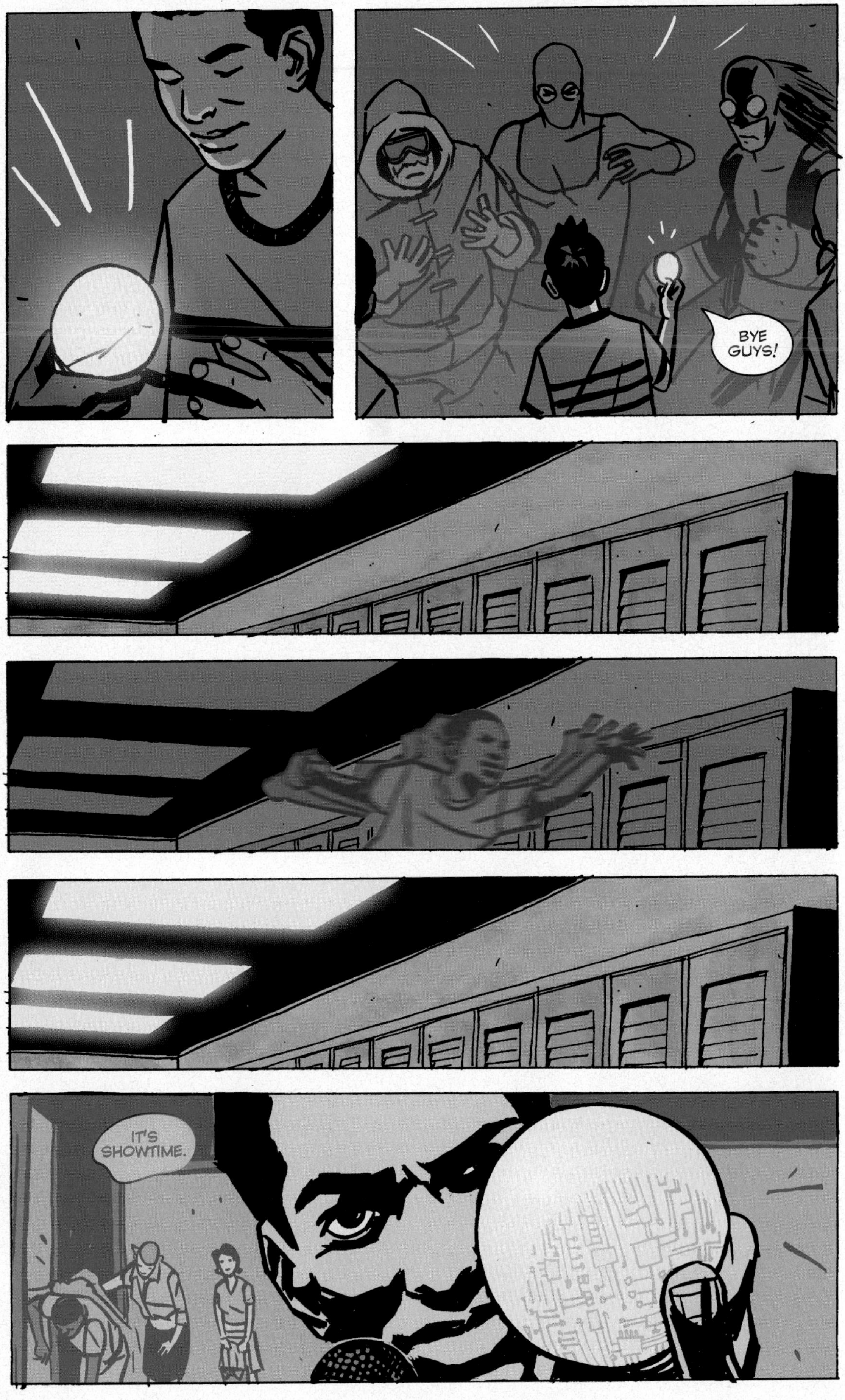
BYE GUYS!
IT'S SHOWTIME.

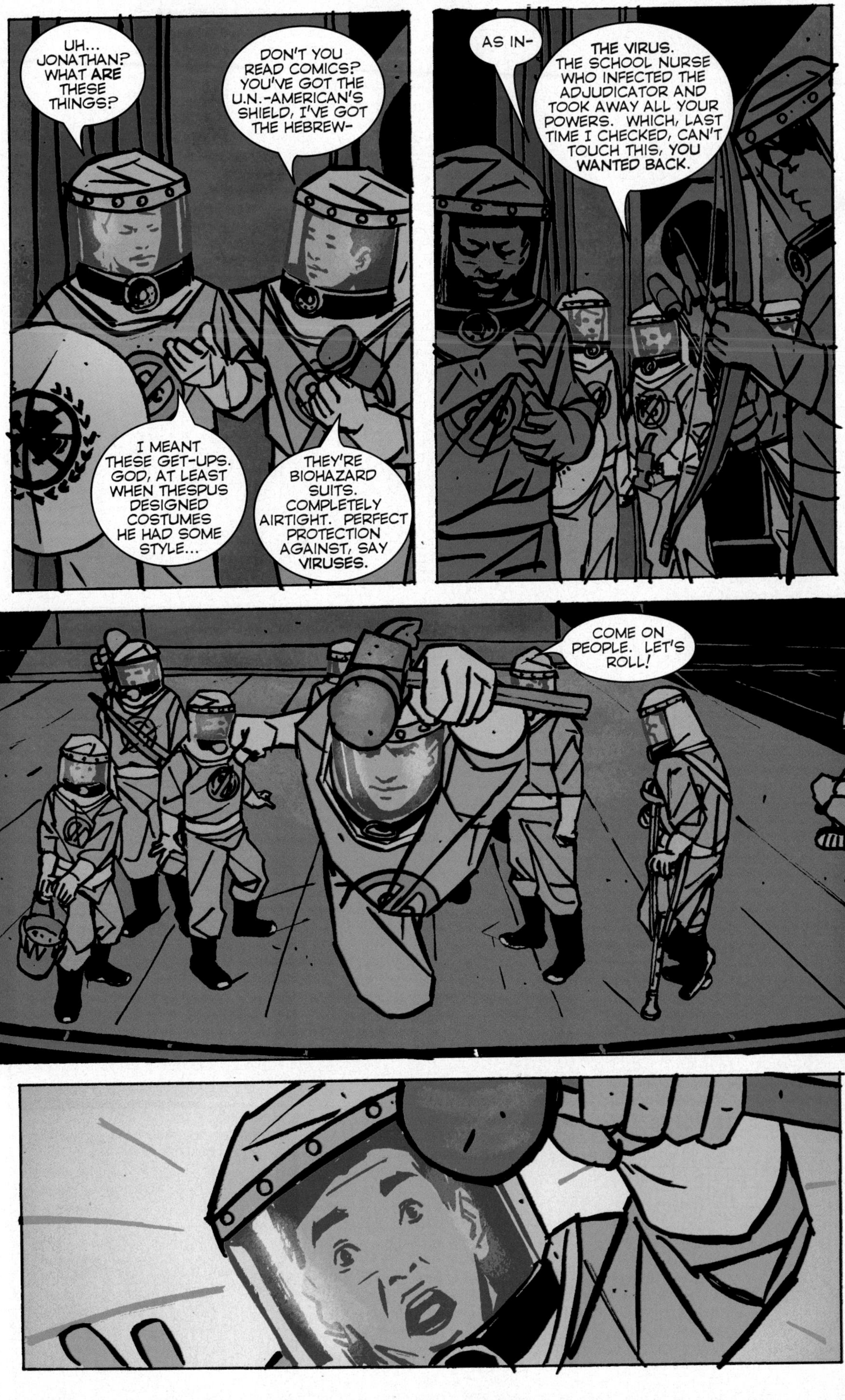
UH... JONATHAN? WHAT ARE THESE THINGS?
DON'T YOU READ COMICS? YOU'VE GOT THE U.N.-AMERICAN'S SHIELD, I'VE GOT THE HEBREW-
I MEANT THESE GET-UPS. GOD, AT LEAST WHEN THESPUS DESIGNED COSTUMES HE HAD SOME STYLE...
THEY'RE BIOHAZARD SUITS. COMPLETELY AIRTIGHT. PERFECT PROTECTION AGAINST, SAY VIRUSES.
AS IN-
THE VIRUS. THE SCHOOL NURSE WHO INFECTED THE ADJUDICATOR AND TOOK AWAY ALL YOUR POWERS. WHICH, LAST TIME I CHECKED, CAN'T TOUCH THIS, YOU WANTED BACK.
COME ON PEOPLE. LET'S ROLL!

THIS WAS YOUR PLAN? THE COSTUMES, THE WEAPONS...THEY'RE HOLOGRAMS.

HARD LIGHT HOLOGRAMS. ENHANCED BY SOLID SOUND. YOU SAID IT YOURSELF.

YEAH, BUT THEY ONLY WORK ON STAGE.

COME ON. DO YOU THINK I MADE THE BLUR RUN ALL THE WAY TO THE NURSE'S OFFICE AND BACK FOR NOTHING?

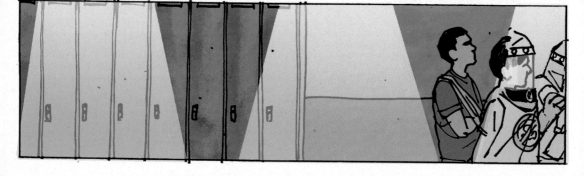

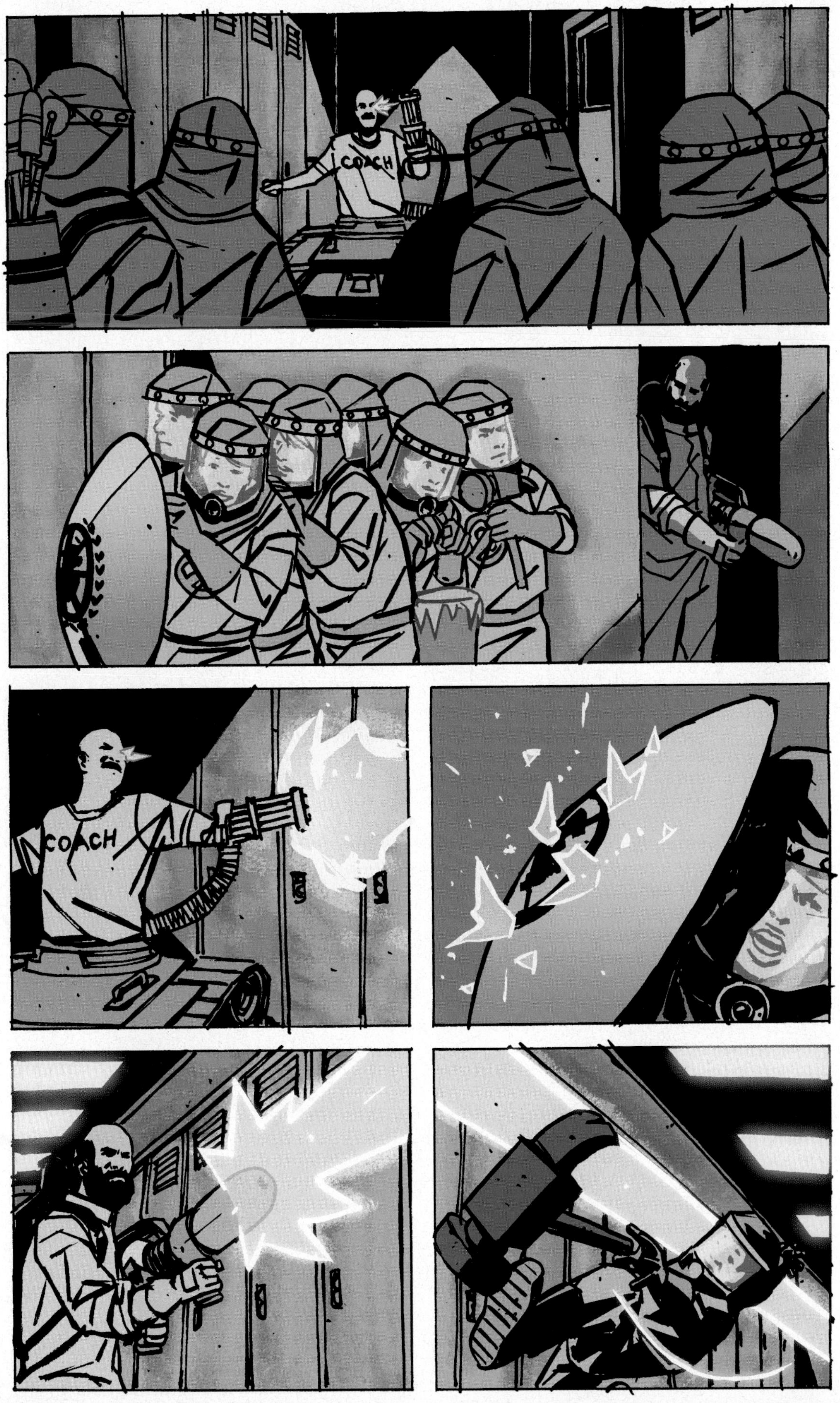
COACH
COACH

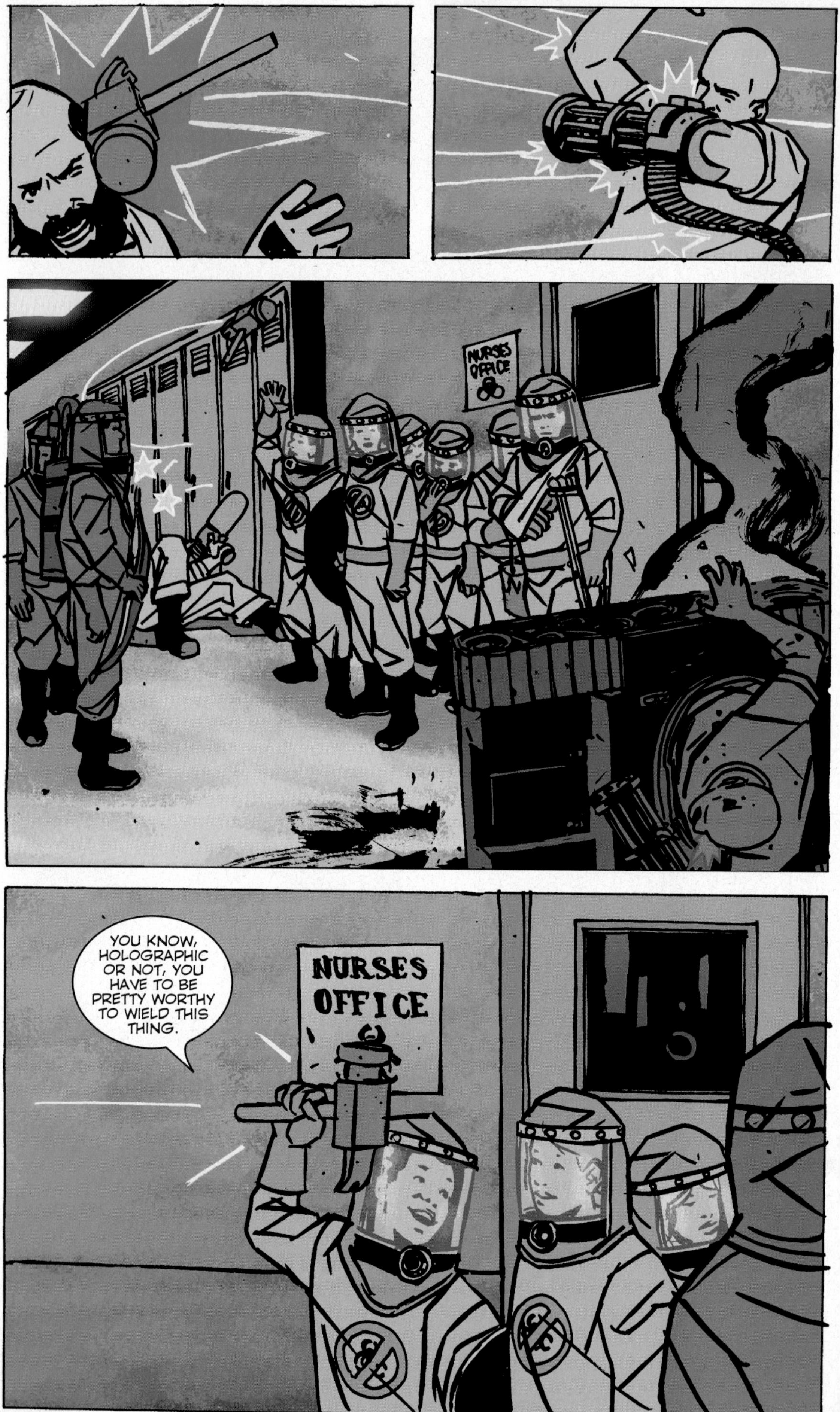

NURSES OFFICE
YOU KNOW, HOLOGRAPHIC OR NOT, YOU HAVE TO BE PRETTY WORTHY TO WIELD THIS THING.
NURSES OFFICE

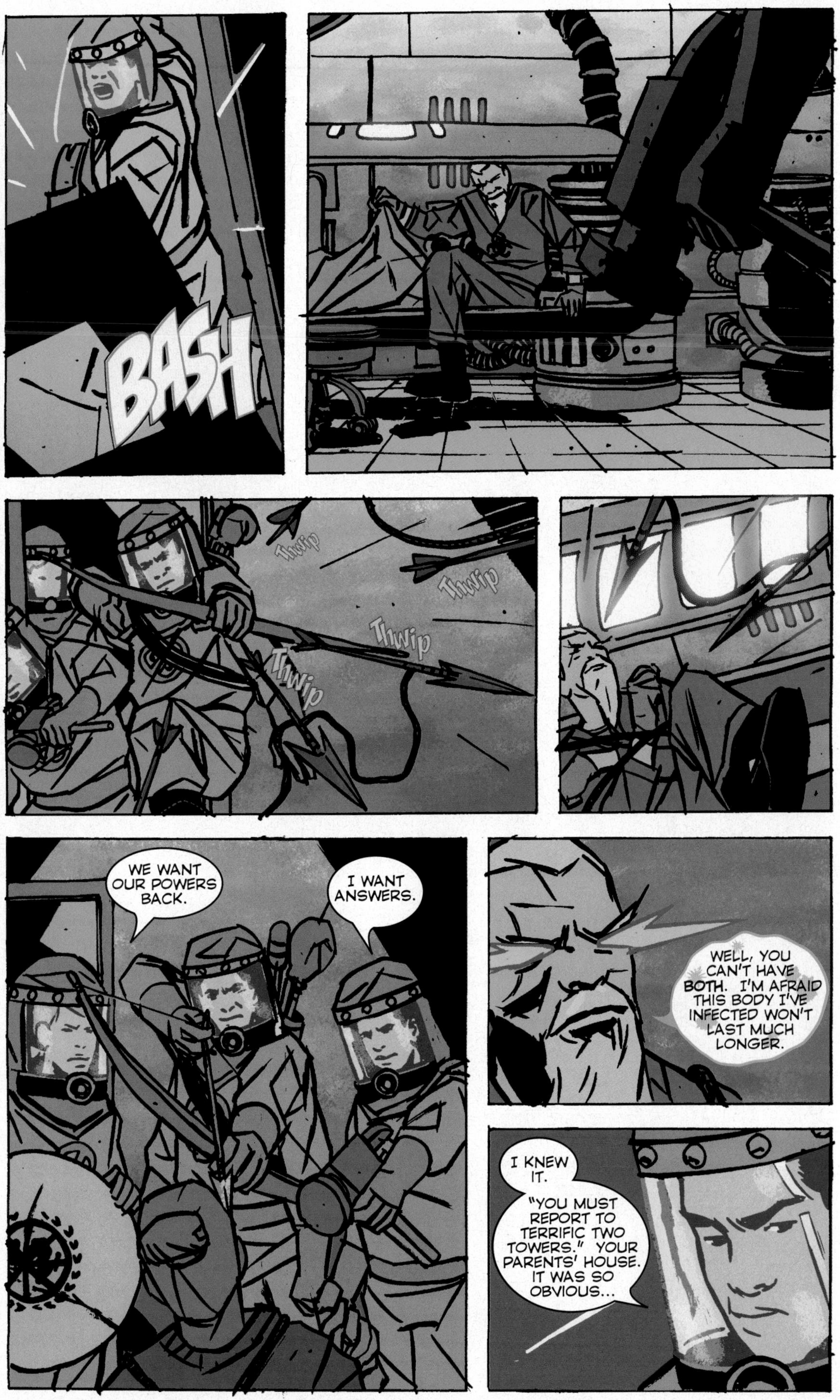
BASH
THWIP
THWIP
THWIP
THWIP
WE WANT OUR POWERS BACK.
I WANT ANSWERS.
WELL, YOU CAN'T HAVE BOTH. I'M AFRAID THIS BODY I'VE INFECTED WON'T LAST MUCH LONGER.
I KNEW IT.
"YOU MUST REPORT TO TERRIFIC TWO TOWERS." YOUR PARENTS' HOUSE. IT WAS SO OBVIOUS...

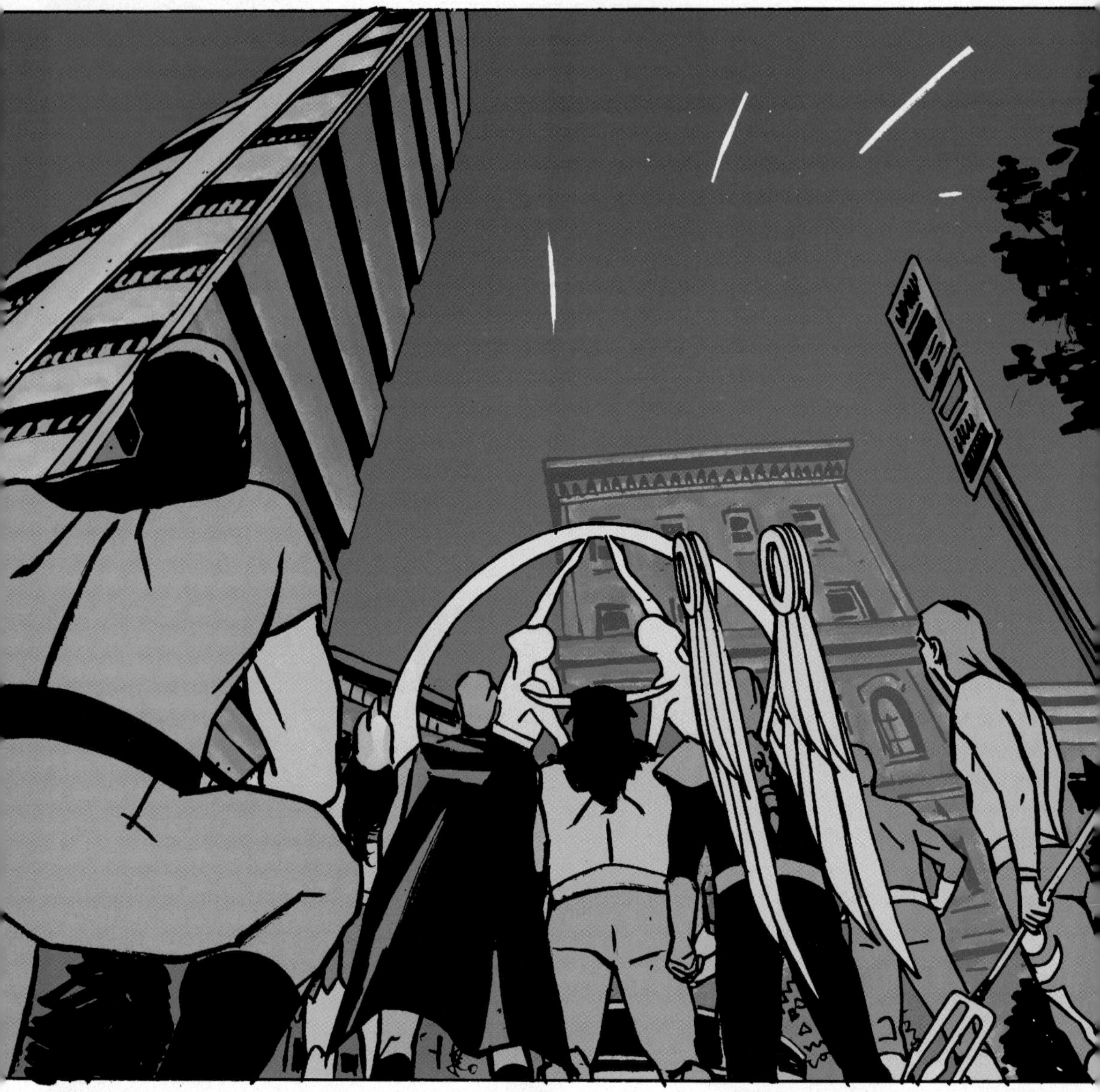

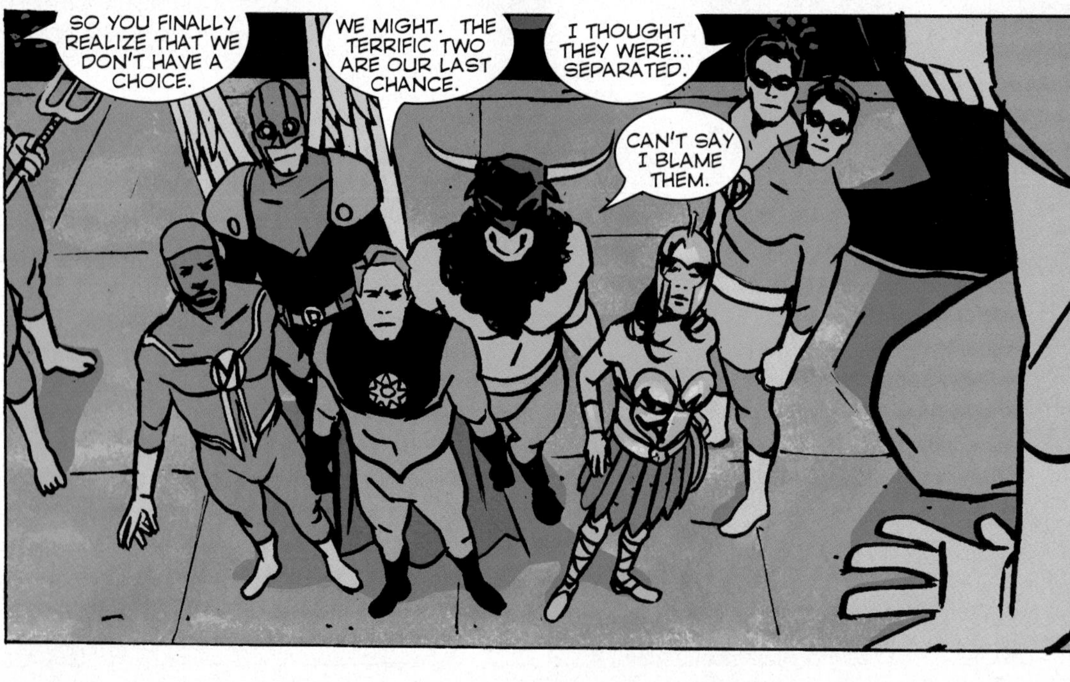
SO YOU FINALLY REALIZE THAT WE DON'T HAVE A CHOICE.
WE MIGHT. THE TERRIFIC TWO ARE OUR LAST CHANCE.
I THOUGHT THEY WERE... SEPARATED.
CAN'T SAY I BLAME THEM.

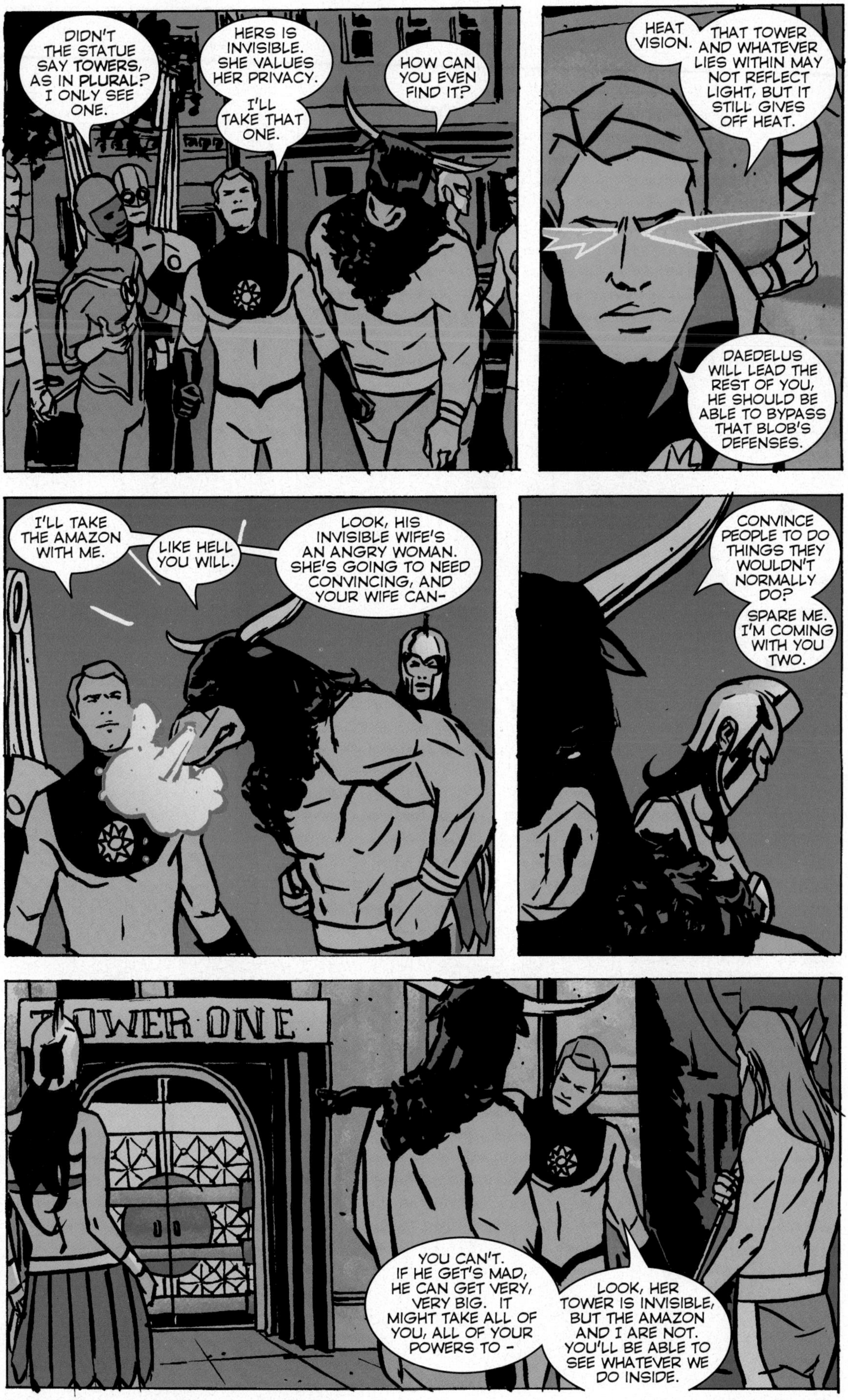

DIDN'T THE STATUE SAY TOWERS, AS IN PLURAL? I ONLY SEE ONE.
HERS IS INVISIBLE. SHE VALUES HER PRIVACY.
I'LL TAKE THAT ONE.
HOW CAN YOU EVEN FIND IT?
HEAT VISION.
THAT TOWER AND WHATEVER LIES WITHIN MAY NOT REFLECT LIGHT, BUT IT STILL GIVES OFF HEAT.
DAEDELUS WILL LEAD THE REST OF YOU, HE SHOULD BE ABLE TO BYPASS THAT BLOB'S DEFENSES.
I'LL TAKE THE AMAZON WITH ME.
LIKE HELL YOU WILL.
LOOK, HIS INVISIBLE WIFE'S AN ANGRY WOMAN. SHE'S GOING TO NEED CONVINCING, AND YOUR WIFE CAN-
CONVINCE PEOPLE TO DO THINGS THEY WOULDN'T NORMALLY DO?
SPARE ME. I'M COMING WITH YOU TWO.
TOWER ONE
YOU CAN'T. IF HE GET'S MAD, HE CAN GET VERY, VERY BIG. IT MIGHT TAKE ALL OF YOU, ALL OF YOUR POWERS TO -
LOOK, HER TOWER IS INVISIBLE, BUT THE AMAZON AND I ARE NOT. YOU'LL BE ABLE TO SEE WHATEVER WE DO INSIDE.

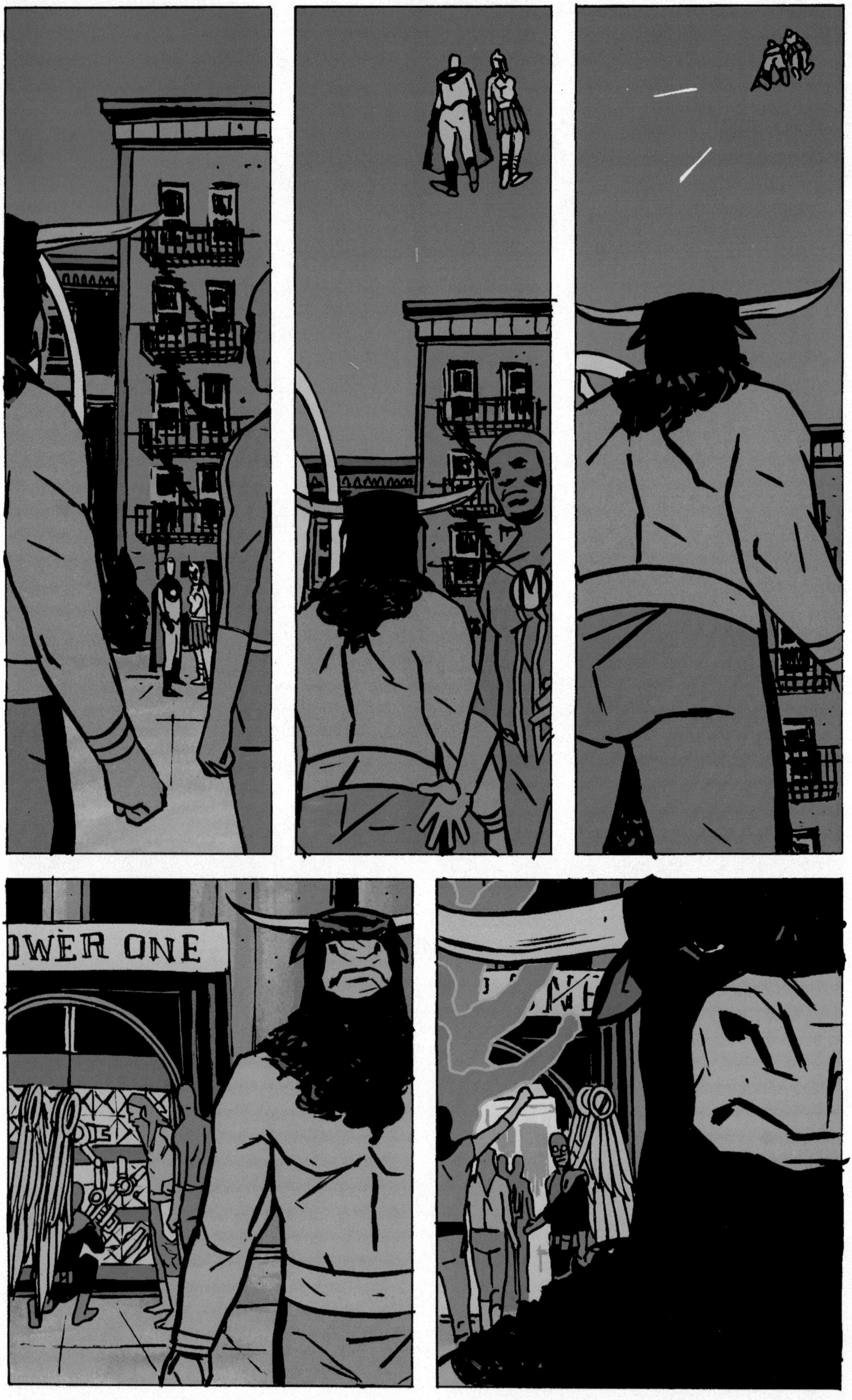
OWER ONE

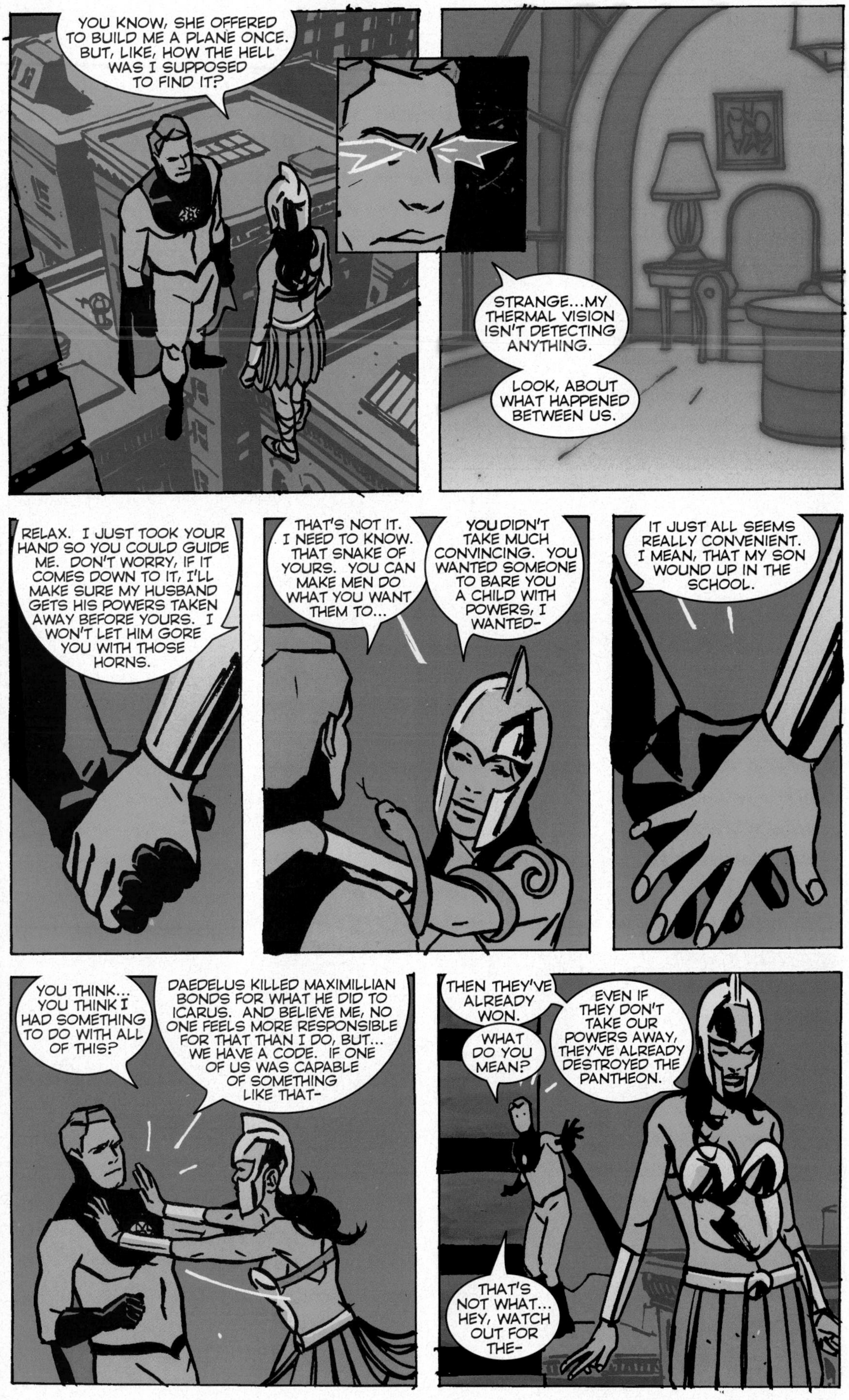
YOU KNOW, SHE OFFERED TO BUILD ME A PLANE ONCE. BUT, LIKE, HOW THE HELL WAS I SUPPOSED TO FIND IT?
STRANGE...MY THERMAL VISION ISN'T DETECTING ANYTHING.
LOOK, ABOUT WHAT HAPPENED BETWEEN US.
RELAX. I JUST TOOK YOUR HAND SO YOU COULD GUIDE ME. DON'T WORRY, IF IT COMES DOWN TO IT, I'LL MAKE SURE MY HUSBAND GETS HIS POWERS TAKEN AWAY BEFORE YOURS. I WON'T LET HIM GORE YOU WITH THOSE HORNS.
THAT'S NOT IT. I NEED TO KNOW. THAT SNAKE OF YOURS. YOU CAN MAKE MEN DO WHAT YOU WANT THEM TO...
YOU DIDN'T TAKE MUCH CONVINCING. YOU WANTED SOMEONE TO BARE YOU A CHILD WITH POWERS, I WANTED-
IT JUST ALL SEEMS REALLY CONVENIENT. I MEAN, THAT MY SON WOUND UP IN THE SCHOOL.
YOU THINK... YOU THINK I HAD SOMETHING TO DO WITH ALL OF THIS?
DAEDELUS KILLED MAXIMILLIAN BONDS FOR WHAT HE DID TO ICARUS. AND BELIEVE ME, NO ONE FEELS MORE RESPONSIBLE FOR THAT THAN I DO, BUT... WE HAVE A CODE. IF ONE OF US WAS CAPABLE OF SOMETHING LIKE THAT-
THEN THEY'VE ALREADY WON.
WHAT DO YOU MEAN?
EVEN IF THEY DON'T TAKE OUR POWERS AWAY, THEY'VE ALREADY DESTROYED THE PANTHEON.
THAT'S NOT WHAT... HEY, WATCH OUT FOR THE-

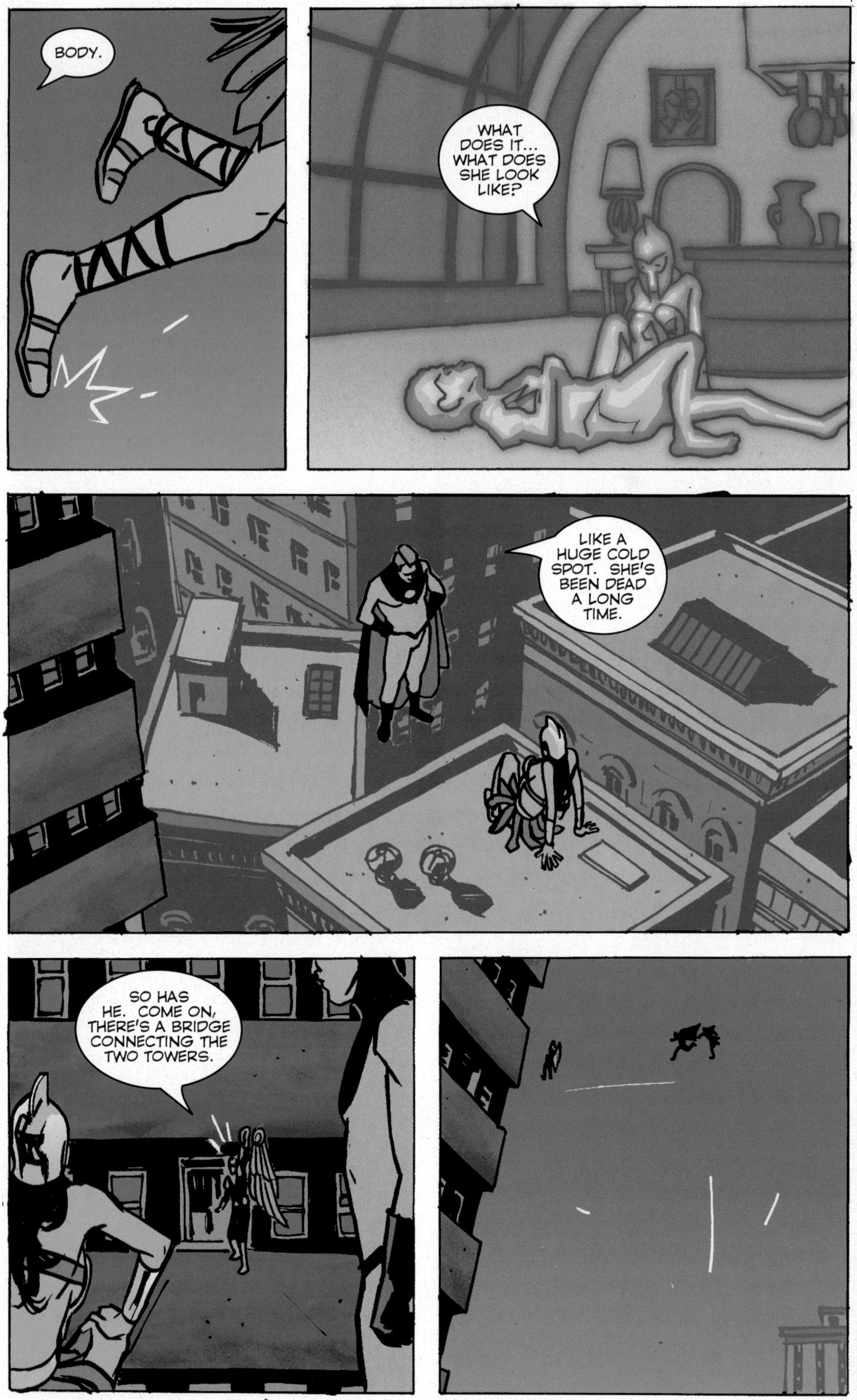
BODY.
WHAT DOES IT... WHAT DOES SHE LOOK LIKE?
LIKE A HUGE COLD SPOT. SHE'S BEEN DEAD A LONG TIME.
SO HAS HE. COME ON, THERE'S A BRIDGE CONNECTING THE TWO TOWERS.

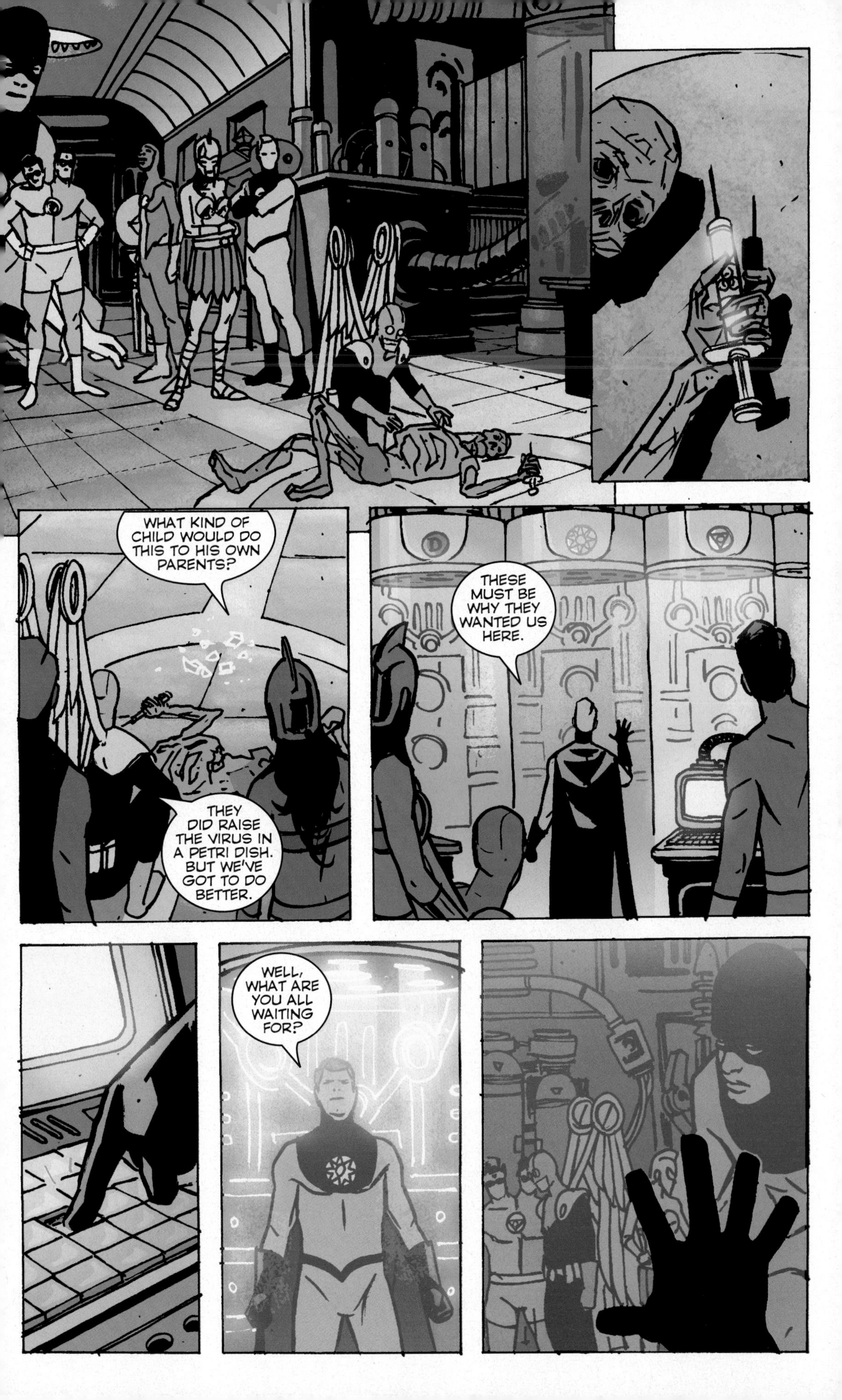
WHAT KIND OF CHILD WOULD DO THIS TO HIS OWN PARENTS?
THEY DID RAISE THE VIRUS IN A PETRI DISH. BUT WE'VE GOT TO DO BETTER.
THESE MUST BE WHY THEY WANTED US HERE.
WELL, WHAT ARE YOU ALL WAITING FOR?

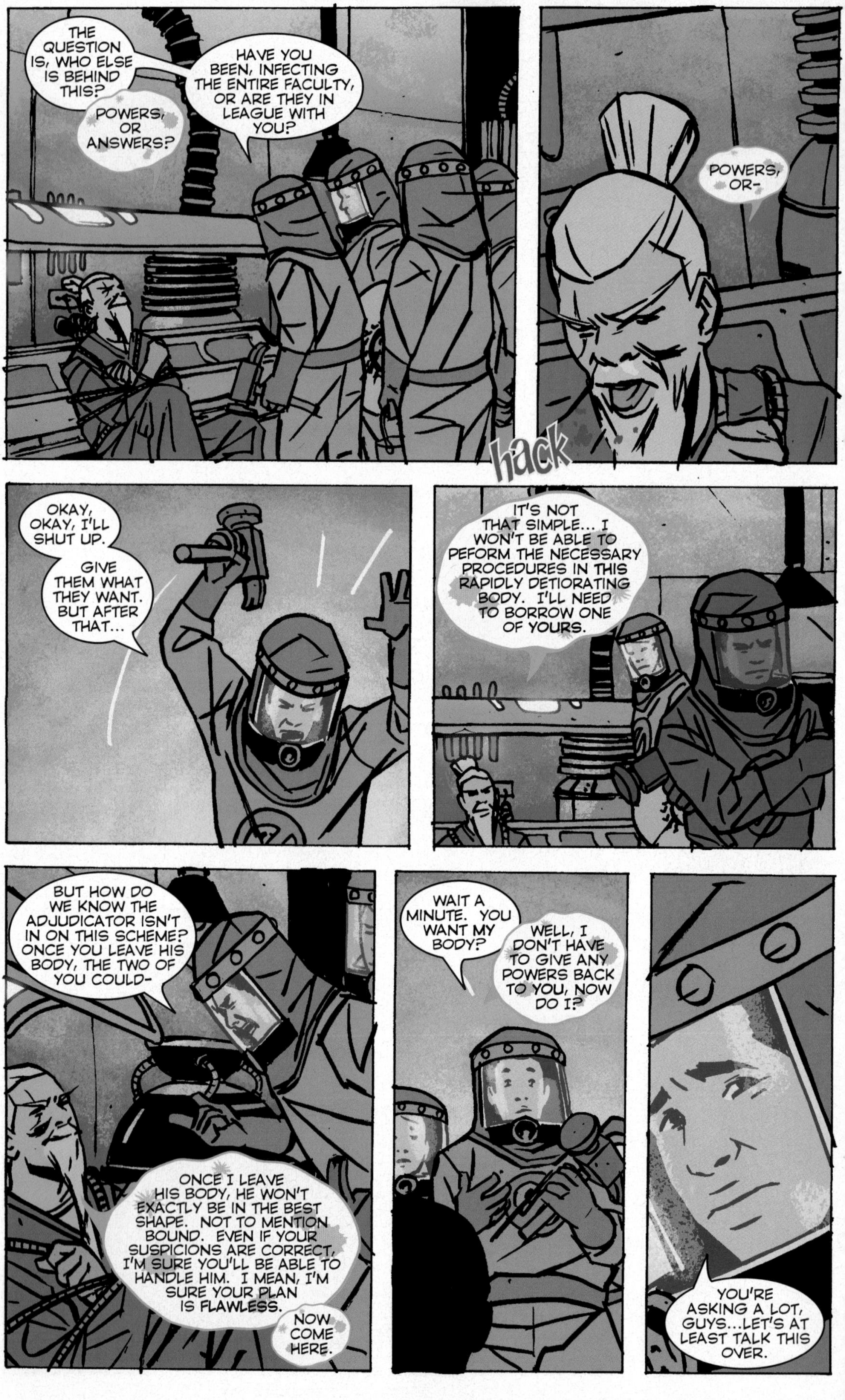

THE QUESTION IS, WHO ELSE IS BEHIND THIS?
HAVE YOU BEEN, INFECTING THE ENTIRE FACULTY, OR ARE THEY IN LEAGUE WITH YOU?
POWERS, OR ANSWERS?
POWERS, OR-
hack
OKAY, OKAY, I'LL SHUT UP.
GIVE THEM WHAT THEY WANT. BUT AFTER THAT...
IT'S NOT THAT SIMPLE... I WON'T BE ABLE TO PEFORM THE NECESSARY PROCEDURES IN THIS RAPIDLY DETIORATING BODY. I'LL NEED TO BORROW ONE OF YOURS.
BUT HOW DO WE KNOW THE ADJUDICATOR ISN'T IN ON THIS SCHEME? ONCE YOU LEAVE HIS BODY, THE TWO OF YOU COULD-
ONCE I LEAVE HIS BODY, HE WON'T EXACTLY BE IN THE BEST SHAPE. NOT TO MENTION BOUND. EVEN IF YOUR SUSPICIONS ARE CORRECT, I'M SURE YOU'LL BE ABLE TO HANDLE HIM. I MEAN, I'M SURE YOUR PLAN IS FLAWLESS.
NOW COME HERE.
WAIT A MINUTE. YOU WANT MY BODY?
WELL, I DON'T HAVE TO GIVE ANY POWERS BACK TO YOU, NOW DO I?
YOU'RE ASKING A LOT, GUYS...LET'S AT LEAST TALK THIS OVER.

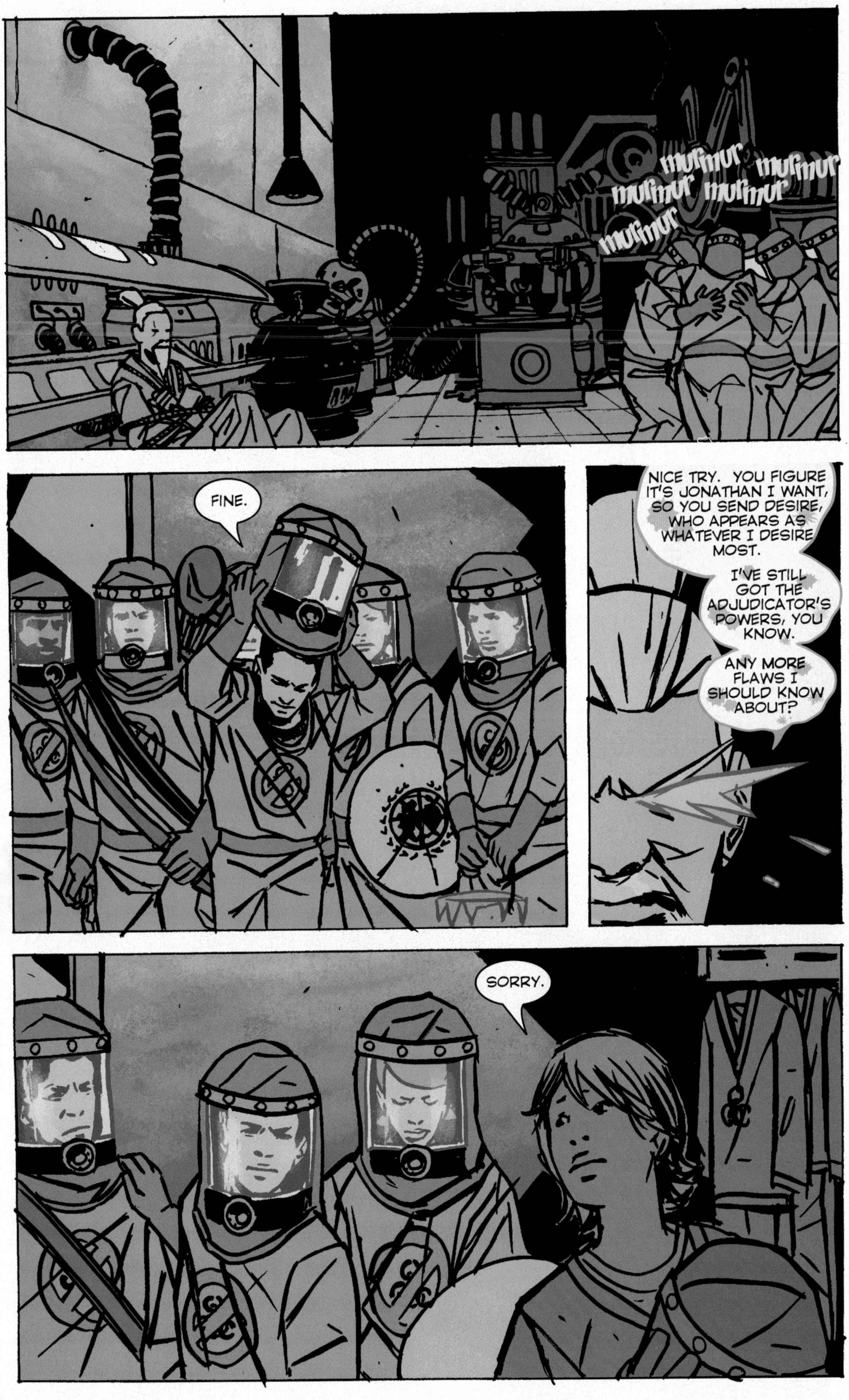
murmur murmur murmur murmur murmur murmur
FINE.
NICE TRY. YOU FIGURE IT'S JONATHAN I WANT, SO YOU SEND DESIRE, WHO APPEARS AS WHATEVER I DESIRE MOST.
I'VE STILL GOT THE ADJUDICATOR'S POWERS, YOU KNOW.
ANY MORE FLAWS I SHOULD KNOW ABOUT?
SORRY.

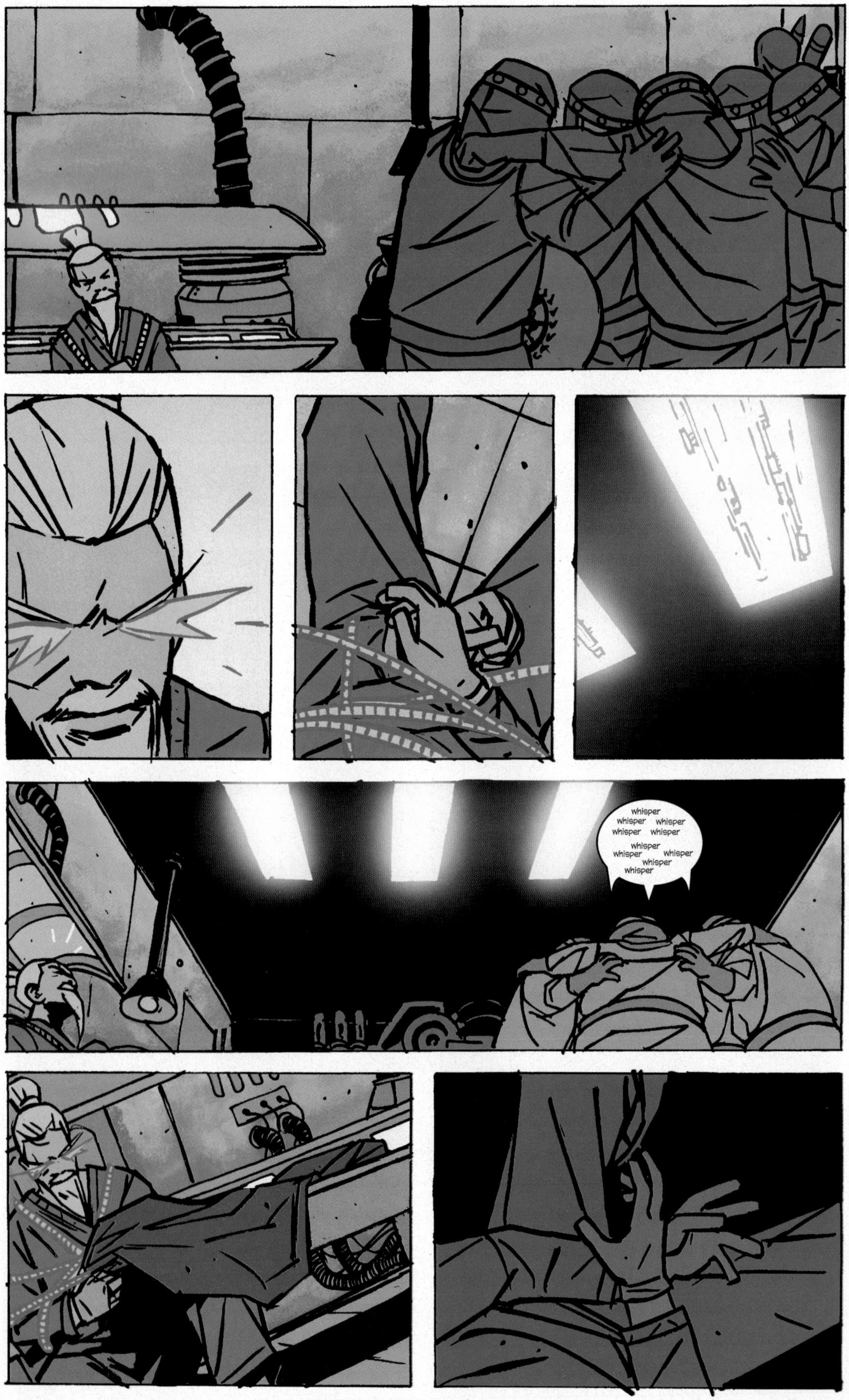
whisper whisper whisper whisper whisper whisper whisper whisper whisper whisper

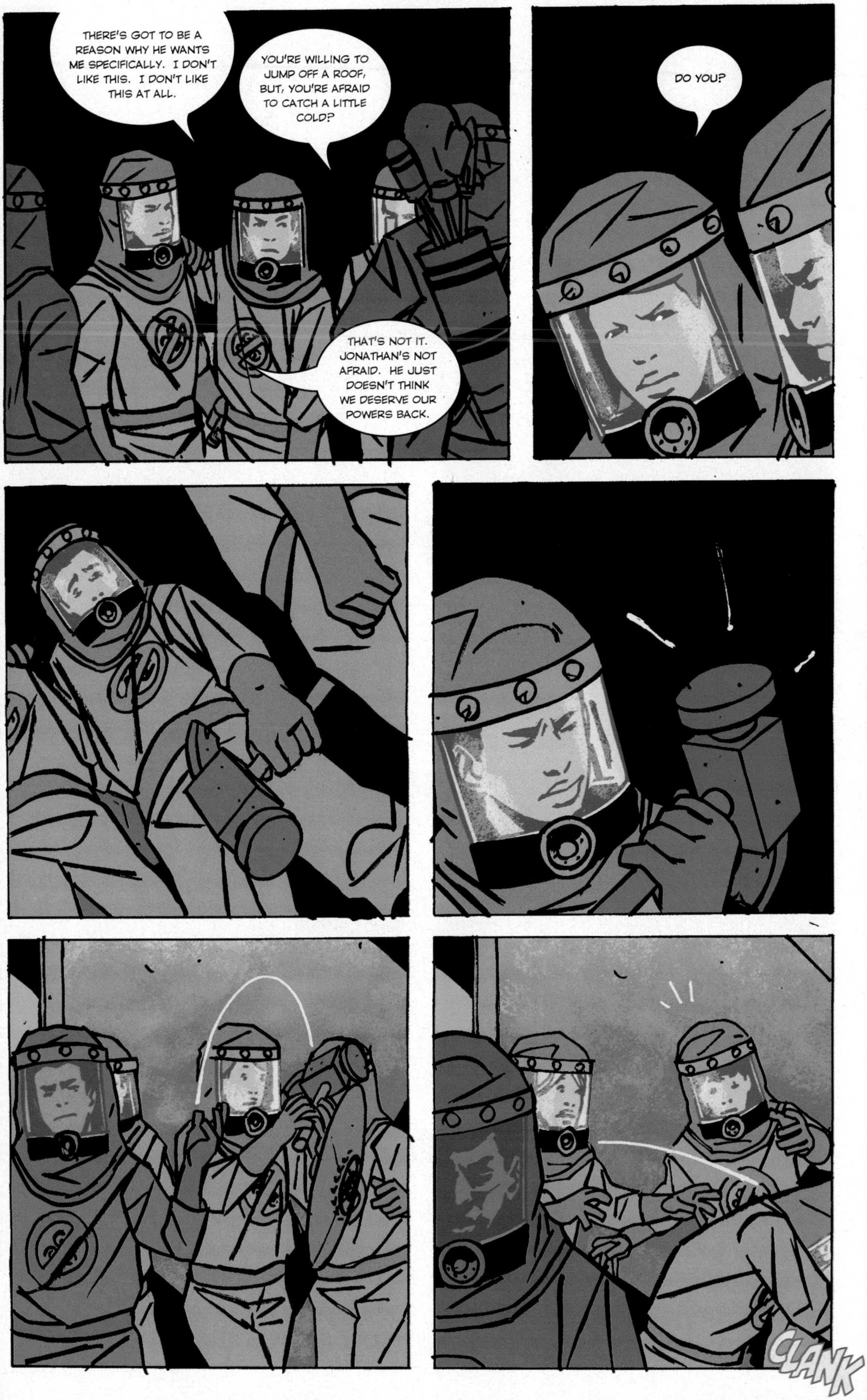
THERE'S GOT TO BE A REASON WHY HE WANTS ME SPECIFICALLY. I DON'T LIKE THIS. I DON'T LIKE THIS AT ALL.
YOU'RE WILLING TO JUMP OFF A ROOF, BUT, YOU'RE AFRAID TO CATCH A LITTLE COLD?
THAT'S NOT IT. JONATHAN'S NOT AFRAID. HE JUST DOESN'T THINK WE DESERVE OUR POWERS BACK.
DO YOU?
CLANK

QUIT STALLING. YOU'RE KILLING ME HERE.

LITERALLY.

YOU GUYS MAKE ME SICK.

NO.

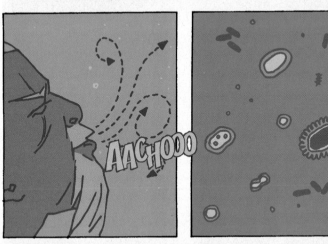

AACHOOO

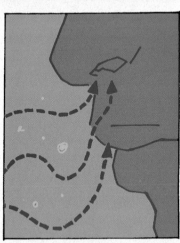

I DO.

WHO'S FIRST?

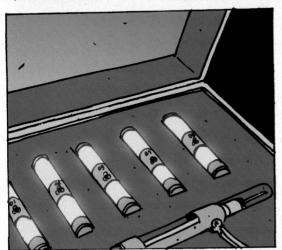

IF ANYTHING HAPPENS TO ME, IF THE VIRUS TRIES ANYTHING...RUN. DO WHAT JONATHAN SAID, GET OUT OF HERE.

MY BOYFR– THE BULLY'S NEXT.

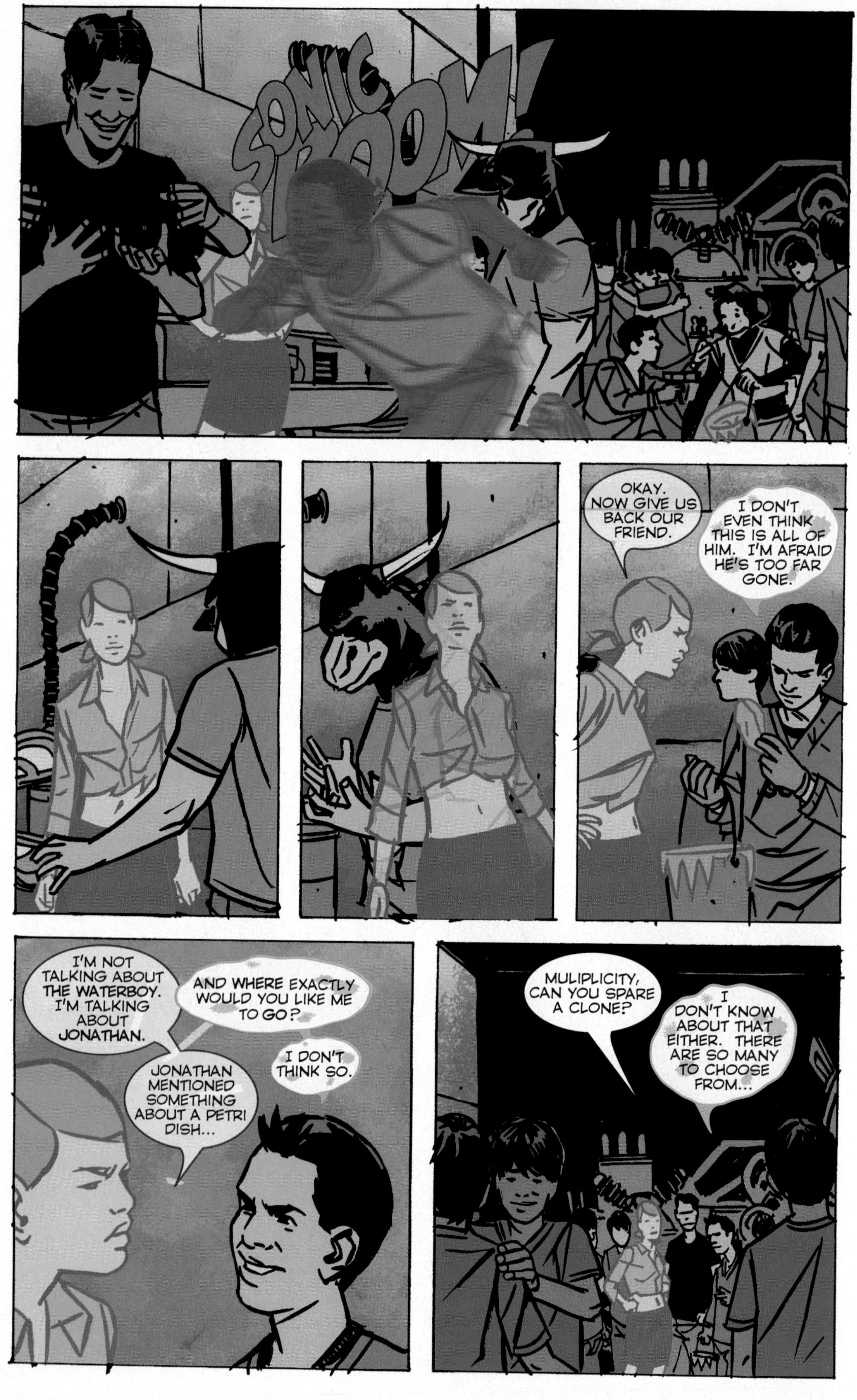
SONIC BOOM!
OKAY. NOW GIVE US BACK OUR FRIEND.
I DON'T EVEN THINK THIS IS ALL OF HIM. I'M AFRAID HE'S TOO FAR GONE.
I'M NOT TALKING ABOUT THE WATERBOY. I'M TALKING ABOUT JONATHAN.
AND WHERE EXACTLY WOULD YOU LIKE ME TO GO?
JONATHAN MENTIONED SOMETHING ABOUT A PETRI DISH...
I DON'T THINK SO.
MULIPLICITY, CAN YOU SPARE A CLONE?
I DON'T KNOW ABOUT THAT EITHER. THERE ARE SO MANY TO CHOOSE FROM...

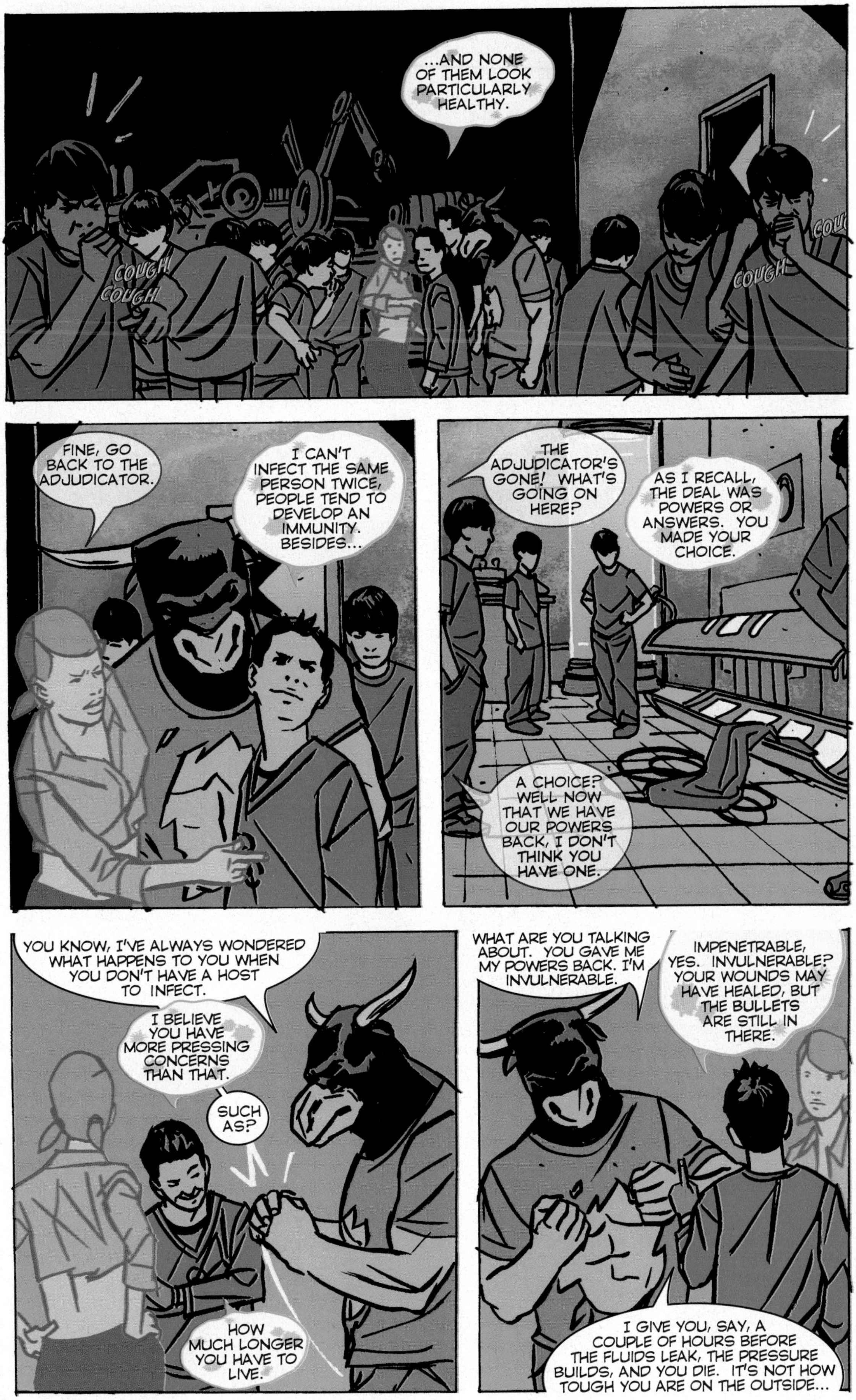
...AND NONE OF THEM LOOK PARTICULARLY HEALTHY.
COUGH COUGH
COUGH
COUGH
FINE, GO BACK TO THE ADJUDICATOR.
I CAN'T INFECT THE SAME PERSON TWICE, PEOPLE TEND TO DEVELOP AN IMMUNITY. BESIDES...
THE ADJUDICATOR'S GONE! WHAT'S GOING ON HERE?
AS I RECALL, THE DEAL WAS POWERS OR ANSWERS. YOU MADE YOUR CHOICE.
A CHOICE? WELL NOW THAT WE HAVE OUR POWERS BACK, I DON'T THINK YOU HAVE ONE.
YOU KNOW, I'VE ALWAYS WONDERED WHAT HAPPENS TO YOU WHEN YOU DON'T HAVE A HOST TO INFECT.
I BELIEVE YOU HAVE MORE PRESSING CONCERNS THAN THAT.
SUCH AS?
HOW MUCH LONGER YOU HAVE TO LIVE.
WHAT ARE YOU TALKING ABOUT. YOU GAVE ME MY POWERS BACK. I'M INVULNERABLE.
IMPENETRABLE, YES. INVULNERABLE? YOUR WOUNDS MAY HAVE HEALED, BUT THE BULLETS ARE STILL IN THERE.
I GIVE YOU, SAY, A COUPLE OF HOURS BEFORE THE FLUIDS LEAK, THE PRESSURE BUILDS, AND YOU DIE. IT'S NOT HOW TOUGH YOU ARE ON THE OUTSIDE...

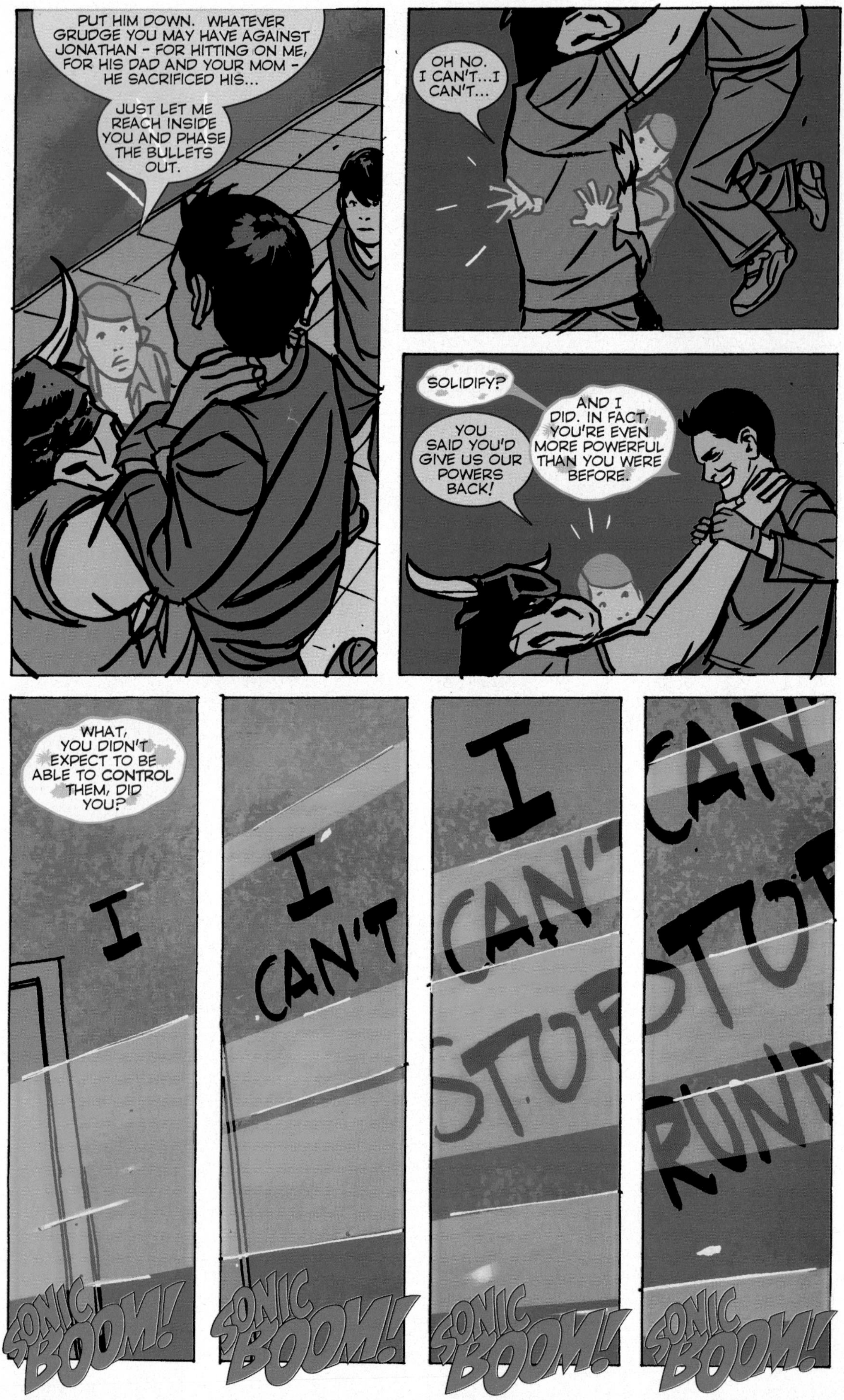
PUT HIM DOWN. WHATEVER GRUDGE YOU MAY HAVE AGAINST JONATHAN - FOR HITTING ON ME, FOR HIS DAD AND YOUR MOM - HE SACRIFICED HIS...
JUST LET ME REACH INSIDE YOU AND PHASE THE BULLETS OUT.
OH NO. I CAN'T...I CAN'T...
SOLIDIFY?
YOU SAID YOU'D GIVE US OUR POWERS BACK!
AND I DID. IN FACT, YOU'RE EVEN MORE POWERFUL THAN YOU WERE BEFORE.
WHAT, YOU DIDN'T EXPECT TO BE ABLE TO CONTROL THEM, DID YOU?
I
I CAN'T
I CAN'T STOP
CAN'T STOP RUNN
SONIC BOOM!
SONIC BOOM!
SONIC BOOM!
SONIC BOOM!

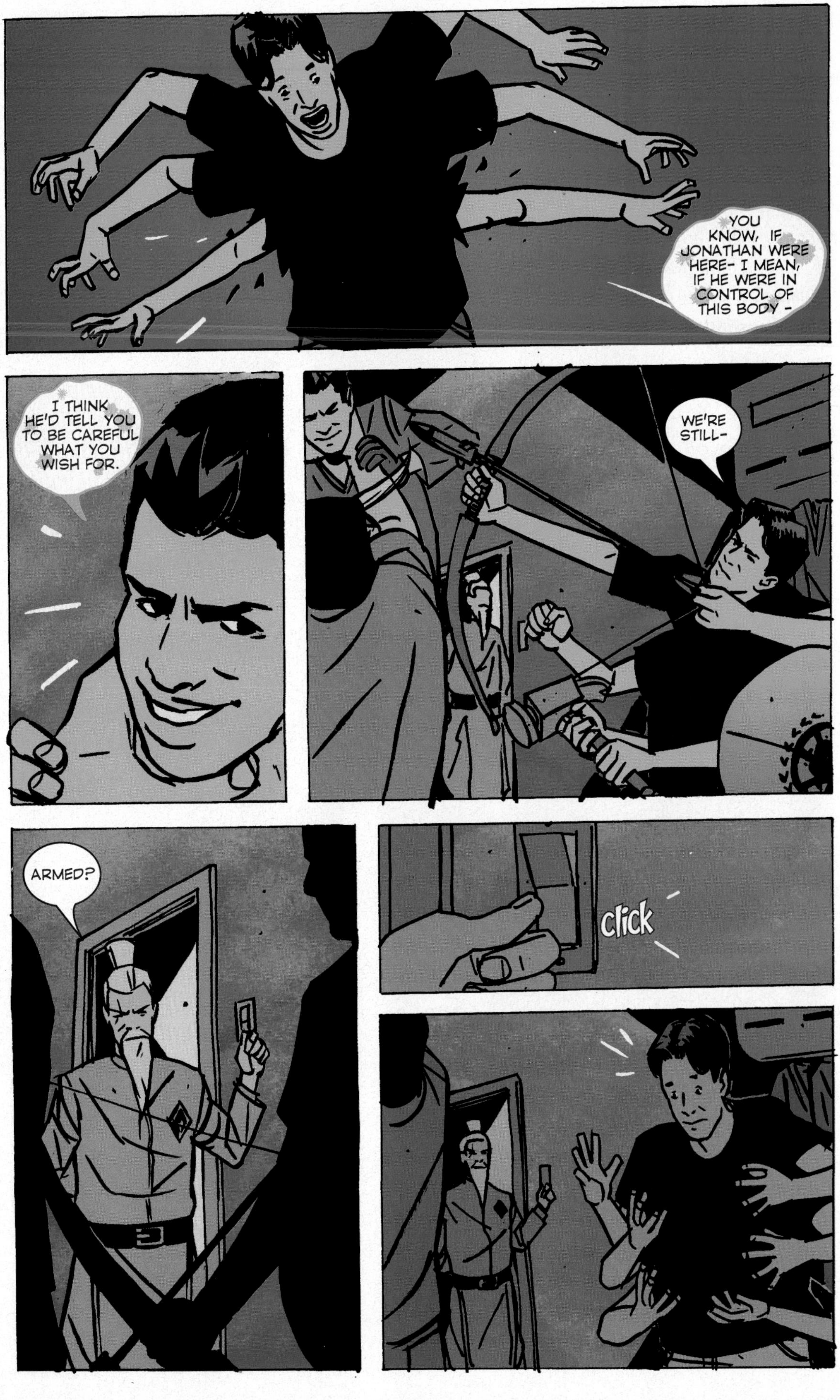

YOU KNOW, IF JONATHAN WERE HERE- I MEAN, IF HE WERE IN CONTROL OF THIS BODY -
I THINK HE'D TELL YOU TO BE CAREFUL WHAT YOU WISH FOR.
WE'RE STILL-
ARMED?
CLICK

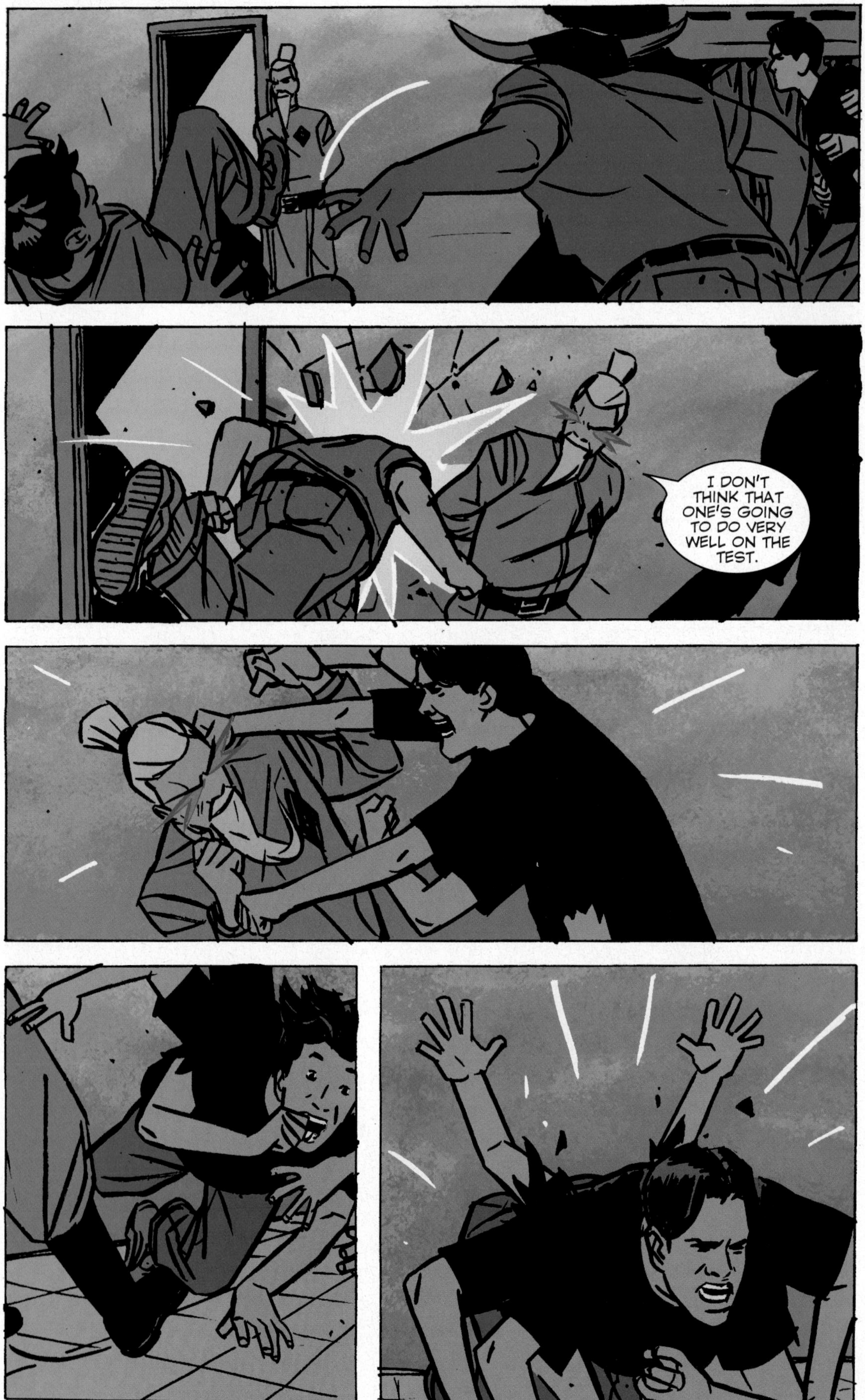
I DON'T THINK THAT ONE'S GOING TO DO VERY WELL ON THE TEST.

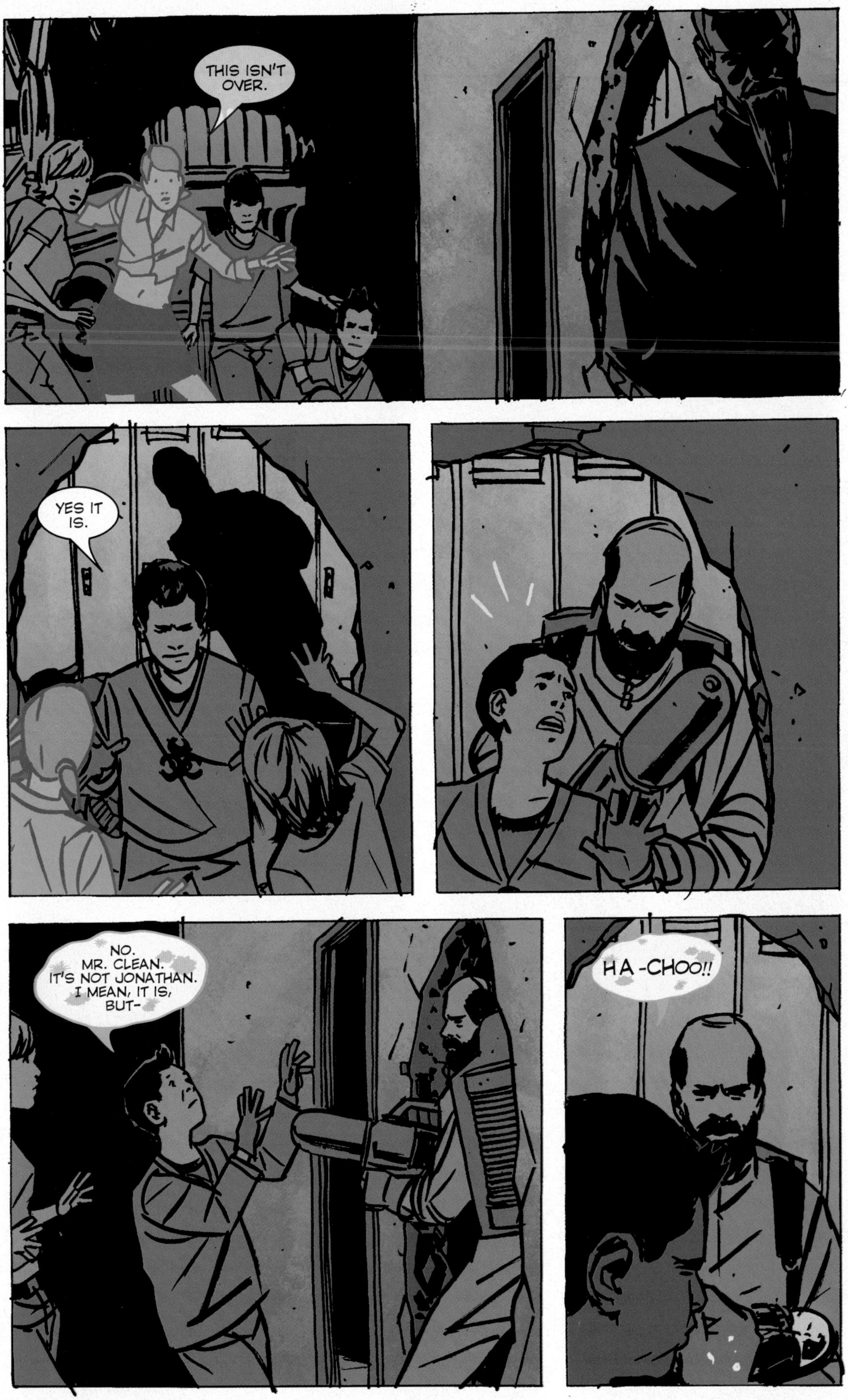
THIS ISN'T OVER.
YES IT IS.
NO. MR. CLEAN. IT'S NOT JONATHAN. I MEAN, IT IS, BUT-
HA-CHOO!!

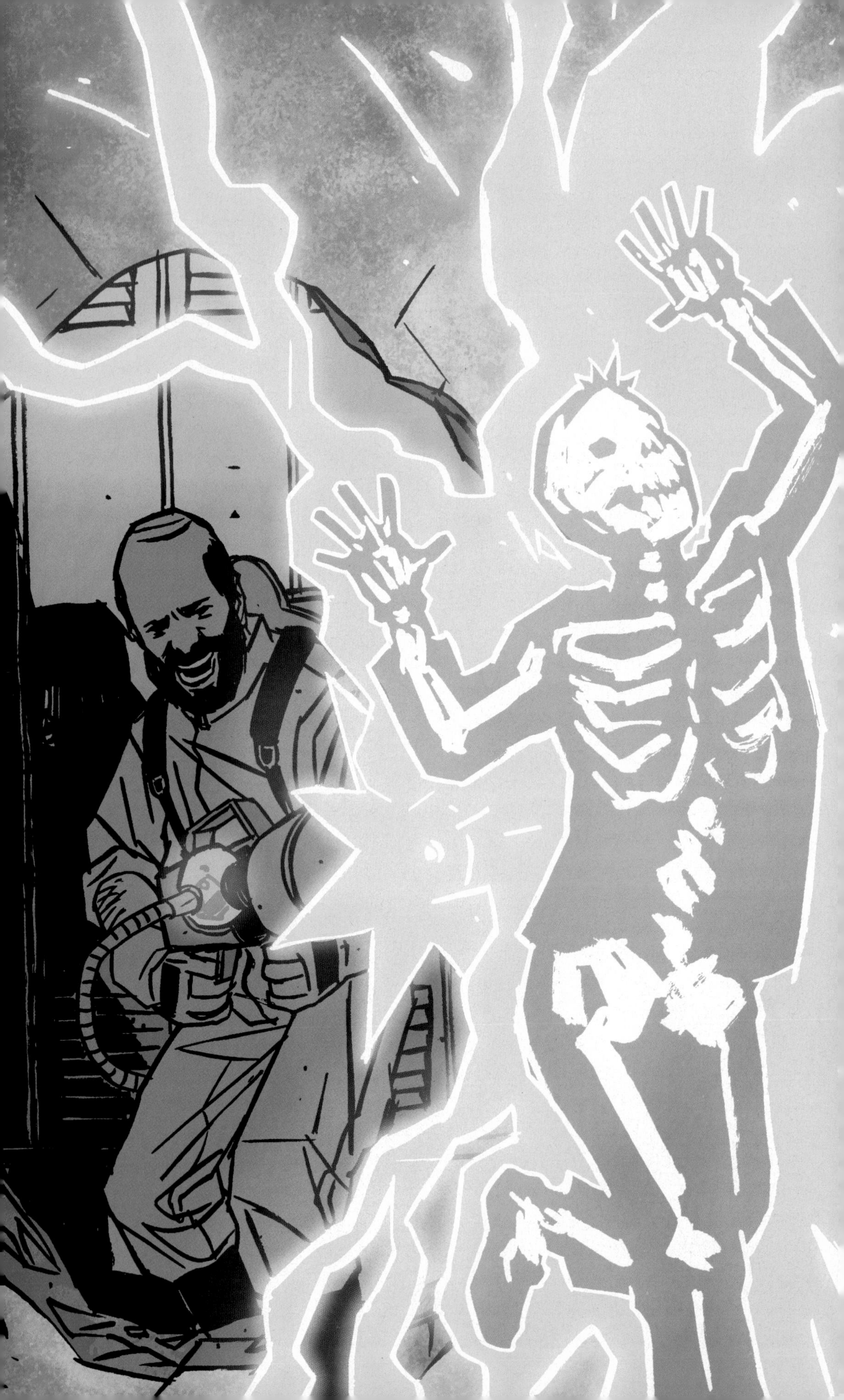

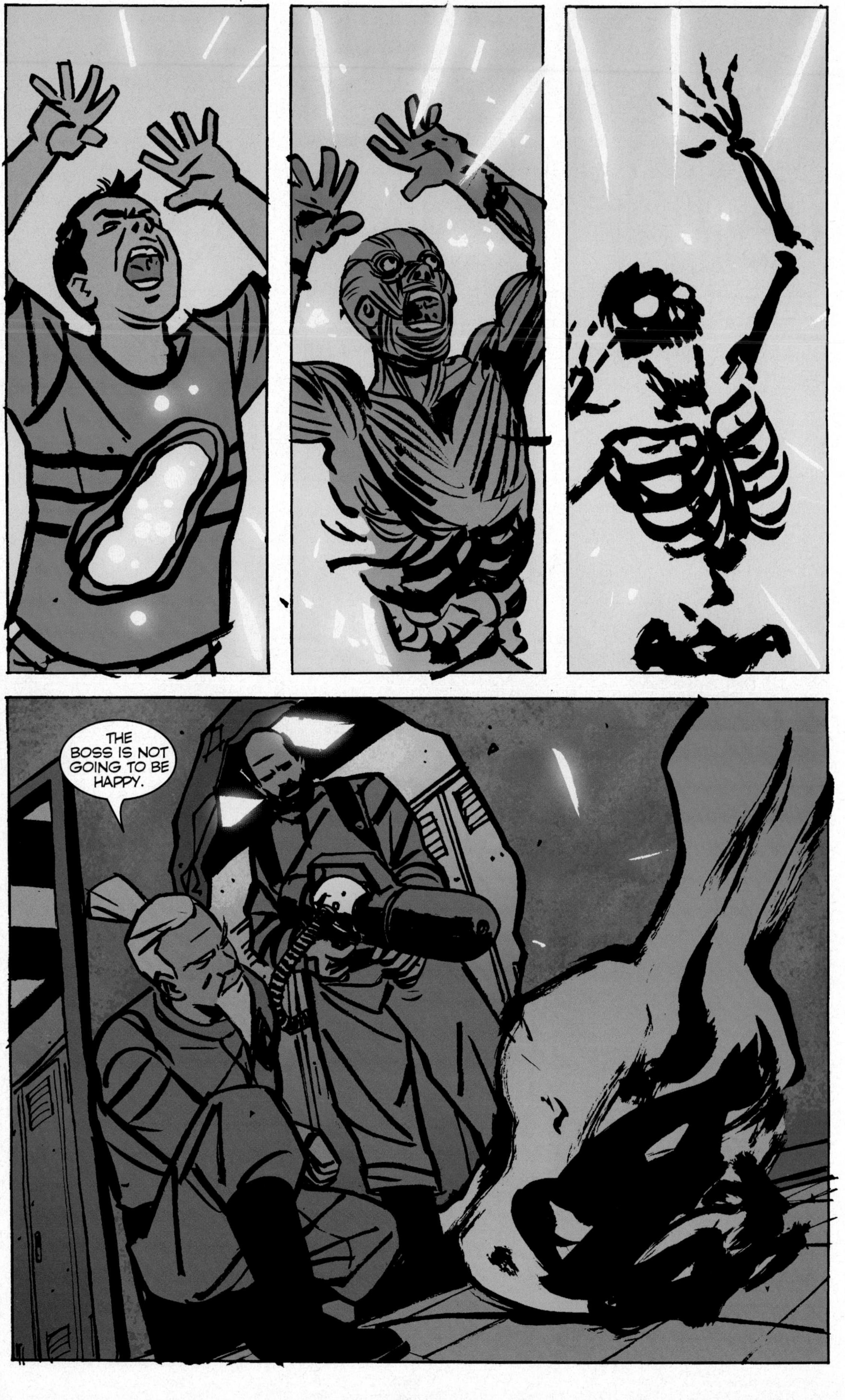
THE BOSS IS NOT GOING TO BE HAPPY.

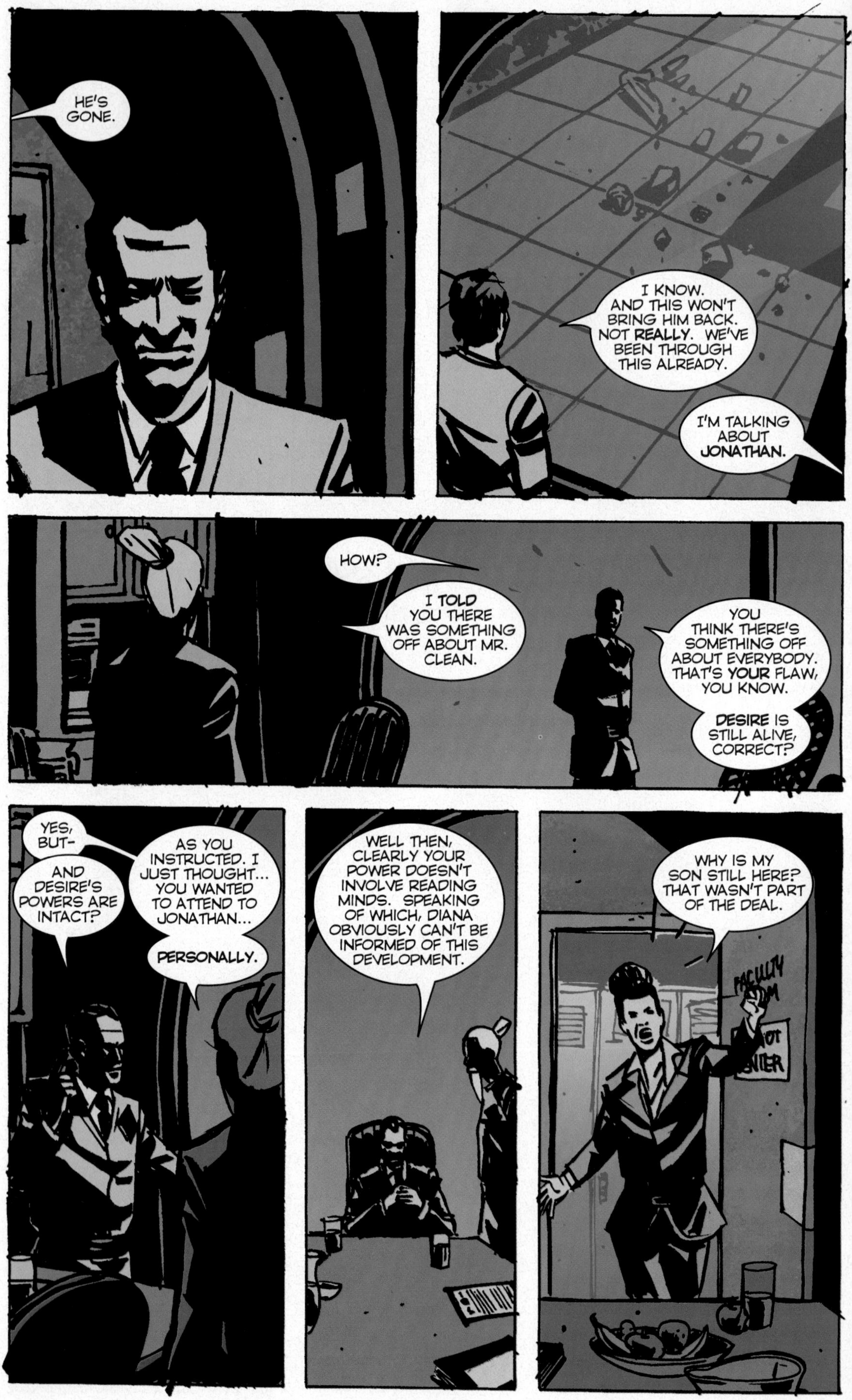
HE'S GONE.
I KNOW. AND THIS WON'T BRING HIM BACK. NOT REALLY. WE'VE BEEN THROUGH THIS ALREADY.
I'M TALKING ABOUT JONATHAN.
HOW?
I TOLD YOU THERE WAS SOMETHING OFF ABOUT MR. CLEAN.
YOU THINK THERE'S SOMETHING OFF ABOUT EVERYBODY. THAT'S YOUR FLAW, YOU KNOW.
DESIRE IS STILL ALIVE, CORRECT?
YES, BUT-
AND DESIRE'S POWERS ARE INTACT?
AS YOU INSTRUCTED. I JUST THOUGHT... YOU WANTED TO ATTEND TO JONATHAN...
PERSONALLY.
WELL THEN, CLEARLY YOUR POWER DOESN'T INVOLVE READING MINDS. SPEAKING OF WHICH, DIANA OBVIOUSLY CAN'T BE INFORMED OF THIS DEVELOPMENT.
WHY IS MY SON STILL HERE? THAT WASN'T PART OF THE DEAL.

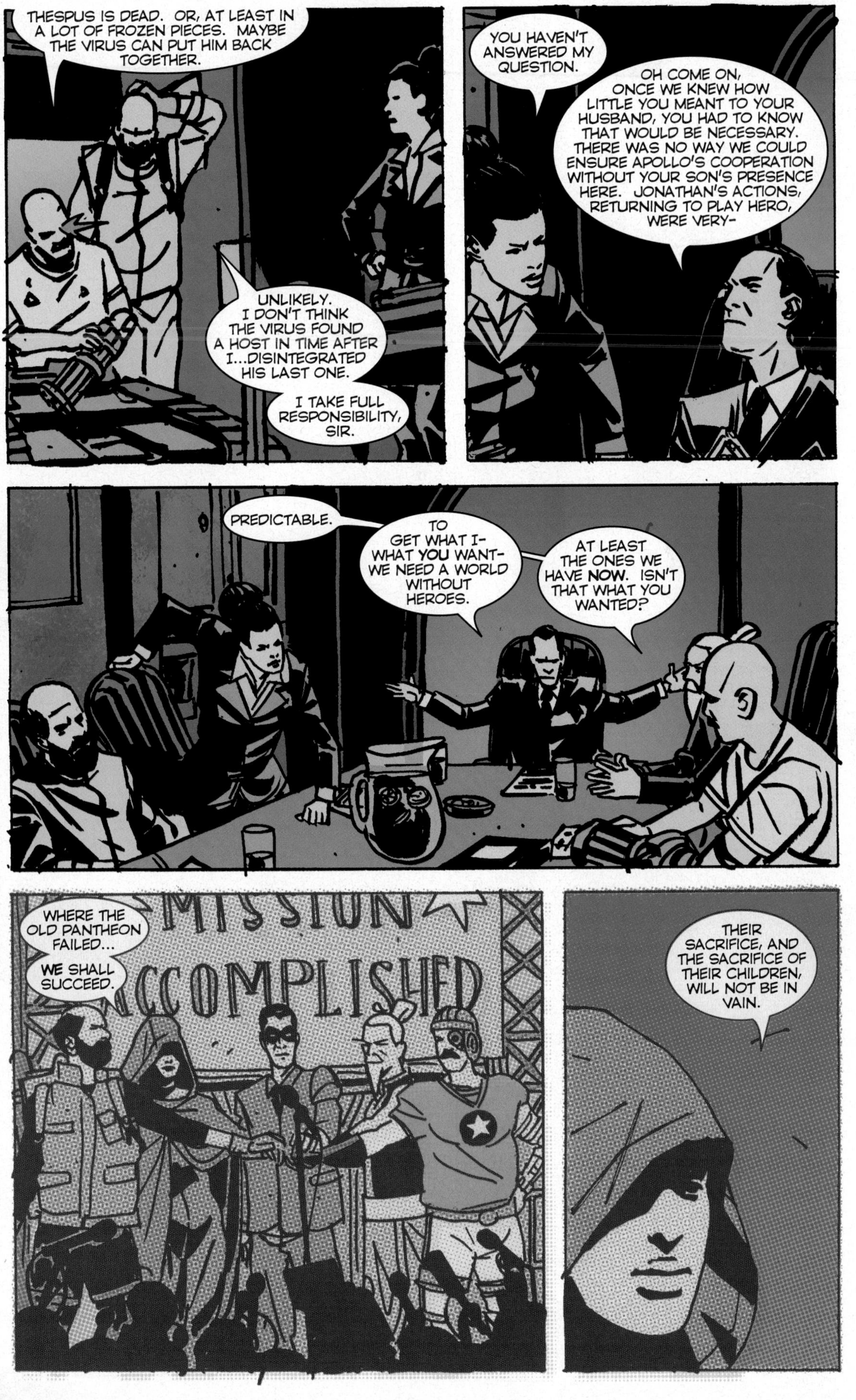
THESPUS IS DEAD. OR, AT LEAST IN A LOT OF FROZEN PIECES. MAYBE THE VIRUS CAN PUT HIM BACK TOGETHER.
UNLIKELY. I DON'T THINK THE VIRUS FOUND A HOST IN TIME AFTER I...DISINTEGRATED HIS LAST ONE.
I TAKE FULL RESPONSIBILITY, SIR.
YOU HAVEN'T ANSWERED MY QUESTION.
OH COME ON, ONCE WE KNEW HOW LITTLE YOU MEANT TO YOUR HUSBAND, YOU HAD TO KNOW THAT WOULD BE NECESSARY. THERE WAS NO WAY WE COULD ENSURE APOLLO'S COOPERATION WITHOUT YOUR SON'S PRESENCE HERE. JONATHAN'S ACTIONS, RETURNING TO PLAY HERO, WERE VERY-
PREDICTABLE.
TO GET WHAT I- WHAT **YOU** WANT- WE NEED A WORLD WITHOUT HEROES.
AT LEAST THE ONES WE HAVE **NOW**. ISN'T THAT WHAT YOU WANTED?
MISSION ACCOMPLISHED
WHERE THE OLD PANTHEON FAILED...
WE SHALL SUCCEED.
THEIR SACRIFICE, AND THE SACRIFICE OF THEIR CHILDREN, WILL NOT BE IN VAIN.

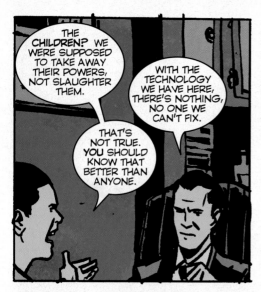

THE CHILDREN? WE WERE SUPPOSED TO TAKE AWAY THEIR POWERS, NOT SLAUGHTER THEM.

WITH THE TECHNOLOGY WE HAVE HERE, THERE'S NOTHING, NO ONE WE CAN'T FIX.

THAT'S NOT TRUE. YOU SHOULD KNOW THAT BETTER THAN ANYONE.

THIS PLAN WAS FLAWED FROM THE BEGINNING.

FLAWED?!

AND I THINK IT WOULD BE BETTER IF YOU ALL JUST FORGOT ABOUT IT.

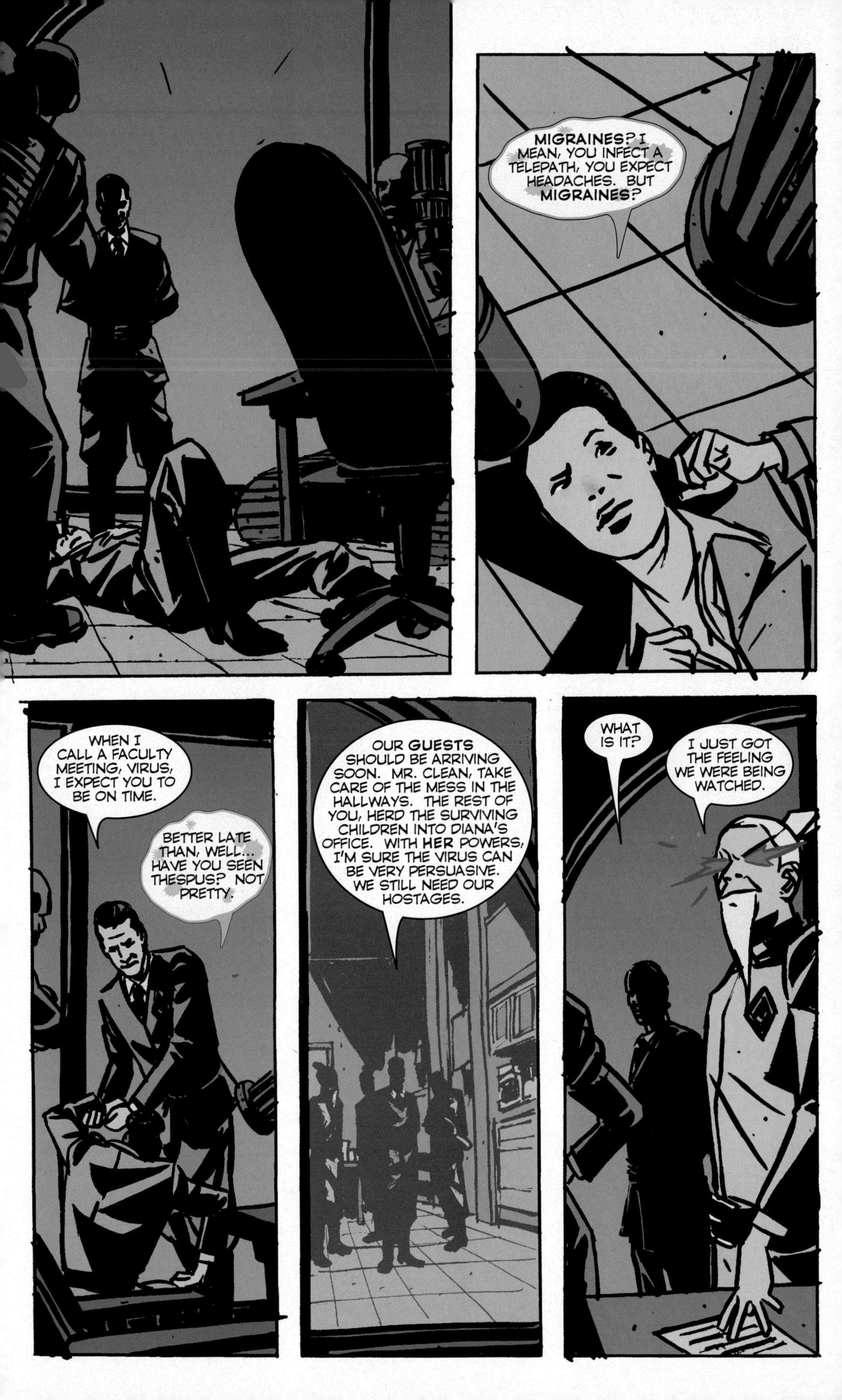
MIGRAINES? I MEAN, YOU INFECT A TELEPATH, YOU EXPECT HEADACHES. BUT MIGRAINES?
WHEN I CALL A FACULTY MEETING, VIRUS, I EXPECT YOU TO BE ON TIME.
BETTER LATE THAN, WELL... HAVE YOU SEEN THESPUS? NOT PRETTY.
OUR GUESTS SHOULD BE ARRIVING SOON. MR. CLEAN, TAKE CARE OF THE MESS IN THE HALLWAYS. THE REST OF YOU, HERD THE SURVIVING CHILDREN INTO DIANA'S OFFICE. WITH HER POWERS, I'M SURE THE VIRUS CAN BE VERY PERSUASIVE. WE STILL NEED OUR HOSTAGES.
WHAT IS IT?
I JUST GOT THE FEELING WE WERE BEING WATCHED.

HOW AM I SUPPOSED TO EAT? OR DRINK?

SINCE WHEN ARE YOU WORRIED ABOUT FOOD? YOU'RE ANOREXIC!

I AM NOT!

I'M GOING TO DIE!

SO AM I!

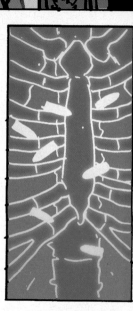

WORSE, WERE GOING TO DIE AS VIRGINS, BULLY.

I THOUGHT I WAS THE ONLY ONE IN THE SCHOOL. HIM TOO?

GREAT. FIRST I'M GOING TO DIE, THEN I'M GOING TO DIE OF EMBARASSMENT. LOOK AT ME. I USED TO BE PERFECT.

WAIT. WHEN YOU LOOK AT DESIRE, YOU SEE YOURSELF?

POSSIBLY EVEN GAY.

THAT'S SICK.

YOU NARCISSISTIC SON OF A - JONATHAN?

WHEN YOU LOOK AT DESIRE NOW YOU SEE JONATHAN?

THAT'S CHEATING. WE ARE SO BREAKING UP.

I DO NOT, AND EVEN IF I DID, IT WOULDN'T BE-

UH...I DIDN'T SAY ANYTHING GUYS.

YOU'RE ALL VIRGINS? THIS REALLY IS A HIGH SCHOOL FOR ABNORMAL TEENS.

THE PANTHEON

JONATHAN? YOU'RE ALIVE? BUT HOW? AND WHY CAN'T WE SEE YOU?

THE PANTHEON

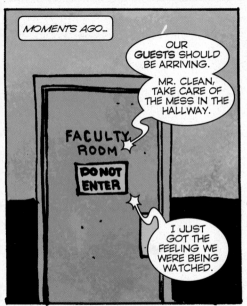

MOMENTS AGO...

OUR GUESTS SHOULD BE ARRIVING.

MR. CLEAN, TAKE CARE OF THE MESS IN THE HALLWAY.

FACULTY ROOM

DO NOT ENTER

I JUST GOT THE FEELING WE WERE BEING WATCHED.

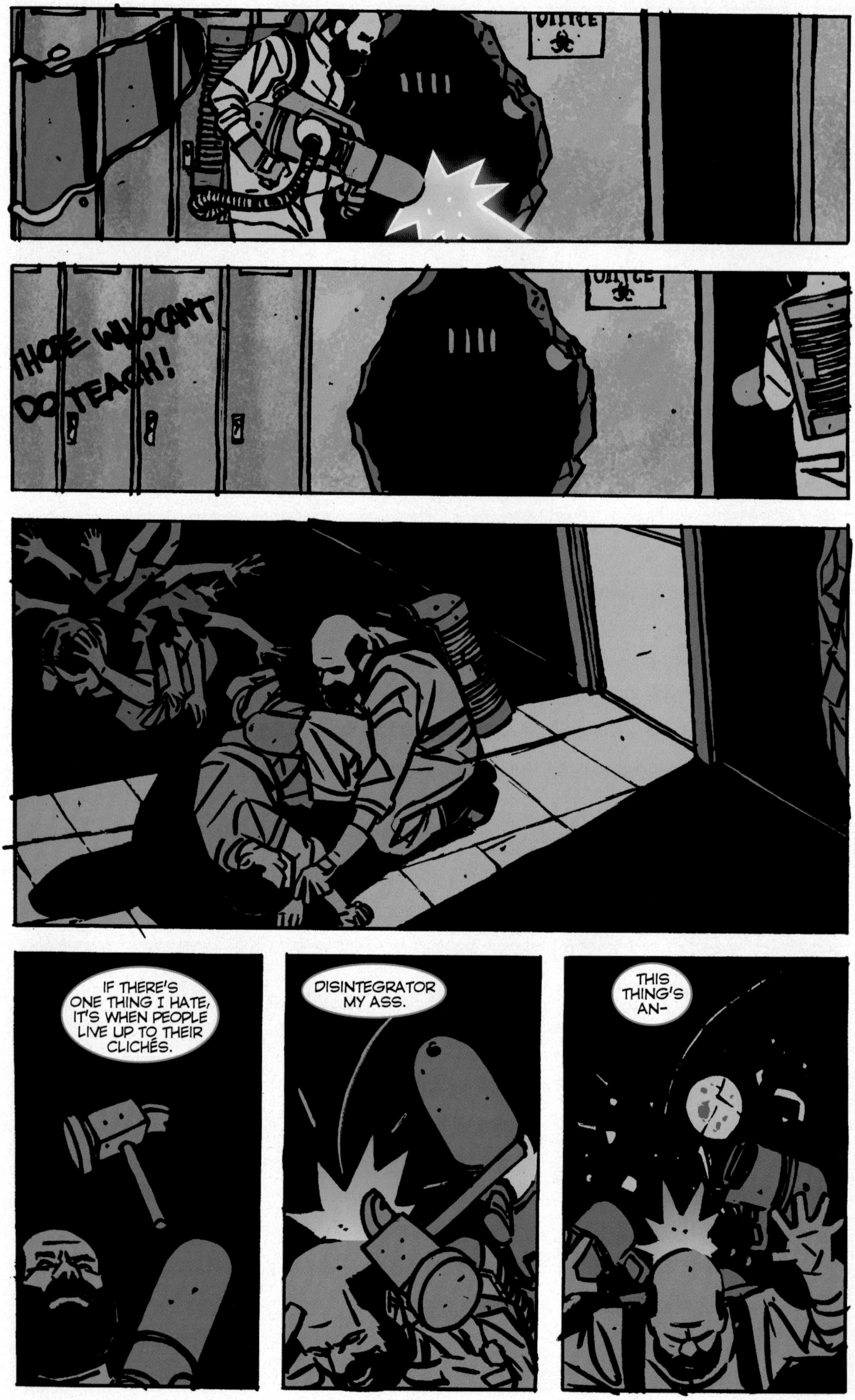
THOSE WHO CAN'T DO TEACH!
IF THERE'S ONE THING I HATE, IT'S WHEN PEOPLE LIVE UP TO THEIR CLICHÉS.
DISINTEGRATOR MY ASS.
THIS THING'S AN-

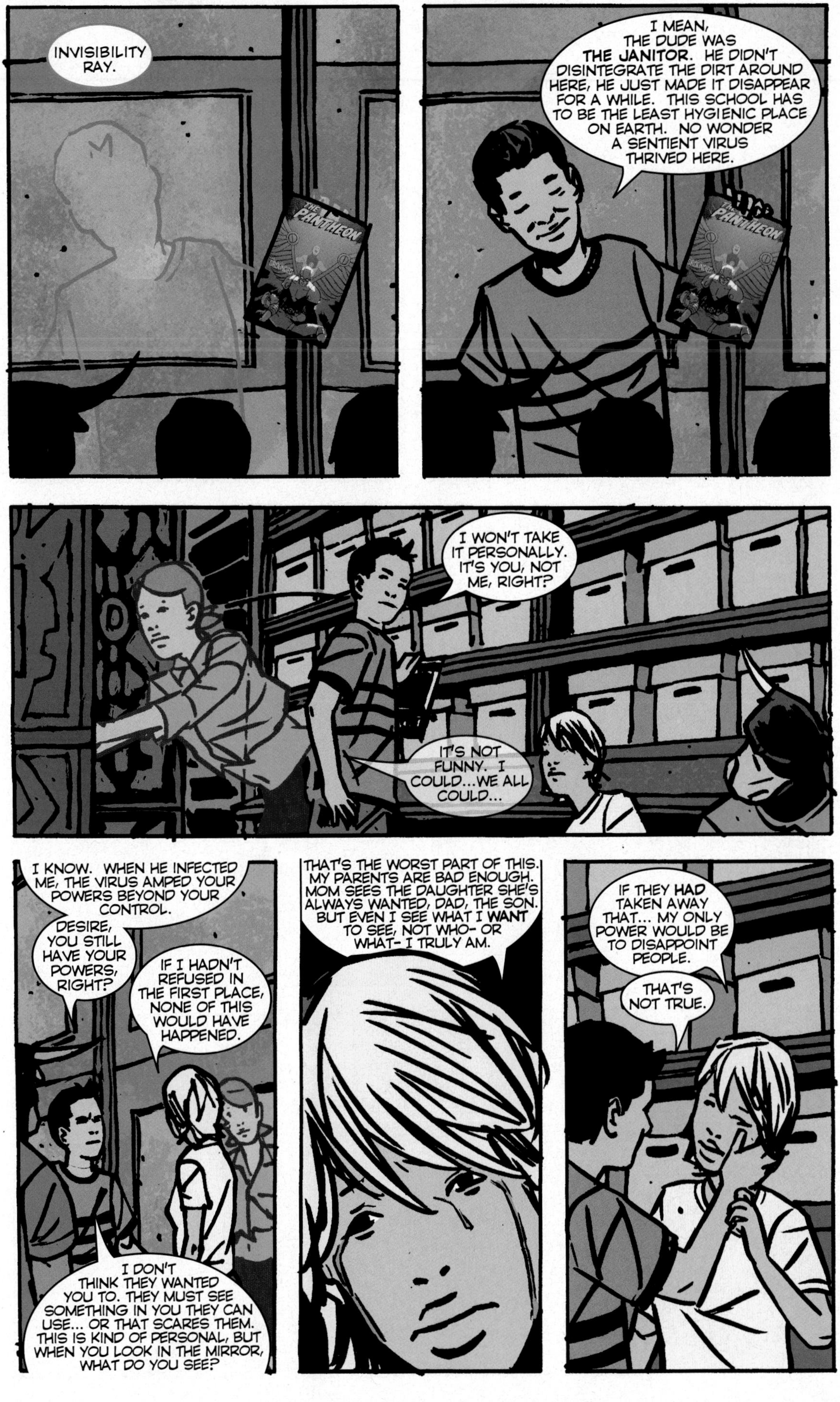
INVISIBILITY RAY.
I MEAN, THE DUDE WAS THE JANITOR. HE DIDN'T DISINTEGRATE THE DIRT AROUND HERE, HE JUST MADE IT DISAPPEAR FOR A WHILE. THIS SCHOOL HAS TO BE THE LEAST HYGIENIC PLACE ON EARTH. NO WONDER A SENTIENT VIRUS THRIVED HERE.
I WON'T TAKE IT PERSONALLY. IT'S YOU, NOT ME, RIGHT?
IT'S NOT FUNNY. I COULD...WE ALL COULD...
I KNOW. WHEN HE INFECTED ME, THE VIRUS AMPED YOUR POWERS BEYOND YOUR CONTROL.
DESIRE, YOU STILL HAVE YOUR POWERS, RIGHT?
IF I HADN'T REFUSED IN THE FIRST PLACE, NONE OF THIS WOULD HAVE HAPPENED.
I DON'T THINK THEY WANTED YOU TO. THEY MUST SEE SOMETHING IN YOU THEY CAN USE... OR THAT SCARES THEM. THIS IS KIND OF PERSONAL, BUT WHEN YOU LOOK IN THE MIRROR, WHAT DO YOU SEE?
THAT'S THE WORST PART OF THIS. MY PARENTS ARE BAD ENOUGH. MOM SEES THE DAUGHTER SHE'S ALWAYS WANTED, DAD, THE SON. BUT EVEN I SEE WHAT I WANT TO SEE, NOT WHO- OR WHAT- I TRULY AM.
IF THEY HAD TAKEN AWAY THAT... MY ONLY POWER WOULD BE TO DISAPPOINT PEOPLE.
THAT'S NOT TRUE.

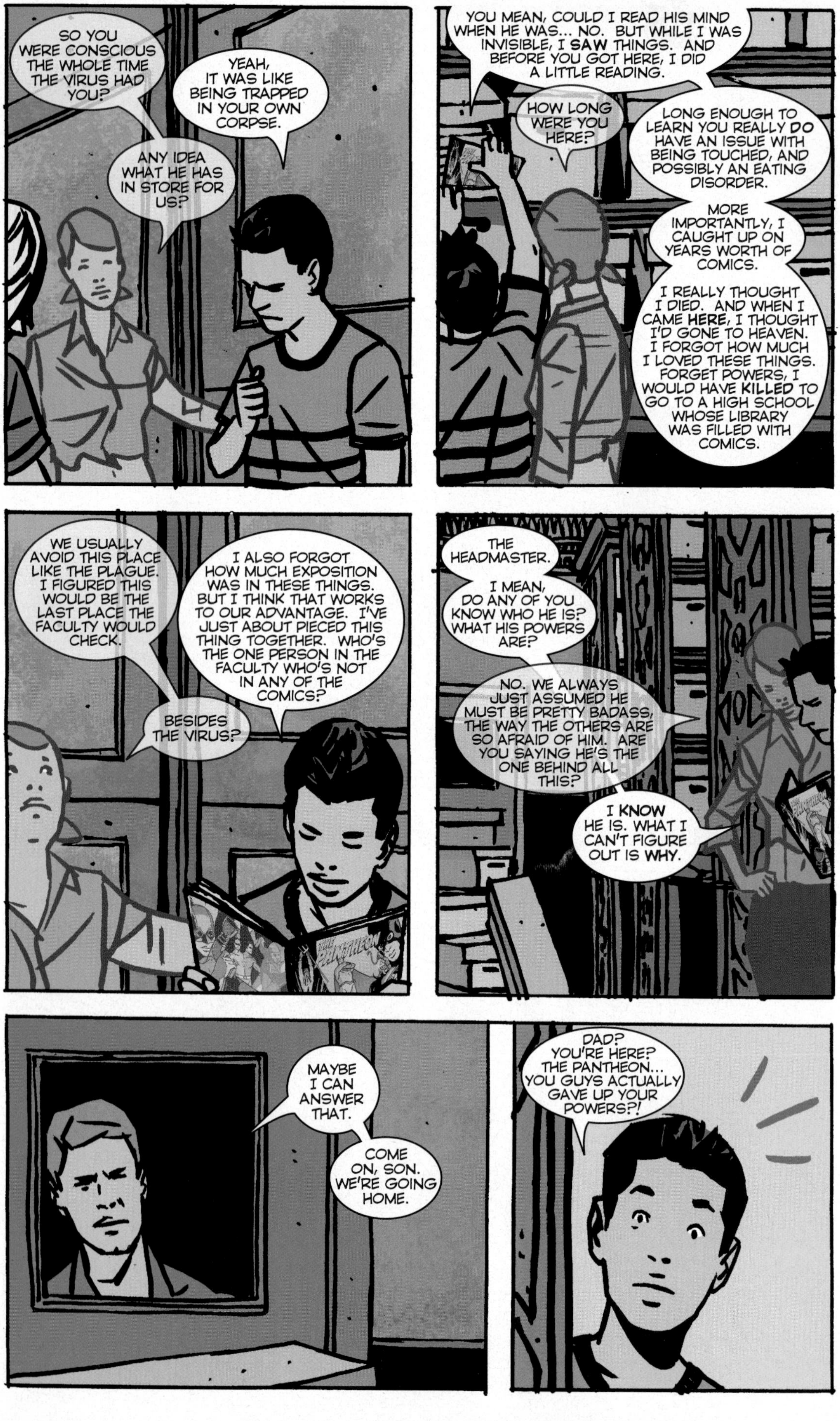

SO YOU WERE CONSCIOUS THE WHOLE TIME THE VIRUS HAD YOU?
YEAH, IT WAS LIKE BEING TRAPPED IN YOUR OWN CORPSE.
ANY IDEA WHAT HE HAS IN STORE FOR US?
YOU MEAN, COULD I READ HIS MIND WHEN HE WAS... NO. BUT WHILE I WAS INVISIBLE, I SAW THINGS. AND BEFORE YOU GOT HERE, I DID A LITTLE READING.
HOW LONG WERE YOU HERE?
LONG ENOUGH TO LEARN YOU REALLY DO HAVE AN ISSUE WITH BEING TOUCHED, AND POSSIBLY AN EATING DISORDER.
MORE IMPORTANTLY, I CAUGHT UP ON YEARS WORTH OF COMICS.
I REALLY THOUGHT I DIED. AND WHEN I CAME HERE, I THOUGHT I'D GONE TO HEAVEN. I FORGOT HOW MUCH I LOVED THESE THINGS. FORGET POWERS, I WOULD HAVE KILLED TO GO TO A HIGH SCHOOL WHOSE LIBRARY WAS FILLED WITH COMICS.
WE USUALLY AVOID THIS PLACE LIKE THE PLAGUE. I FIGURED THIS WOULD BE THE LAST PLACE THE FACULTY WOULD CHECK.
I ALSO FORGOT HOW MUCH EXPOSITION WAS IN THESE THINGS. BUT I THINK THAT WORKS TO OUR ADVANTAGE. I'VE JUST ABOUT PIECED THIS THING TOGETHER. WHO'S THE ONE PERSON IN THE FACULTY WHO'S NOT IN ANY OF THE COMICS?
BESIDES THE VIRUS?
THE PANTHEON
THE HEADMASTER.
I MEAN, DO ANY OF YOU KNOW WHO HE IS? WHAT HIS POWERS ARE?
NO. WE ALWAYS JUST ASSUMED HE MUST BE PRETTY BADASS, THE WAY THE OTHERS ARE SO AFRAID OF HIM. ARE YOU SAYING HE'S THE ONE BEHIND ALL THIS?
I KNOW HE IS. WHAT I CAN'T FIGURE OUT IS WHY.
MAYBE I CAN ANSWER THAT.
COME ON, SON. WE'RE GOING HOME.
DAD? YOU'RE HERE? THE PANTHEON... YOU GUYS ACTUALLY GAVE UP YOUR POWERS?!

EARLIER...

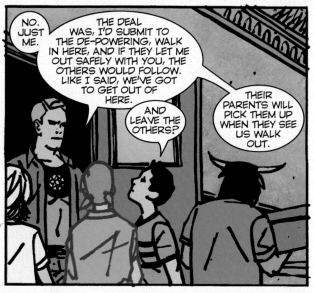

NO. JUST ME.

THE DEAL WAS, I'D SUBMIT TO THE DE-POWERING, WALK IN HERE, AND IF THEY LET ME OUT SAFELY WITH YOU, THE OTHERS WOULD FOLLOW. LIKE I SAID, WE'VE GOT TO GET OUT OF HERE.

AND LEAVE THE OTHERS?

THEIR PARENTS WILL PICK THEM UP WHEN THEY SEE US WALK OUT.

AND WHAT IF THEY DON'T?

WE'LL HAVE CALLED THEIR BLUFF.

WHAT IF THEY LET US OUT, BUT NOT THE OTHERS?

THEN AT LEAST WE'RE SAFE.

EACH PARENT MADE THEIR CHOICE IN THIS. TOO OFTEN I CHOSE MY JOB OVER YOU, AND COME CLOSE TO LOSING YOU ONE WAY OR THE OTHER. I'M NOT GOING TO LET THAT HAPPEN AGAIN. LET'S GO.

HOW CAN YOU LET THEM WIN?

YOU SAW FOR YOURSELF, THE FACULTY DON'T WANT TO RULE THE WORLD, THEY JUST WANT TO REPLACE US.

THE WAY WE'VE BEEN CONDUCTING OURSELVES, SLEEPING WITH EACH OTHER'S SPOUSES, KILLING SUPERVILLAINS... MAYBE IT IS TIME FOR NEW BLOOD.

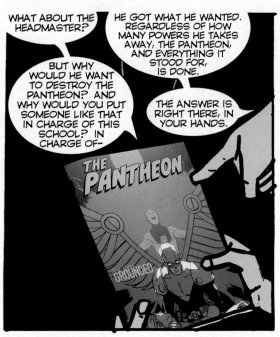

WHAT ABOUT THE HEADMASTER?

HE GOT WHAT HE WANTED. REGARDLESS OF HOW MANY POWERS HE TAKES AWAY, THE PANTHEON, AND EVERYTHING IT STOOD FOR, IS DONE.

BUT WHY WOULD HE WANT TO DESTROY THE PANTHEON? AND WHY WOULD YOU PUT SOMEONE LIKE THAT IN CHARGE OF THIS SCHOOL? IN CHARGE OF—

THE ANSWER IS RIGHT THERE, IN YOUR HANDS.

THE PANTHEON

GROUNDED

SO YOU'VE FOUND ME OUT!

IT MATTER'S NOT, YOU'LL NEVER USE YOUR POWERS AGAINST MAXIMILLIAN BONDS, A DEFENSELESS CIVILIAN.

NOW LET ME GET BACK TO CONQUERING THE WORLD.

YOU GUYS ARE GOING TO LET HIM GO? JUST LIKE THAT?

WE DON'T HAVE ANY CHOICE. THAT'S WHAT SEPARATES PEOPLE LIKE HIM FROM PEOPLE LIKE US.

THAT'S RIGHT. PEOPLE LIKE YOU. NOT ME.

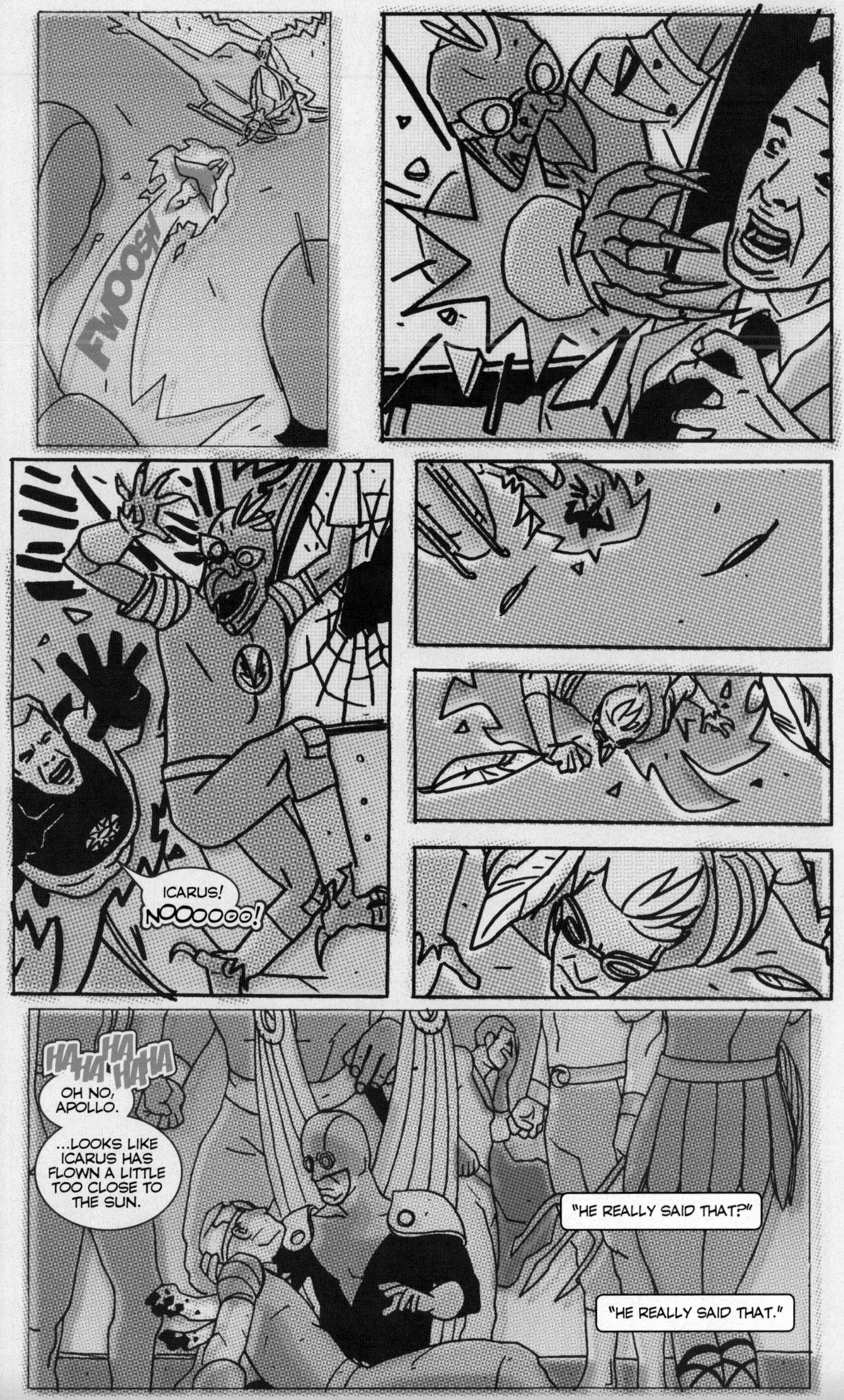
FWOOSH
ICARUS! NOOOOOO!
HAHAHAHAHA
OH NO, APOLLO.
...LOOKS LIKE ICARUS HAS FLOWN A LITTLE TOO CLOSE TO THE SUN.
"HE REALLY SAID THAT?"
"HE REALLY SAID THAT."

ding dong

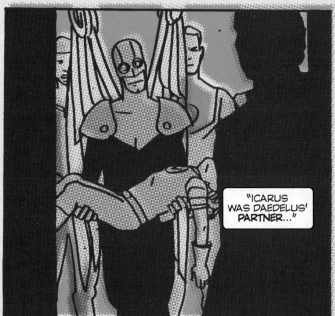

"ICARUS WAS DAEDELUS' PARTNER..."

"BUT HE WAS THE HEADMASTER'S SON."

I'VE BEEN CARRYING THIS AROUND WITH ME... THE TRUTH IS, I DESERVED TO HAVE MY POWERS STRIPPED AWAY A LONG TIME AGO. BUT THE REST OF YOU...THAT'S WHY WE HAVE TO GET OUT OF HERE. NOW.

I UNDERSTAND WHY YOU DID WHAT YOU DID. YOU DIDN'T HAVE A CHOICE.

BUT I DO NOW. THIS IS NOT ABOUT SOME CODE OF CONDUCT, THIS IS ABOUT SAVING LIVES. AND REALIZING WHICH ONES ARE WORTH SAVING.

BUT WHAT I DON'T UNDERSTAND IS, WHY PUT SOMEONE LIKE THAT IN CHARGE OF THIS SCHOOL?

YOUR MOTHER. SHE OFFERED TO—

MAKE YOU FORGET.

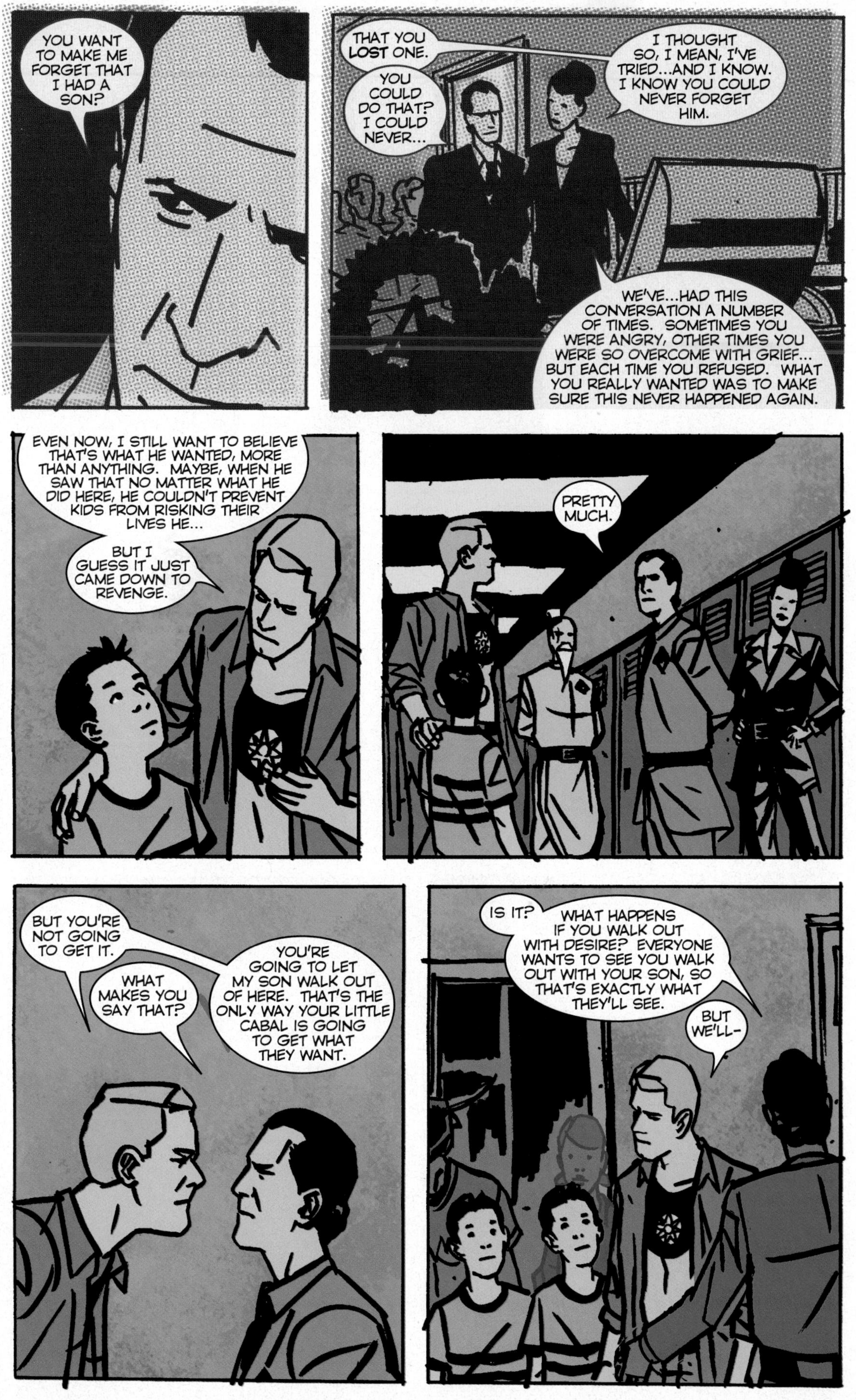
YOU WANT TO MAKE ME FORGET THAT I HAD A SON?
THAT YOU **LOST** ONE.
YOU COULD DO THAT? I COULD NEVER...
I THOUGHT SO, I MEAN, I'VE TRIED...AND I KNOW. I KNOW YOU COULD NEVER FORGET HIM.
WE'VE...HAD THIS CONVERSATION A NUMBER OF TIMES. SOMETIMES YOU WERE ANGRY, OTHER TIMES YOU WERE SO OVERCOME WITH GRIEF... BUT EACH TIME YOU REFUSED. WHAT YOU REALLY WANTED WAS TO MAKE SURE THIS NEVER HAPPENED AGAIN.
EVEN NOW, I STILL WANT TO BELIEVE THAT'S WHAT HE WANTED, MORE THAN ANYTHING. MAYBE, WHEN HE SAW THAT NO MATTER WHAT HE DID HERE, HE COULDN'T PREVENT KIDS FROM RISKING THEIR LIVES HE...
BUT I GUESS IT JUST CAME DOWN TO REVENGE.
PRETTY MUCH.
BUT YOU'RE NOT GOING TO GET IT.
WHAT MAKES YOU SAY THAT?
YOU'RE GOING TO LET MY SON WALK OUT OF HERE. THAT'S THE ONLY WAY YOUR LITTLE CABAL IS GOING TO GET WHAT THEY WANT.
IS IT?
WHAT HAPPENS IF YOU WALK OUT WITH DESIRE? EVERYONE WANTS TO SEE YOU WALK OUT WITH YOUR SON, SO THAT'S EXACTLY WHAT THEY'LL SEE.
BUT WE'LL-

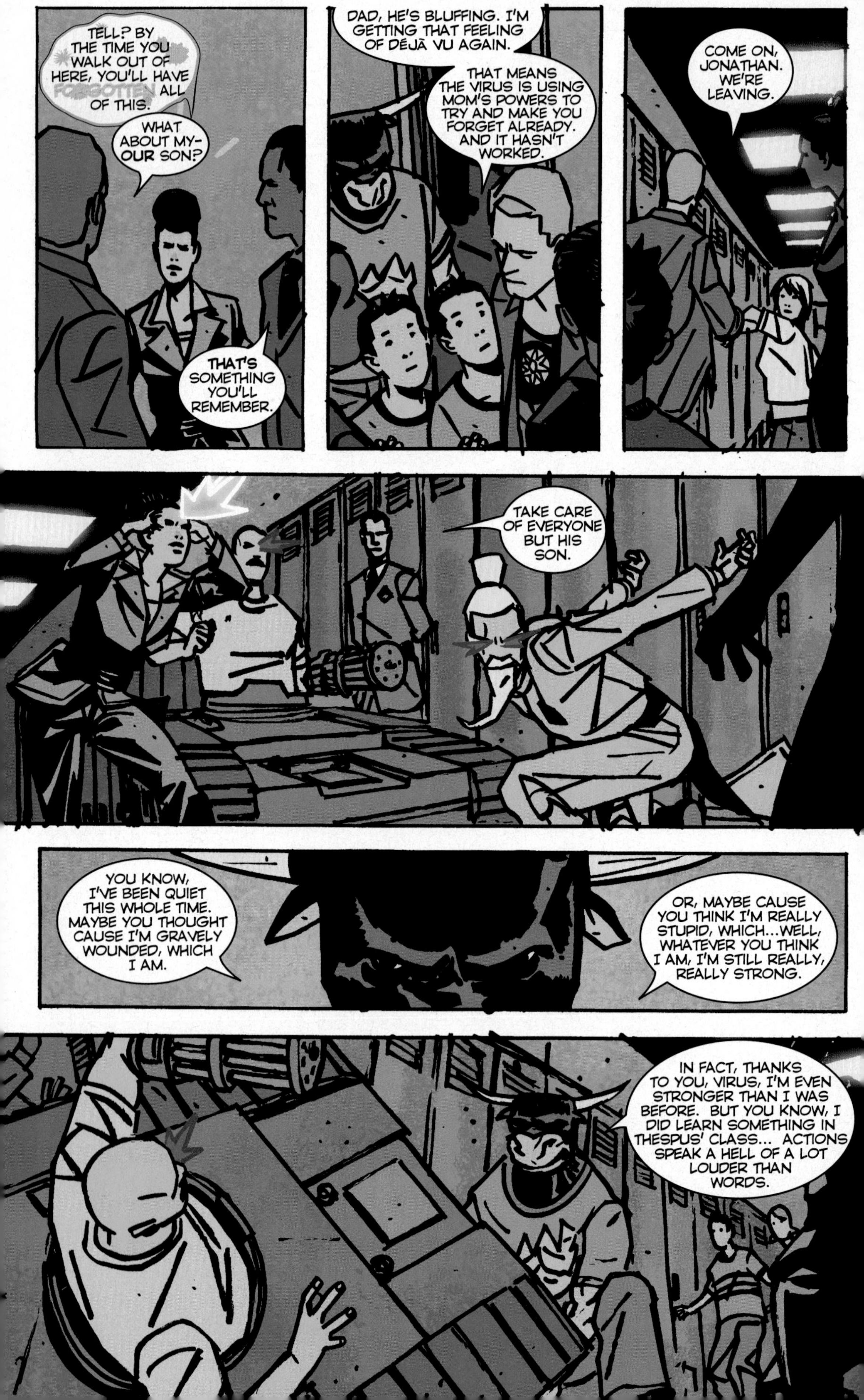
TELL? BY THE TIME YOU WALK OUT OF HERE, YOU'LL HAVE FORGOTTEN ALL OF THIS.
WHAT ABOUT MY- OUR SON?
THAT'S SOMETHING YOU'LL REMEMBER.
DAD, HE'S BLUFFING. I'M GETTING THAT FEELING OF DÉJÀ VU AGAIN.
THAT MEANS THE VIRUS IS USING MOM'S POWERS TO TRY AND MAKE YOU FORGET ALREADY. AND IT HASN'T WORKED.
COME ON, JONATHAN. WE'RE LEAVING.
TAKE CARE OF EVERYONE BUT HIS SON.
YOU KNOW, I'VE BEEN QUIET THIS WHOLE TIME. MAYBE YOU THOUGHT CAUSE I'M GRAVELY WOUNDED, WHICH I AM.
OR, MAYBE CAUSE YOU THINK I'M REALLY STUPID, WHICH...WELL, WHATEVER YOU THINK I AM, I'M STILL REALLY, REALLY STRONG.
IN FACT, THANKS TO YOU, VIRUS, I'M EVEN STRONGER THAN I WAS BEFORE. BUT YOU KNOW, I DID LEARN SOMETHING IN THESPUS' CLASS... ACTIONS SPEAK A HELL OF A LOT LOUDER THAN WORDS.

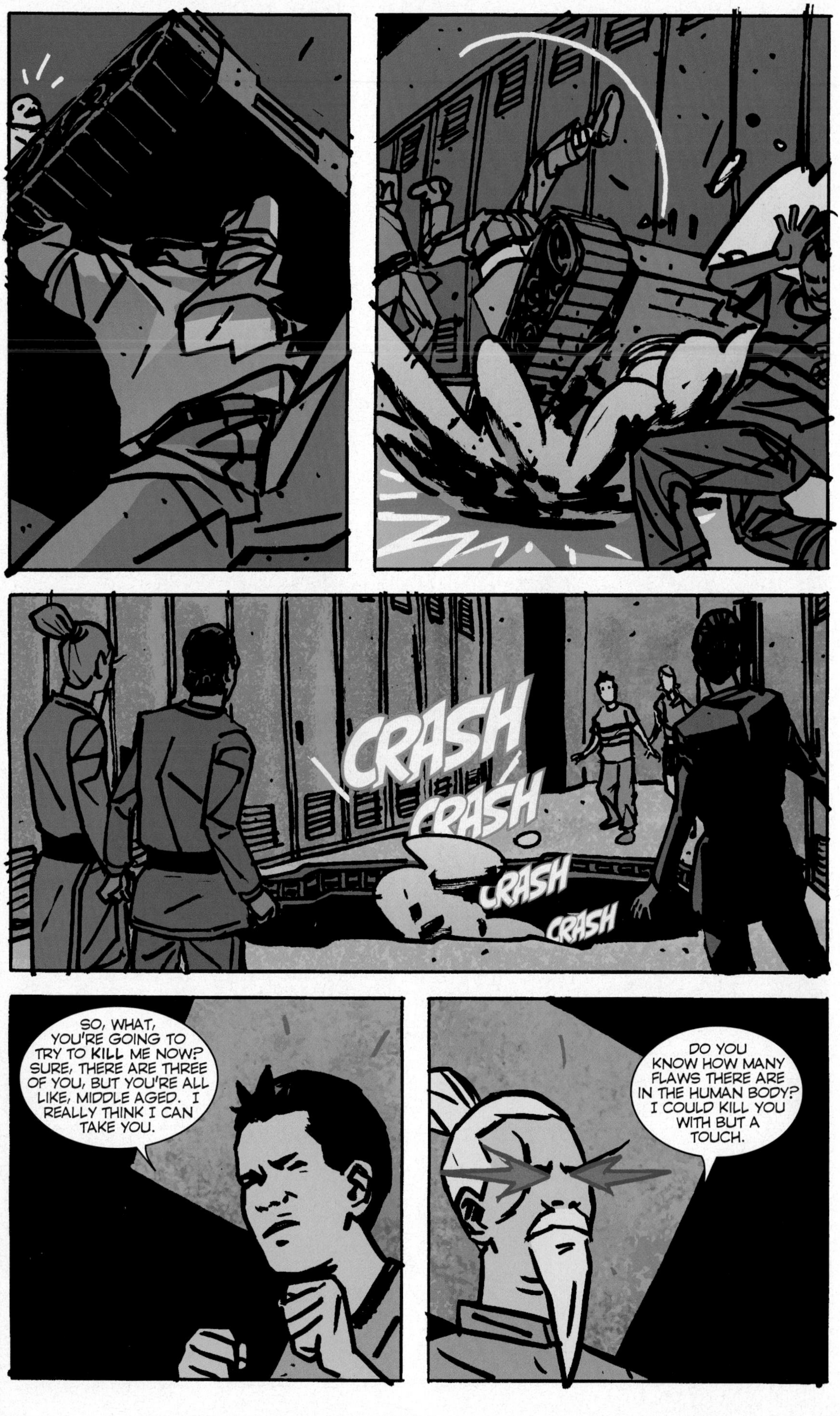
CRASH
CRASH
CRASH
CRASH
SO, WHAT, YOU'RE GOING TO TRY TO **KILL** ME NOW? SURE, THERE ARE THREE OF YOU, BUT YOU'RE ALL LIKE, MIDDLE AGED. I REALLY THINK I CAN TAKE YOU.
DO YOU KNOW HOW MANY FLAWS THERE ARE IN THE HUMAN BODY? I COULD KILL YOU WITH BUT A TOUCH.

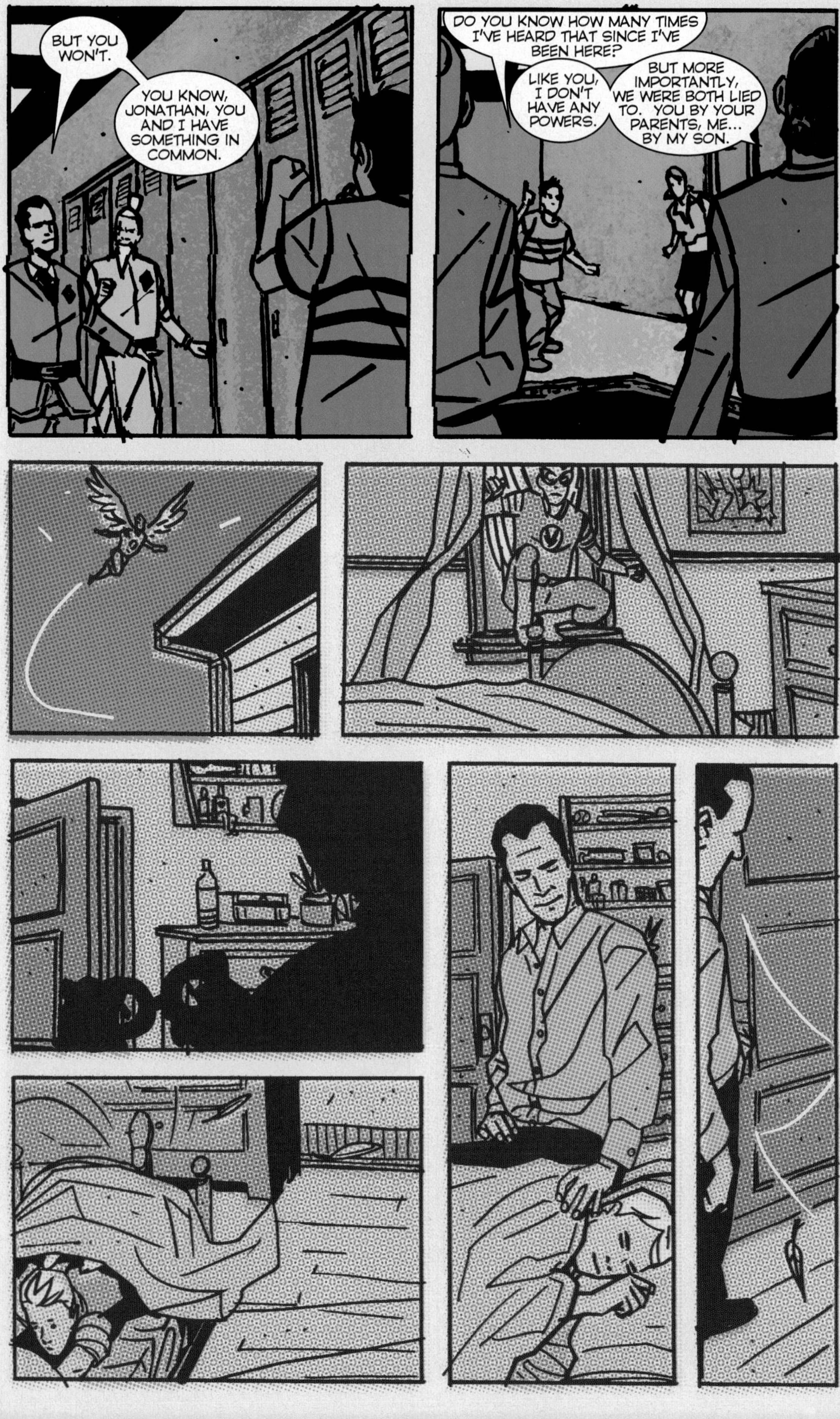
BUT YOU WON'T.
YOU KNOW, JONATHAN, YOU AND I HAVE SOMETHING IN COMMON.
DO YOU KNOW HOW MANY TIMES I'VE HEARD THAT SINCE I'VE BEEN HERE?
LIKE YOU, I DON'T HAVE ANY POWERS.
BUT MORE IMPORTANTLY, WE WERE BOTH LIED TO. YOU BY YOUR PARENTS, ME... BY MY SON.

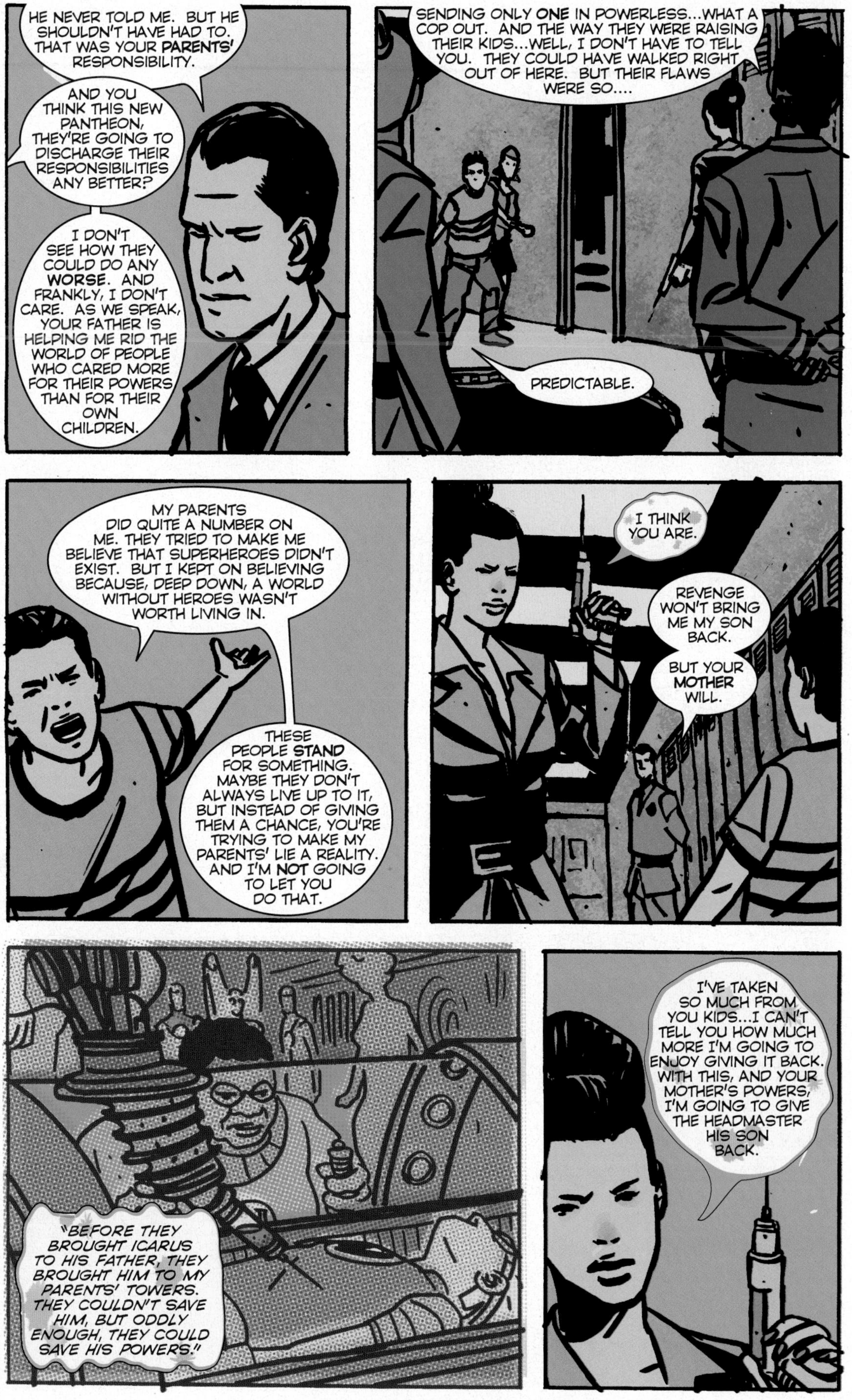
HE NEVER TOLD ME. BUT HE SHOULDN'T HAVE HAD TO. THAT WAS YOUR **PARENTS'** RESPONSIBILITY.
AND YOU THINK THIS NEW PANTHEON, THEY'RE GOING TO DISCHARGE THEIR RESPONSIBILITIES ANY BETTER?
I DON'T SEE HOW THEY COULD DO ANY **WORSE**. AND FRANKLY, I DON'T CARE. AS WE SPEAK, YOUR FATHER IS HELPING ME RID THE WORLD OF PEOPLE WHO CARED MORE FOR THEIR POWERS THAN FOR THEIR OWN CHILDREN.
SENDING ONLY **ONE** IN POWERLESS...WHAT A COP OUT. AND THE WAY THEY WERE RAISING THEIR KIDS...WELL, I DON'T HAVE TO TELL YOU. THEY COULD HAVE WALKED RIGHT OUT OF HERE. BUT THEIR FLAWS WERE SO....
PREDICTABLE.
MY PARENTS DID QUITE A NUMBER ON ME. THEY TRIED TO MAKE ME BELIEVE THAT SUPERHEROES DIDN'T EXIST. BUT I KEPT ON BELIEVING BECAUSE, DEEP DOWN, A WORLD WITHOUT HEROES WASN'T WORTH LIVING IN.
THESE PEOPLE **STAND** FOR SOMETHING. MAYBE THEY DON'T ALWAYS LIVE UP TO IT, BUT INSTEAD OF GIVING THEM A CHANCE, YOU'RE TRYING TO MAKE MY PARENTS' LIE A REALITY. AND I'M **NOT** GOING TO LET YOU DO THAT.
I THINK YOU ARE.
REVENGE WON'T BRING ME MY SON BACK.
BUT YOUR **MOTHER** WILL.
"BEFORE THEY BROUGHT ICARUS TO HIS FATHER, THEY BROUGHT HIM TO MY PARENTS' TOWERS. THEY COULDN'T SAVE HIM, BUT ODDLY ENOUGH, THEY COULD SAVE HIS POWERS."
I'VE TAKEN SO MUCH FROM YOU KIDS...I CAN'T TELL YOU HOW MUCH MORE I'M GOING TO ENJOY GIVING IT BACK. WITH THIS, AND YOUR MOTHER'S POWERS, I'M GOING TO GIVE THE HEADMASTER HIS SON BACK.

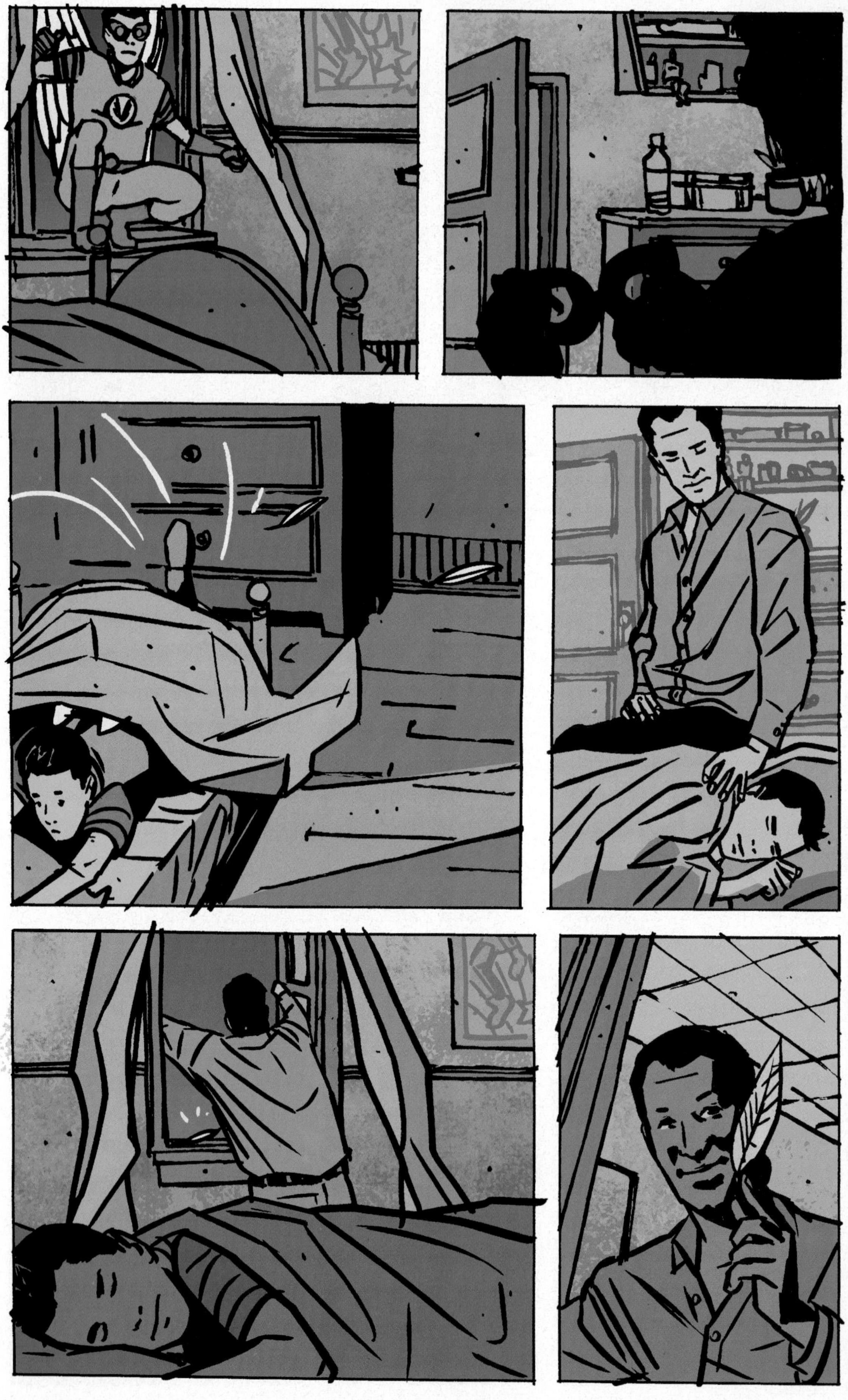

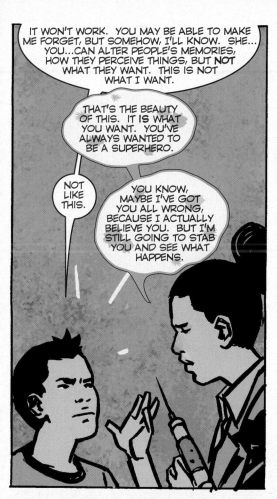

IT WON'T WORK. YOU MAY BE ABLE TO MAKE ME FORGET, BUT SOMEHOW, I'LL KNOW. SHE... YOU...CAN ALTER PEOPLE'S MEMORIES, HOW THEY PERCEIVE THINGS, BUT **NOT** WHAT THEY WANT. THIS IS NOT WHAT I WANT.

THAT'S THE BEAUTY OF THIS. IT IS WHAT YOU WANT. YOU'VE ALWAYS WANTED TO BE A SUPERHERO.

NOT LIKE THIS.

YOU KNOW, MAYBE I'VE GOT YOU ALL WRONG, BECAUSE I ACTUALLY BELIEVE YOU. BUT I'M STILL GOING TO STAB YOU AND SEE WHAT HAPPENS.

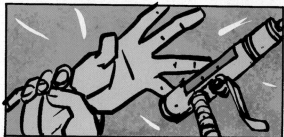

OH, FOR GOD'S SAKE. I'M JUST GOING TO KILL THE BOY.

VIRUS, USE DIANA'S POWERS AND MAKE THE HEADMASTER BELIEVE THAT'S WHAT HE WANTED ALL ALONG.

SURE. I CAN DO THAT.

NOOOOOO!

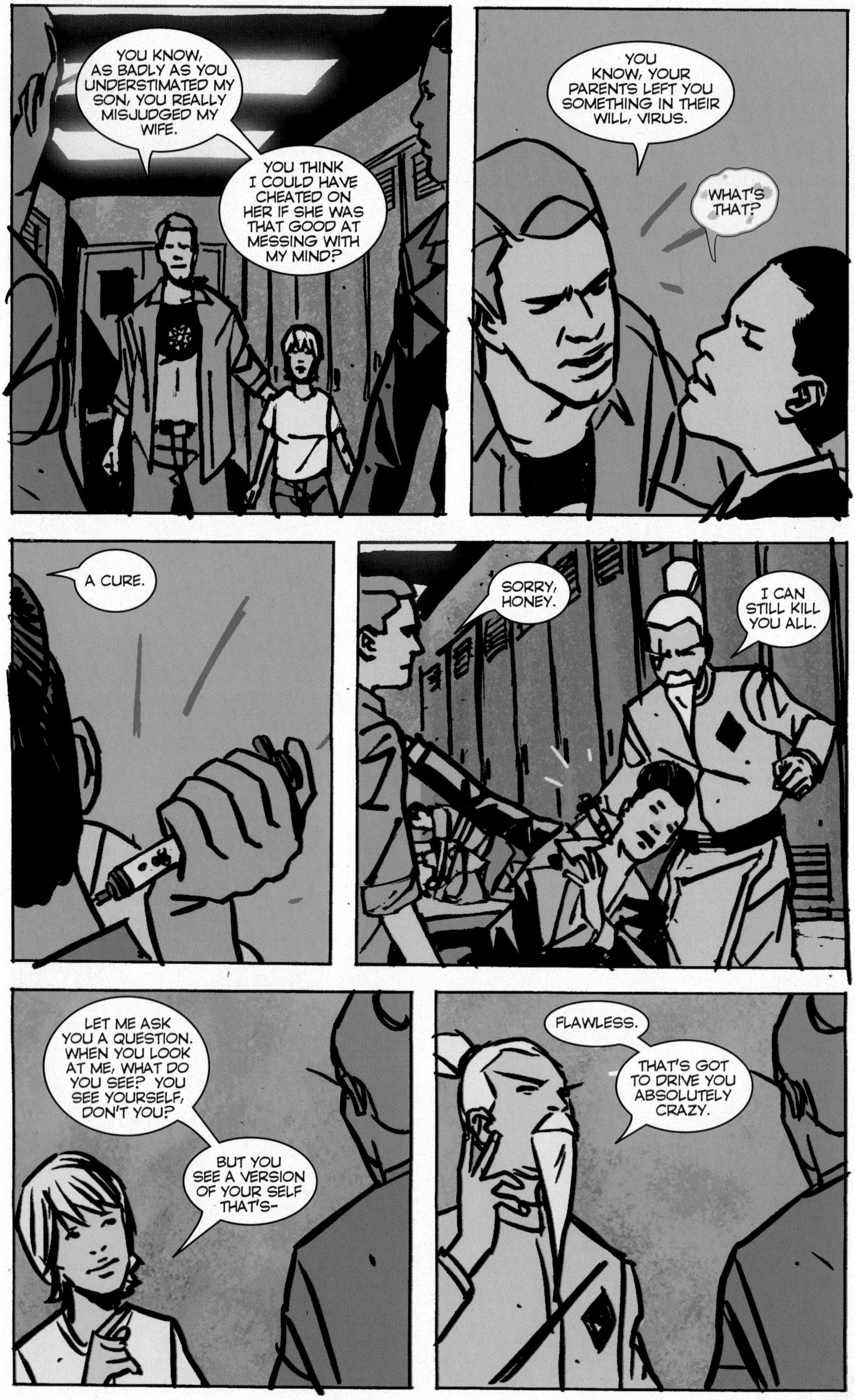
YOU KNOW, AS BADLY AS YOU UNDERSTIMATED MY SON, YOU REALLY MISJUDGED MY WIFE.
YOU THINK I COULD HAVE CHEATED ON HER IF SHE WAS THAT GOOD AT MESSING WITH MY MIND?
YOU KNOW, YOUR PARENTS LEFT YOU SOMETHING IN THEIR WILL, VIRUS.
WHAT'S THAT?
A CURE.
SORRY, HONEY.
I CAN STILL KILL YOU ALL.
LET ME ASK YOU A QUESTION. WHEN YOU LOOK AT ME, WHAT DO YOU SEE? YOU SEE YOURSELF, DON'T YOU?
BUT YOU SEE A VERSION OF YOUR SELF THAT'S-
FLAWLESS.
THAT'S GOT TO DRIVE YOU ABSOLUTELY CRAZY.

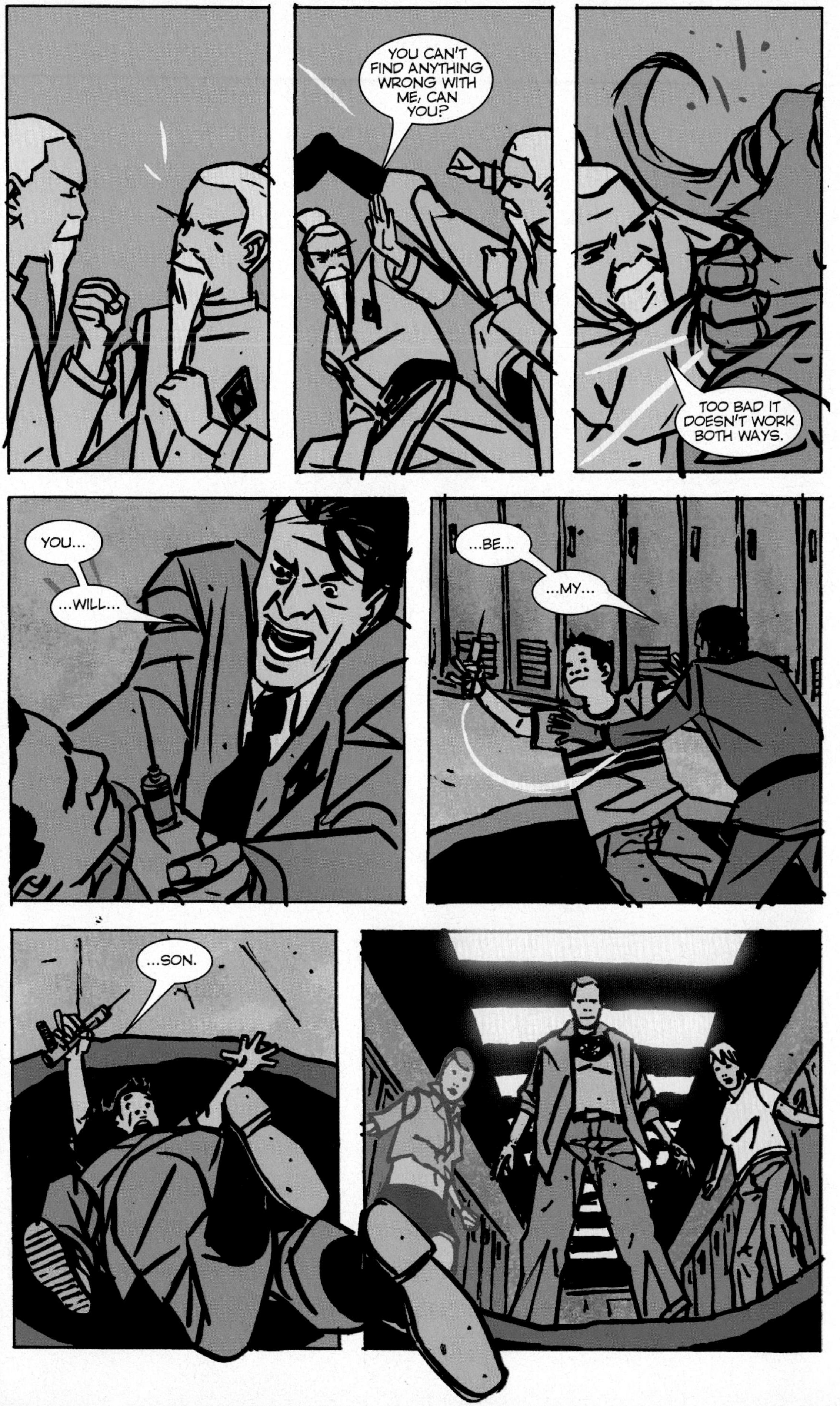
YOU CAN'T FIND ANYTHING WRONG WITH ME, CAN YOU?
TOO BAD IT DOESN'T WORK BOTH WAYS.
YOU...
...WILL...
...BE...
...MY...
...SON.

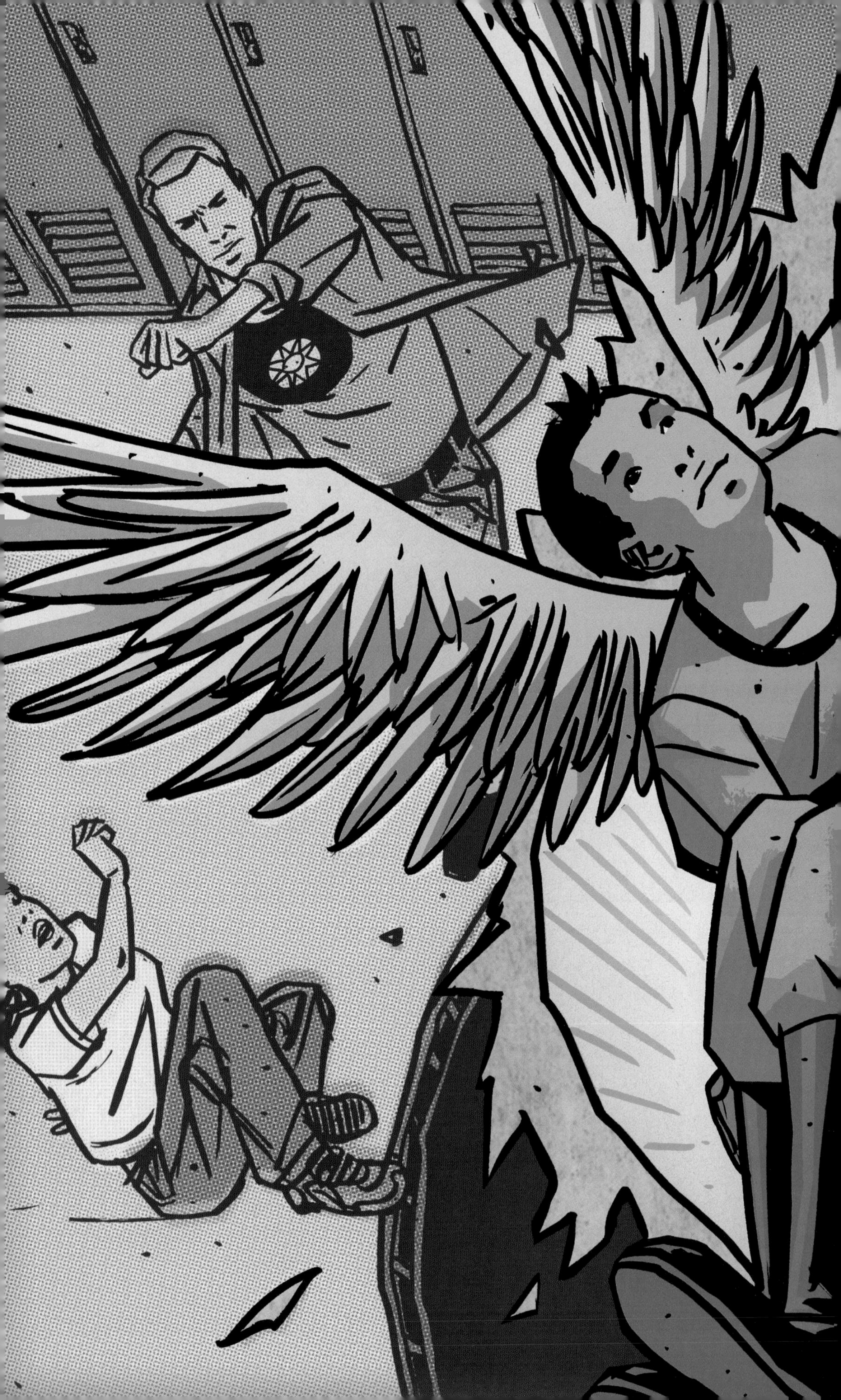

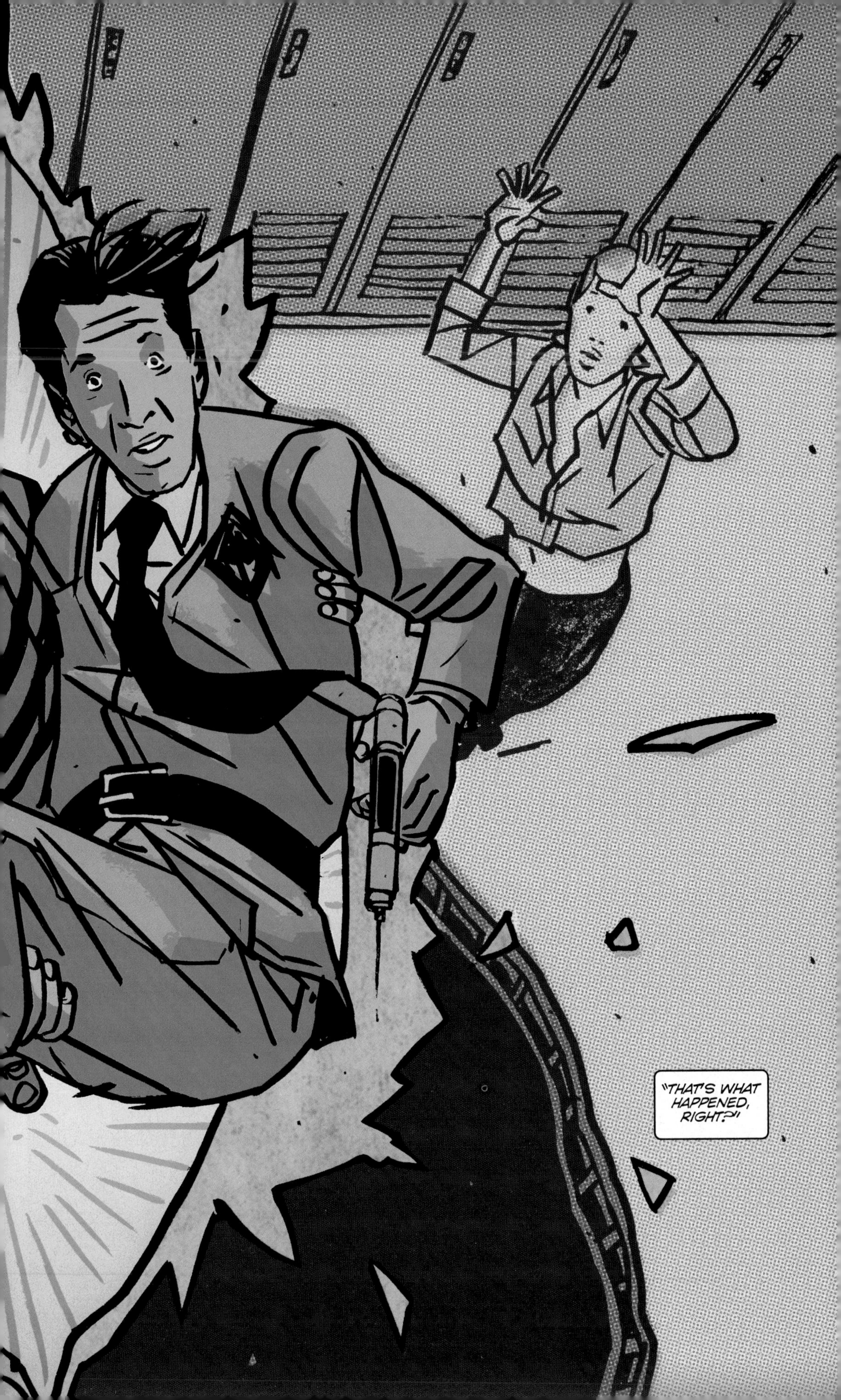
"THAT'S WHAT HAPPENED, RIGHT?"

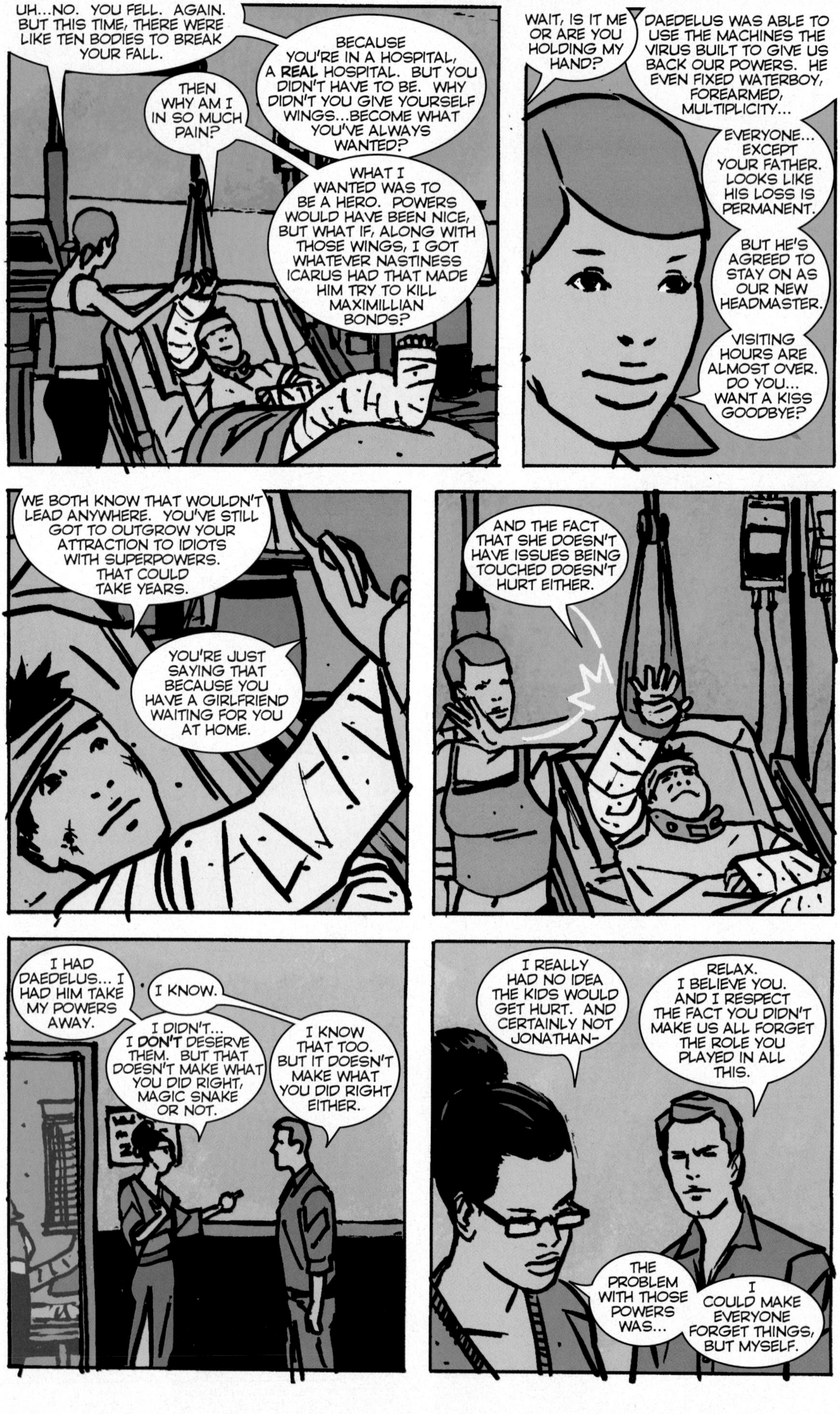
UH...NO. YOU FELL. AGAIN. BUT THIS TIME, THERE WERE LIKE TEN BODIES TO BREAK YOUR FALL.
THEN WHY AM I IN SO MUCH PAIN?
BECAUSE YOU'RE IN A HOSPITAL, A **REAL** HOSPITAL. BUT YOU DIDN'T HAVE TO BE. WHY DIDN'T YOU GIVE YOURSELF WINGS...BECOME WHAT YOU'VE ALWAYS WANTED?
WHAT I WANTED WAS TO BE A HERO. POWERS WOULD HAVE BEEN NICE, BUT WHAT IF, ALONG WITH THOSE WINGS, I GOT WHATEVER NASTINESS ICARUS HAD THAT MADE HIM TRY TO KILL MAXIMILLIAN BONDS?
WAIT, IS IT ME OR ARE YOU HOLDING MY HAND?
DAEDELUS WAS ABLE TO USE THE MACHINES THE VIRUS BUILT TO GIVE US BACK OUR POWERS. HE EVEN FIXED WATERBOY, FOREARMED, MULTIPLICITY...
EVERYONE... EXCEPT YOUR FATHER. LOOKS LIKE HIS LOSS IS PERMANENT.
BUT HE'S AGREED TO STAY ON AS OUR NEW HEADMASTER.
VISITING HOURS ARE ALMOST OVER. DO YOU... WANT A KISS GOODBYE?
WE BOTH KNOW THAT WOULDN'T LEAD ANYWHERE. YOU'VE STILL GOT TO OUTGROW YOUR ATTRACTION TO IDIOTS WITH SUPERPOWERS. THAT COULD TAKE YEARS.
YOU'RE JUST SAYING THAT BECAUSE YOU HAVE A GIRLFRIEND WAITING FOR YOU AT HOME.
AND THE FACT THAT SHE DOESN'T HAVE ISSUES BEING TOUCHED DOESN'T HURT EITHER.
I HAD DAEDELUS... I HAD HIM TAKE MY POWERS AWAY.
I KNOW.
I DIDN'T... I **DON'T** DESERVE THEM. BUT THAT DOESN'T MAKE WHAT YOU DID RIGHT, MAGIC SNAKE OR NOT.
I KNOW THAT TOO. BUT IT DOESN'T MAKE WHAT YOU DID RIGHT EITHER.
I REALLY HAD NO IDEA THE KIDS WOULD GET HURT. AND CERTAINLY NOT JONATHAN-
RELAX. I BELIEVE YOU. AND I RESPECT THE FACT YOU DIDN'T MAKE US ALL FORGET THE ROLE YOU PLAYED IN ALL THIS.
THE PROBLEM WITH THOSE POWERS WAS...
I COULD MAKE EVERYONE FORGET THINGS, BUT MYSELF.

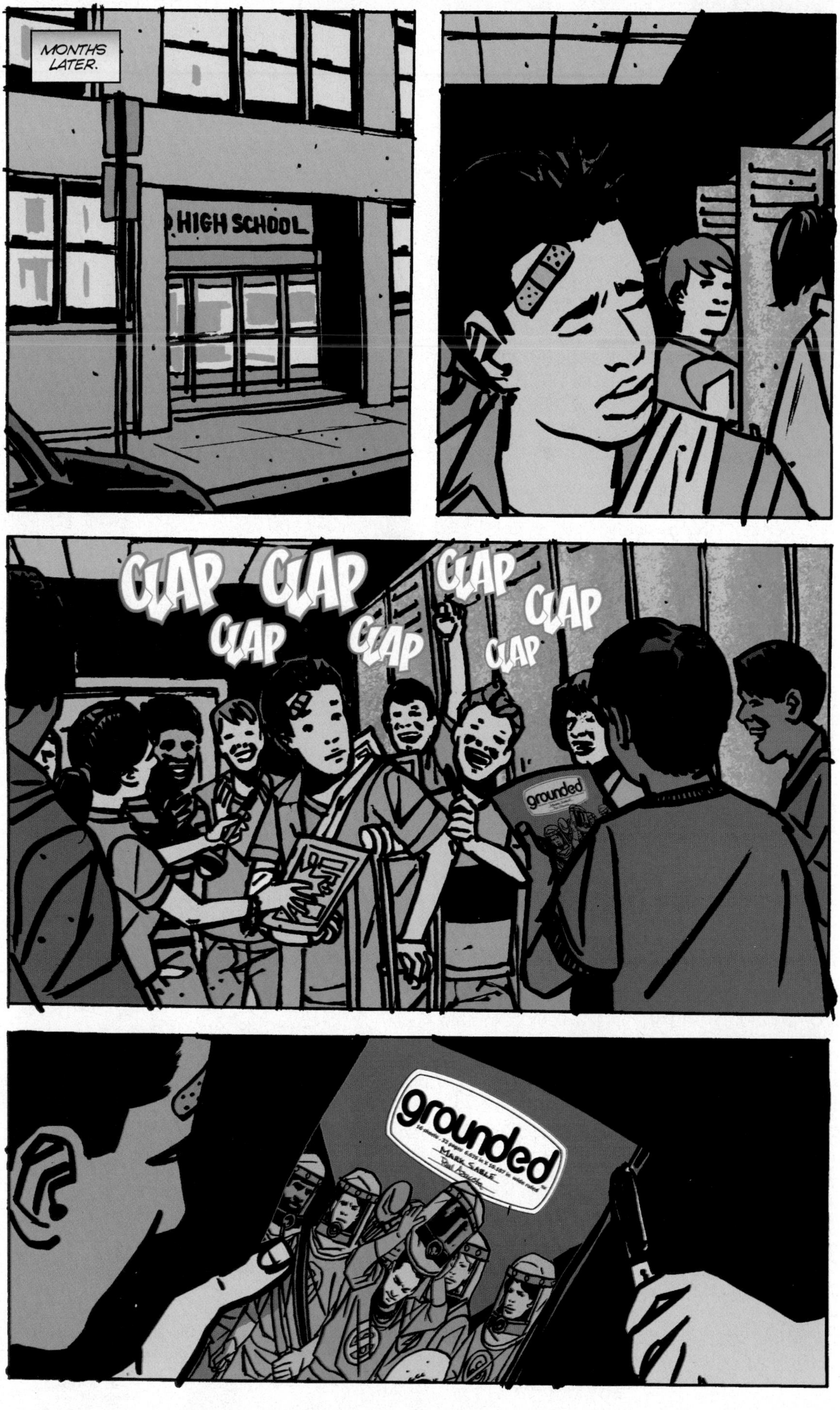
MONTHS LATER.
HIGH SCHOOL
CLAP
CLAP
CLAP
CLAP
CLAP
CLAP
CLAP
grounded
grounded
MARK SABLE

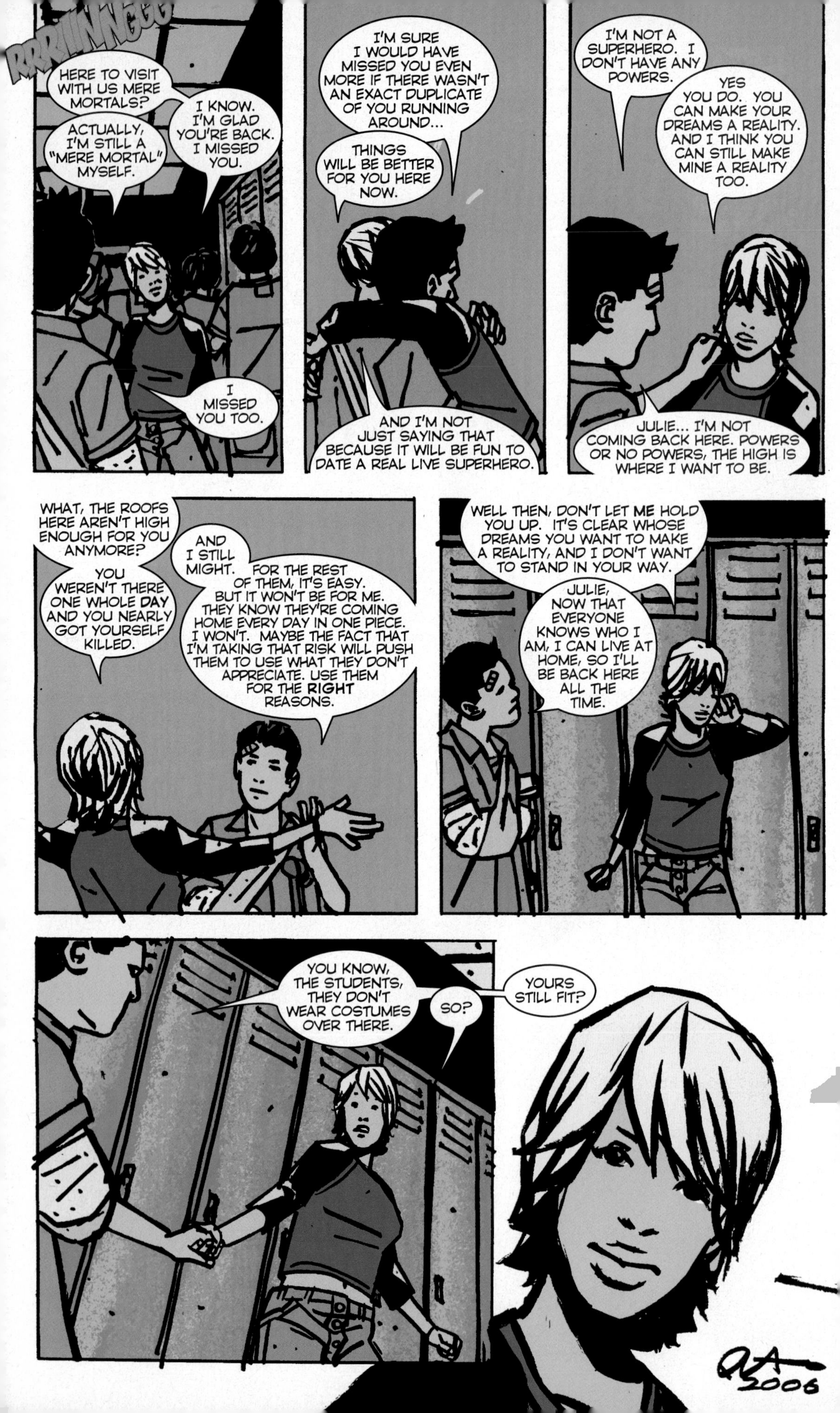
RRRIIINNGGG
HERE TO VISIT WITH US MERE MORTALS?
ACTUALLY, I'M STILL A "MERE MORTAL" MYSELF.
I KNOW. I'M GLAD YOU'RE BACK. I MISSED YOU.
I MISSED YOU TOO.
I'M SURE I WOULD HAVE MISSED YOU EVEN MORE IF THERE WASN'T AN EXACT DUPLICATE OF YOU RUNNING AROUND...
THINGS WILL BE BETTER FOR YOU HERE NOW.
AND I'M NOT JUST SAYING THAT BECAUSE IT WILL BE FUN TO DATE A REAL LIVE SUPERHERO.
I'M NOT A SUPERHERO. I DON'T HAVE ANY POWERS.
YES YOU DO. YOU CAN MAKE YOUR DREAMS A REALITY. AND I THINK YOU CAN STILL MAKE MINE A REALITY TOO.
JULIE... I'M NOT COMING BACK HERE. POWERS OR NO POWERS, THE HIGH IS WHERE I WANT TO BE.
WHAT, THE ROOFS HERE AREN'T HIGH ENOUGH FOR YOU ANYMORE?
YOU WEREN'T THERE ONE WHOLE DAY AND YOU NEARLY GOT YOURSELF KILLED.
AND I STILL MIGHT. FOR THE REST OF THEM, IT'S EASY. BUT IT WON'T BE FOR ME. THEY KNOW THEY'RE COMING HOME EVERY DAY IN ONE PIECE. I WON'T. MAYBE THE FACT THAT I'M TAKING THAT RISK WILL PUSH THEM TO USE WHAT THEY DON'T APPRECIATE. USE THEM FOR THE RIGHT REASONS.
WELL THEN, DON'T LET ME HOLD YOU UP. IT'S CLEAR WHOSE DREAMS YOU WANT TO MAKE A REALITY, AND I DON'T WANT TO STAND IN YOUR WAY.
JULIE, NOW THAT EVERYONE KNOWS WHO I AM, I CAN LIVE AT HOME, SO I'LL BE BACK HERE ALL THE TIME.
YOU KNOW, THE STUDENTS, THEY DON'T WEAR COSTUMES OVER THERE.
SO?
YOURS STILL FIT?
2006

Sketchbook

This is where it all started. The first time I drew Jonathan. He's come a long way and really came to life for me during the series. This first one was actually based on my little brother which is why I guess people always think I'm just drawing myself in high school.

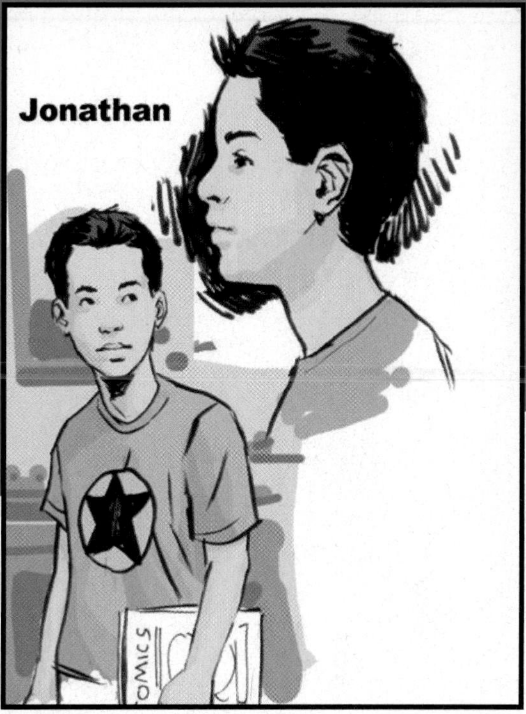
Jonathan

Below is the small sketch I tentatively handed over to Mike Oeming so he could do the issue one cover. I was really amped he agreed to do it. I'm also glad he took my crappy "Batman: Death in the family" homage and kicked it up a notch. Mike is awesome!

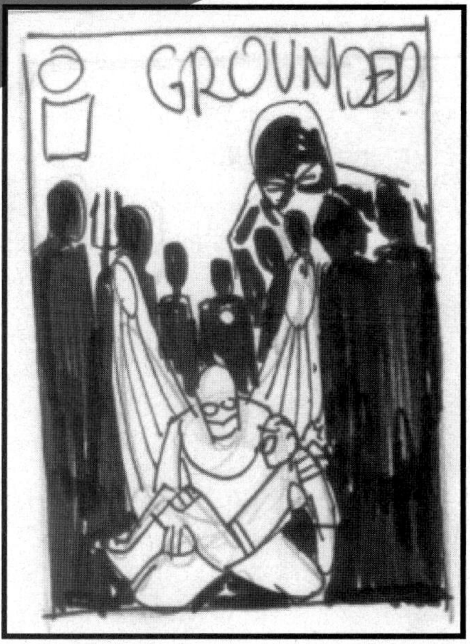
GROUNDED

These two at the bottom are my designs for the High and the Terrific Two Towers. With the High Mark and I really just wanted to blatantly rip of the Hall of Justice from the old Justice League cartoon. I changed it a bit so Warner Brothers doesn't come after our collective hide but we're still shameless. The Terrific Two Towers was something I had to actually think about. Mark just wanted two massive towers and I added the statue to help make it look more interesting. I still like the overall design a lot.

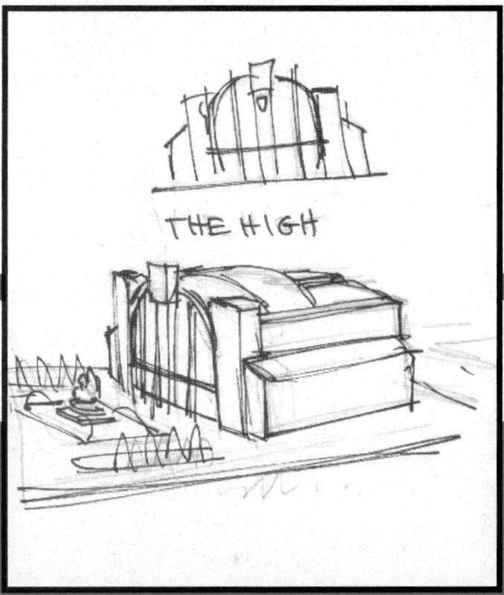
THE HIGH

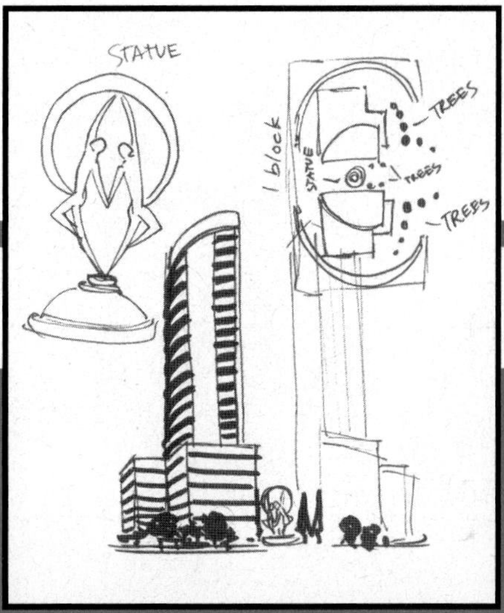
STATUE
1 block
STATUE
TREES
TREES
TREES

On the left is a good example of my process. I'm not big on doing tight pencils and I've always heard the best way to ink is not think of it as tracing (thanks Kevin) but continuing the drawing with ink. I also add a lot of things in the inking stage that you can't really express with a pencil.

Below is another example of rough pencils to inks. All of my favorite artists are not only pencilers and inkers but they have a good energy to their inks (something I'm still working on). Working with a loose pencil stage really helps me be more expressive when I ink. Being that I have to add so much, and drawing it for the first time, in ink it doesn't tend to become stale in the inking stage. Plus I was never really good at "pretty inking" so I guess it works out.

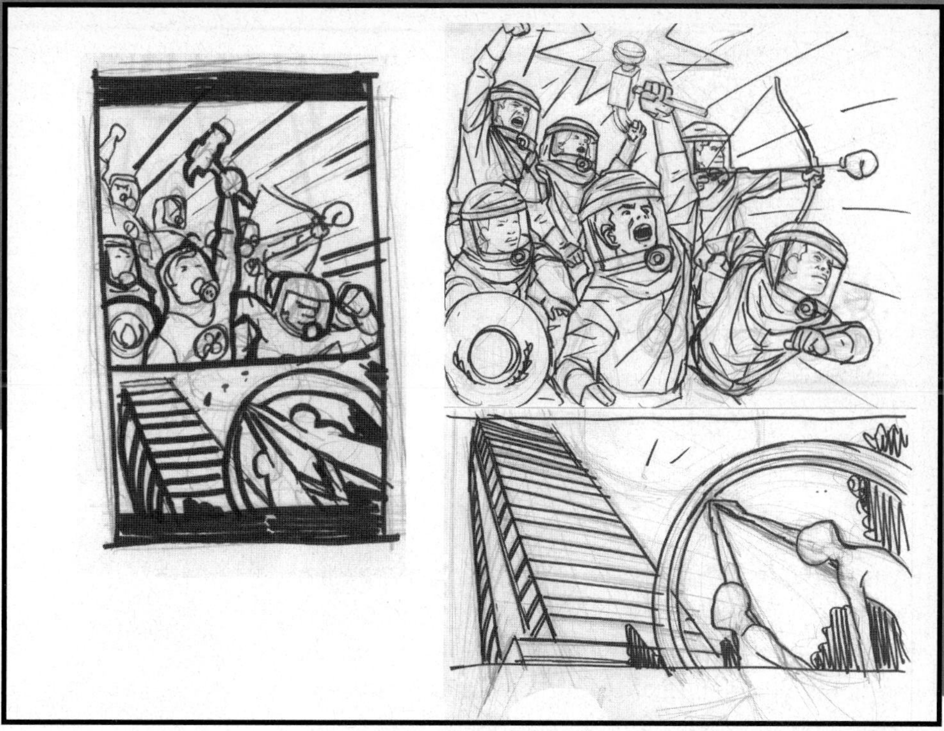

This one was a lot of fun. I remember Mark's notes being something like "think Bryan Hitch Ultimates cover". So after a few attempts I came up with the composition you see here. I think it has a lot of energy and I was glad I could keep some of that in the final cover. I added the bit at the bottom to keep it in line with the previous covers. I thought it was best to go with something really calm to juxtapose all the action on top. I think it works.

- PAUL

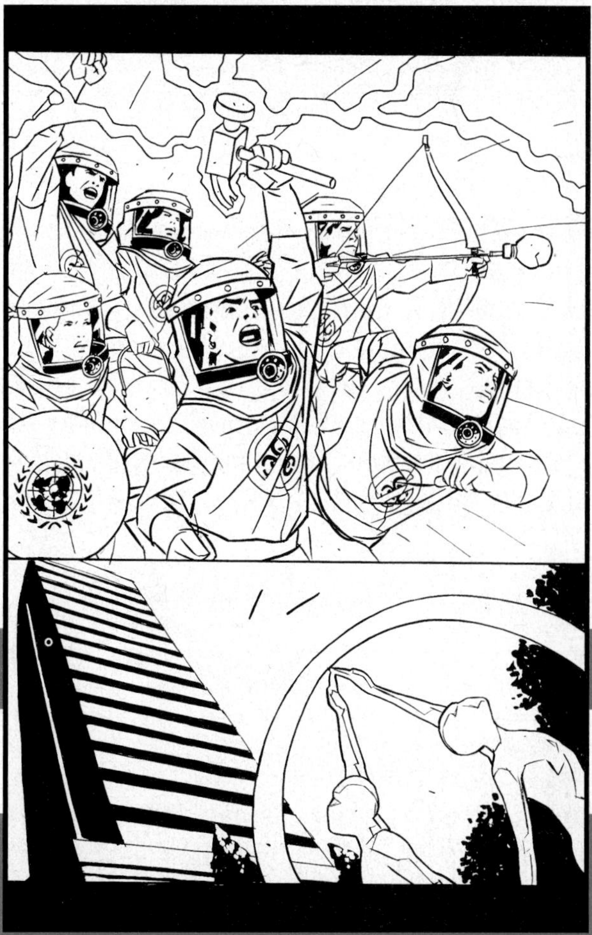

MARK SABLE

Mark Sable, writer for stage, screen and television, holds a B.A. in English from Duke University, an M.F.A. in Dramatic Writing from N.Y.U.'s Tisch School of the Arts and a J.D. from the University of Southern California, but he is best known for being the only man to have worked for both Howard Stern and Charlie Rose. Future comics work includes HAZED, a dark comedy about sororities and eating disorders from Image Comics (think "Heathers" or "Mean Girls" set in college).

PAUL AZACETA

Born and bred in New Jersey, Paul has wedged his way into the comic community. Having first worked for Marvel Comics, Paul moved on to Image Comics and GROUNDED. His main focus now is working on new interesting projects and never losing the ability to stretch himself artistically.

NICK FILARDI

Nick Filardi grew up in New London, CT listening to Small Town Hero, watching Batman the Animated Series and fending off ladies. After graduating from Savannah College of Art and Design in 2004, he colored for Zylonol Studios under Lee Loughridge in Savannah, GA while maintaining the pretense of working an "office" job. Currently living in South Philly with his three-legged dog, Deniro, he also colors for DOLL & CREATURE, NYC MECH, GODLAND, and THE CROSS BRONX.

KRISTYN FERRETTI

Kristyn is an art director/graphic designer for film and multi-media at a firm in NYC. In her spare moments you can find her lettering & designing books like this one.

IVAN BRANDON

Ivan is the co-creator of 24seven, THE CROSS BRONX, NYC MECH and the upcoming GIMME DANGER and THE HEAVY.

For more GROUNDED, please visit us at:
www.groundedcomic.com or www.imagecomics.com